AROUND CINEMAS

A

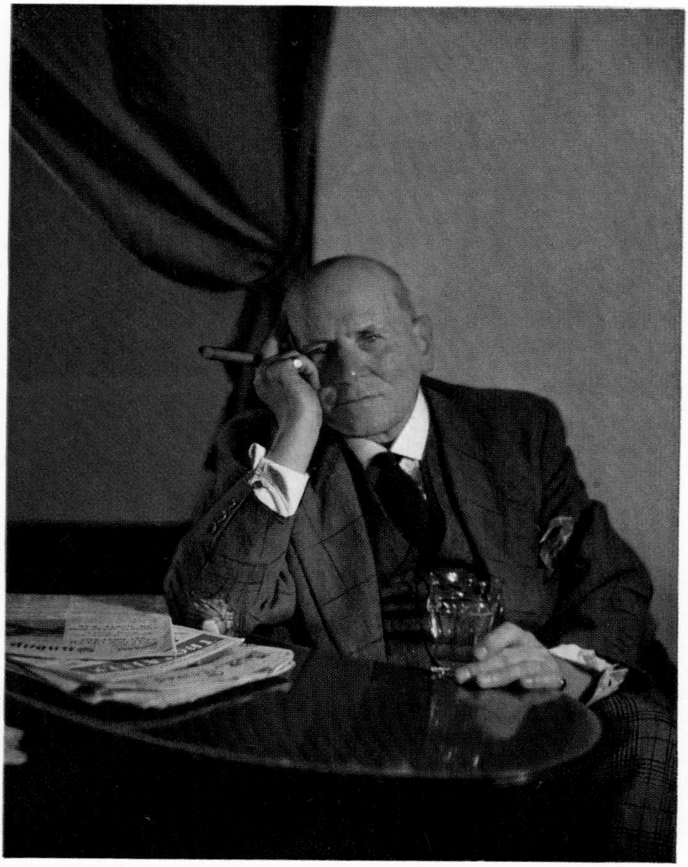

AROUND CINEMAS

(SECOND SERIES)

By

James Agate

24

HOME & VAN THAL Ltd
1948

First published 1948

Printed in the Netherlands by
Holdert & Co. N.V., Amsterdam

To

Percy Cudlipp

ACKNOWLEDGMENTS

My thanks are due to the Proprietors of THE TATLER for their courteous permission to reprint these articles, all of which have appeared in their paper. Also to Mr. Frank Dunn for his kindness in reading the proofs and to Mr. Alan Dent for making the Index.

NOTE

This book, like its forerunner, is not intended to be documentary, educational, didactic, comprehensive. It makes no claim to be anything more than a series of essays written round and about some of the three thousand films I have seen during the last twenty years.

June 22nd, 1946. J. A.

CONTENTS

1

ALAS, POOR PHOENIX !

1928

I PROPOSE shortly to like a film and to tell readers of THE TATLER all about it. But that can only be when the innovators, talkie-mongers, and Empire-breakers give me a week's breathing-space. At the moment more urgent matters are to hand—that is if there can be anything more urgent than enjoying oneself. Progress, like poverty, makes us acquainted with strange bedfellows. The lion, we are told, will one day lie down with the lamb. But who would ever have thought that the lion of Metro-Goldwyn-Mayer would one day lie down with the shade of the late-lamented Mrs. Ormiston Chant. That lady was the first Empire-breaker, as this lion is its last. I do not suppose that the present generation remembers anything at all about that Amazon of the 'eighties. Yet I remember her well. It was my fortune to know Mrs. Ormiston Chant personally. Among the preachers who visited the chapel which I attended as a boy was this distinguished reformer. I remember that she was severe of aspect and august in manner, and that she appeared in the pulpit without a hat—a thing which in those days was considered remarkable. God, she said, had given woman one covering for the head, and there was no reason to invent another. I remember that she spoke extempore, without notes, and at great length, both in the pulpit and at a subsequent luncheon at my father's house, throughout the whole afternoon, and again at evening service. She stayed with us, and at midnight her volubility showed no decrease. My schoolboy studies had just reached *velocity* and *acceleration,* and the good lady seemed to me to be the living personification of these phenomena. I recollect nothing more about her except that to have joked in her presence would have seemed like brawling in church.

It was this meddlesome woman who destroyed one of the things which made England at the end of last century what she undoubtedly was. Conquering generals, unconquerable subalterns, colonials, men who had carried our far-flung banner to the ends of the Empire—all those returning from abroad made it their first pleasure to look in at the house with the proud name, turn their backs on the stage, and quiz the ladies of the Promenade who, in the twenty years since their last visit, had not altered by so much as a day. It may well be that visitors to the New Empire will still want to turn their backs on what was once the stage. But alas, there will be no one, not even an old crony, to quiz! The old house was a hub of empire, a rendezvous, a place where a man of cities might meet other men of cities. It was a civilised place. Now who in his sane senses expects to be able to hobnob in a place either ghostly with silence or raucous with movietone, and without a bar? *Ichabod!* I understand to be the Hebrew for *the glory has departed!* I wish I knew the Hebrew for the converse, which appears to be very much in the minds of Metro-Goldwyn-Mayer. At the opening of the New Empire there was some sort of ceremony whereby each of the Metro-Goldwyn-Mayer stars in the Metro-Goldwyn-Mayer studios in Hollywood said that his or her heart was beating in tune and time with that of the vast audience assembled in the Empire of the glorious past, and hoping for a still more glorious future. What hypocritical bunk! There can be no glory about a picture-palace except dividends. Doubtless the sleek young Jews hovering about the place will see to that.

Let it be said that the builders and renovators have done nothing to destroy the charm of the old theatre, which was always one of the most beautiful in London. They have enhanced it. Certainly the entrance-hall, when you have once got past the miserable *guichet,* is a magnificent apartment. But that wicked gate with the paybox on the very pavement is an abomination. The Old Empire flung wide-open doors to the entire world; the New Empire has no door to fling. Lack of taste could go no further. The old theatre seemed to say, "It's your presence we want!" The new theatre merely demands your shekels. Inside, I repeat, all except the performance is well; and that in time may be well also. Let me describe in some little detail what took place on Tuesday evening of last week. I will begin with the orchestra. This is large and probably good, though, doubtless at the behest of Metro-Goldwyn-Mayer, it must accomplish irritating things. It performed the prelude to *Cavalleria* reasonably well, though why it should be subjected to hydraulic tricks during performance is beyond my comprehension. There was to be more of this nonsense. After the Mascagni the orchestra made mass attack upon an incredibly foolish foxtrot or something of the sort. In the middle of this a grand piano rose by mechanical means from the floor, remained poised long enough to allow its embarrassed attendant to deliver himself of a few passages of parlous banality and then sank. Presently the playing department of an organ began to bob up and down, while the lights in the theatre were similarly manipulated. Are such monkeyings necessary? The organ, by the way, struck me as possessing the least pleasant tone I have heard among these cinema devices. It was like the old hurdy-gurdy plus the *voix-céleste* stop, which appeared to be in permanent use. The dignity of the church organ had gone, and in its place was a tone which I can only describe as musty. It should be said, in justice, that the organist was careful to play nothing which might properly be performed on an organ. The day is presumably far off when the cinema organist will realise that the characteristic quality of his instrument is the opposite of the staccato.

After the orchestra and the organ came a demonstration of movietone which in my opinion demonstrated movietone out of existence. We saw and heard an Italian baritone singing "Largo al Factotum." That is to say we saw him all right but heard as much of him as though we had been late for a performance at Queen's Hall and were listening through closed doors. I am not enamoured of vitaphone, but say candidly that, with all its faults, it is at least a hundred times better than movietone. There followed a sort of Armistice gazette. The jolly parts of this with the old soldier-songs were taken at least three times too fast. The serious parts were better, though I objected very strongly to the callousness which plunged us from the mood of "Abide With Me" into the antics of a jazz-drummer via something called *Night-Lights in Prague*. This was immediately followed by a close-up of an intoxicated duck. A management possessed of even the rudiments of taste would have followed the Armistice pictures with a nature-study or some few moments of quietude. One sitting near me, whom I took to be an ex-soldier, simply said, "Oh, damn!" and hobbled out of the theatre. *Trelawny of the Wells*, the feature of the evening, turned out to be the usual disservice to Sir Arthur Pinero, despite the dental charm of Miss Norma Shearer. Some day I shall have something to say about the Americanisation of English plays. In the meantime Sir Arthur may like to know that he is credited with such felicities as: "What did you have to come here for, you old polar bear?"

2

MR. BENNETT'S FILM

1929

"JANET," said Miss Betsey Trotwood on the occasion when her nephew turned up dirty and bedraggled, "Mr. Dick sets us all right. Heat the bath!" Mr. Arnold Bennett resembles Mr. Dick in that he is accustomed to setting everybody right about everything. Who that did not know himself to be the perfect mentor could have put forth those suave little booklets instructing people in the art of self-management, the conduct of friendship and marriage, the manner of becoming an author, of living on twenty-four hours a day, of making the best of life, of attaining mental efficiency, literary taste, and all the rest of it? Our Mr. Dick is not only a pragmatist, he is the Great Panjandrum of pragmatism. What more natural then than that he should turn to the films and give that misguided industry a gentle but firm push in the right direction? I have great pleasure in saying that *Piccadilly* is, all things considered, a good film. It is certainly a good film in the sense that it is over too soon and that I should be quite pleased if there were another hour of it. But I shall be frank, and say that this film is not nearly as good as I expected it would be. It needs not Mr. Bennett, descended from Olympian heights, to concoct this little tale of a night-club proprietor's intrigue with a Chinese scullery-maid.

May I at this point ask Mr. Bennett whether he considers such an intrigue to be more characteristic of Piccadilly than of the Cannebière at Marseilles and similar thoroughfares in Vienna, Budapest, or any towns which harbour proprietors of night-clubs and Chinese scullery-maids? When I first read that Mr. Bennett's film was to be called *Piccadilly*, I thought of all the things which he, as a novelist, might do with such a theme—how he might take the people debouching from the Tube on to Piccadilly Circus and follow them to their homes, or a selection of them. I imagined that he might give us a little file of figures coming up from the bowels of the earth and declaring that he would work out for us the lives of an arbitrary number of them, say the seventh, eleventh, and sixteenth. It would have been good to see the procession one by one and to wonder what the protagonists would be like when their turn came. Or I thought that Mr. Bennett might choose Piccadilly on Mafeking Night, in the throes of war fever, on Boat Race Night, on the afternoon of a Cup Final. Perhaps he would burn down for us the London Pavilion. Perhaps he would compare the lives of the loungers in the bow-windows of the clubs with the existences of the sprawlers on the grass in the park opposite. Strictly speaking, I suppose Piccadilly is all that street which stretches from Piccadilly Circus to Knightsbridge. Mr. Bennett's film ignores this stretch and concentrates singly on the Circus. His screen-play is all about the underworld, which means that it is not characteristically English but cosmopolitan and would do anywhere. Watching it, I rather felt as I should feel if Mr. Bennett wrote a novel about a Polish countess strangled in Bursley by a Czecho-Slovakian baron and called it *Love in the Five Towns*.

But I have a more serious complaint, which is that Mr. Bennett does not appear to have realised what a film-play might and ought to be. The sub-titles which he has "written specially" would doubtless be excellent if they were sentences in a realistic novel. As film titles they are unwitty and unarresting, and therefore bad. Nor can I believe that Mr. Bennett thinks like a scenario-writer. But for the multiplicity of the settings there is nothing in *Piccadilly* which could not be acted on the stage. I will even say that if a play could have twenty or thirty changes *Piccadilly* would be more effective on the stage. Except for one scene in a night-club, another in a Limehouse saloon, and a third in a coroner's court, everything which takes place is a dramatic snippet concerning only two or three people, and always happening in a room. In this respect *Piccadilly* is inferior to *Underground,* where there were obviously things which could never by any stretch of imagination be put upon the stage. Did we not have views of gasometers, or something that looked like gasometers, with people scaling them? *Piccadilly* is inferior, scenically, to *Sorrell and Son,* which had out-door London for its background. Mr. Bennett gives us nothing of Picca-dilly except an occasional shot showing the electric signs which disfigure, or enliven, the Circus. My point—to which I stick—about this film is that if a few shots of the Café de la Paix were substituted for the Pavilion, and a *boîte* in Montmartre for the Limehouse pub, the film could be presented under the title of *Boulevard.*

A delicious performance is given by Mr. Charles Laughton as a dullard epicure. This is insanely interrupted and almost destroyed by repeated throw-backs to an irritating vamp whom we had been quite content to leave amusing herself in the ball-room. But piecing the bits together, Mr. Laughton's performance is a little gem. Judging from the size of the letters in the programme, the star in the cast is Miss Gilda Gray, with whose photograph that booklet also presents us. For this portrait Miss Gray has adopted Sarah Bernhardt's famous pose in *Azaël.* Indeed she has been said to resemble the great actress, and in my judgment would do so if Sarah had been unremarkable, colourless, and totally devoid of tempera-ment. Frankly, Miss Gray's acting seems to me to be neither praise nor blameworthy. It just doesn't interest me. However, since we are always told that criticism should be constructive, let me suggest to this actress the next time she has to appear at an inquest to make confession of murder, and being garbed like Miss Thorndike in *The Trojan Women*—let me suggest that Miss Gray should discard a dozen or so of her bracelets. At first we see a weeping woman clad in cloak of inky velvet whose folds she holds to-gether with a piteous naked forefinger. Presently one of the folds slips, and at once we behold an arm flashing diamonds from wrist to elbow. The truth of the matter is that Miss Anna May Wong and Mr. King Ho-Chang run away with all the honours that are going. I hardly know any European type of beauty which could stand up against Miss Wong's strange, disturbing loveliness. "Elle était là roulant des choses en sa petite tête de sphinx, ou peut-être, ne pensant à rien, mais gardant cette belle et charmante pose héréditaire de ces peuples nobles et songeurs, la pose hiératique des statues sacrées." I take this sentence from Maupassant's exquisite short story, "Châli." Miss Wong acts with enormous perception, while Mr. King Ho-Chang outplays everybody except Miss Wong.

3

ENGLAND'S DARLING

1929

I SUPPOSE that some day I shall be able to enter the Piccadilly Theatre without hearing Mr. Martinelli bellowing "On With the Motley." But that day is not yet. And I suppose, too, that some day I shall be able to attend this theatre or picture-house without my attention being claimed on behalf of the black races. But that also is apparently not yet. For at the Piccadilly the management thought fit to preface the new picture about Nelson with a film entitled *Dixie Days,* in which a number of the uncomeliest negroes and most villainous negresses I have ever seen squalled a selection of their too-familiar spirituals. After this we entered upon the film about Nelson which Messrs. Warner Brothers have thought fit to call *The Divine Lady.* But that is the film way. The film industry cannot conceive anything in this world except from its sexual aspect. A film about Napoleon would be called *An Ill-Starred Queen,* just as one about Julius Cæsar must masquerade as *The Serpent of Old Nile.* By their womenfolk we shall know them. But I am not sure that under the title of *The Divine Lady* one finds Lady Hamilton more easily than one finds Nelson. For the title has the maximum infelicity of attributing to her qualities which were by no means hers. She was not divine and not at all ladylike. I imagine her to have been a large-hearted, capable, courageous woman overflowing with temperament, and possessing a sense of mischief and plenty of wit and brains. If you were to ask me to describe Emma Hamilton in terms of other women I should say Nell Gwynne, Peg Woffington, with just a trace of Becky Sharp, and the whole enacted by Mrs. Jordan. Probably she had large hands, and Romney tells us that she had a large mouth. I believe her manners to have been as broad as her heart, and that the last thing she would have done would have been to cry. In other words, a thoroughly decent, sensible woman who would not make a bad ambassadress and was the ideal mistress for a sailor.

Then consider Nelson. There is no getting away from the fact that the English will never consent to admire a great man for what he really is, always preferring to worship some image of what they would have preferred that great man to be. I suppose that if a plebiscite were taken to decide who is the greatest Englishman who ever lived Nelson would poll half the votes, the remainder being split between Tom Cribb, the Black Prince, W. G. Grace, Alfred the Great, Shakespeare, and whoever it is that is Captain of the 'Spurs. It is with the greatest difficulty that we can wean ourselves from the idea that the greatest of all Englishmen was not a cricketer, and we make up for this by deciding that always and in all circumstances he must have "played the game." I suppose the popular notion of Nelson is a composite figure made up of Galahad, a nautical brother of Hannibal's, and Cyrano de Bergerac, the whole to look like an imitation of Sir Johnston Forbes-Robertson by Mr. Nelson Keys. Yet how much more interesting the real Nelson must have been. What people will hardly ever believe about Nelson is that he was a sailor who took to the sea at the age of twelve. Still less do we like to realise that Nelson married a widow on a foreign station, pensioned her off, and with Sir William Hamilton and Lady Hamilton set up a triangular household—which course of conduct, as was long ago pointed out, if it had occurred in a play by Ibsen would have been regarded as altogether too un-English to be thinkable. Add Nelson's well-known flamboyance and passion for the limelight, that magnificent talent for braggadocio which inspired that bit of purple about a Peerage or Westminster Abbey, a positive genius for stage-managership, and a manner of handling the English language which would not have disgraced Sir Thomas Browne and was probably the envy of Robert Louis Stevenson. Remember with all this that Nelson was a sailor, and therefore never quite grown-up—in other words, a great glamorous boy. It is the boyishness in him which excuses his overweening vanity and that faculty for seeing himself as hero which never left him.

How much of these characters are we vouchsafed in *The Divine Lady*? The answer is, of course, nothing at all. The Emma Hamilton of Miss Corinne Griffith is a limp, over-manicured rather tiresome beauty with habits of falling on to men's left shoulders—we see her do it in turn with Greville, Hamilton, and Nelson—plucking at harp strings, and allowing herself to be made love to in floods of tears. Part of the production is vile, for I do not believe that Emma, on hearing that Nelson must go to England, clutched at a bunch of roses, swooned on a sofa, and interposed her bouquet between Nelson's lips and hers. Nor do I think she would have telepathic knowledge of the moment when Nelson receives his musket-wound. But then I do not believe in anything concerning Miss Griffith's Emma, from whom all the gusto and the riot have departed to give place to a Niobe-like proficiency in tears. Mr. Victor Varconi is harmless as Nelson, whom, by the way, he does not even begin to resemble. But as a pasteboard hero he does well enough. The film does not make it very clear whether Sir William Hamilton was a *mari complaisant* of genius—which is probably the truth about him—or a bone-headed idiot, or a hyprocitical mixture of the two. But then Mr. H. B. Warner, who plays the part, has obviously been in a difficulty about it since in one scene he has to go to bed leaving his wife to the amorous care of his crony, and in the next must admit that neither he nor his Queen could in future recognise her Ladyship. Mr. Warner extricates himself very handsomely from his difficulty by throwing over it a cloak of impenetrable moral grandeur. The battle scenes are good, though the Nile is done very much better than Trafalgar, which appears to have been a ten-minutes' scrap. Far too little dramatic preparation is given to the closing episodes, too much of the film being taken up by Miss Griffith. The musical accompaniment is very well devised, but the whole effect is spoiled by the fact that it reaches us in canned form, there being at a conservative estimate at least ten times less effect than with the same score played on an actual orchestra. Such parts of this film as are "talkie" would be lamentable if they were not ludicrous, it being perfectly obvious throughout that somebody else is singing for Miss Griffith, who merely opens and shuts her mouth like a fish gasping on a bank. With this difference, that the fish does it at the right time.

4

A FIRST-CLASS FILM

1929

THE proper way in which to look at a gift-horse is to gaze at him full in the mouth, since you cannot glean much from his tail. One or two cinema managements have come forward with the declaration that having discovered the existence of a public which still prefers silent pictures to the screamies they propose to revert to the old love and incidentally restore the orchestra. "But ow?" asked Mrs. May. And, modelling myself upon that good lady, I shall ask, "But for how long?" And, being in an unusually inquisitive mood, I shall further demand to know "Why?" Is this discovery of what I may call the Silent Public in any way motivated by the fact that the cinemas in question do not happen to be in possession at the moment of what they regard as a good screamie? I should like to be satisfied about this for I cannot help regarding my silent gift-horse as altogether too good to be true. These things being said in straightforward, manly fashion—there being nothing of the snake-in-the-grass about the present writer—let me congratulate the management of the London Hippodrome upon a really first-class silent picture. This is the film entitled *The Wonderful Lie.* It is a U.F.A. film, and the fact that I am capable of disliking some Germans is not going to prevent my saying that what makes this film so admirable is its quality of German thought and purpose. Our former enemies do not make the mistake of composing films for scullery-maids; they assume a certain level of intelligence in their audiences, and thus their films automatically become, say, 1,000 per cent better than those obviously written with an eye to the inmates of asylums, criminal or otherwise. We heard a great deal about German atrocities in time of war; why does nobody talk about American atrocities in time of peace? The question is indiscreet, and we will pass on.

Please may I say that I am not blind to the fact that *The Wonderful Lie* is a little over-coloured and frankly Ouidaesque. But I submit that it is the business of this kind of film to be quite perfectly Ouidaesque. It has been laid down that in any novel the characters who go in search of hidden treasure must find it, and I would lay it down that the film producer who goes in search of the exotic at St. Petersburg must also produce it. I shall permit myself to quote the first sentence of the synopsis of this story obligingly given on the programme for the convenience of those unable to believe their eyes. This is the sentence: "All St. Petersburg knew Nina Petrowna, noted for her beauty, notorious for her lies, the mistress of a Colonel of Cuirassiers." Now, in the name of Hackney Marshes and the Cromwell Road, can anything be more enchantingly less like life as it is lived in this early-closing, Dora-ridden metropolis? Colonels of Cuirassiers may or may not be seen sunning themselves in Albany Street or Birdcage Walk; but where are our Nina Petrownas? That again is by the way. Presently a handsome young Cornet joined the Colonel's regiment. Visiting what the programme pudically calls "A famous rendezvous for beautiful women and wealthy lovers"—the kind of place which in simple old London forces half the police into evening dress, with what result to the more imaginative of our younger officers Parliament discusseth not—the Cornet beheld at a night-club Mlle. Petrowna, and stared at her so long and so hard that the child was forced to tell her tyrant that the young man was an old playmate. I cannot recount the story in detail. Sufficient to say, perhaps, that though Nina slipped the latch-key into the Cornet's hand, and waited for him at midnight in a costume utterly neglectful, that young man was conscious of nothing contrary to his conceptions of the virginal. He did not, as the soldiers say, "rumble." And not rumbling, he spent the night in the armchair, while on the other side of the door, with her head against the handle, and squatting on the hard, cold parquet, slept Nina Petrowna. Next morning they shared one breakfast egg; from which the Colonel deduced the worst. So Nina, leaving behind her jewels and furs and taking with her only her principles, went to live in a horrid little apartment, where she had trouble with the local Gas Light and Coke Company. Whereupon the Cornet, to provide pennies for Nina's meter, played poker for thousands of roubles. And cheated. This was the Colonel's opportunity. To prevent her Cornet from being drummed out of the regiment Nina promised to go back and live with her old keeper, and the picture here took the familiar turn whereby women aching for their lovers spurn them for their good, and revert to somebody else. I have shed far too many tears over Bernhardt's third act in *La Dame aux Caméllias* to gibe at Nina's behaviour here. It was clear that the picture would presently end miserably, and I was conscious that the gathering gloom was enlivened by the recollection of a line from Mr. Rex Evans' least pardonable ditty: "You'll end up in *la piscine*, which is French for swimming pool." Instead, Nina ended on the sofa, at the foot of which was lying one of those bottles of the shape and size to hold exactly one fatal dose and be extracted from the corsage at the appropriate moment. I submit that it is quite proper that film heroines should carry what Ethel Monticue would call "a file of prussic in case."

I have admitted that this story is too highly coloured. At the same time one has only got to read the Sunday newspapers to realise that there are districts in London where practically nothing else ever happens. Only, of course, the Colonel would be some elderly stockbroker with a golf handicap of twenty-four, the lady fortyish and loud in voice and hair, and the young man a sheepish dancing cad with an expression and a motor-car pinched from his betters. No, *The Wonderful Lie* will stand the test of probability quite well, thank you. The story is straightforwardly told, the photography is brilliant, and everything about the picture is entertaining. Brigitte Helm is an extraordinarily handsome creature who is not in the least pretty. She has thicker ankles than Greta Garbo, as the last shot in the picture tactlessly demonstrates, but she has greater powers of expression and a line of face which would qualify her to play Brünhilde if the need should unfortunately arise. She is a good actress, Franz Lederer is a sufficiently good actor to make us believe in the innocence of the Russian Army, and if I fault Warwick Ward at all it is because he is so obviously an English major instead of a Russian colonel. But as an English major, hard-bitten and hard-biting, he is excellent. The whole point about the picture is that it is free from the imbecilities of human speech. Nina Petrowna does *not* chirp: "Say, Cornet, you're some kid," and the Cornet does *not* reply, "Baby, I'm just mad about you." Instead of the ineffable dialogue there is some more than effable music, brilliantly played by the Hippodrome Symphony Orchestra. The score has been put together by Mr. Louis Levy, and is a remarkable piece of cinema work. In fact I am in two minds about going again to see this film.

5

PARIS IDOL

1929

"CURIOUSER and curiouser," said Alice in some connection or other. I can never stop wondering what that heavenly young woman would have said if she had had leisure to inspect the films, which, as time goes on, become funnier and funnier in a strictly subconscious way. The other evening I fought my own way into a seat at the Plaza during an exordium by Mr. Henderson. Personally I venture to hope that our cinemas are not destined to become that dreariest of battlefields—the political arena. Mr. Henderson's witty remarks were, however, brief. Or could it be that the operator took advantage of a pause for breath to switch us on to a picture of diving belles in Florida? Which was hardly the same thing. After this we had a bird's-eye view of the Jamboree, which was succeeded by a spectacular affair wherein some two dozen of Mr. John Tiller's young ladies were largely involved. Then came the *pièce de résistance* of the evening, a film called *Innocents of Paris*. "Paris," a rhetorical sub-title screamed at us, "is a palace of delight, a temple of bewilderment, a haunt of leisured lure." I do not vouch for the exact words, but that was the sense of them. What I do vouch for is the last label tied on to the old city by our scenario-writers whom, apparently, nothing escapes. I vouch for this label because in the dark I drew out a pencil and shirt-cuffed it. "Paris," said our subtitler, anxious to drive his nail home, "Paris is the place of ultimate sophistication." Now, what on earth are the gallery boy and girl to whose intelligence the film is singly dedicated going to make of the phrase "ulimate sophistication"? I am reminded of a conversation which a Saturday-Reviewer of the 'nineties professed to have overheard in a Paris café. "Marcel declares that his love for me is platonic," said one gay lady to another. "Dis-moi, ma chère, qu'est-ce que c'est que l'amour platonique?" Her friend replied: "L'amour platonique? Je ne sais pas au juste. Mais pour moi ça doit être quelque sale cochonnerie." Similarly I imagine Mavis turning to her squire in the remoter and upper darknesses and asking anxiously: "Sy, Bert, wot's a ultimate sophisticator?" Bert, making a wild shot, replies: "A bloke wot goes wiv more than one tart!"

The film, when at last one came to it, turned out to be the most childish thing in invention which to my knowledge has yet proceeded from the childlike cinema mind. Maurice, a young Parisian rag-and-bone merchant, was trundling his barrow by the side of the Seine when his attention was drawn by an elderly one-legged scoundrel to a child floating in the water. Had Maurice been in a boastful vein he would have recounted the remainder of the incident in the words of Cassius, "Accoutred as I was, I plungèd in." The child then explained that this mother had accompanied him into the water, and presently a letter was found on the side-walk. This being opened revealed the mother's intention to commit suicide, and concluded with a few reproaches to her father, whose address was carefully given. "Excellent," said Maurice. "Let's take you to grandpa!" And so saying he deposited the child in the barrow and went off without exhibiting any curiosity whatever as to the drowning mother. The father in question, a rich gunsmith, turned out to be as hard-hearted as the letter indicated. He told Maurice to take the brat away, and bothered not at all about the fate of his daughter. Perhaps this was because he was not hard-up for daughters, as the presence in the house of Louise, one of Mr. Walkley's roguey-pogueys with a tousled head, a cold-cream complexion, and an American accent, sufficiently proved. Hard-heartedness seemed to run in the family. For Louise also showed not the slightest curiosity about her sister floating disconsolate in the Seine, preferring to talk out of window with the departing rag-and-bone man. It must be said here that this thing was a talkie, and that the love affair of this modern Romeo and Juliet was conducted audibly. "Good night," said Louise, adding pertly, "or rather good morning!" Which, I suppose, is the modern shorthand for the balcony scene. In the end the rag-and-bone merchant discovered that he had a voice. So he went on the stage, became a star, flirted with his director's wife, broke Louise's heart in twain, and towards eleven o'clock persuaded that goose that marriage was the perfect seccotine. Now I have no objection to this artless nonsense. But it does seem to me to be really rather silly to talk about ultimate sophistication in connection with it.

Innocents of Paris, of course, is quite hopeless as a film, being as much inferior to *The Singing Fool* as, for the purposes of slobbering sentimentality, the white complexion is inferior to the black. This picture is not meant to be anything better than a vehicle for exploiting the talents of Maurice Chevalier. Here it behoves the critic to tread warily, since it is notoriously difficult for people of one nationality to judge the clowns of another. That a Robey or a Lauder could succeed in Paris or New York seems to me extremely doubtful, and I find it difficult to believe that even the supreme genius of Marie Lloyd would have availed with, say, a Marseilles audience. But let us not take it to ourselves that we have a finer discrimination in these matters than the foreigner. Mistinguett, for example, has never seemed to me to be anything more than an underdressed and over-hatted old lady, very active for her years. One might put it this way, that English buffoonery is a blind spot to our neighbours, and vice versa. It is, then, in the full consciousness of proving the existence of this blind spot that I declare my inability to see, as the phrase goes, anything in Maurice Chevalier beyond a certain boyish charm. Two things have helped him enormously—his likeness to Carpentier and the lilt of his best-known song, *Valentine.* With his straw hat carefully set at the wrong angle he has the charm of the overgrown *gigolo.* But even so that likeableness is better on the stage than on the screen, for none of Chevalier's warmest admirers is going to pretend that he films well. The screen distorts that large underlip into something like ugliness, the complexion is pasty, and the voice just nothing at all. There was never any more than an amiable pretence that Maurice could sing, which pretence the film neatly abolishes. Nevertheless this French star has the one quality which transcends all others—the quality of being a success. If there is in you so much as one drop of the milk of human kindness you cannot refuse success to anybody coming on to the stage prepared so obviously to receive it. Maurice expects your plaudits, and you can no more refuse them than you would snatch a cup of water from a thirsty child. This film persuades us that it is a good thing for Maurice Chevalier that he has long been the idol of Paris and threatens to be that of London. For if he is not an idol he can be nothing.

6

"THE TAMING OF THE SHREW"

1929

BRAVO Hollywood! Or rather, bravo Hollywood up to the very moment when, at the end of the film, Miss Mary Pickford gives a huge wink in *The Shrew,* and in one fell swoop of her eyelid destroys the whole meaning of the play. The wink occurs at the moment of Katharine's exhortation to the married women to submit to their husbands. Now we may hold many things about this speech. We may hold that it is horribly out of date, that Ibsen's *A Doll's House* has rendered it unfit for public utterance. We may hold that the speech—and this is my own view—was the poet's way of getting some part of his own back in the matter of his unhappy marriage. But whatever we may think, there is no doubt that in the play Katharine is perfectly sincere. She means what she says, for if she does not the whole play must be pointless. Katharine really is "ashamed that women are so simple, to offer war where they should kneel for peace." Not so Miss Pickford. She tips the women the wink. This wink might be interpreted in two ways, first that she is but seeming tamed, and second, that the tamed creature can wheedle more out of the master than a virago can ever hope to accomplish by violence. But it is poor criticism to supply interpretations to something which ought not to exist at all. Miss Pickford's wink is definitely wrong, and I suggest that the audience when they hear Katharine's submissive speech should divert their attention from the screen. It is quite simple, the women can begin to powder their noses, the men can dive for their hats.

For the rest of Miss Pickford's playing I shall say that it is admirable in intention. Physically, of course, she does not look the part, and can never hope to look it. No actress who really looks like the flower should really hope to be convincing as the serpent under it, and Lady Macbeth when she asked her lord to perform the double function must have known that she was asking too much. Miss Pickford cannot hope to be at once the world's sweetheart and the world's worst-tempered woman. But it is enormously to her credit that she tries to forget about the first, and pretends to be the second. She assumes a malignant scowl, and it is as though a baby were momentarily unhappy about something; she batters Petruchio with her fists, and the operation is as inadequate as taking a pea-shooter to the Rock of Gibraltar. It is said that Carnera is never happier than when lusty coal-heavers or brawny men from the stone quarries are letting drive at his solar plexus; such fillips add zest to his day's enjoyment. Or you might think of another metaphor and say that our darling's storms bear the same proportion to Katharine's rages that the gentle ruffles in the Round Pond bear to the angry rollers of the Atlantic. All this is not to say that Miss Pickford doesn't try. She tries extremely hard, but you can see that she is trying just as plainly as in some village theatricals you can see that the vicar's daughter is trying to be a peccant wife. But there is no question of trying about the Petruchio of Mr. Douglas Fairbanks. Some actors have played this part with their brains, others with their natural fire, others with their animal spirits, others yet again with their mere presence. Mr. Fairbanks plays the part in all these ways put together. He is magnificent equally as an unconsidering tomboy and as a considered tyrant. His facial expression is good, his physique is of course more than adequate to all the demands made upon it, and his voice is excellent. In fact, I have no hesitation in saying that Mr. Fairbanks might transfer his performance to Stratford without conveying any notion of discrepancy.

Whether the screen version could be so transferred is a more ticklish matter. The version used is Garrick's, normally produced under the title *Katharine and Petruchio*. And though it be true that one-third of a loaf is better than no bread, it cannot be denied that to lop off two-thirds of Shakespeare is to mutilate that author considerably. Bianca, for example, disappears from the play after her first five minutes. We do not see the dressing scene, and just as we have got well and thick into the middle of the piece we discover that the film has only a few feet left to run. The wagering by the husbands of the other married women is omitted, and so too is a good half of Katharine's great speech of submission, the result being that the play as a play appears lop-sided. But what there is of it, as Mr. Robey would say, is good, incontestably good. There is no suggestion anywhere that the scene is not Padua or the time the sixteenth century. Or perhaps I should say that there is no suggestion throughout that the film is not what a Warwickshire poet, writing in the sixteenth century, thought of certain goings-on in Padua. The film makes a high-spirited rollicking entertainment at which nobody need be ashamed at being found. We have been told how a young American stenographer sitting next to her beau at a performance of *Romeo and Juliet* desired more particular information concerning Tybalt. "Say," she is reported to have asked, "who's the guy?" And her cavalier answered as precisely as gum-chewing operations permitted: "Cousin to the skoit!" For readers who have no American I suggest that "skirt" in this connection means Juliet. There is nothing of this mentality about Hollywood's treatment of Shakespeare's play.

Let me repeat: Bravo Hollywood!—without inquiring too closely into whether this manifestation of interest in the masterpieces is to be the be-all and end-all of our two artists' aspirations or whether it is the prelude to larger enterprise. If so, it might be interesting to conjecture what other plays are apt to be potted. Obviously the tragedies will have to be left out for the simple reason that our Mary can never hope to be a tragic actress. The Roman histories, too, will have to go by the board, for I do not see our little friend as either Calpurnia, Cleopatra, or Volumnia; and frankly so far as the English histories are concerned one would not have that girlish posy as Doll Tearsheet. This leaves the comedies. Rosalind? Possibly, but there is no part for Mr. Fairbanks unless we are to see the fight with the lion! Viola? M'yes. Perdita? If you like. Miranda? By all means. Portia? Not on your life. Isabella? Heavens, no! Beatrice? All I will say in anticipation is that the Benedick of Mr. Fairbanks would be worth going a long way to see. However, the present film is a venture equally gallant and sensible, and I will call readers' attention to the fact that its sponsor calls himself not Otto K. Grabbenbosch but Charles B. Cochran.

7

PRANCING NIGGERS

1930

MORGAN EVANS, a Caerphilly collier, goes for a jaunt, and with his year's savings in his pocket, to the neighbouring city of Cardiff. There he falls for a siren in what it is polite to call a gaming-saloon, who induces him to play dice with her bully. Morgan loses all his money, starts "creating," and in the disturbance accidentally kills his brother Owen, who has come to look for him. He puts the body in a cart and returns home, where there is a wake, in the course of which he "gets religion." When next we see Morgan he is a revivalist preacher, ambling pietistically through South Wales villages on an ass. In the course of his wanderings he meets the siren and the bully, with the latter of whom he has a bout of fisticuffs. Next we are treated to revivalist scenes of great frenzy, including baptism by ducking. And now the siren re-appears. She will be ducked, and nothing shall stop her from being ducked. Morgan obliges, and presently carries the dripping and now hysterical trollop to a tent where, having by some miraculous process become completely dried, she proceeds to vamp the poor evangelist in the best Jeanne-Eagels-cum-Rosalinde-Fuller manner. "Love's fire heats water, water cools not love." Our Morgan, well-read miner though he is, presumably has not got as far in the sonnets as this.

The same night, when the revivalist meeting is at its full height Morgan and the siren steal away into the Glamorganshire jungle. When next we see the pair they are married, and Morgan has gone to work in the local stone quarries. But Mrs. Morgan has taken to deceiving him and with her former bully. Morgan surprises the pair, who try to get away in a buggy, and there is a midnight chase in the course of which Morgan brings about Mrs. Morgan's death. Finally he throttles the bully, and we get momentary glimpses of him in gaol, whence as the result of good behaviour he is sent back to rejoin his mother and sweetheart in the dear little town of Caerphilly. Surely this story, put nakedly, is all rather tosh, the sort of tosh which generations ago, and translated into Manx, served as a basis for some seven hundred grandiose pages by Sir Hall Caine. What do we glean from it? Do we glean that revivalist ministers, before they start redeeming other people, should be quite sure that they themselves have permanently put away the world and the flesh? But we knew that from *Rain* if we did not know it before. Do we glean that the line between religious hysteria and erotic emotionalism is a very fine one, particularly when the victim is rolling about on the floor? But surely it needed no Mr. King Vidor and 5,000 supernumeraries come from California to tell us this? Are we to glean that a natural trollop will, in spite of duckings, not revert to type? Or that you can get away with three homicides provided that two are in the nature of an accident, and that your intentions are of the best throughout?

These are the questions which we should ask ourselves if *Hallelujah* were really a film based upon life in the Welsh mining-districts. But *Hallelujah* isn't. It is based upon life in the cotton-fields of Georgia. Morgan Evans is really Zeke, a flower of negro chivalry *à la* Paul Robeson; his brother is called not Owen but Spunk; the trollop is called Chick; her bully, Hot Shot; while the scenario is composed by some man, woman. or child of the name of Wanda Tuchock. The whole film is a strange mixture of good and bad. Mr. Daniel L. Haynes, who plays Zeke, is obviously a fine actor, and Miss Nina Mae McKinney, who plays Chick, is a vamp of the most precious allurement. The revivalist scenes are extraordinarily well done. But here I think film critics are a little inclined to lose their heads. When the late Beerbohm Tree stage-managed his crowds in *Julius Cæsar* he did his job of work quite as well as Mr. King Vidor, and nobody talked about "synthetic emotion." Mr. Vidor does the same kind of thing with 5,000 men instead of fifty. Then again I think my colleagues are inclined to confuse the size and difficulty of an undertaking with the interest of its result. The programme tells us of the difficulty Mr. Vidor had to get the right measure of emotion out of a crowd which either went off into real hysterics of its own or stood about like sheep. Personally I don't care if it took Mr. Vidor ten years to train these niggers; all I know is that ten minutes is all I can stand of nigger ecstasy. But the revivalist scenes went on and on, and again on, and then some more, till in the end I became completely bored. Further, this preponderance throws the whole picture out of gear. For it is surely ridiculous to spend two hours watching a lot of negroes jogging up and down, and less than one minute in showing the result of religious hysteria upon the negro mentality, that result being imprisonment for manslaughter. Also I am completely tired of expositions of the negro by whites. It may be that Mr., Miss, or Master Wanda Tuchock—or can it be Mrs.?—is a coloured "pusson." But even so I feel that the directing mind is that of Mr. Vidor who in this film observes the negro from without, in exactly the same way as Mrs. Harriet Beecher Stowe. And between you and me, dear reader, between Mr. Vidor's sentimentality and that of Mrs. Stowe there is not a pin to choose. But the greatest fault with *Hallelujah* is the sound production. Whether from too much amplification or other reason, the voices at the invitation and midnight performance at the Empire had all the old horrible sea-lion quality. So much so that I could not distinguish one word in three. The lighting and the photography are on the whole poorish. Nevertheless, and despite all the foregoing, I declare *Hallelujah* to be the very film for the tired white business man or woman who desires, after the labours of the day, to lay a jaded head upon the perfumed bosom of the South. All others, if they think like me, will find it a little dull. But the subsequent champagne, meringues, and tongue-sandwiches were wildly exciting, and among those present I observed Mr. Leslie Henson and Miss Cicely Courtneidge.

8

BRIBERY AND CORRUPTION

1930

THE whole point about bribery is that it consists of both cause and effect. If there is no effect then the cause becomes innocence itself; in other words there is no harm in taking bribes so long as you are not corrupted by them, because, dear reader, such bribes then merely become gifts. Now I hope I can lay my hand on my heart and swear that like all my colleagues in the theatre I have never been corrupted. But which of us can say that he has never been bribed? I cannot—on the strict understanding that the word "bribe" has the harmless sense given to it above. I still have among my collection of oddities—the sort of collection which Hilary Jesson in Sir Arthur Pinero's play alludes to as his quaint museum, "old ballroom trophies, the blood-stained handkerchief of a matador, the cigarette half-smoked which has been pressed to the lips of an empress"—I still treasure a letter from my good friend, Charles Cochran, written on one of those occasions of dire extremity and collapse which constitute so regular a part of C.B.'s charm. This is the letter:

Dear James,—I have retrieved two bottles of tolerable champagne from my private room at the Oxford, and three of excellent Burgundy from the back of the stage at the Pavilion. A most dear lord has sent a noble haunch of venison, and I have seen something of a brace of pheasants. There is the nucleus of a feast here, after which the deluge! Will you come? Yours in all weathers.—C. B.

After supper we fell to admiring the treasures of that charming house, and I was lucky enough to spy on the floor, with its face to the wall, a lithograph by Picasso, "The Mountebanks." It was a study in starvation. I took an enormous fancy to it. Then C. B. made a speech. He said, "There are two reasons why I cannot give you that lithograph. The first is that you are a dramatic critic; the second is that the picture is not mine but my wife's. On the other hand, I do not suppose that I shall be producing anything for at least two years, and I am certain that my wife will never forgive me if I fall below her standard in these matters. The picture is yours." And with truly Spanish generosity—for he had just returned from Spain, where, if you admire a man's hat, he will take it off and thrust it into your hands—C. B. pushed the picture under my arm. He would take none of my so feeble denials. This picture now hangs on one of the walls of the den in which I am writing. Beneath it is a case containing Henry Irving's press-cutting scissors and a knife found under Shakespeare's house. These were given me by Seymour Hicks. In my bedroom are two photographs of Irving and Ellen Terry in the actual frames in which they hung for twenty-five years, one on each side of Irving's make-up table at the Lyceum; Irving's dresser gave them to Lady Martin-Harvey who gave them to me. I possess a portrait of Marie Tempest with an inscription which makes it more valuable to me than a frame studded with rubies, and a little tea-table which once belonged to Marie Lloyd. And a lot more little things. As critic for the B.B.C. and through the ether I have received one brace of grouse and, at various times, eleven bottles of cough-mixtures.

Since I have gone into business as a film critic I have not done so well, the total to date being meagre—to wit, one spirit-flask, one dozen bottles of champagne of a brand and year other than my favourite, one hundred middling cigars, fifty mediocre ditto, and twenty-five ditto which were damnable. And I hereby beg to announce that I am at any time prepared to receive what Lewis Carroll called un-birthday presents. I am contemplating taking a country cottage for the coming summer, if any; and if it pleases Heaven and the film magnates to rain grand pianos, gramophones, portable garages, tantaluses, lawn-mowers, garden-hedge clippers, and other trivia, I shall accept same. At the same time I beg to announce in a slightly louder tone that I have a most convenient memory for forgetting names, that I never know what company is producing what film, and that the effect of the gift or bribe would be to make my judgment a great deal harsher and stricter all round. The silly people who think that critics are affected by bribes never seem to realise this. They do not realise that the critic who criticises the performance of a friend takes excessive care to be rigorous, whereas if the actor in question is an enemy or a person repugnant to the critic he will take infinite pains to be generous.

The foregoing considerations have been evoked by an article in *The Saturday Review* entitled "Light on the Film Trade," with the sub-title, "Entertaining the Critics." Discussing the dinners which often precede the private show of a film, the writer says: "But in order to bring home more clearly the implications of the banqueting habit in film circles, one must draw a parallel with the theatre and imagine a costly meal being prepared for the dramatic critics, at which, one and all, they fell to heartily, before approaching, with joyful murmurs, the arduous task of witnessing the play, and the process, still further removed from the cold pheasant, of pronouncing upon it. One may well ask whether such a thing would be tolerated in the English theatre, and whether it is desirable in the cinema." The answer is that such a thing has been tolerated in the theatre, witness Irving's little suppers of cold chicken and champagne which did not, however, make a single critic think or write one ha'porth the better of the actor's Lear. The writer in *The Saturday Review* declares further: "There is probably no critic of the films in London who has not at some time reviewed an important picture on an unaccustomed diet of caviare and champagne." My answer is that I personally am completely accustomed to caviare and champagne, and inclined to be sick of both. The whole point is that responsible critics will write responsible criticism however they are treated, and that the writers of film gossip will in all circumstances write film gossip.

9

"SHOW OF SHOWS"

1930

WHEN will these American boosters realise that boosting, except to the completely stupid and uninitiated, does infinitely more harm than good? Good wine needs no bush, and to bring the entire forest of Birnam all the way from Hollywood in order to advertise a thin, unimportant little wine is to invite condemnation for that which otherwise might get off lightly enough. Cannot Hollywood realise that in this country we know something about revue? We do, in fact, know a great deal more about revue than apparently does Hollywood. We know about revues of all kinds; about those examples of design, colour, rhythm, and intelligent entertainment for the grown, sophisticated mind which are identified with the name of Charles Cochran. Mr. de Courville has taught us all about spectacle; Mr. Nelson Keys, Mr. Charlot, and Mr. Jack Hulbert about intimate delight; and Mr. Archie Pitt and Miss Gracie Fields all that we need know about rollicking fun and humour. A week ago every film critic was deluged with advertising matter to suggest that in *Show of Shows* he was to see something of which the world held no parallel. Let me recount exactly what I saw at the Tivoli and let me also pray the reader to believe that I write as one who has been a fervent admirer of revues of all kinds ever since this art-form came into existence.

Revue may be divided into its component parts roughly as follows: colour with which is included spectacle, sound, and the revue items including singing, dancing, and thumbnail examples of comedy and drama. Under the heading of colour I shall say that *Show of Shows* is colour-photography in its crudest, most garish kind, the resulting impression being that a child of seven has been let loose with a shilling box of paints. If a condition of good photography is good focussing then I shall say that this revue wholly fails, for there is no definition except in the close-ups, the majority of the big scenes being blurred and the participators unrecognisable one from another. Whether this is a result of too big a screen or the angle of vision, I am not technician enough to say; but I took the trouble to move from the side of the house where I was sitting to the plumb-centre of the theatre and found no improvement. In the matter of sound the revue has only one good tune, the one entitled "Singin' in the Bath-Tub," and incidentally the matter of this song is unimaginably inane. Further, the whole of the music is woefully reproduced, its volume being of the feeblest and its quality of the tinniest. This leaves the items, and here it is obvious that the American producers have once more succumbed to what they suppose to be the universal passion for celebrities, whether the celebrity does anything worth while or not. Georges Carpentier is raked in to sing a ditty so poor that it humiliates me to write of it, after which he lies on the floor and does physical jerks in the company of a hundred chorus-ladies. Then Richard Barthelmess appears and introduces eight pairs of sisters, each of which appears to have less talent than the preceding pair. I forget who introduces Miss Winnie Lightner who sings in her bath-tub, and all I remember of this artist is that with all her boisterousness she does not begin to have one-quarter of the talent of a Maisie Gay. Rin-Tin-Tin, the dog, then introduces a Chinese fantasy in which Miss Myrna

Loy thinly pleases, after which a number of chorus-ladies climb up and down step-ladders in a manœuvre which might be creditable to junior boys from a training-ship exhibiting at the Naval and Military Tournament. The feat is not graceful, not difficult, and not entertaining, and what it is there for heaven alone knows! Presently for no reason whatever Mr. John Barrymore introduces Shakespeare, the Duke of Gloster, and himself, after which he spouts the "Ay, Edward will use women honourably" soliloquy. This is quite well done, but why do it at all, for it miserably shows up everything that precedes and follows it?

And now I come to Miss Irene Bordoni, a *chanteuse* who devastated this country in *Little Miss Bluebeard*. The manner and methods of this artist were so miraculously foreseen by Huysmans in his description of the music hall that I cannot deny myself the pleasure of an abbreviated quotation: "To match the sounds which issued from her throat the singer had four gestures; one hand on her heart, the other down by her thigh—right arm in front, left arm behind—the same action reversed, both hands stretched out towards the public. She bawled the verses left and right alternately, opening and shutting her eyes according as the rasping melody was doleful or trivial. From the back rows where Désirée sat, her mouth, wide open for the last verse, had all the blackness of a cavern. The singer gave off her last note and bowed once more. Then picking up her skirt and with a last grin and smirk she trotted off to a deafening cannonade of bravos and encores. Désirée was pale with admiration. To begin with the verses had a sense of sentimentality. Again, the singer seemed to her to be lovely as a queen, with all her bracelets and ornaments and the undulating skirt. It was obvious that the cheeks were rouged and the eyelashes pencilled, but what with the lights and the scenery the woman seemed to get some sort of enticement into her performance." Strangely enough the audience at the Tivoli seemed to have a greater sense of humour than Désirée, and the singer's performance provoked not a little derision. Indeed for her Huysmans might have written the concluding lines of his sonnet:

Et c'est là cependant
Que toi, mon seul amour, toi, mes seules délices,
Tu brames tous les soirs d'infâmes ritournelles,
Et que, la bouche en cœur, l'œil clos, le bras pendant,
Tu souris aux voyous, ô la Reine des belles!

A certain liveliness sprang up in connection with the performance of some coloured dancers, after which the *compère* appeared without his trousers and conducted a lengthy argument with a chorus-lady, the solecism being the entire point. But the complete ineffectiveness of the show is to be judged by the fact that, according to the programme, appearances were made by Miss Beatrice Lillie and Miss Louise Fazenda without my noticing them. Going through the revue item by item, I can only think of six which could have found a place in any first-class London revue. These were an acrobatic turn, some negro dancers, the Barrymore recitation, the *compère*—amusing for so long as he was trousered—the old-time episode entitled *A Bicycle Made for Two,* and a really brilliant finale. It is quite possible that *Show of Shows* may please chawbacons in the Cotswolds who have never seen two hundred women together except at an annual fair. But this is a standard of criticism which readers of this paper will not ask me to take into account. I like revue just as much as I like liqueur brandy. But to boost this revue outrageously is like offering one a marvellous balloon-glass, and then pouring into it a cognac of indiscernible aroma. Frankly, if Messrs. Warner Brothers had said: "This isn't a bad little hotch-potch. Why not while away half-an-hour at it?" I should have written entirely differently. No one who wants praise for his mole-hill should hold out promise of a mountain. This is what Messrs. Warner Brothers, when they boosted this film, did.

10

ON HOLIDAY

1930

PARIS is a city which one likes despite, or perhaps because of its faults. The pen with which I write this is worse than any to be found even in an English post office, and the blotting-paper has not been changed since I occupied this bedroom a year ago. I know, because I can recognise an old signature, and remember that the blotting-paper was dirty then. It is not dirtier now; it could not be. But the hotel is clean, though not to that horrid degree connoted by the word "scrupulous." There is, at least, none of that horrid *confort moderne* about it, the sort of thing which Mr. Arnold Bennett preaches as Elysium, or next door to it. And then I adore the proprietress, an old maiden lady who looks as though she had come out of Balzac's "Le Cabinet des Antiques." Proust might have used her. Mademoiselle, for I know her by no other name, has been sitting at her little cash desk since the beginning of the century, always complaining cheerfully of the weather, the Government, the taxes, the exchange, and her rheumatism, but still the embodiment of French content. I should still recognise Paris without its obelisks, its triumphal arches, and its innumerable columns to this and that departed glory. But a live dog is better than a dead lion, and to see Mademoiselle is of more moment than the effigies of Louis and Napoleon. Their sun has set; hers still shines, and the time has not yet come when one could say that it shines wanly. On the whole I should call Mademoiselle rather a gay old thing, indescribably ancient, and bemuffled and bemittened and hung about with little gold chains, but still gay. Gaiety is the one trait of which the French will never cure themselves; and, indeed, to use the word "cure" in this connection is to betray the characteristic Anglo-Saxon phlegm. I was reading the other day one of D. H. Lawrence's last essays, that one which deals with London's inherent melancholy. That essay came very forcibly to mind as the train approached the Gare St. Lazare. I prefer that way because it is cheaper, less crowded, and more leisurely, thus discouraging that type of American who wants to "do" London and Paris in three days, and wipe up Brussels and Madrid before the end of the week. As you approach St. Lazare you skirt an enormous cemetery bringing to mind what the A. B. wrote in his diary: "I think what chiefly fascernates me about funerals is that it is not me in the corpidge." But we were talking about D. H. Lawrence. Now nobody, not even the French, can prevent a cemetery from being solemn, not to say dull. But at the far end of this gloomy place was an enormous wall upon which was emblazoned the sign "Jambon Cadillac." It was really some other name, but that will probably do. In these things it is the spirit that matters. The wall was part of a building, and on the return wall was another sign, "Saucisson Cadillac." It was as though, and as when, Charles Lamb said to the tombstone, "I am alive, I move about, I drink and eat the sausages and hams of Monsieur Cadillac. Know thy betters!" But there are some things in Paris which are not gay, and among these is to be reckoned the service in some restaurants. To-day one, or rather two, lunched in the Bois, not the wood of Boulogne, but that of Vincennes, the idea being to attend the aviation display. We found a delicious little place —by which I mean a large, rambling untenanted place. We peered about for a bit to find that everybody had deserted the restaurant and betaken himself to the edge of the lake or river, or whatever it is that flows through this landscape. This, according to your turn of mind, maks you think of the painter Renoir, or the writer Maupassant. Our meal was modest. *Hors d'œuvres,* including presumably the sausage of M. Cadillac, a sole *meunière,* a chicken, and the usual dessert. The cooking, the sunshine, and the bottle of Cos d'Estournel were alike perfect, but I give the reader my word that it took the establishment from a quarter-to-one to a quarter-past-three to serve this modest repast! However, one was on holiday and one was not pressed, as the old actor who was impersonating a waiter took occasion to remind one.

It was towards the end of this meal that I suddenly remembered that I had this article to write. And then the horrid fact began to come into my consciousness that I had not, before leaving London, seen a film upon which to deliver myself portentously and at length. Somehow or other I had not been in the mood for *All Quiet on the Western Front,* and I make readers my apology for an omission which I hope to repair next week. It is true that there had also been *Sergeant Grischa* to which I had determined to give the slip, as it were, on the sly. And now I do not know for a certainty that I shall ever see this film. For I take Mr. Sydney Carroll as an admirable guide to the pictures, and one whom I would as willingly follow as any. Mr. Carroll does not bother himself very greatly about "screen values", "rhythmic planes", "ideated impressionism", and all the rest of the silly jargon which brings so much of film criticism into line with modern art criticism. But there is a good deal of horse sense about my doughty colleague, and opening my *Sunday Times* I read the following:

> If I had a dog that always put its tail between its legs I would call it "Sergeant Grischa." For it would remind me of one of the greatest curs I have ever seen in human form on the films. Whatever moral the deviser and director of this gloomy, pestilential bit of nonsense, adapted indifferently from Arnold Zweig's story, had in view, I don't know. I cannot see what good object there can be in showing an American-voiced Russian giving a series of alternate exhibitions as a cry-baby, a coward, and a self-centred shirker, geared up at last into calmly facing death at the hands of a firing squad. For my own part I was glad to see *Grischa* finished.

For me that settles it. I know now that I shall not see this film. It also settles one question which has long perplexed me. Is film criticism of any practical value? Do people go to a film or stay away from it because it is praised or condemned in the papers? Well, here is a case of one critic who has, on the strength of a single notice, kept away at least one person from visiting a film.

However, I must be getting to my muttons as the French very nearly say. If returning, why not getting, in the first instance? I determined to spend the rest of this glorious afternoon at some French cinema. Which? With comparative ease I declined the chance of seeing Clara Bow in *Amour des Gosses.* Nor did I seem to care much about *Visages Oubliés* with Clive Brook, or even *Le Chien des Baskervilles.* There was a slightly too familiair ring about all three. So I went haphazard to the Cinéma de la Madeleine where a year or so ago I saw the ever-exquisite and never-to-be-forgotten *Ombres Blanches,* known over in England as *White Shadows.* The first film told the story, half comic and half sentimental, to which the cinema has wholly accustomed us, the story of the eternal triangle, the passionate crime, the trial, the acquittal, and the reunion of two hearts never more to be separated. Only, in this ultra-Parisian case, the film was acted entirely by dogs! The judge was a bloodhound, sombre, melancholy, and all-wise, and he was superb! The wife, too, who committed the murder, was the most life-like little lady-dog imaginable! The main piece of the afternoon was a thriller, and I must confess to having slept as soundly as if I had been at home.

11

LOYALTIES

1930

IN one of his wickedest parodies Mr. Max Beerbohm made Mr. George Moore wonder why when people talked to him of Tintoretto he always found himself thinking of Turgenev. One of my disabilities as a writer is that I always want to write about something other than the job in hand. This afternoon I went to the pictures to see Lillian Gish, not because I supposed she would be particularly worth seeing these days, or because I wanted to hear how she mishandled the English language, but out of loyalty to an old affection. And of course the word "loyalty" suggested another train of reflection, for as I write the newspapers are buzzing with news of the deposition of Chapman, an act which seems to me, of all the revolting and insensate things ever done by a selection committee, the most revolting and insensate. By the time these lines are printed it will be too late in the day to analyse Chapman's past achievements. I shall refer only to that catch at Lord's which got rid of Bradman in the second innings, as to which I hold that a man who could make catches like that should be played for England till palsy prevents him from putting one hand against another. But the point which moves me most is the matter of loyalty to a Captain with a record in Captaincy unbeaten by any who ever led an English team. Other papers have the comparison with military matters, and alleging that the most brilliant General who is out of luck must be deposed, have sought to apply the analogy to Test Captains. This seems to me to confound warfare with mimic warfare. It may be vitally important who wins a campaign or a battle; it is not *vitally* important to anybody or anything, except the circulations of newspapers, whether eleven young Englishmen beat eleven young friends from Australia or vice versa. The greatest evil in this absurdly exaggerated exaltation of Test Matches—an exaltation artfully manufactured by the newspapers to their own profit—is that we are all likely to forget that cricket is after all a game. Upon battles the welfare of nations depends, or is said to depend, as we can easily see from the fact that England, which won the last war, has now more unemployed than all the other countries who took part in it put together. Or near enough. But no child in the slums is more hungry or less educated because Mr. Bobby Jones did four rounds at Sandwich in some three strokes less than a lot of other people who might have been more usefully engaged. Incidentally I desire it to be remarked that I am a keen golfer. Nobody in England would be a less good citizen because Australia contrives to make 1,087 runs as against England's miserable total of 1,086. I also desire it to be remarked that I shall be in Brittany before the first ball of this match is bowled and am arranging for the score to be telegraphed twice a day and at the conclusion of each innings. In other words, I have the normal Englishman's frantic desire that we should win this match. Or had—until they deposed Chapman. What happens now I do not really much care. I shall not cancel the arrangements about the telegrams, but I say quite frankly that I would rather have lost the match under Chapman than win it under anybody else. The whole proceeding seems to me to be so essentially ignominious. By the time these lines appear we shall know what luck has attended Mr. Wyatt. It is said that anybody can govern in a state of siege, and this may be equally true of a state of panic. In my humble opinion panic was never more openly declared than in this decision to choose for Captain one who has no experience of Test cricket. Let there be no mistake. I do not deny that Wyatt may at the moment be in better form than Chapman. My point is that I would rather lose with Grace than win without it. Readers may ask what all this gush has to do with Gish. The answer is—nothing whatever, except that mention of this charming little actress started the subject of loyalty.

What is this mania possessed by the film industry for presenting well-known plays under another title? The film in which Miss Gish is appearing at the Marble Arch Pavilion bears the innocuous title of *One Romantic Night,* and to this film I went in all good faith, never dreaming that I was to be bored once again with the work of that ineffable Hungarian, Ferenc Molnar. The film turned out to be *The Swan* all over again. Surely the ordinary play-goer has a grievance here, for I conceive that anybody who has spent one evening at any play does not want on the following night to have the same play foisted upon him under another name. In my view the film was shockingly acted, these American film players apparently knowing as much about the way royalty behaves as the average cab-horse knows of the Royal Mews. I have always adored Miss Gish, but on condition that she is surrounded by a snowstorm, brutal parents, or hordes of lascivious Chinese. Her eyes are still that enormous distance apart upon which all wistfulness depends; her nose is still one sixty-fourth part of an inch too short, and her mouth not quite where it should be. In other words, I am still in love with her. But that does not prevent me from recognising that the upper housemaid is the extremity of this actress's social range. I had difficulty in getting a programme, so the always courteous management of this house arranged to obtain one for me at the end of the performance. Opening it as I write, I discover that it is a programme having to do with some other show! I mention this understandable detail merely because it precludes me from knowing who the other players were. The actress who played the Princess's mother had features with which I was completely familiar but I could not allocate them to their owner. Vaguely I associated them with the massive termagants of slapstick comedy and the heedless recipients of a wash-tub's contents. As a queen, reigning or otherwise, the actress in question seemed to me to be completely unthinkable, though of her skill in humbler parts I have many delighted recollections. The Prince in this film can never be a satisfactory creature, though there was no reason for presenting him as a howling cad! The vilest middle-class American was spoken throughout, and it was perhaps significant that as the entertainment wore on the sparse audience thinned itself perceptibly. I shall in future very carefully examine the titles of the films produced at what I have always regarded as my favourite picture-house. If, for example, I see anything calling itself *The Gipsy's Lady* I shall at once say to myself, "Ha, ha! Molnar's *Liliom*! No, you don't!" And I shall immediately hie me to somewhere where they are performing *The Red Tunic*—and discover, of course, that this is only Molnar's *The Guardsman.* I have only two requests to make of the film industry. First, that they tell us what plays their films are derived from; and second, that they desist from perpetuating the masterpieces of the more crashing of Hungarian bores.

12

"BILLY THE KID"

1931

THE new film at the Empire purports to tell the life-history up to the date of his marriage and retirement into domesticity of a brave and chivalrous bandit endeared to the public of Mexico by the name of Billy the Kid. Being a bit of a realist I propose to give the facts about a good-looking, black-hearted, homicidal maniac, who never retired, never married, was sentenced to death, escaped, and was ultimately shot in the dark by Sheriff Garrett. William H. Bonney was born in New York on November 23, 1859. The family, consisting of father, mother, and two boys, of whom Billy was the elder, migrated to Kansas where the father died. The mother then took her two boys to Colorado, where she married a man called Antrim, who at once took her and Billy to Santa Fé, New Mexico, whence when Billy was nine years of age they moved on to Silver City. At the age of twelve our hero successfully brought off his first murder. Watching a rough-and-tumble in a bar he observed that one of the participants was a man who some three months earlier had insulted his mother. With Billy to observe was to act, and taking advantage of a moment when the man was about to fell his opponent with a chair, the boy rushed in under his arm and stabbed him to death. Flight to Arizona followed, where he and another young brigand encountered three Indians in the neighbourhood of Fort Bowie. I give Billy's own account of what followed: "It was a ground hog case. Here were twelve good ponies, four or five saddles, a good supply of blankets, and five pony loads of pelts. Here were three bloodthirsty savages, revelling in all this luxury and refusing succour to two free-born, white American citizens, foot-sore and hungry. The plunder had to change hands—there was no alternative—and as one live Indian could place a hundred United States troopers on our trail in two hours, and as a dead Indian would be likely to take some other route, our resolves were taken. In three minutes there were three 'good Injuns' lying around there, careless like, and with ponies and plunder we skipped. There was no fight. It was about the softest thing I ever struck." At Fort Bowie he next killed a soldier blacksmith with whom he quarrelled at cards. At the age of seventeen Billy took part in what is known as the Lincoln County War, a bloody and complicated business concerning grazing-rights in which Billy fought sometimes on one side and sometimes on the other. This was gangster warfare and in no way more respectable than the Chicago feuds of the present day. Even then, it appears, rival thugs took one another for rides, but always on their own horses and sometimes under a flag of truce. Finding a rival drunk in a bar the Kid complimented him on his revolver, put the weapon out of action, returned it to the owner, provoked him to a quarrel, and when the drunken man had fired harmlessly, whipped his own revolver out and shot him through the brain. There was another dreadful occasion when the Kid proposed to a posse which was out to capture him that if they would agree to exchange hostages he would consider the question of surrender. The exchange was made and a very decent young blacksmith, one Jimmie Carlyle, recently come to the territory and much liked by everybody, was handed over to the Kid, who proceeded to make him say his prayers, and then tortured him by shooting all round his head. At the noise of this the posse sent word that if they heard another shot they would presume that Carlyle had been killed, and take immediate revenge on their hostage. Then one of the guns belonging to the police-party went off by accident, whereupon Carlyle, fearing that his own life would be taken, jumped through the window of the block-house and was riddled with bullets before he reached the ground. The Kid afterwards expressed great regret for this misunderstanding, but it was this murder which chiefly brought about his loss of popularity.

Ultimately the Kid surrendered to the police for reasons which might weigh with a Jack Diamond, and was sentenced to death for the murder of Sheriff Brady. Brady held a warrant for the Kid's arrest; so the Kid hid behind a wall and murdered the Sheriff in cold blood as he was on his way to the court-house. Unfortunately Lincoln County did not at that time possess a gaol which would have held a cripple. The Kid had no difficulty in procuring arms and killing his two warders, one with a bullet from his revolver, and the other with thirty-six buck shot. There is no doubt that Sheriff Garrett, who had charge of the prisoner, was responsible for these deaths, since to allow a rogue of the Kid's ability to roam virtually fetterless about a gaol well-stocked with firearms was asking for trouble. The Kid now made his way towards Fort Sumner where he was allowed a few weeks' rope. Ultimately he was rounded up by Sheriff Garrett and two police-officers. Garrett discovered where the Kid was in hiding, rounded him up in some old buildings, and heard him, declaring he was hungry, ask for a butcher-knife with which to get some beef from Pete Maxwell's. But Garrett got to Pete Maxwell's house first and was hiding by the side of Pete's bed when the Kid came in with a revolver in one hand and the butcher-knife in the other. I shall tell the rest in Garrett's own words: "The intruder came close to me, leaned both hands on the bed, his right hand almost touching my knee, and asked in a low tone,

'Who are they, Pete?' At the same instant Maxwell whispered to me, 'That's him!' Simultaneously the Kid must have seen or felt the presence of a third person at the head of the bed. He raised quickly his pistol—a self-cocker—within a foot of my breast. Retreating rapidly across the room, he cried, '*Quién es? Quién es?*' All this occurred more rapidly than it takes to tell it. As quick as possible I drew my revolver and fired, threw my body to one side, and fired again. The second shot was useless. The Kid fell dead at the first one. He never spoke. A struggle or two, a little strangling sound as he gasped for breath, and the Kid was with his many victims." Somehow or other I do not particularly care about Master Garrett who, in his book about the Kid, admits the wilful intention of shooting him in the back, or in the dark, or in whichever way involved the least risk to his own precious carcase. Bonney was buried in the old military cemetery at Fort Sumner on July 5, 1881, he being a little over twenty-one years of age. This young man is known to have committed twelve murders, not counting Indians! He was a handsome, smiling dago, but I cannot discover that he possessed any virtues except courage and the capacity to shoot straight.

It is perhaps unnecessary to say that Mr. King Vidor's film shows nothing of all this, but prefers to present Bonney as a kind of prairie Valentino sighing for a young woman's eyebrow. The young woman in question even goes so far as to whitewash Bonney with the categorical statement: "You've never killed a man that didn't need killing, and you've made America a better place to live in!" This is, of course, complete and utter punk. Garrett, instead of being shown as the atrabilious, self-justifying police hound, has to become the jovial sportsman who is Mr. Wallace Beery. Mr. Beery connives at Mr. Bonney's escape and, twitching his helmet blue, wafts him to fresh woods and pastures new. This film will do nothing to remove the misconceptions already prevalent about the Kid. How prevalent these are may be adduced from the fact that my colleague, Mr. Gordon Beckles, normally omniscient, writes: "I imagine that the sanguinary Billy looked much more like Mr. Beery than Mr. John Mack Brown." Personally I cannot imagine any murderer in his teens looking like that middle-aged mountain. If Mr. Beckles is interested I shall be delighted to show him an authentic drawing of Bonney which shows him to have looked like a Hippodrome chorus-boy in some revue of the Wild West. As a film having no connection whatever with the real Bonney, *Billy The Kid* will pass muster.

13

A GAYNOR-FARRELL DISAPPOINTMENT

1931

AN actor who has a reputation for power and emotion and whose film record is excellent tells me the following story. Some time ago he rang up one of our British studios which was about to produce a film on a famous subject. The actor did not hope to get hold of the casting-director or any of the high gods who earn large salaries apparently by keeping out of the way. My friend, however, hoped to get hold of somebody. And did, with this result. "Of course we know all about you," said the voice. "Sorry, old man, but there's nothing you could play. You see, old man, *Dreyfus* is a comedy!" I do not propose to mar with comment the stark simplicity of this grand story.

I have been wondering lately whether anybody has noticed the bankruptcy of the American language except in the domain of slang. Happening to find myself the other night in a state of despond at Slough, I turned me from the completely empty and draughty, main, and only street into the entirely full picture-house many degrees warmer than a conservatory in July. There I saw and heard Miss Norma Shearer declare that she had been unfaithful to her husband but the episode had not meant a thing to her. Whereupon the husband declared that his flirtation in the pantry with a vivacious widow, which had been the cause of Norma's defaulting, had not meant a thing to him. I suppose that if they used this wretched phrase once they used it twenty times. Later when Miss Shearer was contemplating suicide or going to live in Chicago, her husband, looking like three of Othello's soliloquies rolled into one, told her to "snap out of it." Perhaps American is still too new a country to have anything to do with so old a thing as language, and perhaps too the fact that America has replaced words by slang derives from the same reason which has driven her to jazz instead of music. Walt Whitman said somewhere that he did not think America could produce any genuine art for another couple of hundred years. I have been unable to find the exact passage, but looking for it the other day I came across something else which has a certain significance in our present connection:

> Certainly, anyhow, the United States do not so far utter poetry, first-rate literature, or any of the so-called arts, to any lofty admiration or advantage—are not dominated or penetrated from actual inherence or plain bent to the said poetry and arts. Other work, other needs, current inventions, productions, have occupied, and to-

day mainly occupy them. They are very 'cute and imitative and proud—can't bear being left too glaringly away far behind the other high-class nations—and so we set up some home "poets", "artists", painters, musicians, literati, and so forth, all our own (thus claimed). The whole matter has gone on, and exists to-day, probably as it should have been, and should be; as, for the present, it must be. To all which we conclude, and repeat the terrible query: American National Literature—is there distinctively any such thing, or can there ever be?

In the meantime America continues to send us pictures as bankrupt of ideas as the talkies are of words. Time was when I counted myself among the more frantic admirers of Janet Gaynor and Charles Farrell, Janet for her Wendyishness, Charles for a curious compound of nervous strength and a capacity for being hurt. This was in their silent days. Then came the talkies, and I shall never forget how Janet's speech drove me headlong from the theatre. In this respect she has much improved, or perhaps it is the sound-production which has now become so perfect that in *The Man who Came Back*, trade-shown this week at the Cambridge Theatre, Janet has been allowed to speak throughout in something approaching a whisper, and so avoids raucousness. Farrell's voice is neither pleasant nor unpleasant; any bus conductor might possess it without occasioning remark. He has, however, entirely lost his charm, and throughout this long film not one single moment of his acting gave me any of the old pleasure. Janet appears considerably older, and all that is left of her appeal is the pathetically twisted mouth. She has been badly directed in this film, at least to the extent of being allowed to display two of the ugliest and grubbiest little paws imaginable.

And then the story! Stephen Randolph, the drunken heir to millions, takes a chorus-girl for a trip in an aeroplane and proposes marriage—a freak which costs Stephen's excessively vulgar father 25,000 dollars. The old man then ships off his son to San Francisco. But Stephen, to quote from the programme, "is dissatisfied, and accuses his father of having spoiled him with over-indulgence and a lavish education which made him miss all the real fellowship of college life." Judging from other films the real fellowship of college life consists of playing football with Clara Bow. But let that pass. Stephen goes to 'Frisco and falls in love with Angie, a cabaret dancer whom he proposes to take back to New York with him. Angie is overjoyed, but on hearing that she is to go not as wife but as mistress becomes "bitterly disillusioned." In the meantime Stephen has committed forgery, so his father ships him off to Shanghai. Arriving at that port by sailing-vessel, Stephen discovers the bitterly disillusioned

Angie installed as principal bait in a Chinese opium-den, the maiden having contrived to undergo ten years' degradation in the space of, allowing for her voyage also, about six weeks. So Stephen reclaims Angie and they both ship themselves to Honolulu where, in a flower-covered bungalow on a pineapple plantation, they live for three years. Further complications arise in the course of which Angie, again to reclaim Stephen, who has broken his pledge of reformation, pretends again to have resorted to opium. So he duly horsewhips her in the course of which she drops her Chinese kimono and dope-sodden grin to reveal spotted muslin and the Janet-smile. It was only a trick and as the whipping left her unmarked we can assume it to have been neither for weal nor woe. Then Angie ships Stephen back to New York and remains behind with an oily Lothario who turns out to be old Randolph's private detective. And since Angie, while Stephen is on probation in New York, leads a life of purity at which the flowers themselves would be abashed, why then Angie is presently gathered to the bosom of Stephen in the opulent saloon-lounge of Randolph *père*, who regrets that the boy's mother, being in heaven, must deny herself the pride of making the young woman's acquaintance. At this the dress-circle at the Cambridge Theatre vulgarly guffawed, the politer stalls being content to titter.

Some publicity-literature informs me that "under the direction of Raoul Walsh the elusive appeal of Janet Gaynor is vividly enhanced." If enhanced means what I think it does, this was not possible. I am further told that "to the romantic boyishness of Charles Farrell is added force and power." My remark about this is that we are asked to accept force and power in place of the romantic boyishness which has entirely disappeared. Judging by this film Farrell has now become in his screen personality a completely unremarkable, commonplace, and if anything, rather objectionable young man. Janet, too, is on the wane, and this stupid meandering picture was one more in my too-long sequence of Gaynor-Farrell disappointments. For I loved them once.

14

AT BEACONSFIELD

1931

MOTORISTS proceeding along the Uxbridge Road have little to interest them except the tramlines and the occasional though always fascinating lorries of the Ham River Grit Company. Presently, however, they arrive at Beaconsfield, the noble village in whose church Edmund Burke lies buried and in whose purlieus many famous literary people lead a dead-and-alive existence. In fact I see no reason why I should not confess that the dampest cottage in this or any other place is modestly tenanted by the present writer. I say this because it explains why somebody asked me the other day whether I had seen anything of Mr. Chesterton, to which I ventured to reply that one either sees the whole of this distinguished author or nothing. Leaving the Saracen's Head on the left and taking a turn to the right by the White Hart, whose sign at night looks so exactly like a startled cat, one passes two buildings of obvious size and importance. One looks inscrutably romantic and belongs to the local laundry; the other, which is of the architectural simplicity proper to bathing-vans, is the Lion Film Studio, to which I was bidden to see some shots of a picture featuring Messrs. Conway Tearle and Robert Farquharson and Mesdames Betty Stockfeld, Louie Tinsley, and Violet Vanbrugh. It is unnecessary for me to say anything here about Mr. Tearle, who in his stockinged feet stands some five foot ten inches of solid glamour. Miss Betty Stockfeld is an extremely intelligent young actress whose undeniable loveliness the film will doubtless reduce in its most expensive manner to expressionless putty. But why Betty? There are certain names which film actresses should avoid since they have a belittling effect, and Betty is one of them. Betty Negri would, I feel, not have traversed continents leaving a trail of broken hearts, and Peggy Garbo is unthinkable. For any actress of real histrionic ambition such names as Binnie, Minnie, and Winnie should be strictly taboo. Miss Stockfeld has recently changed her name from Stockfield, and in my view it is a thousand pities that she has not changed Betty to Beata. But that is by the way.

I was considerably intrigued by the presence of Mr. Farquharson and Miss Vanbrugh. Mr. Farquharson is a many-sided artist, and about as many years ago as he and I put together can remember, showed signs of becoming an intellectual actor of the first rank. On Sunday evenings in the 'nineties he could be found playing Herod for the benefit of audiences drawn entirely from the Café Royal, and strictly disobeying Hamlet's injunctions with regard to this rôle. Even to-day he has no rival in the portrayal of the more exotic emotions. Should anybody desire to revive *The Blood-Drinker's Daughter*, in which Miss Henrietta Petowker made so great a success, there is no doubt who would be chosen to play that fantastic parent. Mr. Farquharson, besides being a fine actor, is an accomplished musician, and I should not be surprised to hear that he could paint, sculp, etch, and woodcut as well. He is master of all the arts, and too good to be the jack of any. It will be extremely interesting to see what he does with the films. I have no doubt that he can stand up to celluloid;

my only uneasiness is as to whether celluloid can stand up to him. At Miss Vanbrugh's presence I completely boggled, for here is one of the few remaining actresses who can present a woman of breeding, and what that has got to do with the cinema Hollywood only knows. Some little time ago I saw on the film another actress of extreme distinction, and all she had to do was to wash her pet-dog. A few days prior to seeing this film I had played bridge with the actress in question who, having re-doubled a grand slam in hearts when we were vulnerable, cost us a fortune which I at least could ill afford. Meeting her at supper a few days after the film I said: "Dear lady, I have had my revenge for that re-double. I saw you last week in *Polluted Streams*." The dear creature, for she is dear in more senses than one, covered her face with her hands, and presently the tears of shame were flowing over her exquisite wrists. I hasten to add that this story has nothing to do with Miss Vanbrugh.

While waiting for lunch I spent a very agreeable time wandering over a floor which was littered with thousands of what appeared to be hose-pipes, and remarked how small the players looked against marble columns obviously made out of linoleum. There followed something which, when we have been ushered by cowboys or Red Indians into our seats to see it, will probably turn out to be acting. I was informed that the rest of the picture was being filmed on board some society lady's yacht at Monte Carlo, and that what I had come in from the muddy Beaconsfield roads to see was part of Miss Betty Stockfeld's bedroom in a hotel at Capri. It was certainly very sumptuous and pretty, and Mr. Tearle and Miss Stockfeld luxuriating in a pink felicity movingly concluded a story of which one did not know either the beginning or middle. My admiration for film actors and film acting at once went up a thousand per cent, for it seems that film actors have to face not only the disconcerting lights and cameras but crowds of stage carpenters, plumbers, and shirt-sleeved supernumeraries, each of whom looked as though he were being acted by Mr. Jack Hulbert in a revue. Presently we adjourned for lunch and were told that the title of the picture is to be *Escapade* if it isn't changed to something else, which was being debated with much animation as I left for London. The whole experience, though delightful, taught me this—that the proper place to see a picture is the picture-house. I am the most easily illuded person in the world, and when at the trade-show I see Miss Stockfeld bathed in melancholy on some divan I shall believe that the house surrounding her is a real house complete with staircases and upper storeys, and that her gaze out of window is upon the sparkling waters of Capri, or Blackpool, or wherever it may be, and not upon the lath and canvas of the studio at Beaconsfield.

The picture which I rushed to London to see was *Laughter* at the Plaza. My principal reason for visiting this picture was that I had not been overwhelmed with publicity guff concerning it, and my invariable experience of films is that the less said concerning them the better they turn out to be. Let me say at once that *Laughter* is one of the best talking pictures I have ever seen. The dialogue and the situations are uniformly witty throughout, and there is no suggestion that the film is a photographed play. It even constitutes its own logic, so that everything in the film is right by virtue of being in that film. There is an admirable moment in which two lovers drenched to the skin break into a bungalow, take off their clothes, and cover themselves with the skins of two bears, one brown and the other polar, which are lying on the floor. If only Miss Negri would occasionally consent to be polar! And if only other film stars would realise that if they will laugh at themselves there is infinitely less risk of their being laughed at. Later the film becomes quite serious and I am not at all sure that you might not call it a tragi-comedy. Miss Nancy Carroll, Mr. Fredric March, and Mr. Glenn Anders act delightfully, and, in short, I advise readers to make a note of this title, and if ever they come across this film again not to omit seeing it.

15

CONCERNING GREATNESS

1931

THE world for some time past has been governed by the spirit of megalomania. Everybody wants to do things on the largest scale. They want to dine at the biggest hotels, make one at a record audience at the biggest success in town, own the biggest cars, fly in the fastest aeroplanes, and if they are involved in a railway smash would not be happy unless it was the biggest in the history of these disasters. Mr. Priestley was pointing out the other day that people have again taken to reading the longest novels, and I hope I shall not be deemed ungracious if I say that the wish, dear J. B., may have been father to the thought! No actress can leave these shores without giving the smartest and most riotous party which has ever made Society ask what things are coming to. As if Society didn't know! No actress can set sail for America in other than the largest steamboat, or one driven by an abnormal number of turbines, since with anything smaller goes loss of reputation—always provided the player in question has any, for in the matter of reputation it equally holds true that to him or her that hath shall be given, and you know the rest. The whole of this last sentence is inspired by the *bon mot* of a charming actress who looks like the flower, but whose sayings suggest the serpent under it. This delightful lady—whom I shall not identify except to say that when she is in the cast no play can fail, and when she is out of it hardly any can succeed—this exquisite creature said to me the other day about her dearest rival whom on her departure for America she had dumped with valedictory flowers into the boat-train at Waterloo: "My dear, it must be a very small part for she's gone by a very small boat!" Having said this, and after bestowing the largest possible tip on the waiter and blowing me the weeniest, teeniest kiss that Sir James Barrie ever devised for unborn fairies, this gracious creature was whisked away in a limousine so large that it appeared to be waiting round both sides of the Ivy Restaurant at once. The theatre is certainly the world for bigness of all kinds, and how much more so the cinema! Personally, I love to hear of enormous sums being spent on films because I know then that there will be something to look at. News has begun to pour in about *Cimarron*, and I have received a letter informing me that this film is not only the best and grandest and most magnificent that has ever been made, but that it is the most terrific, astounding, and cataclysmic that ever could, should, or might be made. This is a statement after my own heart. The man who made it has burned his boats, and the only fault I have to find with his letter is that it was sent through the post in the ordinary way. In my view it ought to have been written in gold ink on Japanese vellum and presented to me on a cushion by somebody in plush after the manner of the Presentation of the Rose in Strauss's opera. I think I should have known how to receive this herald, for I should have taken the tip from that character in Mr. Milne's fantastic play, who, when the butler announced that a knight in armour had called, replied: "Show him in, Timms, and bring the whisky!" With the most astonishing moderation *Cimarron* is proclaimed as having cost £450,000. That is a very cute figure; it would have been so easy and so much less impressive to talk about half-a-million. I understand that we are to see a village which in 1899 was only a collection of wooden shacks grow into the town of 1930. Good! The film is from a novel by Edna Ferber and deals with life in Oklahoma. Good again! I have never been to Oklahoma and I know that I never shall go to Oklahoma. Indeed I would very nearly sooner die than go to Oklahoma. On the other hand, there is nothing after which I hanker quite so passionately as to visit Oklahoma on the films, and until March 7 the refrain will continuously run through my head: "Per cinema ad Oklahoma!"

The figures about the Charlie Chaplin film, *City Lights*, which will have been seen at the Dominion before these lines appear, show this undertaking to be, comparatively speaking, paltry, since only the insignificant sum of £ 300,000 is mentioned! But how good it is to know that Charlie still refuses to break that which was always most golden about him—his silence. I am not sure whether I shall not avoid the opening night, on the theory that an idol is something which one should not get too near to. I have seen portraits of a distinguished, silver-haired elegant, walking in a garden in grave converse with the Prime Minister, and it seems to me that this is part of the price one pays for being Prime Minister. Will Mr. MacDonald ever again be able to see *only* that rapt buffoon and tender zany? Will not his vision of *City Lights* be clouded by the suspicion that he is watching a very great artist, perhaps, *pace* the Chaliapin fans, the greatest artist living to-day? If this be so, am I not happier whose mind has never entertained the thought of the meticulous analytical artist knowing why he wears those boots, exactly how stiff should be that arm from which the cane depends, and calculating the wryness of his smile? Charlie Chaplin has always seemed to me to be as self-existent as a golliwog or other childish thing; when you have done playing with him you put him away in the drawer with the other toys. This is the greatest tribute that one could pay to any artist—that one should resent his having any life of his own. Charlie on the screen belongs to the nations and the ages, and I strongly suspect that he belongs also to all time, and in as many directions as metaphysicians shall ultimately find that Time runs. It seems to me that Charlie Chaplin *is* as essentially as matter, and that Mr. Charles Chaplin, the guest of kings and what not, does not exist. And if he does, that is his own affair. My evening paper has just hazarded the following: "Most people may not know that Mr. Chaplin is a very good musician. He plays, with varying success, the violin, 'cello, piano, organ, concertina, and certain brass instruments." I did not know this, and now that I do know it I shall make the greatest possible haste to forget it. All I know about Mr. Chaplin, and all I ever want to know, is that, measuring my words and remembering all the great players, he is, in my view, the greatest of them all.

16

"THE ROYAL FAMILY"

1931

THE tiger which has once tasted blood is a puling simile for the actor who has once tasted applause. Fame, we recalled the other day, is the last infirmity of noble mind, and we remember patting Milton on the back for a just sentiment. But that austere poet was probably thinking of dull folk like emperors and statesmen, astronomers and poets, who do their work in the decent obscurity of their closet, whereas the artist, and particularly the actor, is another matter, as Milton must have known if he had ever been in a theatre. I forestall objection by saying that I do not regard a masque in Cromwell's back garden as theatre. Now the actor's desire is not for fame, which is an abstract matter maturing only in the by-and-by; what he wants is that immediate instalment here and now, hot and strong, which is applause. And I should be prepared if Milton were here to argue the actor's right to it on the grounds that no craving can be wrong which is universal. Applause being the very breath of an actor's nostrils, it follows that when for any reason it is not forthcoming the player is left without anything to breathe. It is the subconscious recognition of this which makes audiences applaud the actors though the play may have left them swooning with boredom. For myself I can think of no abdication quite so pitiful as that of the actor who had abdicated, unless it be that of the journalist who had ceased to write. The reader will appreciate that the tawdriness of the actor's acting and the trumperiness of the journalism are not the point. An essayist of some competence has written about a man whose work is done: "I am Retired Leisure. I am to be met with in trim gardens. I am already come to be known by my vacant face and careless gesture." How much more would the great actor in retirement come to be known by the vacancy of his once so intense expression and the carelessness of his once so carefully measured gesture? I am always incredibly affected whenever I read the account of Macready's farewell to the stage, and my emotion is not at all diminished by a sneaking belief that on the stage Macready was something of a bore. "On nous abandonne," said Marguérite Gautier, "et les longues soirées succèdent aux longs jours!" Actresses will not misunderstand me when I say that artists who have desisted from pleasing in any walk of life are in respect of the ensuing tedium very much in the same boat. The player, then, lives by applause and ceases to live, in the sense of declining to mere existence, when that applause is withdrawn. But in all fairness to the player it must be said that as a general rule he gives life to that which gives him life. Most actors prefer to die in harness, and one might say that there is an unwritten law on the subject. I have already compared the profession of the actor with that of the journalist, and that they have one thing in common cannot be denied. Nobody has ever heard an actor say that as he is not feeling very well he does not think he will go down to the theatre. Nobody has ever heard a journalist say that as he is a bit off colour he doesn't think he will turn in his copy. If a journalist is alive, his copy will be there to time; if it isn't, *ipso facto*, he is dead. The same holds true of the actor.

The foregoing is implicit in that extraordinarily good film, *The Royal Family of Broadway*, at the Plaza, which shows the spirit of the old trouper at its most militant, most persistent, and best. But the finest qualities admit of exaggeration, and this continual desire to be in the public eye, and the immense bitterness attendant upon the slightest and most temporary occlusion, has its ludicrous side. *The Royal Family* is really a skit upon the Barrymores, great players all of them, members of a great acting family, and inheritors of a great acting tradition. But this has not prevented them from indulging in an emphasis which in itself almost amounts to burlesque, and needs but very little parodying to become the wildest and cruellest fun. The film begins with Fanny Cavendish driving home from the theatre with her daughter, Julia, who is, of course, Ethel Barrymore. Julia is thinking of giving up play-acting, and is rebuked by her mother, a ruined tower of tragic beauty, who says: "Stuff and nonsense!" in the language and accents of Lady Macbeth plus the three hags in *Richard III*. They arrive home, which is a palatial affair, with full-length Gainsboroughs on the wall and the traditional Sargent drawing of brother Tony (supposed to be John Barrymore), from whom a telegram now arrives saying that he has killed somebody and will be home presently. "Anyone we know?" asks his mother in her rich, royal accents, and it appears that it is only one of Hollywood's movie directors. Presently Tony arrives, worried not on the question of manslaughter, since the director is recovering, but because some Polish film star is suing him for breach of promise. He arrives with a procession of luggage-bearers, but muffled up to the eyebrows in a bearskin the better to remain incognito, and pretending not to know for whose autograph a mob of some ten thousand gathered in the street outside is howling. He too is thinking of giving up the stage, proposing to enter a Kurdish monastery and eat rice; go to Munich and become a fiddler. In the meantime he must have a bath and rushes up the marble staircase followed by his adoring family, to whom he discards even his ultimate garments. So great is Tony's charm, and so urgent his recital of what he has done and is about to do, that they follow him into the bath-cabinet. Mr. Fredric March gives a magnificent impersonation, so magnificent that it is almost impossible to believe that you are not watching Barrymore. The famous nose and the famous insistence upon profile, the charm and the absurdity, the gestures and the dæmonism, the monkey-tricks and the blaze of temperament, all are here and are continuously and devastatingly exploited throughout what is really quite a good story. It ends with the death of the old actress during a performance of *The Merry Wives* and her replacement by her daughter, who has vowed never to act again. As a very great admirer and a personal friend of Barrymore I enjoyed this picture enormously, for with all its cruelty it does nothing to diminish one's sense of Barrymore's greatness as an actor. They say that Ethel Barrymore is not pleased with Miss Ina Claire's performance of Julia. But I can hardly believe this. Miss Claire gives one of the most delicious pieces of acting I have ever seen on the screen, and if Ethel Barrymore is half as good on the stage she must be a very fine comédienne. Lionel Barrymore does not come into the burlesque at all, and I can quite believe that he is the most annoyed of the entire family. He certainly has the most reason to be. The film is based on the work of Edna Ferber and George S. Kaufman, and it is easily the wittiest thing to be seen in London. It is smartly produced, with a brilliant performance of the old actress by Miss Henrietta Crosman. It was preceded on the evening I was there by something called *Heads Up*, a photographed musical-comedy of the most dire inanity, and extravagantly the worst film I have ever seen, but through which I would willingly sit again to see *The Royal Family of Broadway*. I advise readers, however, to find out the time of the latter's showing and look neither before nor after lest they pine at what regrettably is!

17

THE SHADOW OF NORMA SHEARER

1931

ONCE more I read that a number of people, alleged by their sisters, their cousins, and their aunts to be more than normally good-looking, are to be invited to submit themselves to the camera, after which a certain number will be chosen and allowed £ 50 for dress and £ 5 a week what time they are turning themselves into film stars. Well, the rain it raineth every day with a hey, and a ho, and a hey-nonny-no, but I am still doubtful whether in either Bermondsey or Birmingham it rains or is likely to rain beauty and that particular combination of talent and temperament which makes the actress. Or I will put it this way, that the shower of specially endowed genius, if it is going to fall at all, will fall of its own accord and not in consequence of newspaper broadsides. It has been proved that the British White Hope which is going to put America on its back is a myth, and I suggest that the British Lily Maid who is going to make the Middle West sit up is, and will remain, legendary. At least I feel that when the Greta Garbo, the Marlene Dietrich, or the Norma Shearer happens, she happens because she cannot help happening and is not forcibly recruited from the ranks of lethargic sempstresses, dawdling nursemaids, indifferent typists, *et hoc genus omne*. I know a waitress about whom painters rave and before whom poets grow dumb. Eternity is in her lips and eyes—a description for which I take no credit—but the eternal, alas, is not in her mind! Her goal is the mutton-chop, her horizon spinach, and all is dross that is not on the menu. This Helen of the high forehead and low mentality will never be a film star for the simple reason that she is not one already. I am not, never have been, and never will be a believer in undiscovered genius, holding that genius, if it exists, will discover itself—a view which always has, does still, and always will get me into trouble with the sentimental of this world who babble about chance and opportunity. Whereas, of course, the only thing to say about these two is that chance, when it does not offer, is made, and that opportunity exists for those who have the courage to run after it, catch up with it, and seize it by its only too willing neck. Nobody asked either Dick Whittington or William Shakespeare to go to London; the ceiling of the Sistine Chapel did not walk into Michael Angelo's studio and ask to be painted; most triumphant proof of all, they could not prevent Sir W. B. Richmond, or whoever it was, from having himself hauled up to the dome of St. Paul's and daubing that! Genius will out and there is no stopping it, just as there is no forcing it if it is not there.

Some little time ago I was invited to a luncheon party to meet a famous film star and her husband. The first thing that struck me was that the Star was tiny, about a head shorter than anyone else in the room, and consequently entirely lacking in *prestige* or *prestance*. Had you not known who she was, you would have noted her extreme prettiness and then forgotten all about her. She had nothing whatever of the great actress, that something which fills a room when the great actress enters it, and empties it when she leaves. Here let me admit that the comparison is unfair; in fact its unfairness is exactly my point. Everybody has remarked upon the unremarkableness of great writers who come into their pages and nowhere else. They are perhaps not quite so imbecile as painters or musicians, because in private life they still use words which are a part of their trade. But the musician and the painter have nothing wherewith you may connect them with their genius which to them holds out no grappling-hooks. If these are at one end of the scale and the men of letters are in the middle, the great player is at the other end. For the great player is always, even in private life, expressing himself in terms of his stage personality, and the great actor or actress who walks through a door does exactly what he or she accomplishes on the stage. But the film actor or actress has no personality in the flesh; they do not exist until they have put off the flesh and become shadows. This was proved beyond possibility of doubt by Mr. Humbert Wolfe in his lovely poem about Valentino which nothing apparently will induce him to reprint, is buried in *The Bermondsey Book*, in search for which I have spent unavailing years, and which is worth all his output since and all that he is going to put out in the future. (India papers please copy.) Yet as I watched the Star as narrowly as one may through a mist of caviare, *foie gras*, devilled drumsticks, and champagne, I perceived behind that placid mask—something of the indomitable will, the fiery resolution, and, to borrow the triple idiom of Mr. James Douglas, the implacable resolve which Charlotte Brontë noted in Rachel, and was the first impression one received from Sarah Bernhardt. Duse had this quality too. With her it was ineffable, remote, extinct, as though some previous incarnation had possessed it æons ago. But it was there all right. Miss Norma Shearer has something of this quality, though she may not be conscious of possessing it. I know nothing of her history, but am convinced that she did not moon about Minnesota until Carl Laemmle or somebody happened to snap her with his pocket Kodak. It is a quality which does not lie latent until somebody comes along and accidentally discovers it. It is always said that some producer or manager came along and took Gladys Cooper out of the chorus, the implication being that if that person had not had the wit to perceive Miss Cooper, Miss Cooper would still be twiddling thumbs and toes in the front row. That is supremely wrong. It was this quality in Miss Cooper and her own brains which took her out of the chorus. Sybil Thorndike did not wait till Mr. Shaw asked her to play Joan; she acted Galsworthy and Euripides and every good playwright she could get hold of with such application and ferocity that, metaphorically speaking, she seized Mr. Shaw by the scruff of his venerable neck and wrung the part out of him, the poor man gasping that it had been his intention all along. As with actresses, so with film players. Having made it quite clear that Miss Norma Shearer is Miss Shearer's own creation, I shall now do my best to forget that I have ever seen her. In fact I have not seen her, for the charming little lady who sat at lunch and spoke so prettily to us had nothing whatever to do with the film actress whom I have so often and so greatly admired.

By the way, I wonder when the London cinemas are going to wake up and give us a new picture worth writing about. Every Sunday I read lists of the most exciting films which have just been "generally released." What exactly does this mean? Can it be that in London we never see anything except pre-releases? It is always my experience to find that a film is announced as "generally released" and then to be unable to discover it anywhere. Where, for example, is the new film with the first-class battle between two submarines? This is the kind of thing I want to see and write about, and not the old, old sex stuff dished up again with new-sounding titles like *Dishonoured, Disowned, Disgruntled,* and *Disgorged.* Looking down the list last week there simply wasn't anything that I had the pluck to go to see, and I suppose readers will be tired of hearing how I went to the Academy and what I there beheld. In the meantime and until they stow away the Dietrich in the bowels of a convict ship, perch Ruth Chatterton on the top of some mast while pirates spill their gore, or exhibit la Garbo as a powder-monkey directing operations at the Battle of the Nile—until some change is made from the eternal boudoir, will readers please note that my address, telegraphic and otherwise, is the Academy Theatre, Oxford Street, where there is always something worth seeing. This week it is the great film, *The End of St. Petersburg.*

18

"CONGRESS DANCES"

1931

"I AM giddy," said Troilus on a famous occasion. "Expectation whirls me round." This thought might have been in the heads of the crowd panting and pushing for admittance to *Congress Dances,* provided, of course, that thought is a property of cinema-goers. An ironist might with advantage have stood on the pavement outside the Tivoli and contrasted the gay and excited faces of one crowd hoping to be thrilled to the marrow of its bones with the glum visages of the other crowd who had experienced this thrill and found it wanting. I shall not waste time, space, energy, and erudition in declaring that this film throws no great illumination upon the political situation in Europe at the time when Napoleon was making his "get-away" from Elba. The direction of the film is by Herr Erik Charell, and I have not heard it alleged against *White Horse Inn* that that sparkling entertainment fails as a realistic representation of life in modern Germany. Seekers after an elaborate exposition of Metternich's policy at the Congress of

Vienna are not well advised to go to this film for it, for it is as plain as the nose on Herr Charell's face that his genius is for travesty. The only thing to be asked, then, is whether *Congress Dances* is as amusing a travesty as we have the right to expect from Herr Charell. In my view the answer is in the negative, for the reason that the story, the acting, the settings, and the photography are not good enough. Am I then comprehensively condemning this show? I am afraid I am. *Tant pis,* or words to that effect, as Metternich doubtless said when he heard of Napoleon's landing. The one first-class thing in the show is the music, which is catchy and ear-haunting and moreover has inspired Herr Charell to his best bit of production, the shot in which, the Royalties having vacated their seats at the Congress to join in the dance, their chairs nod assent to Metternich's proposals in time to the music. I shall hazard the guess that not all the music is by Schubert, and of course the programme now lying before me contains, so far as I can discover, no clue as to whom one ought to praise for the captivating song which is sung by Christel in her carriage, and taken up by the entire population of Vienna. Miss Evelyn Laye informs me how to clean my aluminium saucepans, and what to do with any butter which should find itself on my carpet. I would not be churlish, and these useful hints shall be cherished against the time when I have an aluminium saucepan, or when senility makes me childish about the butter. But I would sacrifice these hints, Mr. Jack Buchanan's horoscope, and even the reassurance that Miss Ena Baga still presides at the Wurlitzer, for the necessary, and I think harmless, information that I desire.

On the other hand, the programme exhibits a praiseworthy gallantry in maintaining silence as to the author of the story. There are things one does not do, and to name the author of so abject an imbroglio is one of them. Prince Metternich desires to prevent the Czar Alexander from attending his committee meetings, to which end he enlists the support of an equivocal Countess, brilliantly impersonated by Miss Lil Dagover. But the Czar realises that two can play at that game, and arranges for an enchantress of humbler and more endearing charm, who is, of course, Christel, the little glove-seller. Moreover, the Czar is no fool, and travels with a double, who shall impersonate him and so enable him to be in two places at the same time. This, then, is the entire situation of the piece. There is a council-meeting, at four o'clock, Metternich thinks the Czar is having cocktails with the Countess, while Christel thinks the Czar is having tea with her. The Czar's double keeps both appointments in rapid succession and dissatisfies both ladies, while the Czar turns up at the Town Hall after all. The same thing happens at supper-time when the Czar is supposed to be at a ball, and really that is all the story. News comes that

Napoleon has broken loose, and all the monarchs and big-wigs scuttle back to their respective capitals. The Imperial double takes leave of the grand company at the ball and gets into one carriage, while the real Czar takes sentimental farewell of his unsmirched glove-seller and gets into another carriage. Well, the story of *White Horse Inn* was thin enough; the story of *Congress Dances* is thinner still.

Its strength is that there is no little typist or mannequin in London or Nuneaton or North Shields, or wherever this film may percolate, whose bosom will not throb tempestuously at the spectacle of Christel's rise to the position of uncrowned queen unattended by any degradation. Christel, you see, has thrown a bouquet at the Czar and is about to be whipped by the public executioner when the Czar, who has caught sight of her face, comes in person to the police-court and orders her release. Christel is describing her venture to the other shop-girls when a lackey enters bidding her ascend into a carriage and drive triumphantly through the streets of Vienna to that country cottage which the Czar hopes she will do him the honour of accepting. Christel gets into the carriage and goes to infamy singing, and in the audience we may be sure that every little typist and mannequin is singing with her. And rightly. For circumstances alter cases, and there can be nothing infamous about a cottage which is larger than the R.A.C., though built on identical lines and served by even more flunkeys. The journey in the carriage, in which the whole population of Austria participates having learned the theme-song by divination, is another good bit of production. Elsewhere the photography is poor, all the processions looking as if the people in them had "moved," as we used to say in the days of slow plates. Further, too many of the settings struck me as though they had been put up on Saturday and pulled down on Monday. And then the acting, or rather the over-acting! Apparently there has been no power in Berlin, and I should guess there is none on earth, to keep Miss Lilian Harvey still. Where anybody else would walk she dances; when anybody else would smile she grimaces, and her every gesture is executed with the arms akimbo and her elbows at the level of her ears. If there is no human being within range she must coquette with a parrot or a monkey. Alone and by herself she cannot get into a pair of knickers without doing so in a manner to enchant the bed-post. In short, her archness is so overwhelming that at times I desisted from watching and, closing my eyes, thought regretfully on the decorum and reticence of Clara Bow. Mr. Henry Garat gives a middling performance, for as the Czar he has not enough charm, and as his half-witted double is not more than moderately amusing. Anybody who saw Mr. Alfred Lunt in *The Guardsman* will have some idea of what might have been made of this part. Metternich has nothing to do, but even so Mr. Conrad Veidt gives a superb performance for a reason that hardly ever occurs to anybody—the reason that he is a superb actor. I am neither film writer nor film producer. But if anybody will lend me Mr. Veidt and some not arch young woman, the European situation in 1815, the unknown composer, and one-tenth of the money spent on this production, I will guarantee to turn out a more entertaining film. And if I had a singer to sing old Viennese songs, as this film has, I should get a better one.

19

"FIVE STAR FINAL"

1932

IT is an unwritten law of the theatre that plays must not deal realistically or in any way other than sentimentally with institutions which the public is accustomed to regard sentimentally. Up till about 1880 marriage bells were marriage bells and that was that, or rather those were those. Two people who had contracted marriage were supposed to have contracted it fatally like a disease, and a play could only be monstrous which showed either contracting party as cherishing desire towards any but the other contracting party till death did them part. Chorus-girls were either naughty or good; they could not be both. But the film, while appealing to a less sophisticated audience than the theatre, strangely enough took a more sophisticated view. It showed us marriage as the point where divergence begins, and unison as the only soil in which dissension may be shown. It showed us the chorus-girl pouring into her mother's lap the pocket-money obtained from sitting on the lap of her sugar-daddy. Plays which have dealt with the back of the stage and dealt sincerely have always been failures, whereas films which have done the same thing have invariably been successes. Here an explanation occurs to me which the reader may accept or reject according as he likes or dislikes irony. In the previous sentence I used the phrase "dealt sincerely" by which I meant showing the gingerbread without the gilt, and how that which on one side of the curtain is all glamour, on the other side is jealousy, recrimination and drudgery. Now transfer the scene to America since, of course, all English chorus-girls are moral. Your American film shows the American chorus-girl as a hussy, vulgar of heart and common of mind. This is where the irony comes in. Show this in the English theatre and the English theatre will not have it because it is too ugly. Therefore the English theatre will not show it. But show it in the films and the English film audiences dote upon it because that is the film audience's idea of what a film should be. Whence the success in this country of back-stage films.

But human nature can be more complicated still, an example of which is provided by that really magnificent film at the Carlton, *Five Star Final*. Here is a ruthless exposure of gutter journalism at its very worst, and we find the audience indulging with complete equanimity in two delights at once, the delight of the exposure and the delight in the thing exposed. The average person, you see, is able to enjoy the revolting details of a murder, always provided that the person murdered was young, good-looking, and a female. Indeed it is not so long ago that I found myself reading a fascinating account of the discovery of the body of an "attractive" young woman and of which the head was missing! I confess I couldn't help wondering what had prompted the reporter to the word "attractive." I invariably read every word of every murder trial in the country and am perfectly capable towards the end and, as the excitement increases, of skimming the events of that day's trial in the "News," perusing them soberly in the "Standard," and ending up with the "Star" to see if anything more can be gleaned. The world cannot contain any news which in the order of reading I should put before a murder trial. If an earthquake were to pile Bolivia upon Peru, if a tidal wave swamped the West Indies, if a typhoon destroyed Tiflis, even if Mr. Izzy Schumpfelstein, the well-known British film magnate, turned honest—none of these would take precedence over the vital question as to whether Mrs. Megan Evans-Morgan-Jones, of Nantygwlch, had access to that weed-killer. I have admirable sanction for this. Did not Jane Austen stoutly affirm that she cared less about the Battle of Trafalgar than about Marianne Dashwood's twisted ankle, that she cared nothing at all about the death of Sir John Moore, and would not dream of reading Southey's *Life of Nelson* unless her sailor-brother was mentioned in it? At the same time I regard Jane's taste and mine as wholly low. It is to be presumed that newspaper-editors are like that in so far as they are capable of having two minds about anything and everything. Thus the business mind of an editor will make him insist that his reporters shall succulently report all the more loathsome details of a crime, while the spiritual side of him will burgeon forth in a leader regretting the need for such publicity. He may even combine both attitudes in a sentence and cheerily inform us, say, that it is September, and that while the Crumbles are dripping with blood everywhere else the brambles are dripping with dew.

Apparently your low-class English editor cannot get as low as the American, largely because he is more stupid. Your English editor does not see that there is anything contradictory between his revolting news column and his idyllic leader; he is a simple fellow in whose mental make-up both things exist. A thing which everybody must deplore has got to be described and that's all there is to it! But though dealing faithfully with filth as and when it occurs he will not, I think, create that filth in order that the reporting of it shall send up his sales. That is where *Five Star Final* points to something worse in America than anything we can boast over here. Our low rags would be perfectly prepared to make the most of a Nancy Voorhees Case as and when it happened. But the lowest of them would not dig it up again twenty years after. Nor, I think, is there any parallel even in the English gutter press with Isopod, the bogus muck-raking parson. It is improbable that these niceties of distinction will be in the minds of Carlton audiences, all of which I think will be carried away with the vigour, force, and speed of a capital production which has not a word too few or a gesture too many. To me it was particularly interesting to compare this film with the play as it was acted over here. Mr. Edward G. Robinson is a magnificently vital actor. But he does not quite convince me, as Mr. Raymond Massey so subtly did, of his editor's essential fineness of grain, his possession of that ultimate streak of decency which makes him throw up his job. Nevertheless it is a fine piece of acting and Mr. Robinson has us all with him when at the end he hurls that telephone through the glass door of his proprietor's office. I prefer Miss Frances Starr's performance as Nancy Voorhees to that of Miss Louise Hampton if only for the reason that not in any flight of fancy do I see the English actress as an ex-chorus girl deceived or undeceived. On the other hand I thought the young people better played in the play at the Phœnix, as against which must be set the brilliant acting in the film of whoever it is that plays the editor's secretary. But these distinctions do not matter very greatly. What does matter is that *Five Star Final* at the Carlton Theatre is a grand hour-and-a-half of exciting film.

20

"ARROWSMITH"

1932

AS far as I am concerned there is only one real test of any work of art, whether it be a play, a book, or a piece of music. In the case of a play, do I want to come back after the interval? Do I want to know what A is going to do next and B is going to say in reply to C? In the case of a book, do I want to go on reading it? Or do I skip first a line and then half-a-dozen, then half a page and finally whole chapters? In the case of a piece of music, do I, sitting in the Queen's Hall, hope there is a gramophone record of it? It is even the same with pictures—I mean the real things. Do I want to go on looking at them? If somebody to-day were to make me a present of any picture by Rossetti, Burne-Jones, Holman Hunt, Ford Madox Brown, or that arch Victorian bore, G. F. Watts, I should send the donor my thanks and the picture to the sale-rooms. I was brought up on the Pre-Raphaelites plus Watts, and my mind is still haunted with Rossetti's women of the topless necks and Burne-Jones's nymphs of the bridgeless noses. To-day, however, I willingly hang some reproduction of a cauliflower by Van Gogh, of worm-eaten apples by Cézanne, of a creature by Matisse, who, sitting in front of her dressing-table, can scratch the sole of her foot with an arm so long that she does not need to elongate it. I do not say that these pictures are better than those; what I do say is that I decline to look at those and prefer to look on these. So it is with a film, where again the one and only question is: Do I, or do you, want to go on looking at it? I remember a famous dramatic critic who confessed to having left the theatre during a performance of *Romeo and Juliet*, and in the middle of the speech in which Juliet describes the fun she is going to have with Tybalt's bones, because, said he, "the carts in the street were so much jollier!" It is remarkable how few people who are not chained to the theatre or to the film by their critical obligations refuse to take advantage of their freedom. If a book bores me I pitch it into the waste-paper basket or bundle it back to Mudie's. The moment some smirking fiddler-fellow appears, and turning over my annotated programme I espy the name of Vieuxtemps, Wieniawski, Paganini, de Blériot, Sarasate, or Lalo, whose "Symphonie Espagnole" I will not hear again, the moment I am threatened with any of those composers who wrote not music but fiddler's stuff, why then it's me for the open air! But with theatres and cinemas it would seem to be different. However odious and otiose the play or film, however bored or irritated an audience of either kind becomes, nobody ever quits their torment. Once in Spain a gentleman brought a party to the play, and having listened to some twenty minutes of it said loudly and genially, "Well, shall we be going?" and gathering up his party departed. I have never seen that happen in any other country, and the reluctance would seem to spring from the fact that the play- or film-goer, having paid for his seat, is determined to get the last ounce out of it whether it be profit or the reverse.

Judged by this standard *Arrowsmith*, at the Tivoli, must be one of the best films I have ever seen, because nothing would have induced me to leave until it was over, and because though the film lasted an hour and three-quarters, I had the impression that I had been in the theatre for about twenty minutes. But then I fully expected to enjoy it, if only for the reason that Mr. Sydney Carroll did not! Of *Arrowsmith* Mr. Carroll wrote:

> The film tells of a man's ambition to cope with the terrors and evils of bubonic plague, and his active efforts in battling courageously with the scourge on a tropical island in the West Indies. The romance of the picture comes in with the doctor's marriage to a gallant little nurse whom he has met during his early experiences, and whose life becomes forfeit during the struggle. This *Arrowsmith*, however, is just a morbid, pretentious, tedious film pageant of plague and death. It is a melancholy procession of actors, black and white, who all overwork themselves in a vain endeavour to delude the public into thinking that they are real people. It is about as entertaining as a mud bath, with none of its beneficial results.

When I got to the words "mud bath" I knew that I should be really entertained, and that for once the public is on my side is proved by the fact that since this film started showing it has been almost impossible to book a seat for any performance. The only thing which worried me was what I will call the logic of the affair. The doctor in question had in an early part of the picture experimented upon cattle for a disease called "black leg." Inventing a serum to cure this, he took ten cows, giving the serum to five of them and withholding it from the other five. Those which had the serum recovered and those which hadn't, died. This, said the doctor, was the only possible way of proving the efficacy of his serum. But is it? Suppose all the ten cows had been inoculated and recovered. Suppose a dog certified as suffering from rabies were to bite a hundred villagers. Wouldn't the efficacy of the Pasteur treatment be justified if they were all treated and all recovered, or would one have to let fifty die? When the doctor gets to the West Indies where plague has broken out, he injects his newly-invented serum into the black legs of 50 per cent of the natives, leaving the other fifty to die. It seems to me that the logic is not good enough for the sacrifice and that all that was needed to prove the doctor's case was that no person who had been inoculated in time had died, whereby the whole island could have been saved. But also, I suppose, United Artists would have been saved the trouble of making this film.

This question of logic apart, the picture interested me immensely, because the subject-matter was of interest and the photography magnificent, whether realistic or imaginative. In my view the only dull part of the picture was that which Mr. Carroll calls its romance—a lot of tedious stuff about the doctor's wife, one of those clinging nitwits who hamper their husband at every step in his career, and when he must go out to do battle with bubonic plague, insist upon accompanying him and dying on him at his busiest. The part was extremely well played by Miss Helen Hayes, who is not to be blamed for the heroine's tediousness, to many, I doubt not, the picture's saving grace. I liked Mr. Ronald Colman very much too, for he seemed to me not to over-act. It is only fair to say that this film is taken from the novel by Sinclair Lewis, and for once in a way is a screen interpretation of a writer's work instead of a burlesque.

21

HOW NOT TO DO IT

1932

THERE was a great gathering of the tribes at the first-night of what I take to be on the whole the very worst big picture I have ever seen, the Sterling Film Company's screen enlargement of Mr. St. John Ervine's *The First Mrs. Fraser*. At the same time I hasten to congratulate the film company on the virtuosity which it must have needed to turn one of the best plays of modern times into very nearly the worst picture of all time. The usher who showed me to my seat at the Prince Edward Theatre presented me with the largest and ugliest programme I have ever handled, ugly because it was got up in a scheme of that colour which the French call *caca d'oie*. I insist on the size of the programme because it strikes the note of the whole production, the note of monstrous exaggeration. Mr. Sinclair Hill, who directs, appears to think that you can make a cartoon fit to cover the wall of a town-hall by enlarging a thumb-nail sketch, and I respect the intelligence of my readers too much to do more than state the fallacy. Incidentally the noise with which our ears were assaulted during the preliminary assemblage of the guests was easily the most hideous that I had heard until, in the course of the film, Mr. Hill let loose his cabaret. I am really staggered that film directors who spend thousands of pounds to delight our eyes should continue to offend our ears with the woof and bark of machines which have magnified even jazz-music out of all resemblance to itself, the enlarged tone that results sounding like nothing on earth except, maybe, a goods-yard at Derby. Mr. Ervine's play was a neat, domestic and, above all, little affair about people living in, say, Regent's Park or the Cromwell Road. The plot had its improbabilities, or rather one improbability which was of comparative unimportance when the whole thing was kept small, but which we are bound to question when the play is put up to its present size. Let me deal with this improbability first, at the same time assuring Mr. Ervine, if these lines should happen to catch his eye, that in his play as performed in the theatre it seemed to me to be of no importance whatever. The point is Fraser's objection to divorcing his second wife. His first wife divorced him, and he pleads that he cannot divorce his second wife because it would be bad for his business. The whole play is built upon this, and one accepts the casual improbability in the theatre because a play has to be got going somehow. But the thing which is shouted through a megaphone ceases to be casual, and we have to examine it. One understands, of course, that a shop-assistant at Emporiums, Ltd. may be dismissed if he is divorced because Emporiums, Ltd. have the power to dismiss him. But I submit that this is a part of economic and not moral law. Let us suppose that the case was the other way about, and that it was Sylvanus Emporium, Esq., managing director of Emporiums, Ltd., who had been divorced. Why, in such a case, and if the world were ruled by moral logic, should not the assistant call for the resignation of his managing director for misconduct? The answer is that he cannot, because he has not the economic power. To come down to the particular case, why should Fraser fear not the scandal of being divorced a second time, he being again the guilty party, but the scandal of petitioning, which is no scandal? At the worst it is "not good for business," though we do not see why Fraser should bother about this since in the course of the play he proposes to go for a world tour, and afterwards retire to the country, and anyhow in the film owns a town house the contents of which if sold even in the Caledonian Market would provide him with a life-income exceeding that of the Lord Chancellor.

This brings me to this film's preposterous setting, whereby the Frasers are made to inhabit a palace which even Hollywood would consider dandy. The programme tells me that "the value of the furnishing on one set alone is estimated at £10,000. A marble fireplace came from one of the most famous mansions in England; it cost £2,000, and weighs 3½ tons. Beautiful and rare tapestry adorns the walls; and famous art-collectors were persuaded to loan highly treasured bric-à-brac for this scene." My reply to this is that if the setting at the Haymarket Theatre cost as much as one-tenth of that mantelpiece I should be very much surprised, with the further contention that if this film's lavish expenditure on settings was justified, the play which they swamp could not have been worth while! There was mention in Mr. Ervine's comedy of a night-club, necessitated by the fact that the second Mrs. Fraser's lover was engaged there. Mr. Ervine did not show us the club, and we do not want to see it. But Mr. Hill makes it the principal thing in his film. To accomplish this hundreds of girls have been engaged wearing gowns costing 150 guineas apiece and who take part in a modernistic ballet featuring Lady Godiva, Queen Bess, Cleopatra, Nell Gywnn, etc., etc. Mr. Hill may say that the film public insists upon the expensive riot and the transformation of Mrs. Fraser's window-boxes into the Hanging Gardens of Babylon. Agreed. But if so, why not do the whole thing to key and engage for the first Mrs. Fraser a Pola Negri, Gloria Swanson, or some boobyish good-looker instead of a legitimate English actress endowed with that genuine talent which does not photograph? Miss Joan Barry as the second Mrs. Fraser succeeds completely just because she behaves as nobody outside Hollywood or Hanwell ever has behaved. Mr. Ainley is good too, because instead of presenting a business man he duplicates the Book of Tobit's Archangel.

The film has other major faults which are these. The lighting is often shocking. There are only five shots amounting to thirty-five seconds worth looking at pictorially; these include two views of the Thames Embankment, a fishing-scene, a motor-car, and two motor-lorries. Probabilities are flouted, since the lovers, arriving at a country hotel *after a ball,* find the entire village drinking in defiance of the licensing laws and though the hotel is substantial must order their accommodation in the tap-room. Worst of all, the entire cast is camera-conscious, and obviously preoccupied with slowing down the technique of the stage to that of the film. I understand that £80,000 has been spent on this picture, most of it I daresay swallowed up in the cabaret scenes which are more nerve-wracking than Piccadilly Circus on Boat Race Night, and, as aforesaid, have nothing to do with the play. It is by such useless expenditure as this that the film industry is rushing headlong to ruin. £8,000 plus artistic sensibility would have made of Mr. Ervine's charming little play a charming little film. In the meantime Mr. Ervine's play and Mr. Ervine's wit and, above all, Miss Marie Tempest's art have vanished, so that the whole thing is like the Lord Mayor's coach with nobody in it. In my view this film will lose a great deal of money and gain no kudos for anybody.

22

THE ART OF CONSTANCE BENNETT

1932

MR. SHAW is once reported to have said: "My fame is the concern of other people. It has nothing to do with me." That Mr. Shaw could say this is due entirely to the fineness of a mind which has never had any use for notoriety either as spur or guerdon. But, the reader will interrupt, how can you say this when everybody knows that G.B.S. has spent fifty years hunting publicity or laying himself across the track of it? The point is that G.B.S. has sought publicity for his work's sake, just as your divine might stand on his head in the pulpit to draw attention to his message. Now your film star pursues the opposite course. Her fame has everything to do with her. She can have no other concern because she has no mind with which to take concern. I am not dealing now with the male film star who in most cases is an actor as well as a celebrity, whereas your blonde nitwit is hardly ever anything except the exquisite embodiment of no mind.

I was sitting the other day at an alleged Bohemian club—"alleged" because you cannot get a drink there after hours—which has fallen into the bad habit of employing waitresses, who when ugly spoil the food, when pretty distract the mind, and in all cases shake the wine. My co-sitter was Mr. Philip Page, possessor of the prettiest Tudor mansion and the prettiest neo-Georgian wit in England. I had ordered a tankard of bitter and a whisky and soda, and the girl executed the order promptly and correctly. After she had dumped the change on the picturesquely dirty table-cloth Philip Page said impressively: "That girl remembered about the tankard, gave each of us our right drink, and you the right change. No film actress could *have done that!*" This is the exact impression which these platinum nonentities always give me. I have only met one in the flesh. She was an under-sized, insignificant little thing, and at the party given in her honour you had to look round the room twice to find her, and when you had spotted her you would have said she was the born waitress. Oddly enough the heroine of *What Price Hollywood?* is a waitress. Mary Evans, a flaxen beauty, happens to be waiting upon Maximilian Carey, described by Hollywood as "a great but eccentric director." Now the word "eccentric" has different meanings in different countries. In England it has been debased to mean a comedian who is funny with his feet, whereas in Hollywood it just means drunk. Carey takes the girl to a party given in honour of the "world première"—how Hollywood dotes on the grandiose phrase!—of his latest picture. At this point it should perhaps be mentioned that Mary is presented by Miss Constance Bennett, who may or may not be an actress, while Carey is played by that magnificent comedian, Mr. Lowell Sherman. Carey gives Mary a try-out in which she is terrible, but going home that night she rehearses the single sentence of which her part is composed for so many hours that next morning, when she is given another chance, she reveals herself as a world actress and a potential star of such magnitude that the hard-hearted and withal Jewish producer, Julius Saxe, gives her a million-dollar contract. Next, Mary, whose brilliant commonness continues to entrance or appal me—entrance if it is assumed and appal if it is not—falls in love with a millionaire polo-player who conquers her in the Petruchio manner, without any acknowledgment to Shakespeare or whoever it was that Shakespeare bagged his story from. At the end of this scene, in which are used up all Hollywood's reserves of blatant expense, we find Mary sitting down to caviare, champagne, and a full-dress orchestra in her night-shirt, whereby the New Gallery will obviously be crowded for as many weeks as the management desires. After Mary's wedding Carey goes downhill at a speed exceeding all that the textbooks have to tell us about velocity and acceleration. But Mary, whose heart is as golden as her hair, has always loved Carey in a selfless, idealistic way not understood by the common herd in general and her husband in particular. So when she tries to reclaim him in the small hours of the morning the polo-player, whose head is as wooden as his mallet, goes off to Reno to get a divorce. But Mary continues in her good work and, getting Carey out of prison, sets him on the road to reclamation with a glass of hot milk. But the road is too uphill for Carey, who shoots himself. The American press is, of course, not going to minimise the fact of an ex-film director's dead body being found in Mary's spare bedroom, whereupon Mary, who by this time has had a child, retires with the brat and a negro Mammy to the South of France, whither presently the polo-husband repairs, and all live happily ever after.

I have said that I do not know whether Miss Constance Bennett is acting or not. Well, I don't, for the reason that this is the first time I have seen Miss Bennett, and I do not know whether she can play anything except common little waitresses out of common little tea-shops. If she can and if the aspirate in "You 'aven't proposed to me yet to-night," repeated twenty times, is accidental, why then Miss Bennett is a considerable actress. One of the reasons why I am doubtful about this little lady's histrionic powers is her prettiness. She is undoubtedly extremely pretty, and I have never yet known a pretty woman who was a great actress. Great actresses either have great beauty like Mrs. Siddons, Duse and Mrs. Patrick Campbell, or they are frankly ugly like Réjane, or they have strange fascination like Sarah Bernhardt, or an odd assemblage of warring lovelinesses like Ellen Terry. But they are never pretty. You have only to go to Nature to see why prettiness can never be the arena for the conflicts of great passions. Windermere with its dimpled prettiness requires the sun; Wastwater with its gloom and grandeur can alone accommodate the thunder and the lightning. It would be absurd to pretend that the human face is not to some extent the mirror of the mind. Ellen Terry, when she played in *Macbeth*, merely made you want to smack her, and frankly I do not see Miss Bennett as Medea. In fact I do not see her as anything except an extraordinarily pretty and provocative little lady. "Maiden ladies," said Oscar Wilde, "subsist entirely on cake," and I am quite sure that film stars like Miss Bennett subsist entirely upon admiration. In other words, upon their fame. They have nothing else upon which to exist, since the amount of acting which goes into a rôle like that of Mary Evans would not get the stage player through the part of Nerissa, let alone that of Portia. In fact I believe that it requires less skill to give Miss Bennett's performance in *What Price Hollywood?* than it does to wait upon a roomful of Bohemians and bring each his proper drink and change.

23

THINGS THAT AMUSE ME

1932

PERHAPS the greatest joy in my life is the discovery of things not, one thinks, supposed to be funny. Turning the other day to the broadcast programme, I read: "3.25, East Anglian Herring Fishing Bulletin." And again, under the hour of "7.10" my eye caught something which read like "The Future of British Oats. By Sir Biggles Wade," though here I confess to some manipulation of the text. Anyhow I laughed long and loud, just as I laughed on hearing about Mr. Priestley's mishap. Upon this I permit myself a few words, inasmuch as I believe that I have, owing to my own good luck or the B.B.C.'s mismanagement, delivered more wireless talks than anybody else in Great Britain. Not once during six years have I ever gone down to Savoy Hill or Broadcasting House without a spare copy of my talk in my pocket. On two occasions it has been convenient to use these owing to the extraordinary ingenuity displayed by speakers' manuscripts in getting themselves mislaid. I do not think any sane person ought to blame the B.B.C. in this matter. It is a property of things to get themselves mislaid, and personally I should be very much surprised if anybody at a minute's notice could lay his hands on the Treaty of Versailles! But I am surprised that Mr. Priestley, who comes from Yorkshire, and is prepared at any moment to instruct anybody about anything, should not have taken the obvious precaution. Would Mr. Priestley confide a 1,000-page manuscript even to the General Post Office unless he had a copy at home? Very well then. Or again, would he go motoring without a spare tyre? Then why does he propose to go broadcasting without a spare manuscript? Yes, in these dull days life can be made amusing for those of us who know where to look for the funny things, the best place, of course, being where people intend to be most serious. A great place for seriousness is that cinema programme in which you get a minimum of information about the film you have come to see, and a maximum of prognosticatory comment for next week, or next month, or even later. Apropos of that colossal piece of pretentious bunk, Eugene O'Neill's *Strange Interlude*, presently to be shown in a film version at the Empire, I am told that "the sacred, secret processes of thought itself are stripped naked and tossed to the audience in terrific ruthlessness. The result is something that rips the watcher bit from bit." What I want to know is whether the watcher will be allowed to gather up his bits before he departs. I think I must consult Beachcomber.

The film itself, *Skyscraper Souls*, turned out to be the usual portentous jumble about nothing in particular. David Dwight was a boss in the building trade who had not understood Ibsen's lesson that building happy homes for happy human beings is not the highest mission of your architect and builder. I am not surprised, because I have never understood Ibsen's lesson myself. In fact I think it is bosh. Further, I see no reason why a New York architect should not build a skyscraper of 100 storeys provided that the building will stand up, and that people can be found to take rooms on a ninety-seventh floor. I suppose that if Ibsen had written this film he would have found in the skyscraper a symbol of man's cheek in measuring himself against forces stronger than man. Cheek, that is, tempered with the obligation upon man to achieve more than he can. I can perfectly well see this film as an Ibsen play. I can see, and in the mind's eye hear, interminable acts in which architectural discussion as to strains and stresses have their parallel in the strains and stresses of the human soul. I see as clearly as if I were sitting in some repertory play-house, converted school-room, or draughty drill-hall, that fifth act consisting of the skyscraper's roof, a flagstaff, and the naked elements. I can see a trap-door opening and the emerging head of Mr. Franklin Dyall who, clinging to the uncertain flagstaff—since we have been told that the building has a storm sway of 711 feet—addresses to the crowd on the pavement below appropriate remarks on the instability of human affairs. Presently I see the aureoled pallor of Miss Mary Merrall who, doubting that her old man has gone potty, now follows him to the roof. A little later I see the head and shoulders of that grey iceberg which Miss Nancy Price so perfectly simulates. She, of course, is Miss Merrall's sister arrived but now from Norway to ask why Mr. Dyall has not taken the slightest notice of her for fifty-seven years. She has whiled away the time playing with dolls but is tired of that. The battle between the two sisters is now joined since both want to push their master-builder from off the top of the skyscraper, but for different reasons. After a time they look round only to find that Mr. Dyall has disappeared. Whereupon, locked in a sisterly embrace they go over the parapet together. What really happened, of course, was that Mr. Dyall, finding his remarks something interrupted by the thunder and lightning, a sleety drizzle, and the high words of the sisters, had gone quietly down to tea.

It is perhaps needless to say that the film, *Skyscraper Souls,* which has been adapted from a novel by Miss Faith Baldwin, bears but slight resemblance to the foregoing. The master-builder in the film has a wife who takes no interest in him beyond his cheque-book and a mistress who is his secretary and of whom after twenty years he is a little tired. Now this secretary has a little assistant-secretary with a sweet smile and agreeable knees of whom, or of which, Dwight becomes enamoured. At least he proposes to take her yachting, to which the assistant-secretary agrees because she has had words with her humble sweetheart, who is a clerk in a bank forty-nine storeys lower down. But the secretary opposes Dwight's pacific intentions and, Dwight persisting, shoots him. Whereupon the secretary mounts to the roof and dives, platinum first, into the street below. I don't know how it strikes the reader, but it seems to me that this skyscraping business is the purest guff, since there is nothing whatever in this film which could not happen in a building three storeys high. There is the usual nonsense about the speed at which life is lived in New York, which again I do not believe. Indeed, a man who has been there tells me that every New Yorker who has an appointment to keep waits, watch in hand, until he has left himself insufficient time to get there, which means that he will be compelled to put on break-neck speed, and so impress everybody else with his importance. To sum up, I found this film very funny in ways which its producer obviously has not intended. It is well acted, though I think Mr. Warren William should modify his habit of patting ladies where they sit down. The third time this happened I could not help thinking of Mrs. Patrick Campbell who in the Hackett production of *Macbeth* complained about having to sit on a green log in a puce dress while the Thane of Fife did all the talking. "Well, well," said the producer in the accents of mollification, "I'll ask Mr. Hackett to pat you!" Whereupon Mrs. Campbell is said to have replied in tones of infinite melancholy: "I hate being patted!" Thus at least runs the story, for which I do not vouch. But it made me wonder whether the ladies in this film have not equally disliked being patted.

24

GREAT STARS AND LITTLE ONES

1932

IT will be extremely interesting when Mr. Charles Laughton returns to these shores to see whether the crowd queues up for him as it does for a new film star who threatens to become a rival of la Garbo or la Dietrich, or even for a great and familiar actor in a new rôle. I cite Mr. Laughton because I have the sneaking conviction that he is the only approach to a great actor we have left, since he has not required the Shavian drama to prop and bolster him into greatness. The reception accorded to Mr. Laughton when and if he returns will tell us which way the battle swings as between theatre and cinema. I am not referring here solely to the hysterico-epileptic film-fan for whom the hysterico-epileptic film drama is singly devised. For, of course, all films have to be made to please the lowest intelligence, since all the other grades of intelligence put together do not amount to enough people to make any film profitable. The odd thing about the cinema is that even persons of moderate intelligence lose when they enter a cinema what little intelligence they possess. Whenever I go into a picture-house I instinctively feel that I do so for the purpose of gratifying my lowest, or perhaps better simplest, instincts. The word "low" in this country has an unfortunate connotation due to the fact that as a nation we are morality-ridden. Therefore instead of "lowest instincts" it would perhaps have been better to write "least complicated desires", the desire to see things which are both unusual and desirable. Things like sailing-ships, and icebergs, and coral reefs with Honolulu maidens diving therefrom and rescued from the jaws of sharks by Otaheite youths clad only in the flowers of the hibiscus. So much for out-of-doors. Indoors I insist upon Russian courtesans in snow-clad palaces slaking the fever of their passions in golden goblets presented by swart Senegalese. I must have, moreover, dens of Arab vice to which one descends by half-a-dozen steps permitting a shaft of sunlight to cast a moral reflection upon the gloom and that table on which (and because her lover jilted her) some flower of innocence dances for the benefit of Norway's blondest beast, to wit a sailor.

Now lots of people possessed of better brains than mine have the same need when they enter a cinema to love the lowest when they see it. That is why everybody—in your gossip-writer's sense of the word—goes to the cinema. Doubtless if you ask them they will say that they go because the cinema is cheaper than the theatre, because it is more comfortable, and because they can go by bus since there is no need to dress. Such reasons would be good and valid reasons, but they would not be the real ones. People go to the cinema to satisfy the deep-rooted instinct for something spectacular and rare which they cannot see in everyday life. One of the world's greatest plays is Ibsen's *Hedda Gabler*. I would go to Liverpool or to Hull or any of our gloomier centres of industry at the mere whisper of a performance of *Hedda Gabler* by the local repertory company and whether I thought the leading actress was likely to garble Hedda or not. Yet I would not cross the road to see la Garbo garbol her. The fair maid of Spitzbergen, or wherever she comes from, would doubtless be extremely fine as Hedda. But when I go to the films I do NOT want to see Scandinavian ladies behaving unreasonably in outlandish drawing-rooms. What I do want is to see them behaving reasonably on ice-floes, transfixing polar bears with hat-pins and so forth. Or wielding a battle-axe to vindicate the outraged honour of some Viking parent. Or perchance clinging to some forlorn rigging pursued by a nauseating Norseman while Mr. Clark Gable lashed to a mast looks over his streaming shoulders with the request that she will not bother about him! Those things are the proper business of the cinema and all the sensible world knows that they are. They appeal to instincts which are common to the whole of humanity and which can never be cultivated away. That, in short, is the reason why a film star receives a welcome which the world's greatest stage players, the Garricks, the Bernhardts, the Irvings, and even the Chaliapines, have never known.

Looking round the Marble Arch Pavilion the other evening I saw the smartest possible audience. It was a pouring wet night and a patient queue was standing in the rain in the certain knowledge that the show was going to be worth it. And it *was* worth it. These Germans are great film producers, and I take leave to rank Erich Pommer with the best of them. The story of *Tempest* is neither better nor worse than all of Jannings's stories, for the simple reason that it is the same one. My knowledge of German is just enough to enable me to catch the drift of a sentence and then to lose it again. And presently I found myself uncertain whether Jannings had been sent to prison for the theft of an opera-cloak to put round his wife's shoulders or for the murder of the lover who acted as the opera-cloak's deputy. And, of course, the uncertainty didn't matter. What was certain was that there had been a terrific scene which took place at an exhibition of fireworks whereby the pyrotechnics in the garden were matched by the jealous display going on in Jannings's mind. In the end the lover was pursued to the top of something that looked like a windmill, while all around the rockets and the Roman candles and the Catherine wheels fizzed and whirled, and star-scattered both actually and symbolically. Presently Jannings, after convulsions which were surely recorded on the nearest seismograph, hove the lover out of the window so that he fell into a convenient pond, and the waters closing over him continued to mirror the firework-maker's revolving suns and moons. The film then had a moment of complete silence which was matched by the silence in the house. After this Jannings had still to settle with the cause of the trouble who, cowering in pearls and ermine, knew what was coming to her. First Jannings called her every unutterable name, then put the half-Tecla on Miss Anna Sten's lovely throat, whereupon the strangled girl glued her lips to Jannings, and that Colossus remembered that it was bed-time. But that was only half of *Tempest*, for Jannings being sent to gaol either for the cloak or for the windmill incident, Miss Sten carried on, so to speak, with a gigolo who was apparently Jannings's godson. Jannings then unexpectedly emerged from prison and producing a clasp-knife endeavoured to disembowel his godson while rolling with him on the floor. This time the attempt did not succeed, and the film ended with Miss Sten assisting the young gentleman up many, many flights of stairs to bed, while in the courtyard below the Chief of Police was telling Jannings that he couldn't hope to kill all his wife's lovers and that the next or third effort in that direction would be looked upon by the authorities quite seriously. Of Jannings it is unnecessary to speak; he was immense as usual. As for Miss Sten I may say that she is a pretty little girl and a good actress, but that to compare her with la Garbo is ridiculous. She has none of the distinction, the aloofness, the sophistication, the mystery, the genius.

25

CECIL SUPERBUS !

1933

SITTING down to Contract in a country house in Dorset some time ago I cut as partner a venerable individual with a bald head and an immensely long white beard which he folded on his chair before sitting. This arch-druid who looked as though he had himself laid the first stone at Stonehenge exhibited as much knowledge of Contract as a hippopotamus might have of chess. Which did not prevent him from clamantly justifying calls of which a half-witted peahen would have been ashamed. Next day I asked Mr. Mark Hambourg, also a member of the house-party, who my partner of the previous evening had been, and he replied in a roar which would have filled tidal basins: "My boy, he is the greatest living Judas Maccabæus. Unfortunately he plays bridge like Judas Maccabæeus!" This anecdote for the entire truth of which I moderately vouch seems to me to be justified because it is good in itself, and because it leads indirectly to *The Sign of the Cross,* the new film at the Carlton. The connection, which may not at first sight be obvious, is this, that within ten minutes of the conclusion of that film I was sitting down to bridge with the original Marcus Superbus, the actor in question having played the part for four nights before Wilson Barrett took it up. In those years I was living in the provinces and so never saw Barrett in the part, though having vivid recollection of quantity of Tearles and Calverts. I first saw the play in the little manufacturing town of Nelson when I was still in my 'teens, and I at once fell head over ears in love with the charming young actress, Beryl something-or-other, who played Stephanus. What a wonderful play it was, still is, and must ever be since every element of popular appeal is worked for all it is worth and none is omitted! There is romantic love of the King Cophetua and the Beggar Maid order, now translated into terms of Roman prefect and Christian maiden. There is sadism in both the general and the particular. Nothing is more agreeable to the normal theatre-goer than to glut his appetite for horrors while at the same time slaking his sentimentality. It was indeed a touch of genius in Wilson Barrett to add the torturing of the individual Stephanus whom the audience knows to the larger-scale but less identifiable lacerations of the circus. Add hysterico-epilepsy based on genuine religious fervour, refrain from any kind of irony or questioning, and you have an assemblage without parallel for the excitation of popular enthusiasm.

It goes without saying that whatever the theatre did with this material the film must be able to do infinitely better. This film has been objected to on the grounds that it is not a contribution to what may or may not be popularly thought about the early Christian martyrs. My reply to this is that when *Androcles and the Lion,* which is a contribution to such thought, was performed some little time ago at the Old Vic I did not see these objectors present in their thousands. The point, of course, is not whether this film is a good Shaw but whether it is a good Cecil B. de Mille. As to the latter I have no doubt whatever, and I hereby certify that never has Mr. de Mille made himself less ridiculous. The photography is excellent and he has so far succeeded in creating illusion that at times it is possible to imagine that one is seeing the real thing. Of all things in the cinema this illusion of actuality is the most difficult to produce though I think Mr. de Mille has for once in a way made his claim good. His crowd scenes are superb, and I do not think it would be possible for anybody, except possibly Captain Bertram Mills, to criticise the happenings in the circus. One really does believe that the gladiators who salute Cæsar are about to die, and when after the combats their bodies are piled on a truck and carried away one really believes that they are dead bodies. The lions, too, are first-class, and it would seem that in this matter Paramount has got Metro-Goldwyn-Mayer beaten to a frazzle. Here the cinema is magnificent on its own ground since there is no theatre in the world and no artistry which can do for the interior of the Colosseum what the films can do. Great artists like Reinhardt can, of course, suggest the Colosseum; the cinema reproduces it, and to some minds that in itself is a delight. In another connection I am always the first to say that in Shakespeare's play of *Henry V* five soldiers can adequately present the Battle of Agincourt, five because that number splits up into two groups, a pair and a trio, which gives it the air of being a crowd. On the other hand, seven thousand five hundred Paramount supers do convey an excellent idea of a Roman crowd, just as the Colosseum itself would doubtless give an excellent notion of the Colosseum. But Mr. de Mille is to be specially praised for this that, æsthetically considered, he has improved upon the old play. There is a depth of seriousness in the scenes with the old Christians to which the play never attained, and particular praise should be given to Messrs. Arthur Hohl and Harry Beresford for two lovely performances which if the whole thing were turned into a morality-play and performed in a church would need no alteration whatever.

In this case as in all others the difficulty could only be with the principals, since supers of genius abound. Mr. de Mille has been fortunate in his choice. Failing John Barrymore he could not possibly have got a better Marcus Superbus than Mr. Fredric March who after a trifle of uncertainty in the early love-making scenes puts up a courageous and a convincing show. His nose and forehead are grand, and if he is a little shaky about the chin it is presumably because Nature, after all, and not Michael Angelo made him. Miss Elissa Landi, when she was an English actress, was an extraordinarily bad one, in the sense that having any amount of natural emotional power she seemed to have neither the skill nor the desire to discipline it. She is now improved beyond all measure and is now definitely an actress instead of a gifted amateur. She was always amazingly good-looking and has now become intelligent-looking as well. There is one long scene in which while some courtesan monkeys around Mercia, the girl must stand rapt and with her mind elsewhere. Miss Landi does this difficult scene very well indeed, and it is refreshing to realise dramatic tension and to find that it has not been tampered with. As Poppæa Miss Claudette Colbert extricates herself with enormous discretion out of a part which is built up entirely of pitfalls, a part which entrusted to the normal gum-chewing diva would have ruined the film completely. It is impossible to imagine what would have happened if the rôle had been given, for example, to the lady who plays Dacia and whose uncontrolled Americanism reduced me to helpless tears. Tears of the more serious sort were very nearly evoked by the moving acting of Mr. Tommy Conlon who plays Stephanus. As Nero Mr. Charles Laughton enjoys himself hugely, playing that Emperor as the flaunting extravagant quean he probably was.

26

"CAVALCADE"

1933

IN one way the cinema has enormously let me down. Normally the procedure on the occasion of the "world première" of a "smash hit" is to invite about five times as many people as the house will hold, so that when one has finally battled one's way through a seething mob one is asked if one would mind sitting on the stairs or leaning over a balustrade within six feet of the film because the wives of eleven film-promoters are sitting on the seats reserved for one. The film then begins a prompt three-quarters of an hour late and with a first picture having nothing whatever to do with the main item. A cartoon and a news reel follow, after which and in the middle of lunch-time the main attraction condescends to put in an appearance. The whole business of the first showing of *Cavalcade* at the Tivoli was horribly mismanaged. No household troops kept the Strand clear, for the very good reason that it did not need clearing. No police, mounted or on foot, pranced in front of the Tivoli for the very good reason that there was no mob to be controlled. At twenty-five minutes past ten in the morning one arrived, was ushered without confusion into a comfortable seat, and a glance round the house told one that the management had invited enough people to fill all the good seats and no others. At half-past ten to the minute trumpets blared, and at the exact time advertised the film of *Cavalcade* started. In short, the whole thing in its decency, orderliness, and punctuality was as unlike a film première as it is possible to conceive.

In another and much more important way the film industry has let itself up enormously. *Cavalcade* is a grand film in all its aspects. It is a completely faithful reproduction of the spirit and letter of Noel Coward's original work. It conveys to the spectator exactly the same quality and quantity of emotion that the stage play did. It is, having regard to the kind of art aimed at, a work of art, a perfect whole meaning what it says, and even what it takes care not to say. In the matter of its photography, settings, and crowd marshalling it is flawless with the possible exception of two back-cloths which are obviously an intrusion of the studio upon reality. As a message for the times it repeats Mr. Coward's message exactly. As a precipitant of tears this film will not easily be equalled. And last, though of course not least, as entertainment it is superb. It is not a photographed play because Mr. Coward did not aim at a play. But it is a colossal show with a thread of story running through it which I venture to think comes out even more clearly on the film than it did on the stage. Messrs. Frank Lloyd and Winfield Sheehan who produced this play for Fox Films may lay this flattering unction to their souls that never has a film been produced with greater magnificence or better discretion. The picture is totally without any trace of Hollywood, and, though made in America, is bone-English throughout. It is unnecessary to tell readers of THE TATLER what the film contains since I have already said that it is entirely faithful to the stage play. There are two omissions, or perhaps I had better say that I detected only two. One of these is the silent frieze of Hyde Park after the death of the Queen, and it would not surprise me if this had been tried and found ineffective in this medium. The other omission, which I regret less, is that of the drunken party with the undergraduates. As against these omissions must be put the fact that owing to the medium the scenes of war-hysteria are more effective now than they were before.

But none of this praise would have been possible if the directors had not been magnificently served by their cast. Here one must say at once that while one would have wished to see again the extraordinarily lovely performance of Miss Mary Clare, no better substitute than Miss Diana Wynyard could possibly have been found. She has great beauty on the screen as well as in real life, and the direction has posed her so as to make the most of the upper and more exquisite half of her countenance. She grows old beautifully, and though our Mary attained a deeper note of poignancy in the later scenes, Miss Wynyard gives a beautifully felt and well-thought-out performance which holds the whole film together. She has delicious period clothes to wear and carries them like a lady and not like a film star. Miss Irene Browne also wears her clothes with a full sense of their value, and it is a pleasure to note the possession in both actresses of poise and timing. I thought Mr. Clive Brook's Robert Marryot much better than the original, which always struck me as a little weak. Mr. Brook is gallant enough in the early scenes, while in the later ones he grows old and perfectly assumes the grand manner and heartwhole stupidity of the higher command. Perhaps the elder boy might be a little better cast, though admirable compensation is made in the choice of Mr. Frank Lawton, who plays the younger son without over-reminding us of Young Woodley. For those who remember Mr. Fred Groves's Alfred Bridges it is at first a little difficult to accept Mr. Herbert Mundin, though here one must congratulate not only the producer but the player upon not introducing extraneous funniosities to which the part must have invited. Ellen is again in the hands of Miss Una O'Connor, to which she had established a right that it would have been impertinent and impolitic to contravene. Here is a really fine performance in the sense that the character appears to be living before your eyes. M. Sacha Guitry has laid it down with a pettishness which suggests jealousy that the film actor does not act but has acted. Five minutes of this film are sufficient to expose this fallacy. It is a fallacy because M. Guitry was looking at it from the angle of the player rather than of the spectator. It is nothing to the film-goer that what he is looking at took place six or twelve months ago. The point is whether he is induced to believe that the thing he looks at is happening here and now. In this sense *Cavalcade* is real. Or so the audience signified at the Tivoli last Wednesday morning not only by its applause but by its emotion which had been perceptible throughout.

27

KIDS FROM GERMANY AND SPAIN

1933

AS I write, a letter from the world's best golf correspondent and no mean authority on Dickens informs me that Little Nell is a little pig! To which, but that I have sworn to adjure dippings into the French tongue, I nearly replied on a postcard: "A qui le dites-vous?" But is Little Nell any worse than Paul Dombey, or Little Eva, or Master Willie Carlyle, or Miss Alcott's Beth? I would say Yes, a hundred times Yes, because these excessively disliked dying and she adored it. Indeed I feel about Little Nell that if she had survived she would have gone to live at Kensal Green and sat interminably in a bay-window on the second floor. Why on the second floor? To count the leaves better, stupid! I am persuaded that her favourite heroine was Juliet and that she would have loved, waking or dreaming, to inhabit "a vault, an ancient receptacle" and there madly play with her forefathers' joints. In short, in a Freudian age she would have been called not Nell but Necrophila. That is the modern feeling, and I am not at all sure that it was not the old one, with the exception of the miners of Roaring Camp where the test for virility was probably the number of buckets-full shed over Dickens's wan monstrosity. These things being said and agreed to, let me now confess that the handkerchiefs are not made which will suffice me at the bedside of any child who dies in the theatre or even on the screen. Coal-black songsters whose cheeks are furrowed white by the thought of mammies at home, pugilists *distraits* since they are fain to smooth a pillow streaked with infant gold, cow-punchers desisting from wife-beating at the patter of tiny feet, pork magnates who hear that patter vowing to re-cherish their wives—all this guff and hooey enthrals me as it obviously enthrals Americans. I believe that even those American critics who can gaze stonily and for hours together at *Strange Interlude* succumb before the child theme skilfully used. Deny it though both may and will, I feel that at some early showing of *Sonny Boy* Mr. Mencken groped for Mr. Nathan's hand, and that in Mr. Mencken's bosom Mr. Nathan folded all his sadness up. But a truce to these horrors—I do not mean my American colleagues—and my recollection of them!

My present point is to declare how astonishingly good from every point of view is the new film at the Cinema House in Oxford Street, that film being *Emil and the Detectives*. This is not the usual screen adaptation of a story; it is Eric Kästner's story re-lived. It is played almost entirely by children in a manner which suggests that one will have to revise one's whole notions of what acting is or may be. These children are neither stage-conscious nor camera-conscious nor art-conscious, and I would bet the profits on *Cavalcade* to a ha'penny that they have never heard of what our clever young highbrows call "spontaneous rhythm." In plain English, which is the one thing your highbrow young or old cannot write *or even understand*, these children are not self-conscious, or were not self-conscious when the film was being made. They were told to play at something, played at it, and were photographed. And, I beg to suggest, not very differently from the way in which you and I might have photographed them. It was certainly clever of Ufa to show in the scene at the railway-station the *Manchester Guardian* sticking a mile high out of the book-stall. This tiny incident alone "places" the film; you cannot borrow that august seal to set upon rubbish, and the rubbishy producer would not have thought of it. The little Cinema House was crammed full of fashionables and intellectuals as well as people of the humbler sort, and all of us could be heard doting audibly on one of the jolliest, least pretentious, and most plausible stories of child life that has ever been written. The villain, too, was superbly done; there was about him a seedy smartness and a kind of bogus villainy which were beyond praise. Did his eyes squint or didn't they as they began to leer ingratiatingly at Emil from under that incredibly jaunty bowler, and, half-way down the tapering nose, decided to pick his pocket?

I think the whole key to the film is in this actor. The children must not outwit a real bank-robber because they could not. But they can be a match for a story-book villain, which this actor has taken care to be. If this is not intention it is the luckiest chance. It is he who gives the film the value which Kästner intended in his book, though this does not prevent the children from being delightful throughout.

The evening at the Adelphi began with a couple of delicious Mickey Mice, though I should like once more to warn Mr. Disney that he is spoiling his joke by over-elaboration. To my and, I think, to everyone's horror the first cartoon was in colour, which gave it a three-dimensional solidity. Whereas the whole essence of these things consists in their use of two dimensions only. But let that pass. What part of Spain does the Kid come from? Doubtless Mr. Eddie Cantor would have us think Andaloothia, as people who have spent a night in Barcelona insist upon calling it. *The Kid from Spain* is a first-class musical comedy in which, for no rhyme and less reason, hundreds of Cochranic young ladies rise from a single dormitory, divest themselves of silken clouts, and after an appropriate dance plunge into a marble bathing-pool the size of Grosvenor Square. These gaieties continue for a time, after which Mr. Cantor is allowed to become enamoured, though in the endearing process he gets mixed up in a bank-robbery, whereby he is compelled to masquerade as a Spanish bull-fighter. During the early part of the film Mr. Cantor had some good Cantorisms the best of which I take to be: "What's the use of a diploma? Every time you want to look at it you must run upstairs to the attic!" But it was when we came to the bull-fight that he made his real conquest over gravity. There was a glorious moment when he tendered the red cape to the charging bull which passed him harmlessly on the other side. For twenty minutes, or so it seemed, the supposedly enraged animal trotted with lowered head within two inches of the seat of Eddie's pants, whose owner accomplished marvels of agility, if indeed they were accomplished by him and not by a substitute. How much of all this was trick one cannot tell, though I should think it must have been difficult to find a substitute bull! Some of the grandeur and *panache* of the bull-ring was also recovered, and the whole entertainment was ripping in our sense and not the matador's. In fact the film for me had held so much of the sense of danger and escape that I was quite startled when, stepping off the pavement to avoid two evil-looking larrikins, I heard one say: "Don't you believe it, mate. There's a wrong way and a right way to cut a froat!"

28

"CYNARA" AGAIN

1933

HOLLYWOOD has made a pretty good job of what was always a pretty good play. I find that when the piece was first produced I wrote that Captain Harwood and Mr. Gore Browne had "thrown constructional skill overboard and allowed their play to become a stragglesome affair of episodes, strung together as though they were the scenario for a film." I went on to say that "the scene in the baths is probably one of the most inept which has ever fallen from the pen of responsible dramatists; and, indeed, the whole of this first act, which lasts one hour and twenty-five minutes, is empty of contrivance, feasibility, interest, and wit." But surely one of the purposes of the silver screen is to transmute base metal into gold, which proves that I was right and this film is right and all is right as right can be! Has Hollywood overdone the scene at the baths? Perhaps Mr. King Vidor does not know Paddington or he would not have represented that doubtless salubrious district as a gem of rural England. On the other hand Mr. Vidor may very well plead that he ransacked California without finding a spot quite as dingy as London boasts. Anyhow the scene is gay, and it is probably unfair to blame this ingenious producer for permitting himself a tiny splash when everywhere else he has refrained from what might have been an orgy of irrelevant colour. For example, he refrains from giving us anything of that Derby day as a wind-up to which Warlock, to use Mr. Sydney Carroll's word, "betrays" the little shop-girl, Doris, picked up in some angular tea-shop and at the baths awarded first prize for curves and cleanliness. Here I permit myself to question Mr. Carroll's "betrayal" since upon the exact connotation of this word depends the whole meaning of this film. I take it that in the dark ages, say the year before Hardy's *Tess*, to betray a girl meant seducing her either under promise of marriage or by getting her to believe that this is a reasonable thing for nice-minded girls to do with their nice bodies. Both of these Rake's Gambits presupposed an idiocy on the part of the maiden in which your Lothario was seldom disappointed, since these were the days when a rapt and unsullied imbecility was part of the dower brought by every innocent to the marriage bed. The bridal veil was a symbol of the girl's life up to that moment; marriage was to be the eye-opener.

But leaving the mythological past to look after itself, which it didn't, let us return to the present. Warlock tells the girl that he is married, and she on her side tells him that, to put it delicately, this is not her first entry into the courts of love. How, then, can she be either betrayed or seduced? It seems to me that delicate writers like myself are in need of a new word, though there are plenty of good old Anglo-Saxon ones which would do! Warlock does not even lead the girl up the permanent garden, for the good reason that she forestalls him by saying that the affair shall last exactly as long as Warlock wants and no longer. It is her that both play and film go wrong by making the fellow a barrister, since barristers do not fall in love except under proper safeguards, covers, and other indemnities. But a much greater error on the realistic side is to permit the Warlock ménage to be so excessively well off, though this fault is not in principle worse in the film than in the play, except that the Warlocks are better off still! It is a maxim of English custom, though not of common sense, that a man who has offended the community in one way may not henceforward serve it in any other. Years ago this England, disliking the bedroom manners of its greatest Foreign Secretary, had no further use for him; presumably it would rather have been plunged into a war by a bachelor than kept out of one by a gay and moreover elderly dog. A barrister who goes through the Divorce Court would obviously not be allowed to plead in it, and perhaps it is the essence of advocacy to have no personal experience of the kind of cause you plead. Because Doris breaks her pact and hangs on to her man after hanging has become undesirable, Warlock is reduced to penury—or would be but for the fact that his wife's fortune permits them to discuss Doris's suicide, and how it affects them, in Capri's costliest villa. That, however, is the play's fault and not the screen's. After all, one must not expect the film to show greater sensitiveness than the older art, and this explains why the film again shows Warlock giving his little games away by treating Mrs. Warlock on her return from her foreign tour with the scantiest marital courtesy. The husband who on such an occasion tells his wife she is tired, pecks at her forehead, murmurs something about letters to write, and leaves the warm precincts of the cheerful chamber without casting any longing, lingering look behind—only in two arts each fifty years behind the novel could any husband hope successfully to overstep the modesty of nature. In plainer English, in real life he would not get away with it.

Apart from trivial carpings *Cynara* is an excellent film, since as a whole it impresses us with its truth to life. Young women do sometimes behave like Doris, and there are quite a number of wives who take even more persuading than Mrs. Warlock needs to be convinced that the nature of the brute is polygamous, and that man by becoming husband does not desist from being man. The acting is quite first-class, except that Ronald Colman is still a trifle too casual for the slow-moving Warlock though he does his utmost to suppress his natural ebullience. I think, however, that he should have shaved his moustache in view of the fact that English barristers never wear that appendage when it is smart and only when they must look like a walrus anyhow. A lovely performance comes from Kay Francis who, as Mrs. Warlock, keeps her fury at being deceived within reasonable limits. Doris is played by a film actress unknown to me. This is little Phyllis Barry, who has something of the fragility of Miss Celia Johnson and rather more skill in suggesting that she is a shop-girl. The part of Tring is subtly presented by Henry Stephenson, and the quartet work together admirably. Somebody has taken considerable care with the dialogue in which I noted only one Americanism. This is where Doris says "Mind you call me" instead of "Mind you ring me up." I noted no other inaccuracy, except that the driver of the taxi should have lowered his flag. But that is the merest trifle, and will certainly not prevent the Carlton Theatre from keeping its flag flying.

29

NOT A BERNHARDT

1933

THE uncritical are obsessed by two manias. The first is to dislike something not because of what it is, but because of what it isn't. Critics of this sort dislike Thackeray because he isn't Dickens, or even a period comedy because it isn't a musical farce. The contrary mania is to like something because of a fancied resemblance to another thing not even remotely like it. "I adore Suggia's 'cello playing," people will say. "It's so exactly like Rembrandt's chiaroscuro." These are the highbrow idiots, whether congenital or as a result of studious application. But not only the uncritical are affected in this way; there are professional critics equally obsessed. A colleague has been asking whether Elisabeth Bergner is another Sarah Bernhardt, and for those who don't know I permit myself to mention that Elisabeth is the extraordinarily fine German film star now appearing in her first talkie, *Dreaming Lips*, at the little Academy Theatre. The comparison between Bergner and Bernhardt in my view can only be made by somebody who has seen one but not the other, or possibly neither. I have as much hysterical admiration for Miss Bergner as becomes a sober-minded person, but I venture to say that she and Sarah are seas asunder. Bergner's acting comes from the heart, whereas Sarah's came entirely from her love and knowledge of mountebanking. Bergner's sincerity has the power to wound, and her sorrows are real; Sarah's insincerity transported you in a chariot of gilt to a heaven of cardboard, and her griefs were as much an exhibition as Niagara. In an interview Miss Bergner has denied knowledge of technique, which, if I know anything at all about acting, merely means that this exquisite little person was talking through her fair interviewer's charming hat. "I only know that I feel what to do, and then it is done," says Miss Bergner, in my view pulling her interviewer's doubtless exquisite leg. Of course the little German lady may be another Garrick in the sense that she stepped upon the lot, as I believe the cinema stage is called, a mistress of her art. In other words she has been born with technique and doesn't know it, which is quite another matter from thinking you haven't got it.

This film tells once again the oldest story in the world, or what would be if Adam had had a brother, for it is all about a woman who is in love with two men. Gaby loves her husband Peterle in a mothering sort of way, and she also loves one Michael Marsden but in a way the most modern mother would hardly condone. Peterle is the conductor of a symphony orchestra, and Michael Marsden is a great fiddler who has assumed an English name. Marsden looks strangely cosmopolitan, and it has probably never occurred to Englishmen that from a foreigner's point of view that adjective includes his race. I think all little boys at Eton and Harrow, and even some big ones at Oxford and Cambridge, should be instructed that as soon as they step ashore at Boulogne they become "beastly foreigners." But that is by the way. Marsden looks half Belgian and half English, like Ysaye and a taller, thinner H. G. Wells, and I hope nobody who hasn't seen both will write to say there is no resemblance to either.

It is not necessary to insist that as the film is about a virtuoso and a conductor, we are vouchsafed a good deal of the prowess of both. I do however respectfully suggest to Herr Rudolph Forster, magnificent actor though he is, that the next time he portrays a fiddler, he should take lessons in stance and grip. He would then be told that the correct position for the right elbow is close to the side. Apart from this perhaps insignificant detail Herr Forster has successfully accomplished the rare feat of making us believe in his musicianship. One does not, however, quite believe in the programme for this concert. *Qui trop embrasse mal étreint,* meaning that you should not crowd more into a programme than that programme will hold. In this film Marsden is supposed to play the whole of a Mozart Concerto, the whole of the Mendelssohn Concerto, and one movement of the Beethoven. One reflects that the proverb about the half-loaf does not refer to Concertos, and that something must have altered in German taste if a concert can wind up with somebody's cadenza to Beethoven's first movement: nor does one quite believe in the world fiddler who will come back after this first movement, and in Berlin give an encore, consisting of the kind of musical muck which virtuosi visiting this country regard as suitable for the Albert Hall on Unpleasant Sunday Afternoons. And there my carping ends. The rest of the film is turned by the superb acting of Bergner, Forster, and Anton Edthofer into a tragedy as moving as anything two-dimensional can be.

The piece moves with a beautiful simplicity, and one believes in all that the trio is not only doing but thinking. I should like to take this opportunity of recording my admiration for the extraordinary acting of the two men, which is likely to be swamped in the enthusiasm for Bergner. The part of the fiddler is probably fairly easy, that of the gay, shallow and rather meretricious husband is much more difficult, and if there are more actors like these two out of Germany I should like to see them. They cannot be equalled in Hollywood, and modest Elstree has made no open boast of any talent of this order.

Having said that Bergner is not in the least like Bernhardt it is probably one's duty to say whom, if anybody, she resembles. Well, she reminds me of Pitoëff, except that she is very much better-looking and her face has actual as well as spiritual beauty. She is more than a little like Fay Compton, has something of the wit of Mary Ellis and most of the simplicity of Janet Gaynor. Last, from the crown of her head to the soles of her feet, all over, all through, and all the time, she is a consummate little artist, as full of technique, whether she knows it or not, as an egg is full of meat. In fact fuller, for she does not lack that little bit at the top which is missing in some eggs. Nothing has been left out in the equipment of an artist as brilliant as she is appealing. And besides being a great artist, which is easy, she is a first-class actress, which takes a lot more doing.

30

"KING KONG"

1933

I SURMISE that this is one of those Kinquering Kongs immortalised by the late Canon Spooner. At any rate it kinquered me up to a point. But first I should like to record an impression which I very definitely received, the impression that the enormous crowd at the Coliseum had been gathered together not solely to witness an exciting film but to pay tribute to its old favourite, Edgar Wallace. "The King is dead, long live the King!" was doubtless intended to imply no more than that while the holder of the kingly office departs kingship remains. But it is a cruel saying, nevertheless, and never more cruel than when it is applied to people who are not kings, or kings only in their little world. In his day Edgar Wallace was a king in Fleet Street, for he had about him that largeness which belongs to royalty. Though he had an enormous house in Portland Place he must needs take a suite at the Carlton where double doors were arranged doubtless to prevent the secret of the next play from leaking out. I remember that when I lunched there with him the meal consisted entirely of drumsticks, the result of I know not what holocaust of chickens. It was the old actor Elliston who aroused Lamb's wonder by declaring that at dinner he partook of but one dish "counting fish as nothing"; with like sovereignty Edgar had decreed the culinary banishment of all other parts of the fowl. But then everything about Edgar was Napoleonic, and this included his cigarette-holder which was the longest I have ever seen, his person than which I have known none broader, his manner which was on speaking terms with majesty, his princely poise, his capacity for work, and the gusto which made public proclamation of the goodness of that work. It was again Lamb who upheld that a man was entitled to laugh at his own jokes, since if he did not he would sit like a host esurient at his own table. Then again Edgar bestrode Fleet Street like a Colossus, while between his legs men of alleged greater talent ran about making themselves much smaller reputations. But the most royal thing about Edgar was his munificence which if the age had sufficient gratitude would now be crystallised into a proverb. He gave and he lent, and hardly knew t'other from which, though the recipients of his bounty had a shrewd enough idea. When he died, Fleet Street hearts were heavy, and not only because of the realisation that some purses would be lighter. He impressed his age, and I begin to think that the impression will be a lasting one. Fleet Street has not replaced him because it has now no name with which to conjure. He respected the intelligentsia without having any of their sad limitations. He was the friend of crooks, which is in itself no mean achievement. He was the beau ideal of all that crookdom expects honest men to be. In other words, he had a great heart, and an English one, and all English people knew it. In my view they have now not forgotten that which they knew, and I believe that that memory counts for something in the enormous crowds which are now flocking to the Coliseum. *King Kong* is presumably the last work that we shall see of one who was genuinely a little master, and there is a sense in which the Coliseum première was a memorial service.

My difficulty is to know from what angle one should look at this picture. As a story of a monster surviving from prehistoric times and to whom dusky and remarkably prepossessing young maidens are offered up as sacrifice lacks all that mystery and sense of the conceivable which marked Rider Haggard and all the other first-class workers in the fantastic. This business of shipping an extraordinarily vulgar maker of movie-pictures to an unexplored island is altogether too perfunctory. Nor do I think very much of the monster when we get to him, largely for the reason that too much is claimed for him. I am prepared to believe in Hotspur's feat of plucking bright honour from the pale-faced moon, but with the best will in the world I cannot accept this outsize gorilla plucking bright aeroplanes from that bit of sky which belongs to the American pale-face and sending them hurtling to earth. The whole effect of these scenes was to make me feel dizzy. There is a girl in this film, and for an excellent reason. It is all very well for Kong to wreck an overhead railway in the way in which a child will wreck a toy train, and this together with the fact that the golden-haired girl lies in the palm of Kong's hand gives a fairly accurate notion of the scale in which Kong is imagined. But human nature being what it is, our interest in such a picture inevitably centres in the monster's interest in the golden-haired girl, and the film censorship being what it is, it is obvious that Kong must be as sexless as the largest teddy-bear that ever enlivened tot's cot. The poor fellow is allowed nothing at which the tenderest innocent should mewl or puke, and one wonders why he doesn't make his dinner of the girl since she can afford him no other entertainment. At one gulp, too, since a twenty-foot mouth is not going to make two bites at a five-foot cherry. But no! The girl had to be preserved at the end, so that Kong may die not through being riddled with machine-gun bullets but because he has looked upon the face of Beauty. This is all the more odd in that since he first made the acquaintance of the young woman he has been doing nothing else.

Where the film is really good is in the skill with which the monster has been made to work. There is a magnificently contrived fight between Kong and a megalosaurus. The scenery, too, is extremely well contrived, and I should imagine that the animal noises were recorded in some amenable zoo. Technically the double photography is excellent, and my only criticism of the whole film is that not at any moment in it is the note of terror struck. It is all just very good fun, and my view is that Wallace had a first-class idea and that Hollywood spoiled it by biting off even more than a brontosaurus could chew. Indeed at moments intended to be horrific I heard more than a suspicion of laughter. If, however, the film fails as a provoker of sheer unalloyed terror it succeeds as extravagant entertainment, though here again I go back to the earlier part of this article and my belief that it is the general sense of indebtedness to this film's author which has saved it. This, however, may be a purely personal view and the film certainly gives you its money's worth though not, I think, in the currency claimed for it. Visitors to the Coliseum should on no account miss *Esmeralda,* which is one of the very best burlesques I have ever seen on the stage or screen. It is certain that between the two nobody can be bored.

31

"DINNER AT EIGHT"

1933

I THOUGHT *Dinner at Eight* pretty well acted when it was done in play form; the screen version at the Palace knocks that performance silly. It also knocks into a cocked hat the absurd notion that first-class actors know nothing about team-work, the highbrow idea being that nincompoops and noodles by playing constantly together acquire as a body a virtue which they do not possess as individuals. I have never believed and I will not believe this. I will not believe that Little Piddleton's bridge-playing doctor and lawyer with their wives, through living in each other's bosoms, will beat a team of daggers-drawn American and British experts. When anybody speaks highly to me of team-work in the theatre I know in my bones that individually the actors are no good! The cast at the Palace contains nine first-class film stars—the advertisements say ten. They play together magnificently and for me make the story more entertaining than I have previously deemed it. Six out of the nine famous players run away with the film in turn, and the fact that six horses are running away together does not debar those six from constituting a team. Let me take them in the order in which they appear in the programme. First comes Marie Dressler with a performance which is staggering in these paler days and would have been good when I was a boy and actors acted instead of going to parties. Here is the old combination of riotous temperament and rich comedy done with never-failing variety and resource. I can pay Marie no greater compliment than to say that throughout this piece of mingled realism and buffoonery—for your weather-beaten gold-digger is necessarily a tragic figure—this great artist reminds me of Calvé in her last days in *Carmen,* and of Arthur Roberts impersonating a woman, which is pretty much the same thing. But it needs great prose or its echo to do justice to Marie in this part. Let me say, then, that forty years of gold-digging have been to this Carlotta Vance, as to Pater's Monna Lisa, but as the sound of liars and dupes, and live only in the brutality with which they have moulded the changing lineaments, and tinged the hair. Hers is the head upon which all the ends of the world are come, and the eyelids are very weary. Or let me put it another way and say that every young person who wants to know what acting may be should go and see a performance which is equally recommended to any young actress desirous of knowing something about her art.

John Barrymore plays Larry Renault not, I think, nearly so well as Basil Sydney in the stage version, perhaps because he has grown too plump. Mr. Sydney gave the impression of a certain fineness underlying the ravages of time and dissipation, whereas Barrymore suggests nothing more than the good-looking man run to seed. But I do not see the necessity for making elaborate excuses; Barrymore's is the poorer performance, and that's all there is to it! Wallace Beery is excellent as Dan Packard, though here again I preferred Lyn Harding. I shall confess to being surprised beyond measure by Jean Harlow's brilliant and witty performance of Kitty Packard, that compendium of all that is nice in the human body and all that is nasty in the human mind. I had never thought before that Miss Harlow realised the appalling commonness of her sirens. It is now apparent that she does, and the way she turns little lady into vixen is seen to be a miracle of calculated art and malice. As Oliver Jordan, Lionel Barrymore is capital in his assumption of the feckless man of affairs who would let himself and his business run downhill in his desperate effort to catch up with that social climber his wife, well played by Billie Burke. Note that at the play's climax this character is not debarred by her feather-headedness from being in the right. You remember the situation. Mrs. Jordan's husband has got heart-disease, her daughter has been seduced, while her butler has been arrested for stabbing the chauffeur who has been taken off to hospital. All these things are important though none of them is the immediate point, which is the telegram announcing the defection of the English Lord and Lady in whose honour Mrs. Jordan is giving the dinner-party. Minor tragedies sometimes take precedence over major ones, as Macbeth usefully laid down. Mrs. Jordan's relatives and lackeys should have been smitten, seduced and stabbed hereafter. Lee Tracy's portrayal of the little film agent, though lively and authoritative, misses some of the quality which David Burns gave it in the play. That was one of the most exquisite cameos I remember; one does not feel that Tracy is quite Jewish enough to go the length of the little agent's devotion. But it is a lively piece of acting all the same. As the doctor Edmund Lowe suffers from looking a little too like John Barrymore; to permit any shade of resemblance between the characters is the one fault in the direction of this film. Lastly, Madge Evans as Paula Jordan cannot get near the unbearable pathos of Margaret Vines. It seems to me now that when all these additions and subtractions have been taken into account I was wrong in implying at the beginning of this article that the acting in the film knocks the flesh-and-blood version silly. It doesn't if you leave Marie Dressler out of account. But that is impossible; her success in this part is so tremendous that it over-rides any and every other consideration. The film without her would still have been good; with her it becomes one of the finest entertainments that have ever taken place in theatre, music-hall, cinema, circus, or, I would almost add, gladiatorial show at Rome.

It is a rule among publishers not to allow an author to publish books simultaneously, though the same does not seem to obtain in the theatre, where plays by the same author running at the same time are said to encourage each other. Some notion of this kind appears to have dictated the simultaneous appearance in two different films of Marie Dressler and Wallace Beery. My reaction to this is that whereas Marie can stand the double test, Wallace comes out of it poorly. So poorly that I left the Empire at midnight having seen the two films consecutively and hoping that it would be a very long time before I saw Wallace again. He has not half of Marie's variety, or perhaps it may be that *Tug-Boat Annie* is a dull film anyhow. A man sitting behind me murmured that it was at least 25,000 feet too long. There was some justification for this since, Annie's character being quickly established, there remains nothing for the next hour except Marie's futile attempts to prevent Wallace from becoming too beery. The last half-hour livens up owing to a rousing storm at sea. But to me the picture was a disappointment largely perhaps through following on the very exciting *Dinner at Eight*. Intending visitors are recommended, therefore, to reverse the order. In the meantime will American film producers try to realise that it is far better to give too little of a pair of fine artists than too much?

32

THE COMPARATIVE UNIMPORTANCE OF THE FILM STAR

1933

I SUPPOSE that the truth of the matter is that I am not really a film-fan. I am very fond of the cinema and often visit it other than professionally, which is the great test. But I do not attach importance to the cinema actors, one of whom seems to me to be just as good as another. I can never, for example, quite tell the difference between John Gilbert and Ronald Colman though I remind myself that one's nose is too long while the other has a silly little moustache. Unless I look at the programme I haven't the vaguest notion whether it is Gary Cooper or Charles Farrell; if at the end of the picture I see Janet Gaynor crushed in a blacksmith-like embrace I think it is probably neither but Henry Garat. I cannot tell George Raft from James Cagney, or Robert Montgomery from Rod la Rocque. With the women it is worse. If I behold a young woman striped like a zebra, wearing a pill-box of wild ass's skin over one eye, and being hypochondriacally tragic about nothing in particular, why then it must obviously be Joan Crawford. Or if I see a young woman composed entirely of Turkish-delight, then I guess that it must be either Constance Bennett or Jean Harlow, though again I have to look at the programme to know which. The reason is that film players as a class move across the screen without making any more impression on me than I presume a mannequin does on the female shopper. The impact on the male escort is doubtless greater, but that is by the way. The only film artists whom I can, as it were, summon up in the mind's eye are Chaplin, Jannings, Veidt, the two Barrymores, Laurel and Hardy, Lillian Gish, Greta Garbo, Marlene Dietrich, Janet Gaynor, and Marie Dressler. No, reader, you are quite mistaken—I should *not* know either Douglas Fairbanks or Mary Pickford! And I have no clear picture in my mind as to which is Novarro and which was Valentino. Now I suppose that to your real film-fan such a state of affairs is unthinkable and borders upon pose. "What!" the reader exclaims. "Not know Irving and Ellen Terry? The man's not fit to be a critic!" The point, dear reader—and it is so obvious that I am ashamed to make it—is that your average film actor or film actress is not a Henry Irving or an Ellen Terry. Or anything remotely approaching them, for then of course there would be no difficulty. I am persuaded that what it boils down to is that your film-fan bases his affection for his stars not upon their talents as artists but their characteristics as individuals. That is why film-fans are strictly uncritical and why I permit myself to be called a film critic. I care nothing at all as to whether Marie Dressler is Wallace Beery's wife, mother, or daughter, whether she is penniless or a martyr to arterio-sclerosis, or rich beyond the dreams of newspaper-proprietors and in the habit every morning of diving from a chrysoprase balcony into an open-air bath of lapis-lazuli and beryl. I only know the artist and care nothing at all for the woman—which to your film-fan must be the flattest burglary that ever was committed.

This was tremendously borne in upon me the other evening when I went to see the all-British production of *The Fire Raisers* at the Capitol.

Here the cast was composed almost entirely of well-known English actors known to me through scores of plays. And now an odd thing happened. This was that I found myself taking a personal interest in each player. Had they been acting on the stage, I should have surrendered to illusion; here I found myself taking an interest in them outside their parts and to the extent of hoping the best for them in their struggles with the new technique. I think that even if they had not given first-class performances I should have enjoyed their playing because I happen to have known and liked them through scores of other performances. What nonsense to pretend that this was a guilty fire-assessor when one remembered lunching with Mr. Leslie Banks less than a month ago! How could one think in terms of murderous fire-raising thugs when one remembered waving to Mr. Francis L. Sullivan in the Café Royal the previous evening? Mr. Frank Cellier familiar as the lordly owner of immemorial beeves in scores of country-house comedies, Mr. Lawrence Anderson of the noble voice and exquisite presence providing his clothes are of some remote century, Mr. Henry Caine, always a very good actor and never quite getting the parts such good acting deserves. And so one could go through the whole cast. Familiarity in this case breeds excess of admiration. How could one be nasty towards any actor who was nice to one yesterday at lunch? Nearly all the dramatic critics of my acquaintance have spent their lives trying to get into famous theatrical clubs; my wonder is how having got into them they can possibly continue to exercise their critical functions. It may be said that grapes are sour; my answer would be that over-sweetness is not the first property to be demanded of a dramatic or any other kind of critic.

Therefore I would say that an English critic familiar with the players of the English stage is the last person to say whether *The Fire Raisers* is or is not a good film. Because I know and like the players it seems to me to be an extraordinarily good picture. Now all film-fans like all film stars, which is the reason why, dear film-fan, all pictures must be extraordinarily good pictures. There is this to be said of the film at the Capitol, that it is an interesting subject and one which is very much on the carpet at the moment. The fire scenes are extremely well done though the authors have had some difficulty in tidying up the end of their story. Mr. Sullivan as the fire-raiser is shot by Mr. Banks, the criminal fire-assessor, after which Mr. Banks decides to make a funeral pyre out of the building to whose firing he was a party. But what about the assistant thugs? Murder has been committed, and it really seems that something should be done about it. But there is a great deal of virtue in eleven o'clock, and perhaps films need never be as logical as stage plays. People going out of the theatre almost invariably discuss the play, whereas in the cinema they forget the film in the very act of diving for their hats. Films, in other words, come like shadows, so depart. At the very best they can never be more than the ghost of the real thing. If a minor criticism be permitted it is that the people who cast actors and actresses for a film should be careful never to get two alike. There were two female characters in *The Fire Raisers*, the boss's wife and the boss's secretary. Throughout the entire evening I was never clear which was which. And I can only hope that the boss did not share my difficulty! Both seemed nice capable young women whom one would never know again. My suggestion is that the directors should have helped a numskull like myself by making one woman plump and fair and the other skinny and dark. I can only say that the one I occasionally took to be the secretary seemed to me to be the better actress.

33

LA DIETRICH'S LATEST

1933

DURING his last illness Old Man Czepanek insisted on his daughter Lily reading aloud the Song of Songs. Hence the title of the Carlton's new film. As he was dying he would probably not feel up to explaining the mystical nature of that canticle which with any other interpretation is hardly suitable reading for a young girl. To the pure, however, all things are notoriously pure, particularly to Saxon blondes. So Lily came away from Old Man Czepanek's grave having got by heart only the nicer passages, which she was in the habit of reciting in and out of bed and season. She took the train to Berlin, whose railway-station can never have seen a less gawky village maiden or one more beautifully manicured and eyelashed. One felt that Lily had come from a farm where even the pigs were made of Dresden china. This is the place to say that Lily was acted by Marlene Dietrich, who having founded her career on sophistication has obviously wanted to see what would happen if the foundation-stone was removed. To my mind this is rather like a race-horse seeing if it can run slowly, or a juggler pretending to drop things. There are, however, many people who like to see great actresses playing at being little girls, and to these all that followed must have given considerable satisfaction.

Lily now went to live with her aunt who kept a book-shop and who lived opposite Richard Waldow, an impecunious sculptor who was mad about the torso. His studio was littered with Venuses rising from sea-waves and

Herculeses descending into stables, and to him Lily seemed the exact embodiment of Youth Not Knowing What Was Coming To It. So Lily very obligingly took off her clothes and put them on again. And it was May, and the cherry-trees were in bloom, and Heidelberg was round the corner, and there was a boating expedition, and Lily had a frock of sprigged muslin and wasn't afraid of soiling it when she flung herself to earth, and Richard didn't care what happened to the knees of his trousers, and other people besides aunts lay tumbling in the hay, and it was all very like a Shakespeare lyric set to music by Schubert. But Lily, far from being the light o' love Richard seemed to expect, turned out to be a prudent puss babbling of marriage. So Richard, with a career to make, chucked the girl, who was taken over by Richard's patron, the Baron von Merzbach, an elderly millionaire colonel anxious to devote the rest of his life to making a Baroness and a lady out of Lily. Two of the oddest things in the cinema are the persistent way in which it harks back to the stories of the masters, and its knack of doing the least possible with them. Nobody in connection with this sentimental orgy—and I cannot help it if this includes Hermann Sudermann's original novel and Edward Sheldon's less original play—seems to have realised that the Baron von Merzbach's passion for Lily is the Baron de Nucingen's passion for Esther Gobseck all over again. I am not suggesting that pages of Balzac's dialogue should have been put into the mouths of this film's characters. A great actor like Jannings would have given something of the madness and pathos attaching to the last passion of an exhausted roué. Indeed the parallel is nearer than I thought since, the sculptor being the exact counterpart of Lucien de Rubempré, the trio is complete. But very little is made of von Merzbach by Lionel Atwill, and it is no argument to say that the material was not there; it would have been there if Jannings had played the part and if necessary Reuben Mamoulian, the director, would have been sent to fetch it! Given Atwill's playing and incidentally Mamoulian's direction, it was difficult to believe that Lily, unless she was a hopelessly vulgar little chit, would have married the Baron merely to score off her absconding lover by being a Baroness. That is shop-girl mentality, and first-class direction would have seen that something more was necessary to make it other than an insult to our intelligence. After Lily had undergone the necessary schooling Richard was invited to the baronial mansion, where the Baron was intentionally rude to the former lovers though for no discoverable reason. This so upset Lily that, with Duse-like abandon, she wandered after dinner through a lot of trees to the cottage of her riding-master whom she had that very afternoon thrashed for what servant girls call "presuming." The riding-master was about to presume again when the cottage caught fire, and Lily, being rescued, headed straight for the Berlin gutter. This resort, being film-wise interpreted, meant picture hats and late suppers in a Bitter-Sweet kind of cabaret.

Here we had a flash of the old Marlene singing hoarse nonsense with an air of horse sense. Presently Richard discovered her and took her back to his studio, where Lily seizing a convenient crowbar demolished the statue of herself with appropriate orchestral lamentations from Tschaikowsky's Pathetic Symphony. Richard said that he was prepared to let it go at that—these were his actual words—and kneeling on the floor gathered to his arms the prone Lily, the train of whose dress Mamoulian had carefully arranged in folds that Chanel or Molyneux would have approved. Surely this is the mark of the unimaginative director; ordinary observation should have suggested that women who fall to the floor do so in an untidy heap. The last shot revealed Richard embracing Lily, having apparently forgotten all about the young riding-master and willing to re-enter his career with the addition of a slightly soiled Baroness.

Of la Dietrich in this part I am content to say nothing except that she simulates the negation of herself as cleverly as Miss Marie Tempest would doubtless do if she were asked to play Gilbert's Patience. Of Lionel Atwill's performance something has already been said. Alison Skipworth as Lily's rum-drinking aunt makes a great deal out of a very little. If I am chary of expressing any opinion about Brian Aherne's performance as Richard, it is because I do not see why an actor possessing the minimum of facial expression should be chosen for a medium requiring the maximum. He is a fine figure of a man and would doubtless be first-class in those Alaskan melodramas in which backwoodsmen felling trees in snowstorms to slake equatorial passions whirl gleaming axes round bronzed shoulder-blades. But as the artist-amorist torn between two kinds of clay, this actor seems to me to be not more vital than one of his own statues. Altogether a disappointing picture though the management made every effort to enhance it by inviting one to attend an hour before it started and endure a series of preliminary films which were positively ghoulish in quality. But even their cessation did not make me feel that *The Song of Songs* is anything other than a second-rate film.

34

"THE PRIVATE LIFE OF HENRY VIII"

1933

PUBLISHERS will tell you that in the matter of historical novels it never rains but it pours. Let them publish a novel on Mary Queen of Scots and at least six more manuscripts on the same Queen will arrive before the month is over, including two by Miss Marjorie Bowen and three by Mr. George Preedy. Two years ago it was impossible to take up any book which was not about this over-written Queen. Then came Elizabeth's turn, and for the last two years every drawing-room has been blasted with ecstasy for the Virgin Queen, with whispered conversations beginning: "Of course, my dear, what was really the matter with Elizabeth . . . ." The world, being still Tudor-minded, has now turned its attention to Bluff King Hal, and the present film consists in showing how each of Henry's six wives called his bluff. *The Private Life of Henry VIII* is an excellent film and a credit to British production, always presuming that Mr. Alexander Korda is British. First let me say something about this film's presentation. The façade of the Leicester Square Theatre was flood-lit by, if my eyes did not deceive me, lamps reposing on lorries stationed in Leicester Square—in my view an unwarrantable interruption of traffic which would not be tolerated in the case of a theatre proper. Inside was the usual childish parade of attendants who may be disguised at the will of the management, and according to the picture, as gondolieri or Volga boatmen, buccaneers or deep-sea divers, gladiators or Little Boys Blue. On this occasion they were buckramesque. In the foyer, at a tepidarium's temperature, was assembled the usual film-première crowd, all that assemblage of blonde nitwittery and vacant squirehood, tempered here and there by the polite world's more venturesome spirits. Presently, meaning in about twenty minutes, the phalanx deeming itself sufficiently seen moved on to the hotter room of this Turkish Bath, to wit the auditorium. There we were regaled with one of those entertainments devised, it would appear, solely for the purpose of taking all dignity out of an evening. This was a haphazard and arbitrary review of early film stars with a running commentary in one of the most hideous voices that even Hollywood has ever canned. This was followed by a Silly Symphony and a Mickey Mouse cartoon in, of course, the wrong order. Then four trumpeters appeared, made a foolish noise, and went off. This sort of presentation infuriates and disgusts me not only because it offends me personally, but because it diminishes what is trying to be an art. The management may well say: "Show us how to do better." I will tell them. The way to do it is this. Let the flood-lighting, the camera-clicking, and the picturesque attendants remain as they are; these are toys to please the gaping crowd outside the cinema-doors. The changes I would have made were upstairs. I should have begun with the National Anthem played by a full flesh-and-blood orchestra, and followed that with a short travel film of the most exquisite quality procurable, accompanied by good music. I should then have demanded from my orchestra a shortish piece of extreme virtuosity. Indeed I should probably have invited an English composer of merit to prepare specially for this occasion a fantasia of national airs celebrating England's greatness. As it was, the film began in an atmosphere of cheap scent, cheap jewellery, and cheap-jackery, which was not improved by the intolerable facetiousness of the film's opening remarks. We were told that the film would take no notice of Katherine of Aragon who was a person "of no particular importance". Marvellous is the mind of man, and wonderful the mentality of your film producer who can deem Katherine's scenes in Shakespeare's play not to come within the scope of Henry's private life. This remark being quickly followed by that of a lady-in-waiting that the King's love-life was responsible for the phrase "chop and change" made us think that we were in for a horrid evening. Fortunately this humorist had now shot his bolt, and the rest of the dialogue was allowed to continue on a level so utterly mediocre that no sentence could be better or worse than any other.

Actually the film began with the death of Anne Boleyn, and it needs a world as insane as that of the cinema to conceive that Henry's relations with Katherine and Anne were too unimportant to be included in the survey of his private life which was presumed to begin when Anne Boleyn laid her head on the block! Anybody not in the film world would have realised that the great tide of emotion in Henry's life was more than half spent at the point when this film begins. Perhaps whoever conceived this film was making a virtue out of necessity, the private life of Henry being largely a tragic affair and the business of the present film being to provide an uproarious comic rôle for Mr. Charles Laughton. That Mr. Laughton does it well goes without saying. He has everything which Holbein and tradition have lent to this monarch except royalty. It is, perhaps, unfair to ask Mr. Laughton, who must play Henry in undress, to insist upon what he may be like when he is dressed up. But it is the part of a great actor whose authors have let him down to supplement them or shove them out of the way for a moment while he gives the audience that in which they have failed. In respect of kingship Mr. Laughton's portrait will not for a moment stand up to that of Mr. Frank Vosper in Mr. Clifford Bax's play, and it was Mr. Laughton's business to see that it should. In the matter of brusque bonhomie, royal rages, and sheer Rabelaisian comicality combined with suggestions of a little boy caught stealing jam, this Henry is excellent. But on the whole it is no more than what one expected of him, which in the case of a really great actor means that he has failed. For the really great actor always gives you something which you did not anticipate.

History has been twisted to give Miss Elsa Lanchester a grotesque chance as Anne of Cleves, and the other wives were goodish. Mr. Korda's production is really first-class, and I shall give the palm of the entertainment to this and to the Thomas Culpepper of Mr. Robert Donat who is in the period, in the Henry James sense. Everybody else in the film is pretending to be Tudor and, in Mr. Laughton's case, pretending very well. Mr. Laughton took his bow at the end, which in my view was almost as much of a mistake as to make a public entrance and submit to be clapped on the back by scores of people he didn't know. Here again the film-world has no sense of values. Proper publicity, did they but know it, would have been to produce on some other night in the week with Mr. Laughton safely under the Old Vic's lock and key.

35

STORM OVER EISENSTEIN

1934

RUMMAGING in an old cupboard the other day I brought to light an old copy of THE TATLER published in the Dark Ages, to wit the autumn of 1928. The talkies had just started and one of my many immediate reactions to the intolerable innovation was that it would abolish the film orchestra. I wrote: "No film that I have ever seen has, by itself and unaided, occupied more than a quarter of my theatre-going mind. How in the absence of music am I to divert the remaining three-quarters? Drink? I am not in the habit of going to the cinema in a state of intoxication. Dope? I do not know where to get any. Sentimental dalliance with the young lady next to me? She invariably turns out to be an aged gentleman with spectacles and a beard." But five years have passed and I withdraw some of the foregoing. In those five years I have seen films which have occupied the whole of my mind, and in predicting the abolition of the orchestra I did not foresee its tinned brother. It was because I had just cleared out my cupboard that this old article was fresh in my mind when the same evening I went to see Eisenstein's *Thunder Over Mexico* at the Marble Arch Pavilion. And then, joy of joys, I realised that the film was going to be all-silent! It is true that the canned music persisted. Ever and anon I reflected how much better a flesh-and-blood orchestra would have been with a score chosen suitably from the classics. I hankered, too, after that air of the living theatre which is always given by the shaded lamps in the orchestra under which we know are warmly lit music desks. How much better is such a theatre, even if it is only a film-theatre, than the sad gully debouching on no-man's-land and terminating in a sheet! The music for Eisenstein's film seemed to me to be neither good nor bad nor yet indifferent; it was just nothing at all.

Now about Eisenstein. Among the things which to me are constant marvels is the enormous amount of knowledge about things happening outside this country which come so naturally to all my film colleagues and not at all to me. Is it that these clever people are in themselves knowledgeable? Or do they acquire knowledge, and how? Or is it thrust upon them, and by whom? Every little inky boy who can hardly blow his nose, let alone spell, seems to know all about Eisenstein. Yet like them I, too, go about the world and keep my eyes open. Nevertheless until this week I have gleaned nothing about Eisenstein, known vaguely to me as the producer of *The Battleship Potemkin.* This film has never to my knowledge been produced anywhere where I could go to see it. But I sense and have read that it is a good one. There is a prologue to *Thunder over Mexico* in which Mr. Upton Sinclair tells us something about it. In its full length the picture would take seven hours to exhibit, and when Eisenstein tried to return to America with thirty-five miles of film in his waistcoat-pocket he found himself forbidden to re-enter America. Mr. Sinclair does not tell us why, though all my colleagues seem to know that it was because Eisenstein did not see what Hollywood saw in Dreiser's *An American Tragedy.* Where Hollywood saw a lurid sex-drama, the Russian found a terrific indictment of the capitalist system, and said so. One could not expect Mr. Sinclair as a 100 per cent American to help in spilling these revolutionary beans, and so quite rightly he kept mum. What he did tell us was that Eisenstein was not allowed to re-enter America for the purpose of cutting his film, and that Russia refused to receive the film, which would have permitted Eisenstein to cut it at home. So Hollywood cut it for him, and in my view did not cut it well. We were turned out of the Marble Arch Pavilion at a quarter to eleven, after an hour and twenty minutes of the film, which on the general aspect was not long enough for a film of rare and astounding beauty. But there was a particular reason why the film was too short, and I shall assign it to the fact that the ending is wholly unintelligible, there being nothing to connect this story of private tyranny with that picture of revolutioned and modern Mexico with which the film concludes. That missing quarter-of-an-hour before eleven o'clock should have been used to show how out of a multitude of private injuries a national sense of injury was created, and how that led to Revolution with the consequent destruction of the old régime and the setting up of the new. "No montage!" said a young friend of mine, shaking his undergraduate head.

The beginning of the film is lovely, and I could have done with at least another mile of those enchanting antiquities recalling one's boyhood enthusiasm for Montezuma's Daughter. But one felt that this could not last long and that presently we should have to pay attention to the inevitable story. This tells of a Mexican peasant who submitting his bride-to-be for the approval of the landowner hears that she has been raped by the landowner's brother. Actually such a peasant would, one presumes, shrug his shoulders, dry the young woman's tears, and use the incident to throw up against her whenever in future years she started nagging. He would certainly not strike the lord of his flesh, or even the lord's brother, knowing that the result would certainly be some barbarous form of torture and death. Here, however, would be no film. So the peasant in question and two others who have taken his part are buried up to the chin and trampled to death by galloping horses. And Eisenstein is much too cunning a producer to fail to see that while awaiting execution the three may as well assume a grouping which takes the mind back two thousand years. Then without explanation we are shown a new Mexico which appears to consist entirely of boilers and boiler-scrapers. This as it stands is meaningless but it is too short to dull the effect of what, pictorially speaking, must be one of the most beautiful films ever made.

36

"LITTLE WOMEN"

1934

SOME little time ago the papers were all predicting that the Bright Young Things would presently go out of fashion. It was ever thus. When the 'nineties petered out it was in favour of the excited earnestness of Mr. H. G. Wells and the sober, practical philosophy of Arnold Bennett. George Moore used to be fond of declaring the exact spot in Piccadilly or street-corner in Mayfair at which he had made discovery of a masterpiece. I remember the exact moment at which I first decided that the 'nineties had definitely passed away. The Midland Hotel in Manchester had just been opened and I was wilfully committing the extravagance of dining alone and in solemn state in its delightful French restaurant, so unlike the chop-houses of which even your hard-headed, economically-minded provincial sometimes gets a little weary. I had taken with me *Kipps* which had just been published and of which people were beginning to talk. The first twenty pages made me oblivious of the food, while the next twenty made me forget the wine, and presently I was in a state of complete mental and spiritual intoxication. According to the 'nineties there was nothing left in the world worth doing. "Let's go to a theatre," said Algernon in *The Importance of Being Earnest,* and Jack answered: "Oh no, I loathe listening!" Would he go to the Club? Jack hated talking. Would he trot round to the Empire? Jack couldn't bear looking at things. What, in fine, would Jack do? The answer was: "Nothing!" But in nineteen-hundred-and-something the fashionable inertia has passed away and given place to feverish if middle-class acitivity. There was still something in the world worth doing. As it was in the early days of this century, so it was predicted a few months ago that the same thing must happen all over again. Just as the age of *The Yellow Book* had collapsed, so all that *Vile Bodies* stood for must pass away. Sitting the other evening at the Regal it really looked as if this prediction had come true. Here was no picture of gangsters, night-club, and all the spurious jollity and very real vulgarity to which Hollywood has inured us since the mechanical side of the talking film has become perfect. To my mind the debasing influence of most of the pictures turned out by Hollywood is best shown by the fact that we have lost all sense of their vulgarity, just as your drunkard may be perfectly convinced that he is a teetotaller in everything except name. Many a hardened drinker when asked how much he takes will answer "Practically nothing," and quite fastidious people now come away from the pictures persuaded that what they have seen has been practically in good taste.

The house on the night I attended was filled to capacity to witness the film made out of a book of which to-day's young people know nothing. *Little Women* was first published in 1868 and at once became popular. It was still a comparatively fresh work when I first made its acquaintance round about 1888, when it rapidly ousted from my affections such stories as *A Peep Behind the Scenes, Edith Vernon's Life-Work, The Wide, Wide World, Queechy, The Lamplighter, Lilian's Golden Hours* (a title which I suggest to Miss Braithwaite for her Reminiscences), *Won by Gentleness* (of which I remember no more than that a baronet called Sir Gervase fell off his horse, caught his foot in the stirrup, and was bumped along cobblestones to the baronial hall), and, of course, *Little Lord Fauntleroy*. To me, Meg, Jo, Beth, and Amy were and still remain as real as though I had lived with them; Mrs. March, Laurie, and Mr. Bhaer are only a little less so, while Mr. March always was and still is a poor and non-existent fish. When the four girls came on the screen the other evening I knew exactly which was which and even took upon me to correct one or two young people in my neighbourhood who confused Meg with Amy. Some of them even seemed inclined to give a Freudian explanation for Jo, that single-minded, single-hearted tomboy who just couldn't love handsome Laurie but could become second mother not only to Mr. Bhaer's five children but to Mr. Bhaer himself. It was a delightful evening, and I thought that the picture, which ran a full two hours, might well have been longer. It captivated the young people in the house as well as the old, and this is to be attributed to the producer, George Cukor, for having had the good sense to allow Miss Alcott and her characters to tell their own story. If the picture has a fault it is that so much insistence on Beth's attack of scarlet fever deprives her death of some of its pathos; no audience is going to take that fence twice. Beth, Meg, and Amy are charmingly played by Jean Parker, Frances Dee, and Joan Bennett. But there is something more to be said for Katharine Hepburn who plays Jo. I am always very chary of estimating the powers of any player whether on stage or screen on the strength of one or two performances, and I have only seen Miss Hepburn three times. The first was in *A Bill of Divorcement*, when she attracted attention by her raging ugliness and the stark dissonance of her speech. The next film was *Morning Glory*, where at times she looked amazingly beautiful and revealed herself as at least a capable actress. Now comes this film in which she adds to all that is demanded by the part of Jo an insight, a vision, and a spiritual tenacity good enough for Emily Brontë. If Miss Hepburn has not genius, she has something very near it.

37

"JEW SÜSS"

1934

OBVIOUSLY the first thing is to congratulate Gaumont-British on the enormous amount of care, archæology, and money that they have spent on mounting this super and, I am afraid, super-boring *Jew Süss*. Always, of course, supposing that any energy expended in this way is a matter for ongratulation. My own view is that it is a colossal and unnecessary mistake. It all began, I suppose, with Henry Irving when for his production of *Faust* he insisted upon having an exact replica of the gates of Nuremberg. To one of my way of thinking any old-fashioned-looking gates would have done equally well, just as anything vaguely Roman will do for the Senate house in which Cæsar was murdered, and anything vaguely Egyptian suffice for Cleopatra's palace. Some day somebody will film *Antony and Cleopatra,* and then I suppose somebody will be sent to Egypt to count the number of bricks in the Great Pyramid and see that the same quantity is delivered at Shepherd's Bush. The programme informs me that "carriages, baggage-carts, coffins and cradles were all built in the studios and are meticulous reproductions of originals." Is it supposed that one in a thousand of the visitors to the Tivoli cares tuppence whether, say, the baggage-cart belongs to Pomerania in the 17th century or Thuringia in the 18th? The programme goes on: "Among other things a complete garden was created in the studio with eight tons of peat moss and more than twenty thousand flowers." I confess to being considerably worried as to whether the peat moss was exactly the same as the kind that grew in Germany in the days of Jew Süss. Had it differed by one fraction of an iota I feel sure that such pleasure as I had in the evening would have been ruined!

One more quotation should make my point, for in this instance the programme is actually apologetic: "The only feature of *Jew Süss* that is not literally accurate is the leash of eight magnificent Great Danes. The hounds of the days of Jew Süss are extinct and Great Danes were used as the best possible substitute, but even they were dressed for their parts. Their huge spiked collars are exact reproductions of the collars worn by the hounds of Württemburg." In my view a considerable proportion of the £120,000 which this film is said to have cost could have been saved by turning the scenery and costumes over to Mr. Oliver Messel or Mrs. G. E. Calthrop. It was Mr. Messel who dressed the stage so wittily and amusingly for Mr. Cochran's production of *Helen!* Now how would the film industry have coped with that? I imagine that they would have engaged somebody from the Institute of Civil Engineers, or whatever the body is called, and sent him all the way to Greece with a sextant and theodolite in order to determine exactly how topless were the towers of Ilium. Next they would have despatched Sir Flinders Petrie to excavate the plains of Troy in order to discover a battle-axe and shield of the period from which correct copies might be made. After this I suppose they would consult the President of the Toxophilists' Association in order to make quite certain of the shape of the arrow which got Achilles in the heel; and glass-houses would be erected for the cultivation of myrrh, spikenard, or whatever Helen may be supposed to have put in her bath.

However, the fashion is against me, probably because people dislike using their brains. "What!" exclaim the directors of Gaumont-British. "Haven't we used our brains in getting our archæology absolutely correct?" The answer is that they have used them too much. When Mr. Messel and Mrs. Calthrop design scenery and dresses they are content to put on the stage a witty thing, after which they trust the audience to use its brains to see how wittily they have done. This is exactly what film audiences dislike doing; they infinitely prefer sitting back freed from the necessity of doing any thinking and secure in the knowledge that £ 20,000 or £ 30,000 has already been spent to save them the trouble.

There is no need for me to give the plot of this film for the reason that everybody except myself knows it, whereas I, not having read the book and not intending to, am not very clear what that plot is. Oddly enough, I do not find the programme helpful here since it flagrantly contradicts itself. A note on the middle page represents Süss as a noble fellow with his thoughts turned to his people, whereas an article on an earlier page suggests that he was a grafter and opportunist who richly deserved the end which he finally got. Whichever version be preferred, in my view the film is slow-moving and dull, though worth sitting through for the execution at the end and the utterly delightful *Peculiar Penguins* which follow. I wonder, by the way, whether the Tivoli will consider going pro-Christian for a bit, as I am really getting rather tired of these Wandering Jews, Rothschilds, and Süsses. Besides, in my case it is preaching to the converted. I am, and always have been, a pro-Jew or more accurately an anti-anti-Semite, and my particular dislike of the recent orgy of Jew-baiting in Germany is that it is going to lead to a great many more films extolling that people at unbearable length. Put it another way. Armenian massacres are bad enough; but they would be worse still if they were to let loose a flood of films about Armenians, delightful though those people undoubtedly are.

Jew Süss is capitally played except that we weary of Mr. Conrad Veidt before the end, and that Mr. Frank Vosper goes through the most appalling passions without a trace of them on his beautifully cold-creamed face. The best acting came from Sir Cedric Hardwicke, and it was a pity we saw so little of Miss Haidée Wright. The other women I thought poor, with the exception of Miss Pamela Ostrer. It was her director, of course, who insisted that a young woman who has fallen half a dozen stories on to a tulip-bed should look like Millais' Ophelia only on dry land.

38

THE WAR AT THE RIALTO

1935

REALLY it is difficult to say whether war pictures—even the authentic ones—do or do not achieve the end for which they are shown. The day after I had seen *Forgotten Men: or The War As It Was,* which is a stringing-together of actual photographs taken during the actual fighting—in view of the number of fake war pictures one is compelled to stress this—I said to a famous black-and-white artist: "Go and see this picture and you will never consent to another war." He replied: "I shall never consent to another war whether I see the picture or not. I have seen enough." He went on to tell me how, chatting in a club-lounge in a little county town near London, at one moment there were six talkers, and a moment later all that was left of the other five was a stomach sticking on a wall. My friend had escaped because of a little girl whom he had thrown to the floor for safety and whom he was holding down while the Zeppelin passed. It is possible that readers have been revolted by the foregoing incident; I intended them to be. During the War Arnold Bennett made the same plea, urging that the most gruesome particulars as to what really happens in battle should be published as widely as possible. He maintained, and I agree with him, that if war is ever to be stopped at all, it can only come through the realisation of every man, woman, and child of what it really is and entails. How many people are aware that there are war-victims still living to-day whose injuries are such that their relatives have never been allowed to see them? "Whatever," said Bennett, though I cannot guarantee his exact words, "whatever is not too bad for Civilisation to sanction should not be too bad for Civilisation to read about." It is the old question of moral cowardice, which was raised, I think by Mr. Shaw, in connection with capital punishment. The point was that any voter who does not instruct his Member to take immediate and active steps to abolish capital punishment should be prepared to take the hangman's place at the next execution.

It is fair to say of this picture that it is grim but, with very few exceptions, not gruesome. I still think that if the War were no worse than it is represented here, one would be entitled to class it as no worse than the last of the bearable agonies of mankind. You see men riddled by machine-guns and falling on their faces, or sent to earth with the breath drawn out of them for ever by a shell. Or you see a man leap a trench, receive a bullet in mid-air, and fall into the ready-made grave. But much of this film is not more than an amplification of the first line of one of the poems in *A Shropshire Lad*: "Shot? So quick, so clean an ending?" This film shows us very little of all that part of the horror which was not quick and not clean. It shows us nothing of the men burned by liquid flame, or agonising for days on barbed wire. Nothing of soldiers retching their guts out, turning green and yellow, and finally dying from the first gas-attacks. Though there are horrific things in this picture they attack only our tragic sensibilities and not our nerves and senses. There is a shot of a young soldier de-lousing, but watching him we continue to sit in our clean linen. There is plenty of mud, but we remain seated in a picture-house smoking our pipes in comfort, whilst the cigar of the man next to us smells good. Now consider that the death which throughout the years was at any soldier's elbow is not symbolised in those war cemeteries. The death which stalked them was not tidy, symmetrical, and moving like something in a tragedy. In actuality, this death was indescribably foul, grotesque, and meaningless. The man who knew that it might meet him at any time knew also that, though it might bring him glory, it would come without pomp and without circumstance.

To compass high resolve, to steel yourself to the worst that can befall while yet your body is healthy, well-fed, and well-housed, and your mind clean and easy—this is one thing; but it is another thing to carry out that resolve when your nerve is shaken and your mind dismayed, when you are cold and hungry, filthy and rain-soaked, with your nostrils full of a sickening stench, and that stock of patience which gave out long ago must still meet the demands of such minor things as indigestion, toothache, boils. *De minimis non curat lex*, but it is a mistake to suppose that war takes no account of little things. That is why if and since the aim of *Forgotten Men* is discouragement one could wish that it had been much less bearable. I feel sure that, if the recent exhibition at Dorland House had been a cinema-film, few could have seen it through without fainting or vomiting, whereas the effect of the film is akin to that exhilaration which proceeds from high and poignant tragedy. War is different from the tragic masterpiece in this, that it is poignant but not high.

Another thing which truth compels me to set down is that this film is less poignant than it would have been if our minds had not been vitiated by so many sentimental war pictures. I remember one in which there was a moving incident of an English boy dying in a shell-hole and tended by a wounded German. In the invented picture one knows all about the individual, his old mother at home, his sweetheart, the letters he will never receive or be able to answer. In the actual film we have to jog our minds to realise that every one of the hundreds of deaths which occur in it happens to an individual whose story would move us did we but know it. The film, then, is in some ways like a railway accident which, happening, say, in China, does not appal us as much as smaller accidents happening at home. It is just because this film is real, and not a work of art, that we have to go much farther to meet it than a work of art demands. Perhaps this explains why the most effective sequence is the sinking of the "Blücher." The great ship is heeling over and hundreds of men are in the sea swimming towards the English boats which are putting out to save them. And then the Zeppelin appears, the war-code consenting to the sacrifice of the drowning German sailors in the effort to destroy the English boats which are then driven off. That is a terrible sequence, and such as a great dramatic artist might have conceived! No praise can be too high for the sober commentary of Sir John Hammerton which accompanies the film.

39

"LORNA DOONE"

1935

NOT everybody knows that the novel, *Lorna Doone*, on its first appearance was a complete flop. Then an English Princess married the Marquis of Lorne, and the British public in some way connected the two events. The book ran through edition after edition, and the author's fame was made, though, consistent with its first view, the public still persistently declined to read anything else by Blackmore. I well remember when and where I first read *Lorna Doone*. It was during the bitter winter of 1891, and I was a small boy at school and very homesick. We had separate cubicles and every night I used to snuggle up against the hot-water pipes and read this book until the lights were put out. I fell in love with Lorna that winter, and have never been out of love with her. This constancy to Lorna is, I think, the experience of most readers and is in some measure attributable to the extraordinary beauty of her name. And then again Lorna gives one the impression that her creator had no trouble with her. Stevenson has a passage which all novelists ought to know by heart: "Readers cannot fail to have remarked that what an author tells us of the beauty or the charm of his creatures goes for nought; that we know instantly better; that the heroine cannot open her mouth but what, all in a moment, the fine phrases of preparation fall from round her like the robes from Cinderella, and she stands before us, self-betrayed, as a poor, ugly, sickly wench, or, perhaps, a strapping market-woman. Authors, at least, know it well; a heroine will too often start the trick of 'getting ugly'; and no disease is more difficult to cure." Lorna never sickens for this complaint. Her beauty and her charm are unquestioned and unquestionable. Stevenson goes on: "Who doubts the loveliness of Rosalind? Arden itself was not more lovely. Who ever questioned the perennial charm of Rose Jocelyn, Lucy Desborough or Clara Middleton, fair women with fair names, the daughters of George Meredith? Elizabeth Bennet has but to speak, and I am at her knees." Lorna has but to pity the little boy who cuts his feet in the eighth chapter and I, too, am on my knees.

How artful was old Blackmore to keep us waiting so long for Lorna how like a dramatist, confident that his heroine is worth waiting for! Shakespeare does this, you know, with Juliet, and a whole act passes before Sudermann's Magda appears. But I think that if guessing in this matter should be attempted at all, the secret of this book is to be found in its portrayal of pure love. From the moment John Ridd sets eyes on Lorna we realise that they are to be lovers till the end of time. Consider this:

> I have never heard so sweet a sound as came from between her bright red lips, while then she knelt and gazed at me; neither had I ever seen anything so beautiful as the large dark eyes intent upon me, full of pity and wonder. And then, my nature being slow, and perhaps, for that matter, heavy, I wandered with my hazy eyes down the black shower of her hair, as to my jaded gaze it seemed; and where it fell on the turf, among it (like an early star) was the first primrose of the season. And since that day I think of her, through all the rough storms of my life, when I see an early primrose.

That note, once struck, is never departed from. The insistence on John's slow and heavy nature does something besides describe John; it describes Lorna. Who can doubt that she was the quicker-witted of the two, and that while physically he was her protector, it was not she who leaned upon him, but he upon her? Indeed, it is not too much to say that Lorna mothers him from the moment of their first meeting to the end of their lives. She is little, and if you like to imagine her as frail of stature no one will quarrel with you. At the same time in comparison with her lover she is infinitely wise, and as the book goes on a kind of queenliness grows upon her.

It is this elder gravity in Lorna which makes her so difficult to cast. Miss Victoria Hopper in the film at the Adelphi has none of it; she is never at any time throughout the picture anything more than a timid frightened little soul. In my time there have only been two actresses who could possibly have stood up to Lorna and given us all of her many-sidedness. The first is Ellen Terry, and the second is Mona Limerick. There was no resemblance between these two actresses; yet both would have played

Lorna perfectly. We all know what Ellen Terry would have done with her, whereas Mona Limerick is the cherished recollection of the few. She was acting in Miss Horniman's company round about the same time as Mr. Basil Dean, who probably remembers her. My best recollection of her is Mr. Masefield's Nan, of which character, said Montague, she made a tragic figure of the order of Hardy's Tess: "Her natural incapacity for suspicion, her blindness to her lover's poorness of spirit, her own frank sanity of instinct, her gallant generosity in affection, the touch of grandeur in her revenge, which to her is not mere wreaking of a private hate but the rescue of other women from her own griefs—all this is nobly conceived and its expression splendidly wrought. Acted as she was last night, Nan stands out white and columnar from among the creeping things of the dark place she moves in." I think this gives not so much a picture of Lorna as an extension of what Blackmore's heroine could have been had she been placed in the predicaments devised by more tragic novelists. She is not the merely pretty, witty little thing who is the heroine of Crockett's *The Lilac Sun-Bonnet,* and the actress who is to give us Lorna and the whole of Lorna must be of sufficient stature to suggest that if called upon she could play both Nan and Tess. Mr. John Loder has no difficulty with the hero, who has only to be big and stupid. This is a part within the capacity of more actors than I should care to name, and I am only surprised that Mr. Basil Dean, having chosen a delightful little player who is completely wrong as Lorna, did not go the whole hog and looking round for his Ridd bethink him of Mr. Ernest Milton. Where the picture entirely succeeds is in its lovely delineation of the Devonshire landscape, except that Exmoor looks as if it had been transported to Russia. Perhaps the cameraman came from there? The other characters all look as if they had got into their clothes in Wardour Street and then taken a Green Line bus to the Doone Valley. Also, they are much too period-conscious, singing ye olde Englishe songes in ye olde Englishe voices, and with the air of a famous choir hoping its date isn't going to clash with Ye Olde Englishe Folke-Dancers.

40

SOME NONSENSE—AND DAVID COPPERFIELD

1935

THE Savoy Hotel was a good place to be in on a recent Sunday, for it was in that literary caravanserai that the Critics' Circle had its Annual Dinner. Mr. Ivor Brown in the chair made an admirable presidential speech, largely about Miss Marie Tempest, who was the Guest of Honour dividing it equally into witty things and wise ones. Among the latter was the statement that Miss Tempest was first and foremost a professional; she always knew what she had to do, and she always did it. I should like to suggest a definition of the difference between the professional and the amateur which I have never seen put forward. A professional is a person who can do his job when he doesn't feel like it; an amateur is a person who can't do his job when he does feel like it. It is odd, by the way, how few professional after-dinner speakers there are, how all speakers seem to delight in proclaiming their amateur status. The reader knows what I mean, how speaker after speaker will get up and describe the shock they had on receiving the invitation to make a speech, their misgivings ever since, and the agonies they are now suffering. After wasting five minutes in dithering, the next twenty will be devoted to delivering a masterpiece of marshalling and cogency to apologise for which is an obvious act of hypocrisy. I remember an occasion on which I had to follow that one of our actresses who, after Dame Madge Kendal, is the best speaker in the profession. On this particular occasion she annoyed me by giving a display of diffident collapse as graceful as, and even more complicated than Pavlova's Dying Swan. I began my speech by saying: "Ladies and gentlemen,—Nobody in London enjoys public speaking more than Miss X—— and myself." But I have given up all ambition that way, since it is humiliating to spend a fortnight working up one's brilliant impromptus only to read in next day's paper: "Mr. Agate suitably replied."

Very little time was wasted at the Critics' Circle Dinner. The guests got quickly down to the business of slanging the critics, who were made to look very small beer indeed. Miss Diana Wynyard told with great relish her experience during the last few months, that of emerging every evening from the stage-door of Wyndham's Theatre, exactly opposite the stage-door of the New Theatre, where Mr. Gielgud is still playing Hamlet, to find an army of autograph-fiends with its back towards her. The most startling speech was made by Mr. John Maxwell, who talked of the cultural influence of the films and drew a picture of the Lancashire mill-hand leaving work in silk stockings and with her face nicely made-up, all owing to the influence of Hollywood, which had enabled her to glimpse something of the best in life! At this a critic, who shall be nameless, spilled his champagne and was violently pulled down by better-behaved guests on each side of him.

The chatter about *David Copperfield* still goes on, and if I appear to be discussing it a little belatedly it is because its first-night happened after last week's number had gone to press. I hasten to agree that film magnates cannot regulate the production of their magnum opuses entirely with regard to the convenience of THE TATLER and its readers. My colleague, Mr. Sydney Carroll, has used the occasion to unburden himself of a piece of criticism which inspires me with awe. Mr. Carroll says: "The director, George Cukor, has, I think, been a little too anxious to follow on the heels of Dickens, for the truth must be faced that we have outlived these melodramas of undiluted sentimentality and fantastic diction. The players strove not unsuccessfully to conquer their material and mould it into something approaching nature, but the effect on the whole was like looking at life in the Victorian era through distorting mirrors and magnifying glasses." Let me draw Mr. Carroll's attention to that volume by Mr. Chesterton entitled *Criticisms and Appreciations of the Works of Charles Dickens,* and that passage in which this most devastating critic and greatest admirer of the world's first novelist says: "I have been talking about the omissions of Dickens. I have been talking about the slumber of Dickens and the forgetfulness and unconsciousness of Dickens. In one word, I have been talking not about Dickens, but about the absence of Dickens. But when we come to him and his work itself, what is there to be said? What is there to be said about earthquake and the dawn? He has created, especially in this book of *David Copperfield* he has created, creatures who cling to us and tyrannise over us, creatures whom we would not forget if we could, creatures whom we could not forget if we would, creatures who are more actual than the man who made them." And again: "But Micawber is not a man; Micawber is the superman. We can only walk round and round him wondering what we shall say. All the critics of Dickens, when all is said and done, have only walked round and round Micawber wondering what they should say." Mr. Carroll has not wondered, and has said. He has found that the diction of Dickens, which includes that of Mr. Micawber, is fantastic. Your film director should not allow Mr. Micawber to say, for example: "Under the impression that your peregrinations in this metropolis have not as yet been extensive, and that you might have some difficulty in penetrating the arcana of the Modern Babylon in the direction of the City Road—in short, that you might lose yourself—I shall be happy to call this evening, and install you in the knowledge of the nearest way." The way in which Mr. Carroll would have Mr. Micawber talk is, I suppose, something like this: "Say, kid, I guess you're kind of hazy about this quaint old burg!" and so on. I believe, and I think everybody else except Mr. Carroll believes, that despite all the exaggeration, caricature, over-drawing or what you will, of the characters in *David Copperfield,* the first and last impression of this great masterpiece is its abiding truth. It is a commonplace of literary criticism that these characters, or most of them, are truer to us than the actual people we know and live with. I do not know what Mr. Carroll means by "outliving" a book like this except in the sense that we have outlived *Tom Jones* and in non-fiction, Boswell's *Johnson*, or Pepys's Diary, or any great work which faithfully depicts contemporary manners.

I will not wrong my readers with a description of the film at the Palace which they can and will see for themselves. Instead I would like to stress the admirable point made by Miss Lejeune that the principal difficulty of the adapter must have been the change from the first person to the third. In the book David is not of much importance. He is a character of the second magnitude through whose eyes we behold the creatures of first magnitude abounding in the sense of their glorious and riotous selves. In the picture the interest largely devolves upon David, and it is the people surrounding him who become of secondary importance, an effect which is enhanced by the astounding virtuosity of the child-actor, Master Freddie Bartholomew. Among the real successes are Mr. Dick and Mrs. Micawber, but nothing in the world is going to make me praise or even approve of the Micawber of Mr. W. C. Fields. Here I only see a brilliant low comedian dressed up in Micawber's toggery and exciting laughter by bringing to Micawber the qualities of Fields, the famous low comedian. On the other hand, the fact that Fields remains true to Fields will make for this picture's popularity, because I am convinced that what to-day's public wants is not Micawber but Fields. On the first-night, whenever this Micawber appeared the crowd in my vicinity first uttered a yell, then listened for the words which were supposed to provoke that yell. Apart from Micawber, I think the picture is a good one, and on the understanding that no first-class novel can ever make a first-class picture!

41

TOUJOURS LA BERGNER

1935

AN actor who says, "Get out of my house!" will point, almost invariably, to one that he shakes his fist at, the object of his wrath. Contrariwise, should your layman tell an enemy to leave his house I hold it unlikely that he will accompany his command by any gesture more significant than the twitching of an eyebrow. And which of us, not being a war-lord, is ever prompted to shake his fist, however mailed and however potent? This co-ordination of thought and gesture is a convention which Miss Elisabeth Bergner rejects and is admired for rejecting. In the interests of dramatic realism it would appear that she is determined never to let her left hand know what her right mind is doing. It is almost as though she had evolved a set of gestures utterly opposed to the emotions she is called upon to portray, and has yet contrived to portray those emotions in her gestures' despite. Her latest film, *Escape Me Never*, at the London Pavilion, affords close opportunity for the study of Miss Bergner's method. An open hand *gaminerie* of walk enhances it. Her gestures are all of them sufficiently held flat against the face inexplicably accentuates her sarcasm. A certain incongruous to become real, so that unless you are looking for them you will not see them. Undeniably, this is a part of good acting.

The film, like the play, is essentially a starring vehicle that centres in the personality of—I quote the programme—"a strange, impish waif," Gemma Jones. In brief, it tells the story of her love for Sebastian Sanger, musician, choreographer and fundamental cad who, though married to Gemma, has an affair with Fenella McClean, his brother Caryl's *fiancée.* On the night when Sebastian's ballet is born to the London stage, Gemma's illegitimate baby dies. Anybody who is not a Bergnerite *à outrance* may well protest that the baby should have died hereafter. And Miss Margaret Kennedy fails to realise that to any man a baby which is not his is just a baby. Gemma cannot have it both ways. The composer who will run away from his first-night to make a fuss by the cot of another man's infant, already dead, is a bad composer. And if he is a good composer, nothing else matters. I will forgive any liar, thief, forger, bigamist, burglar —I will forgive any man who is any or all of these if he will write me another *Tristan.*

Dr. Czinner, the director, has made the film a model of "emotion re-collected in tranquillity." And that goes for all the cast—including, even, Gemma's baby, who is none of your mewling, puking, transatlantic infants, but a child half as strong and twice as silent, obviously preoccupied with intimations of that immortality he is presently to experience. According to plan the dialogue for the most part is conducted in undertones—a device calculated to bring out the overtones of production in nicely contrasted distinction. Otherwise, the direction is normal, and so redolent of the theatre that one is almost disappointed in Dr. Czinner's essentially cinematic concession, whereby the closing sequences of the film are made to coincide with the film's opening. For her part, Miss Bergner has been obedient to her director-husband's every beck and call. She brings to *Escape Me Never* the same emotional restraint that she brought to *Dreaming Lips* and *Catherine the Great*—so much restraint, indeed, that our higher-browed critics have elevated this player to the rank of Queen of Quietism. In the matter of expressing grief by doing absolutely nothing

Bergner has Duse cold. The rest of the cast are, if possible, even more tranquil than the production itself. We are permitted two enchanting glimpses of Miss Irene Vanbrugh as Lady McClean, once in a dining-room and once in the Dolomites. She is, and was bound to be, equally at home in either. Mr. Hugh Sinclair, as Sebastian Sanger, taking his cue from Miss Bergner, smoulders only with hidden fire—occasionally so hidden that one suspects his being something of a wet rag. He plays an unsympathetic part, redolent of Lewis Dodd in *The Constant Nymph,* which ought to evoke our sympathy if the play is to stand on an even keel. And I venture to say that if Mr. Leslie Banks had played the part there would have been some reasonable balance between the manifestly selfish composer and that nodule of egoistic granite which is Gemma. As Fenella McClean Miss Penelope Dudley Ward acts with deeply conventional gesture and toneless efficiency, and the hideousness of her frocks can only by excused on the theory that if Miss Bergner isn't to look beautiful nobody else shall. I was surprised to see Mr. Lyn Harding, who takes the part of Heinrich the conductor, conducting so tentatively. Twenty-five years ago this very month Mr. Harding played Brutus in *Julius Cæsar* at His Majesty's, and called upon Lucius most trippingly for a song. Yet in the ballet sequence, when the violins come in on the crest of a wave, Mr. Harding's bâton, content to be led rather than to lead, moves only with the occasional timidity of a conductor of the Smithfield and Billingsgate Amateur Operatic Society. During the same programme Mickey Mouse makes his screen début in colours. I understand that Mr. Disney has been sorely perplexed over the problem of choosing an appropriate shade for his hero's pants. In *The Band Concert,* however, this difficulty has been obviated by dressing Mickey in a pseudo-military uniform so voluminous as to conceal the offending garments. The uniform serves also to hinder Mickey's good intentions as the conductor of a zoologically ill-assorted brass band. Nevertheless, undaunted by the length of his sleeves, by the machinations of a hostile wasp, an impertinent little duck and a passing typhoon, he contrives to draw music not only from a genuine cornet but from an ice-cream cornet, too. The typhoon, which bursts upon the brass band in the middle of its performance, provides a disintegrating element that is responsible for one of the Silliest Symphonies I have ever seen. But Mickey himself must look to his laurels. Donald Duck, as an inopportune intruder with an abundance of penny whistles tucked ingeniously beneath cap and wing, steals a scene or two from his superior star. *The Isle of Spice,* a documentary travel film of Ceylon, showed us natives, palm-trees, more natives, elephants, and yet again natives. I preferred the elephants. The photography was generally distinguished—what it lacked in colour being fully compensated by the greater vividness of the accompanying commentary, which described the "sapphire sea" and the "ruby sands" in a manner that left little to be desired and nothing to the imagination.

42

LIGHTEST AFRICA

1935

THE colossal and undoubted success of films like *Sanders of the River* at the Leicester Square Theatre makes me more apprehensive than ever as to the future of the English stage. I went to the second night of this really magnificent film and was in a way horror-struck to see the breathless interest which it aroused and to hear the applause which at the end it evoked. The house was packed from floor to ceiling by an audience of every height of brow. I was horror-struck with a peculiar shade of horror-struckness. When I go to see a play like *Frolic Wind* or *The Old Ladies* I enjoy it, know that it is a work of art, and realise that I enjoy it just because it is a work of art. When I go to a film like *Sanders of the River* I enjoy it, realise that it is grand entertainment like a circus or a rodeo, and know that my enjoyment does not in the least depend upon the work or art which it is not. In other words, I regard theatre-going as one thing, and film-going as another, and do not allow my films to impinge upon my plays. If I were minded to visit a theatre, say, once a fortnight, I should not feel that an evening spent at a boxing-match or at greyhound racing counted as an evening at the theatre, and, as explained above, it is in the spectacular as opposed to the dramatic category that I place the films. It is not in this way that the normal film-goer is given to analysing his pleasures. Because the films are shown in a building built like a theatre, the average play-goer imagines anything he sees on the screen to be a play, and a visit to a film becomes, therefore, equivalent to a visit to the theatre. Again, the theatre which talks about things rather than shows them necessarily calls for a certain amount of imagination on the part of the play-goer, whereas the film, by showing everything, calls for no imagination at all. When in the play about Clive the actors talked about elephants, you had to use enough imagination to conjure up a vision of these pachyderms. In the film they just photographed a lot of elephants, and the lazy spectator could lap them up with his eyes without any necessity to use his mind. Putting all these arguments together, I feel when I am depressed, or under the weather, or when the English summer is threatening, that the theatre is in a very parlous state indeed.

The film made from Edgar Wallace's novel is enormous fun. Wallace fans tell me, however, that the film has ruined the book in turning the character of Bosambo into pure hero, instead of leaving him as an impudent, semi-comic ex-convict, a kind of dusky Sam Weller who has got the length of the white man's foot and used it to kick him into kingship of a powerful tribe. In spite of this it is, I repeat, enormous fun, always providing you are willing to believe in naked or semi-naked savages who speak English among themselves in the heart of the African jungle and in their war-canoes sing a version of the Eton Boating Song to the lyrics of Mr. Arthur Wimperis and the music of the not-more-African Mr. Michael Spoliansky.

Each for all,
Whate'er befall;
All for each
Is what we teach . . .

does *not* sound to me like the kind of chant head-hunters use on their direr expeditions. Mr. Paul Robeson singing this doggerel in the prow of his *praw* is a sight for the gods, or, better still, for the pale-faced braves and squaws in evening-dress at the Leicester Square Theatre preparing to watch their papooses take the field at Lord's in a few weeks' time singing "Forty Years On." If the last sentence is something of a jumble, then I submit it is justified by this film, which in turn is like a page out of Stanley's *Darkest Africa*, a short story by Mr. Kipling in Empire mood, and Mrs. Jellyby's plans for educating the natives of Borrioboola Gha on the left bank of the Niger. This film is all about educating the natives of even less pronounceable places to believe in the supremacy of the British Civil Service. Mr. Leslie Banks admirably plays the hero, indifferently called the Infant or the Nilghai, who after some Old Boys' match modestly relates a tale of exploits to raise the hair and curl the toes of nightgowned little boys who have stolen out of dormitory to cluster round his jack-boots. Sanders is the kind of man whom Stalky, Beetle, and McTurk, and Edgar Wallace and, I verily believe, Mr. Banks, all adore. He has only to lift his walking-stick and *impis* pause in their march. He has only to say Tchk! and a Chaka trembles. Let him but go to the coast for a week-end, or to Europe to be married, and once more the earth thunders with the pad of naked feet rushing battlewards, the air is rent with the beat of tom-tom and ululations of bloodthirstiness. Even the beasts of the field and the fowls of the air seem to know when Sanders comes and when Sanders departs, when the law of the jungle must be kept or may be broken. More simply, this film has some very fine shots of animals!

In a word, the story is such as delighted me in those Rider Haggard and Kipling days to which I am always willing to return, and it is conducted throughout with a niceness that is impeccable. Was ever a loin-clothed African so much the gentleman as Mr. Robeson in this film? Was ever his mate so much the lady as Miss Nina Mae McKinney? Were ever two such children so little grubby and so little sticky? We see the murder of a white man, and the projected murder of two savages, meaning Bosambo and his spouse, which are conducted with a circumspection and a propriety and a total absence of any unpleasant details which would put to shame any London party. In addition to names already mentioned, there was one good little bit of acting by Mr. Martin Walker. But the great things about this film are its frank acceptance of drama as a healthy boy of fourteen understands it, its really superb photography, and some dance and chorus numbers by wild and woolly natives who may have given Mr. Korda some trouble at the outset, but who now could be safely invited to supper in any smart restaurant. In fact, I was surprised to see that at the famous Grill Room where I took my midnight kipper there were, practically speaking, none present.

43

THE CAMELLIAS AGAIN!

1935

IT is one thing to be a boy in London on a hot August afternoon in the 'nineties and see Sarah Bernhardt at the zenith of her powers in the greatest tear-compeller of all time. It is quite another thing to be an old fogey haled out of bed to sit in a cinema, breakfastless, watching a charming comédienne overthrown by a part for which she doesn't begin to have the means. Every actress who has ever essayed Marguérite Gautier has had something with which to essay her, and that something has been pre-eminent of its kind. I spare readers any account of what Sarah was like, first, because I have written enough on the subject, and second, because to-day's young things wouldn't have the vaguest notion what I was talking about. Duse, of course, had the pre-eminent something, and when you get sufficient pre-eminence perhaps it doesn't matter if that something is all wrong. Even Duse's greatest admirers could not deny that she played the courtesan with an ineffability and a *retenue* which would have been overdone even in an abbess. Sorel acted the old play as though it were a man-of-war, with Marguérite Gautier for figure-head. This made her Marguérite too imposing since none of her lovers would have dared to call her "bonne fille." In fact, she made the play largely nonsense. But it was pre-eminent nonsense. Then there was Mme. Ida Rubinstein, who played the part by sheer force of clothes and scenery. I still remember that bed-chamber, a mother-of-pearl sea on whose surface swansdown wavelets rippled, and that Marguérite died in an apartment for whose decoration Africa had been denuded, the world's ostriches had been defeathered, and the Poles denuded of their bears. Yes, it was a pre-eminent bedroom! Pitoëff played the death scene like St. Joan in a nightgown, which did not prevent it from being pre-eminently moving. Tallulah blasted the piece with camellias, and one remembered that Sarah never wore one. Clever though this performance was, it never emerged from the coal-scuttle bonnet in which Miss Bankhead played it, and was occluded by the lemon-coloured trousers worn by Armand on this occasion. Of course, the story of the Lady of the Camellias as we see it now is pure nonsense. Let us go over it yet again. Armand, a young Frenchman of good family, is living with Marguérite, a famous courtesan, and she, having fallen in love with the boy, has decided to give up her profession and live on such crusts as the sale of her furniture and jewels will bring. Armand has no money and apparently no job, and what the pair are going to live on when Marguérite's resources are exhausted is not at any time discussed. Now Armand has a sister who is engaged to be married, and her *fiancé's* family will not allow the marriage unless Armand breaks off his liaison with Marguérite. Whereupon Marguérite decides to sacrifice herself for the sake of a young woman of whose existence she is up to that moment totally unconscious, and upon whom she will never set eyes! She pretends to Armand that she is really in love with a nasty fellow called the Comte de Varville—and Armand is donkey enough to believe her. After which Marguérite dies of consumption.

To-day your highbrow critic will talk about "ancient fuss," "curio from the dramatic museum," "passionate flap-doodle," "mawkish trash." But that is only because your highbrow critic of to-day has never seen the play really acted. I will not agree that if a new Bernhardt were to come among us to-day, to-day's audience, intellectual though it may be, would not suffer the same emotional experience as the audiences did in the far-away 'nineties. The human heart is unchanging, though fashions of thinking may vary; and the purely emotional power of great acting abides. It is no argument against the greatness of the feat which Desclée, Modjeska, and all the others achieved, to say that the play itself is out of date. To argue this way is like saying that because we have invented boats and trains and motor-cars, Hannibal did not perform a great feat when he made his way over the Alps from Africa into Italy. It would take a mighty fine general to do it to-day under Hannibal's conditions, and, therefore, the greatness of Hannibal's achievement endures. So does the achievement of any great actress in this part endure. I remember magnificent performances by Miss Olga Nethersole, Mrs. Charles Sugden, and many others, and I believe that if Dame Madge Kendal were to play the part to-day, at the age of 85, she would send the entire audience home in tears! It would only be safe to say that *La Dame aux Camélias* does not hold the boards when an actress of sufficient power treads them and fails.

Of Mlle. Yvonne Printemps's performance in the film at the Academy I speak grievingly because, like anybody else, I recognise what an exquisite little actress she can be when she is not overweighted. But her charm, as all the world also knows, is that of the *gamine*, and if anything is certain about dashing Cyprians it is that they must dash! Marguérite should have all the glamour of Paris, whereby the richest men in that gay city should be ready to fling fortunes at her feet. But, alas! Mlle. Printemps gives the impression that the part in this piece which she ought to play is that of Armand's sister, for whom the sacrifice was made! She cries very appealingly at times, but the camera is not kind to her, and one should not be tempted to think of Shakespeare's deer down whose long nose the tears coursed in such piteous chase. That heavenly blob which Nature has given this actress for a nose has been worth a fortune to her on the stage; on the screen it is a liability. No, if the old play must really be screened, then it should be by a Hollywood actress who can rise to the sheer acting it demands. Garbo would provide all the necessary glamour, the heartache, and all the rest of it, while Norma Shearer is now sufficient of an actress to cope with the letter scene. This scene, which any actress would give her ears to play, is entirely left out of the present film, together with all Marguérite's reflections upon her profession. An enormous amount was made by Dumas out of the remorse of the courtesan, with long speeches about Heaven forgiving but the World remaining inflexible. Every one of these was omitted also, and in their place we had Mlle. Printemps gadding about an ornamental water in a skiff, and it did not help matters that the barge she sat in was positively wreathed in camellias. It was unfortunate, too, that M. Pierre Fresnay was chosen for Armand since in every scene he played his partner off the set. I thought Marguérite's death scene was pathetic, but only because her delirious imaginings were ingeniously visualised by the photographer. There is, however, no justification whatever for omitting the line: "Ce n'est pas possible que Dieu soit si bon!" And, in short, I can only repeat about this performance the remark of the Scotsman who was with me: "It'll no dae!"

44

"A MIDSUMMER NIGHT'S DREAM"

1935

LET me begin with a word to Messrs. Warner Brothers. A fortnight before the première of *A Midsummer Night's Dream*, and in the anticipation of a big first-night crowd, my secretary telephoned for seats and was promised them. As they did not arrive the Editor of this paper spent the greater part of the day before the performance endeavouring to procure seats for me. He was invariably referred to personages who were not in their offices and whose secretarial young women were invariably discourteous and unhelpful. The same thing happened on the day itself, when it was finally intimated that no seats could be obtained. Since nothing could be done for love the Editor next tried money, and a seat was promptly bought in which I sat in lonely splendour with a small desert of empty stalls all round me. I cannot understand the egregious folly of such mismanagement. A child of ten should know by this time that you cannot muzzle criticism, and that the attempt to do so may turn a bark into a bite. Fortunately for Messrs. Warner Brothers I am not affected. This should be put down not to Christian charity but to complete indifference as to whether any management is ill-mannered or otherwise. I take no interest whatever in managements, and deliberately decline to know who makes what pictures and what artists are tied up with what managements. All I am ever concerned with is the picture, and it was not until I referred to my programme to see what management had been rude to this paper and to me that I realised that the presenters of this picture are Messrs. Warner Brothers. Having noted that fact for the particular purpose I now forget it.

And now to more amusing matter. Surely it was a mistake on this occasion not to dispense with the tinned orchestra, at least for the Overture. All film companies throw money about recklessly without, so far as I can see, ever throwing any of it about sensibly. Why not engage a flesh-and-blood orchestra and conductor of repute to impose silence on the fashionable mob through whose noisy hum those four moonlit chords bringing magic into the theatre could hardly be heard? One of the oddest things of the last hundred years is the degradation of the ear and the exaltation of the eye. A hundred years ago it mattered very little how an actress danced so long as she could sing, whereas to-day's favourites, provided they can dance, are at liberty to sing like sick headaches. The audience at this first-night paid no heed whatever to Mendelssohn's lovely Overture, and it was not until the treacly lights were turned on to the picture's preliminary announcements that they sat up and took notice. In other words, the moment they had something to see they began to listen! And now the point arises—What did they listen to? Well, not Shakespeare's verse, nine-tenths of which is just omitted, perhaps for the very good reason that, with the exception of Mr. Ian Hunter, there is nobody in the cast with the faintest conception of what verse, Shakespearean or otherwise, is, or may be. Mention of the word "cast" brings up the vulgarity, in a literary sense, of the film world. The proper and decorous way of printing this play's cast is to begin with Theseus, Duke of Athens, followed by all the male mortals in descending degree. Then Hippolyta, Queen of the Amazons, followed by Hermia and Helena. Last, Oberon and Titania, with Puck their chief attendant, the whole to conclude with the four speaking Fairies. Look, now, at the way the Adelphi programme does it, though for space reasons I reproduce only the first half:

Dramatis Personæ

James Cagney	Bottom
Joe E. Brown	Flute
Dick Powell	Lysander
Jean Muir	Helena
Victor Jory	Oberon
Verree Teasdale	Hippolyta
Anita Louise	Titania
Hugh Herbert	Snout
Frank McHugh	Quince
Mickey Rooney	Puck
Ian Hunter	Theseus

I beg to point out to Professor Reinhardt that the principal personage in Shakespeare's *A Midsummer Night's Dream* is not Mr. James Cagney. Neither, for the matter of that, is it Bottom. Nor are the actors more important than the characters they represent. Let me tell the Professor and anybody else whom it may concern that to begin your cast of a Shakespeare film with the name of the best-paid actor is just low! As was to be expected, Shakespeare's *A Midsummer Night's Dream* was turned into a Reinhardt's Midsummer Nightmare. Never before has there been such leafery and greenage, such scampage and boundery. Chief bounders were Lysander and Demetrius, for Mr. Dick Powell and Mr. Ross Alexander would have been better employed in some American college film. Chief lady bounders were Hermia and Helena. To put it shortly, there wasn't an ounce of Shakespearean breeding among the quartet. Alone, Mr. Hunter, as Theseus, spoke his lines beautifully and with a sense of poetry.

The best part of the show was the fooling of the Athenian workmen, which is Hollywood-proof. In the matter of the fairies I have very little opinion, except that I see no justification for making Oberon as sombre as though he were playing Death in a mortality play, or King of Night in a German opera. (Mr. Joe E. Brown's Flute was good but not magic enough for that!) Nor can I see why Oberon should bestride a nag worth less than a pound a leg. I thought Miss Anita Louise's Titania excellent if you conceive that sprite as a large and luscious lady attended throughout by American bridesmaids. As for the fairy ballet, I have no opinion at all. They were just foolish, like Victorian illustrations, and I got sick of their eternal drapery and floatage.

Mr. James Cagney's Bottom, though too young, seemed to me superb, and for once the metamorphosis was made credible. The man's an actor! Puck, in England generally played by a widower, has been wisely entrusted to Master Mickey Rooney. This Puck is not a fairy but a laughing, roguish boy, the wrong thing, but exquisite. In other words, the child's a remarkable actor. The music throughout has been beautifully arranged by Dr. Korngold. Readers will forgive me if the foregoing is all a little higgledy; my excuse is that this production is very much piggledy!

45

SHYER AND SHYER

1935

IF ever there was a play which was set in midsummer it is Shakespeare's *As You Like It*. Indeed, it is always a wonder to me that Shakespeare did not call it *A Midsummer Day's Dream*. That this is not everybody's view is shown by an article encountered by accident in a Sunday paper. The film correspondent was discussing Miss Elisabeth Bergner's filming of Rosalind, and he, or more probably she, wrote as follows:

"She sat on a white marble seat beside a pool, with a snow-white pavilion beyond and a white-towered palace stretching away to a pale sky. Silvered cypresses, pale birch trees with their leaves faintly golden, gave the scene an odd, Christmas-tale quality."

Having presided the other day at a debate between Sir Cedric Hardwicke and Mr. St. John Ervine on the subject of Whether Actors Waste their Time on the Screen, I was naturally anxious to learn from this film correspondent what Miss Bergner had done on the occasion of the interview besides sitting on a white marble seat. The next paragraph told me:

"She sat very still, gazing at a locket, in which was the miniature of her father, the banished duke. She sat like that—on and off, as the Frog Footman said—for three hours. During that time something like five shots were taken."

While the cameramen were cerebrating, Miss Sophie Stewart attired as Celia "in the tall pointed head-dress of the Middle Ages" had dropped her brightly coloured shuttlecock into the pond seven times. While Miss Bergner was locket-gazing and Miss Stewart was shuttlecocking, "a party of ducks was urged continually towards the camera by a gentleman in waders, another gentleman in waders skimmed the pool with a large shrimping-net, and a crane stalked coldly out of the pool and up the marble steps of the palace. Two handsome swans were released from canvas covers and urged towards the water." It would appear that not one word of Shakespeare was spoken throughout the whole of these three hours.

Presently, Miss Bergner, presumably tired of acting Shakespeare, began to act a little on her own account. She laughed and whispered to Miss Stewart. She whistled at the swans. She made odd schoolgirl faces at her husband, Dr. Czinner. She begged the assistant-director to let the crane go to sleep. No, reader, I am not inventing this! I am merely repeating what the film correspondent of the Sunday paper told me. And then Miss Stewart took a turn, telling the interviewer how happy it made her to work with Miss Bergner, how Miss B. thinks of everybody, wants Celia's dresses to be as pretty as Rosalind's—I'll bet they're not!—wants Miss Stewart to look her nicest, and to feel contented, and to love the story. The film correspondent then went on to discover that the proposed version of *As You Like It* had a quality about it reminiscent of one of Miss Bergner's early silent films, *The Violinist of Florence.* Miss Bergner cried out and clapped her hands like a child. The reason was that in this picture she wore the mannish costume which she had used for Rosalind in the German version. Here let me break away from the film correspondent to ask how many plays or films there are in which Miss Bergner has not appeared in male costume. In *The Violinist of Florence* she wore the Ganymede costume which in the German version of *As You Like It* she had worn for years. In *Escape Me Never* she spent a whole act in white shorts. In *Catherine the Great* she reviewed her troops in uniform. In *Saint Joan* she, of course, appeared as an armed warrior. We are now to see more of her in mannish guise in the film of *As You Like It,* and I am inclined to lay 100 to 1 that as David in the Barrie play early next year she will make a further excursion out of her proper sex. I want to know the reason for this, because it is obvious that Miss Bergner is too astute a contriver of circumstances to allow herself to be ruled by coincidence. Does she aspire to go down to history as the legitimate stage's equivalent of Vesta Tilley? We should, I think, have a certain disregard for an actor whose reputation rested upon assumptions of womanishness. Why should Miss Bergner insist upon assumptions of boyishness? You may reply that Sarah Bernhardt appeared in man's garb, and quite rightly you may cite Hamlet, l'Aiglon, Lorenzaccio. But those were three parts spread over a great number of years, and in between them Sarah played scores of grown and mature women. We are always hearing of the grown and mature women Miss Bergner has played on the Continent—Lady Macbeth, Hedda Gabler, and so forth. Why is no effort made by anybody to let us poor English see this actress as a grown woman? Is she afraid of her public? The reason I raise the point: it is two years almost to a day since Miss Bergner was hailed by the dramatic critics of London, almost without exception, as a great actress. Those who did not join in the chorus said that while she was obviously an exquisite little actress they must wait for her appearance in a play or part which justified the certificate of greatness. I do not wish to labour the point, but I do emphatically state that greatness in an actress cannot be established merely by looking woe-begone after the manner of a little boy and blushing pathetically at the knees.

In plain English it is two years since Miss Bergner was challenged to justify the ecstatic pronouncements made about her by appearing in a part which would do so. She has consistently refused. Indeed, her policy has been all the other way, and I am told that at the recent Shakespearean Matinée in aid of the National Theatre Appeal she went to extravagant lengths to appear in the guise not of a great and commanding actress but of some piteous little waif remorselessly caught up in the unwanted limelight. Greatness, let me tell Miss Bergner, should be made of sterner stuff. And bigger parts. And less clapping of hands, and less "smiling like a shy schoolgirl." By the way, isn't there a latent danger in these public exhibitions of shyness? There was a time when Sir James Barrie held a monopoly in coyness. Then came Miss Bergner to suggest what two can do at that game. But suppose the public should be fascinated to the point of joining in? Suppose the first-night audience at the promised Barrie-Bergner play should be too shy to turn up? I see a canvas here, worthy of the brush of a Michael Angelo. I see the foyer of His Majesty's Theatre. It is empty save for Mr. Cochran and his ancient, the ever-faithful and well-beloved Major Leadlay. There they stand flanked by flunkeys obeisant in plush and powder. They wait, but the play-going world is too shy to do them reverence. Motor-cars draw up out of which nobody descends. They are empty, having been sent as a mark of respect! "Can we have overdone it?" whispers Charles, and in the vacant foyer his words crackle like artillery. "I wonder!" booms his ally. I repeat that I see a picture here. But I know no artist shy enough to paint it.

46

"RHODES OF AFRICA": A MAGNIFICENT FILM

1936

BRIEFLY, the circumstances of the Jameson Raid are as follows. They are in themselves so interesting and have been so much overshadowed by bigger events that I make no apology for transferring them to paper and doing so in the words of Lady Lugard. The large alien population which had been attracted to the Transvaal by the phenomenal wealth of the Johannesburg gold-fields, conceiving themselves to have reason to revolt against the authority of the Transvaal Government, resolved towards the end of 1895 to have recourse to arms in order to obtain certain reforms. Arming was to take place secretly, and the revolution was to be carried out when the mining population was sufficiently prepared to be in a position to take concerted action. Rhodes, as a large mine-owner, was theoretically a member of the mining population. In this capacity he was asked to give his countenance to the movement; and in so far as his extensive property in the Transvaal suffered from conditions which other mine-owners pronounced to be intolerable, he had the same right as others to decide by what means it was advisable to endeavour to obtain redress. But, as Prime Minister of a British Colony, he was evidently placed in a false position from the moment in which he became cognisant of a secret attempt to overturn a neighbouring government by force of arms. He did more than become cognisant. The subsequent finding of a Cape committee, which he accepted as accurate, was to the effect that "in his capacity as controller of the three great joint-stock companies, the British South Africa Company, the De Beers Consolidated Mines, and the Gold Fields of South Africa, he directed and controlled the combination which rendered such a proceeding as the Jameson Raid possible." He gave money, arms, and influence to the movement; and as the time fixed for the outbreak of the revolution approached, he allowed Dr. Jameson, who was then administrator of the British South Africa Company in Rhodesia, to move an armed force of some five hundred men upon the frontier. Here Rhodes's participation in the movement came to an end. It became abundantly clear from subsequent enquiry that he was not personally responsible for what followed.

There is your English hypocrisy all over. Rhodes, the Prime Minister of a British colony, supplies a well-known hothead like Jameson with money, arms, and influence, allows him to station himself on somebody else's frontier, makes no protest whatever, and then calmly accepts the suggestion that he is not responsible for what follows. The thing is monstrous. Jameson and Rhodes and Joseph Chamberlain intended that there should be war in the Transvaal, and there was war, the onus being shifted on to the wretched Boers by contriving that they should be the aggressors. Even the admirable film at the New Gallery, *Rhodes of Africa,* takes care that the whole thing should start with an alleged attack on the Uitlanders. It is this which prompts Jameson to send a telegram asking for powers to take the strongest punitive measures. Let us be quite clear about this. I am not objecting to the Boer War. In any case I have got to accept it in the way that the lady at Carlyle's dinner-party had to accept the Universe. That big nations shall swallow little ones is not a Christian principle, but I can conceive few things more despicable than Bible-thumping with one hand, and with the other sending money and arms to facilitate the swallowing operation. This is nearly as hypocritical as for an armament magnate to go to church and join in the prayer "Give Peace in our time, O Lord." The film shows this very clearly. It shows Rhodes supporting Jameson through thick and thin. And it shows Jameson sending his telegram saying that he is going to make his raid unless he receives immediate orders to the contrary, and then cutting the wire to prevent receipt of those orders. How much more admirable was old Kruger calmly saying to the excited Boers that when you want to kill a tortoise you wait till it puts its head out! The ambushing of Jameson's force has always struck me as one of Justice's most poetic feats. And now the British Government takes a hand in the hypocritical game. It entirely acquits Rhodes of responsibility for the raid, but finds that he acts in a manner "inconsistent with his duty as Prime Minister of the Cape." Rhodes then went about in a night-shirt of penitence blaming himself "not for having encouraged the revolution, but for having failed to hold the movement so completely in check as to have been able to prevent disaster." The result, of course, is that when English politicians take it on themselves to get up on their hind legs and lecture other great nations on the act of swallowing, I feel a little sick. I should feel less sick if Jameson had been shot and Rhodes hanged! But was not Rhodes a very noble and virtuous man, and did he not leave a lot of money to Oxford University?—the reader asks. The answer is that the private virtues of statesmen are no more the world's concern than their private vices. In his public attitude to the Transvaal, Rhodes was a canting humbug, which this film abundantly proves.

It is a pity that Mr. Walter Huston's Rhodes should look so exactly like Mr. Ramsay MacDonald. As he also makes him act like President Lincoln and look as though he might at any moment burst into Drinkater, I for one must vote this impersonation a failure. On the other and, Mr. Oscar Homolka's Oom Paul is superb, and there is a magnifi-nt performance of Lobengula by Mr. Udansia Kumalo, of Matabele-nd. This is such a good performance because one does not know Mr. dansia Kumalo. It is no good telling me that yonder is a missionary of rts when I know perfectly well it is Mr. Lewis Casson. Nor am I going believe that those impeccable vowel sounds come from a Boer rmer, when I know them to proceed from Mr. Felix Aylmer. Indeed, beautiful is Mr. Aylmer's speaking voice that they have chosen it to eak the film's Epilogue. This is stupid. They should have paid Mr. ylmer five thousand pounds a minute for the Epilogue instead of five undred pounds a week for gumming on false whiskers. Similarly one cognises Mr. Frank Cellier, Mr. Sam Livesey, and many others. Though is is sheerest heresy, there is a lot to be said for getting hold of Boer rmers who are Boer farmers instead of well-known actors whose looks nd voices come back at one from a hundred plays and films. The pro-lem is not easy. If it is going to be art, why bother about real nations? ut if you are going to Africa to photograph real African oxen, why ot photograph a few real African farmers? The real thing is always the etter actor anyway!

47

A HOLIDAY ARTICLE

1936

AM writing this in an entirely unreal country where the greatest charm ith which the human race was ever invested goes hand in hand with he most unblushing roguery. A man should not in a land of Autolycuses ay down his spectacles, relinquish his walking-stick, and expect to pick hem up again. But to steal a man's horse from under his very nose s, to say the least of it, roguish! Fortunately, they were my stick and ny friend's spectacles, but not my horse. Now, where there is no real roperty there cannot be any real loss, and the property of this country s to be unreal. What shadows we are, and what shadows we pursue, was ever truer than here. And here am I, holidaying and smiting little balls ast distances—vast until you measure them in terms of real yards—yet ondemned to write my weekly article on the cinema. Time and tide wait or no man, nor will printing press stay its maw for one lazing time way by the gentlest tide that ever came in from the Atlantic. Foreseeing hat I should be gravelled for lack of actual pictures to enthuse over or get cross about, I brought other material with me to this paradise. Fo surely that is a paradise which consists solely of a championship gol links, washed by the sea, a mountain, and a hotel marked with four o the guide-book's stars and deserving of five? All the same it is incredibl meaning that I still do not believe it that a hotel visitor, resident in hi hotel, cannot order, obtain or consume an alcoholic drink after nin o'clock in the evening! You begin your evening round after tea, say a the comfortable hour of half-past five. You finish about eight, and whisky and soda and a bath take up the next hour or so. At one minut past nine you saunter into the dining-room feeling that a pint of cham pagne will do nobody any harm. "Sorry, sir, but it's against the law!"

The waiter hands you the menu, on the back of which you read: "B Law, Alcoholic Liquor can be purchased or consumed between the hour of 10 a.m. and 9 p.m. only. This Regulation applies alike to Resident and Non-Residents."

The result is that the wash-basin in my bedroom is filled with non vintage Bollinger over which the cold tap ceaselessly runs, the fireplac is stacked with bottled Bass, Haig nods to me from the mantelpiece, Boot winks at me from the dressing-table, while in the boot-cupboard, o whatever it is, I snugly keep the after-dinner brandy. And I challeng Mr. Hugh Walpole to tell me that in the whole of Hollywood, from whic Elysium he has just returned after some two years of coquetting wit the films, he found anything more desperately absurd. Here am I, a sober and quiet-drinking a man as you shall find in the whole of Flee Street, compelled, in sheer self-protection, to furnish my bedroom lik a gangster preparing for a siege!

The material which I brought with me to Ireland was a series o articles in which Mr. Walpole has been giving us his impressions o the "Incredible City." I have never been to Hollywood—and would no unless before I started somebody paid me a competence for life. Yet I fin that I already know by intuition all that Mr. Walpole has divulged. *Of course,* the place is ugly, cheap, tawdry and common. *Of course,* th people are absurd and the business methods insane. What else did Mr Walpole expect? I was talking the other day to Mr. James Whale, th producer of *Show Boat,* and congratulating him on having successfull got the manifold sillinesses of that spoof masterpiece down the publi throat. "Yes," said James, "but even you did not realise that, if the chro nology of the film is correct, the young girl who at the end makes her débu as an opera star must be over sixty, while her mother is past eighty!" I that one sentence lies the whole secret of this film business—the art o passing off things for what they are not. Film actresses are not actresses but dummies, dressed, groomed, producer-pawed, and then shoved about a platform while gum-chewing cameramen take thousands of photographs of which the best are afterwards picked out and joined up. Nor are film actresses beauties in their own persons and apart from their make-up. I once wrote of a great film star: "Miss X has acquired so much poise that she can no longer walk, and has become so soignée that she cannot sit." The week after I had written that sentence I met Miss X. At least, I was ushered into a private room at a large hotel. In the room were cocktails, a score of journalists, a lot of fussing film people from Wardour Street, and some dozen women, one of whom was presently pointed out to me as Miss X. I had not spotted her! She was no height worth speaking of, looked nothing when she was sitting, and less standing, and generally had the air of an upper housemaid. In other words, her topless Divinity was dumpish! The same contradiction pervades and pursues all that film actresses are and do. Nothing is known of Greta Garbo, and lo! it is arranged that nothing shall masquerade as a mystery eclipsing the Sphinx. Another star, twinkling for all she's worth to eclipse Garbo's steady blaze, asks, from beneath eyelids so heavily black-leaded that their owner cannot lift them, why it is that men notice her. "Cannot I lead my own life in peace?" she breathes, in accents so heavily scent-laden that they slam a door at ten feet. A third star has come to Europe to arrange for a pet monkey's divorce. These means failing, some brat must be kidnapped or got the custody of; all for the bedazzlement of typists at Tooting and waitresses from Walthamstow.

Men, of course, have less scope for nonsense, and the way Hollywood "gets" them is to bring about the deterioration of their art. Despite his enormous popular success, Mr. Laughton is not, in my opinion, the outstandingly fine actor on the film that he was, and I feel sure again will be, on the stage. On the screen Mr. Laughton permitted himself to label a bundle of buffooneries "Henry VIII"; in the theatre I feel that he would have resisted this. And I am quite certain that this sensitive artist would never have faced the London footlights as a shock-headed butler with a passion for reciting the speeches of Abraham Lincoln. The point about the pictures is that they are designed to appeal to the greatest number of the lowest intelligence. A picture which does not make this appeal must lose money, and if it loses money it is of no interest to Hollywood. The test of a picture is its reception not by me or Miss Lejeune or the highbrow critics of the weeklies, or even the audiences at the Curzon Theatre and the Film Society. The one and only criterion *for Hollywood* is the reception a picture is likely to meet with in Poplar and Oldham or their Middle-West equivalent in mining districts and seaport towns. If you have been driving rivets into the *Queen Mary* for eight solid and sweating hours, what you want in the evening is not a reproduction of the spirit of Flaubert in a carefully reconstructed version of *Madame Bovary*, but a sight of some magenta-haired waif in a tattered frock scorning gilt-laden jewels thrown at her bare but ruby-enamelled toes. The screen as art cannot interest Hollywood. What interests Hollywood is the screen considered as the equivalent of the fun-fair, coconut-shy, Big Dipper, and the hobby-horses round the steam organ. It doesn't need two years at Hollywood to bring home so simple a truth. I do not say that pictures can never be art. What I do say is that Hollywood can never make them and should not be expected to.

48

RED INDIANS AGAIN

1936

THE film of *The Last of the Mohicans* at the London Pavilion naturally starts a train of childhood memories. I wonder whether people are still writing children's books. And does the modern child read them, either new or old? And, what is more to my purpose, does any little boy or girl to-day sit in a patch of garden-shade, or in winter on a corner of the hearth-rug by the fire, while Nurse reads aloud? Now that I come to think of it, my childhood's stories were all suitable for girls. Later on, when I could read for myself, Captain Marryat, R. M. Ballantyne, and Fenimore Cooper bore me across an utterly boyish sea. But in the earliest time I can remember I had to take my tastes from Nurse, and I will confess that hers were of the sentimental order. My first story, then, was called *A Peep Behind the Scenes*, and it was concerned with a caravan and a travelling showman's golden-haired daughter. My second book was called *Lilian's Golden Hours*, of which all I remember is that the villain got himself locked up in a secret chamber, so that nothing of him remained for discovery except his skeleton. Third came *Little Women*, a book which I have read many, many times since. Elegant Margaret, coquettish Amy, gentle Beth, and warm-hearted, impulsive Jo—here is a quartette of sisters never to be matched. To this day I am not proof against the passing of little Beth. About this same time I listened to a tale called *Won by Gentleness*, which began with a baronet called Sir Gervase being thrown from his horse and dragged along the road by his stirrup-iron. Then came *The Lamplighter*, and then *Queechy*, about which I remember absolutely nothing, except that at the time it was my favourite story of them all. All the same, it was run pretty close by another hearthrug volume of which title and plot have both vanished. Here I am able to conjure up only the name of the heroine and one single sentence concerning somebody else. "Bee" is the heroine's name, and the sentence runs: " 'Home,' cried Julia, and threw herself back in the carriage."

The Last of the Mohicans belongs to a later stage, which included *The Coral Island, The Settlers in Canada,* and *Masterman Ready.* I remember as a boy being enormously moved by it. Yet if anybody had asked me before going to the picture at the London Pavilion to name any of the characters in this tale I think I should have had difficulty. I certainly should not have been able to recall the name of the last Mohican, though I think that much delving into the past might have brought forth the name of Chingagook. (The film spells it rather differently.) I also remember in the book a viperish little beast of the name of Cora. The first thing to be said about the film is that it is a great muddle. Very early on it appears that the English for some totally unknown reason are fighting the French in the unmapped backgrounds of North America. There are also three sets of lesser people. These are the English settlers and the English Red Indians, both lots being noble indeed. Then there is a horde of French Red Indians of the uttermost malignancy. After a time one begins to recognise the French Indians by the fact that they shave their heads all but a central bit, which very much resembles the plume on a Greek helmet. (See any boy's book on the Trojan Wars.) The English colonel has two daughters, or maybe a daughter and a niece. They are called Alice and Cora, and they behave exactly as all English virgins do in a countryside infested by natives who are addicted to rape, with a spot of banditry thrown in. The English virgin doubtless regards herself as Evolution's crowning achievement, with the result that she flaunts her virtue in the world's face very much as the kings in Shakespeare flaunt their kinghood. There's such divinity doth hedge an English virgin that she feels safe in taking her virginity into the unlikeliest places. Are there bandits lurking on the fringe of some Chinese golf-course? Your virgin will saunter with one club and half a dozen balls for a little practice on the remotest green! Does every depression in the desert contain a leering, nasty-minded Arab? Nothing must content your virgin save a stroll in the dusk towards yonder tenantless oasis. Is it common knowledge that hostile Indians are laying two tomahawks to one that they will scalp the English virgin before sundown? Then must she choose that particular afternoon to ride her palfrey in spots so lonely that a famished leopard would be good company. Nothing on earth will induce the English virgin to change her spotlessness for sense. The sands of the desert will grow cold long before the heart of English virginity warms to any sense of what Nature is all about.

It was because they were English virgins that Alice and Cora must sit making daisy-chains on the river bank with the English firing over their heads at the French, and the French firing over their heads at the English. They apprehended no danger from the Indians, in spite of the fact that scalps could be seen drying on every bush. Each, it appeared, was in love with a noble savage. Now, it is all very well to use the phrase "noble savage" in irony; I am not at all sure that there is not something in it. If, as I surmise, there are Red Indians in this piece, they are certainly more noble than the Hollywood film actors who are just nothing except Hollywood film actors. Hawk-Eye, for example, strikes me as having no kind of relation even to such reality as is to be found in Fenimore Cooper. I have no idea who the actor is, but should not be in the least surprised to hear that it is some Hollywood celebrity, whereas Uncas and Chingagook seem to me to be very fine indeed, and to wear about them some of the primeval dignity of Man.

The Indian scenes are done with the feverish activity of Mr. Bertram Mills's men breaking up a circus, which reminds me that I once saw two Red Indians in the flesh at one of Mr. Mills's luncheons, and I sat between them. But which was Mr. Chingagook and which Mrs. Chingagook I was unable to discover. Nor can I discover whether this new film is an extraordinary masterpiece or perfect tosh.

49

REMBRANDT IN LEICESTER SQUARE

1936

IT was sincerely thought and maliciously said by some people that the beauty of the *Kermesse Héroïque* film would swamp whatever Korda might have attempted in his *Rembrandt.* This has turned out to be just not true. The French film, being done in a warm sepia, has extraordinary charm. But when all is said and done it is a little film and a mere anecdote, whereas the other is an immense work unfolding the history of a lifetime. After the first picture the second looks a little grey, and only in that respect has one film hurt the other. For all that, *Rembrandt* is amazingly full of that light which the great master of painting subdued to his supreme purpose. Other painters had used light; Rembrandt was the first to utilise darkness. He added Night to Day. Perhaps there is a little too much light in the film, which dances in perpetual sunshine. Does it never rain in

Holland? Is the mackintosh unknown? I a little felt at the end when the shadows began to close in on the old painter that a trifle more use might have been made of the Pathetic Fallacy. Possibly, nay probably, Korda is right, and perhaps it is even here that he and Laughton have got nearest to the heart of their mystery. A writer has said: "No one among Rembrandt's contemporaries appears to have mentioned his death. He died forgotten, in the deepest poverty, possessing only his clothes and his painting materials. In some ways, despite the pathos of it, this seems a fitting end. He achieved immortal fame by his art, and when life ceased he possessed nothing but the instruments by which he had expounded that art." Let us agree about the "fitting end." But let us also agree that, while fitting to us who read about it, that sort of end may be damnably wretched for him who has to go through with it. Now Rembrandt may very well have gone through with his with gusto, and it would also be fitting that the reckless spendthrift and squanderer of life should in the evening of his day become the most genial of old rogues. Let us remember that there is one thing which the old and destitute can afford as well as the rest, and that is a rich sunset. There is plenty of sunset in this picture, and Laughton's genius makes us perceive that that which sets is indeed a sun.

Rembrandt's life tells the old story of the artist who, endowing the world with imperishable wealth and so enriching it for all time, takes out of the world that which he now needs without petty consideration of the lesser man's by-your-leave. What can it matter to Shakespeare whose work is going to live for ever that he should be already twenty-six legs of mutton in arrears with the butcher? It matters to the butcher, and it can't be helped if that red-fisted churl does not realise that providing legs of mutton *ad lib.* is his part in the creation of world-glory. Why should a master who is going to hang the galleries of the world with jewels deny his wife a gem or two? What, in the long run, does money matter? Rembrandt's difficulties began with the great house he bought for himself in the Breestraat in Amsterdam, and could only have ended with his temperament. To pay for the house he borrowed money at exorbitant interest, and then did not use it to pay off the arrears or even the interest on the arrears. At this point I imagine the reader saying: "You're telling me!" Good reader, rest assured. We who write also know all about it. The film treats this part of the subject a little lightly, and with good reason. For it is to be shown to the English nation, and the English are a nation of shopkeepers, and shopkeepers think in terms of quick returns and not lasting guerdons in connection with somebody else's fame. Therefore, *Rembrandt* is not the tale of a splendiferous rogue and master artist plundering with one hand and enriching with the other. It is the story of a noble spirit baffled and thwarted, rising to heights which his generation dimly perceived, falling into oblivion at the age when most geniuses receive their reward, and at the last finding comfort in that extraordinary verse in Ecclesiastes : "Wherefore I perceive that there is nothing better, than that a man should rejoice in his own works."

But for Elsa Lanchester, whose Hendrikje is a rarefied performance of remarkable spirituality, the film is as it should be, all Laughton's Rembrandt. To say that this is a *tour de force* of resemblance is to say little; the art of make-up is not a major one. But Laughton in this picture does two things which only a great actor—and I am not writing carelessly—could have done. He sets the picture back in time so that we believe in seventeenth-century Amsterdam, and he never for a moment permits any doubt that we are in the presence of a great painter, a great artist, a master spirit, and a genius. The high scorn and the rich display of temperament in the early part of the picture are good. But this is the kind of goodness we expect. What we do not look for is the warm glow of the close. Never, as Stevenson said in another connection, has the end of life been suggested with a finer tact. The greatest feat of all is that, though the playing here is concerned entirely with the spirit, the sheer actor in Laughton has, as it were, brought to his own canvas all that virtuosity with which the master himself limned old age.

50

"THE WHITE ANGEL"

1936

"OH, dear Miss Nightingale," said one of her nursing party as they were approaching Constantinople, "when we land let us go straight to nursing the poor fellows!" But Miss Nightingale had no such pleasant illusions. "The strongest will be wanted at the wash-tubs!" was her reply. It is amusing to compare Lytton Strachey's essay on Florence Nightingale with the account of her which appears in the *Encyclopædia Britannica.* The former has written: "Everyone knows the popular conception of Florence Nightingale. The saintly, self-sacrificing woman, the delicate maiden of high degree, who threw aside the pleasures of a life of ease to succour the afflicted; the Lady with the Lamp, gliding through the horrors of the hospital at Scutari, and consecrating with the radiance of her goodness the dying soldier's couch—the vision is familiar to all. But the truth was different." The *Encyclopædia* agrees—with the exception of the last five words. "She is the subject of a beautiful poem by Longfellow, 'Santa

Filomena,' and the popular estimate of her character and mission was summed up in a particularly felicitous anagram, *Flit on, cheering angel!* The story of Miss Nightingale's labours at Scutari," the *Encyclopædia* goes on, "is one of the brightest pages in English annals. She gave herself, body and soul, to the work. She would stand for twenty hours at a stretch to see the wounded accommodated. She regularly took her place in the operating-room to hearten the sufferers by her presence and sympathy, and at night she would make her solitary round of the wards, lamp in hand, stopping here and there to speak a kindly word to some patient." Yet the story of the hospital at Scutari and what Miss Nightingale found there makes, surely, one of the *darkest* pages in English annals. Again hear Lytton Strachey: "Want, neglect, confusion, misery—in every shape and in every degree of intensity—filled the endless corridors and the vast apartments of the gigantic barrack-house. The very building itself was radically defective. Huge sewers underlay it, and cesspools loaded with filth wafted their poison into the upper rooms. The floors were in so rotten a condition that many of them could not be scrubbed; the walls were thick with dirt; incredible multitudes of vermin swarmed everywhere . . . . As for purely medical materials, the tale was no better. Stretchers, splints, bandages—all were lacking, and so were the most ordinary drugs." To this asylum came the wounded, the dying, and the sick, cases of fever and frost-bite, dysentery and cholera. In the voyage across the Black Sea, which sometimes lasted as long as three weeks, the poor wretches, hardly clothed and blanketless, lay on the naked decks, which were slippery with stale blood. Strictly speaking, Miss Nightingale's labours doubtless make a bright page in English annals; it is the other pages which are foul.

Here it is necessary to make the old, old point. This is that the cinema is primarily a place of entertainment. People go to the cinema not to be instructed in the conditions of military nursing in the time of the Crimean War. They do not go to learn the actual truth about the character of Florence Nightingale. They do not even go to learn all the facts about her career. They go to be entertained, totally indifferent as to whether the subject of their entertainment is Florence Nightingale, Grace Darling, Flora Macdonald, or the Lass of Richmond Hill. This is the one thing which Hollywood knows perfectly. Now, the story of Miss Nightingale, even with the most sentimental handling, is a forbidding one. There is no lover in this story, or not in the sense in which film audiences understand a lover. She was not present at Balaclava, and therefore there cannot be any Clark Gable to take a tearful farewell before obeying the order to charge and to have his dying pillow soothed half an hour later. Hollywood's difficulty, as I see it, has been to make a reasonably sympathetic picture while sticking reasonably to facts. Now, the only way to do this was to limit the number of facts and stick to the most sympathetic interpretation of them. In other words, Hollywood was bound to take the *Encyclopædia's* limited view of Florence, since to take Lytton Strachey's full account would have meant dropping the film altogether. Non-cinema-goers will realise that the real interest in Florence Nightingale's life begins *after* the Crimea, the labours at Scutari being a mere stepping-stone to what was to come. Actually, Florence Nightingale lived on for more than fifty years after the point at which the film at the Tivoli concludes. For after Scutari comes the story of Miss Nightingale's demoniacal possession. It is an old tale now how, broken down in health and virtually under sentence of death, she, from a sick-bed, began a crusade the like of which has never been equalled for ferocity. She declared war against filth and the defects of the military hospital system, and raised her banner of sanitation and reform. She began by attacking the Queen and the Prince Consort; and the Queen, having previously given her a brooch, parried the attack with a compliment.

This is not the place to tell the terrific story of the great battle with Lord Panmure, which ended in the reform of the Army Medical Department, nor of that still more fearful struggle in which nothing less was aimed at than the reform of the War Office itself. It is true that she had Sidney Herbert with her; but then Mr. Gladstone was on the other side, and presently Herbert gave way under the strain and died. Thus ended one of the most tremendous and protracted political wars ever fought. The *Encyclopædia* says simply: "The experience of those terrible months (at Scutari) permanently affected Miss Nightingale's health, but the quiet life she afterwards led was full of usefulness." Its brief little account brings us down to 1862, and Miss Nightingale was not to die until 1910. Volumes could be written about the feverish activities of forty out of these fifty years; the *Encyclopædia* dismisses them in a dozen lines! It is only fair to say that I take my information from the Tenth Edition of the *Encyclopædia,* my companion of many years. It is always possible that Florence Nightingale has been brought up to date. But this makes my point of how right this film is, not only to take up the *Encyclopædia's* view of its heroine, but to stop where it does. I found *The White Angel* noble, moving, and worth while. Between you and me, reader, I am getting a little tired of famous actors who on any pretext, likely or unlikely, will deliver somebody or other's Defence of Warren Hastings. I have consulted the *Encyclopædia Britannica* here also, but it does not seem to know on which side Sheridan delivered his four days' speech, though perhaps this, too, has been brought up to date. Anyhow, it is refreshing to hear Miss Kay Francis deliver something which really is to the point—that speech to Queen Victoria which may be taken as the creed and declaration of faith of the nursing profession. The film ends here, and rightly. A great lady once told me that she was present when Queen Victoria said: "We have been having a deal of trouble with dear Miss Nightingale!" Hollywood has seen quite rightly that its film must be concerned with the ministering angel in Florence Nightingale, and not with the implacable foe of the Queen's Ministers.

51

UN-MAKING HISTORY

1937

ACCORDING to the cinema magnates the whole of history is based on the principle of *Cherchez la femme!* And not only on the principle of seeking the lady but of finding her. English history may be, and in part has been, reconstructed on this principle. William the Conqueror came over to this country because his liaison with the Duchesse de Pontet-Canet was forbidden by Pape Clément. William Rufus was slain by Walter Tyrrell because he made love to the latter's wife. Henry II had Becket murdered because he caught him winking at Fair Rosamund. Richard I went to war with the Saladin to rescue Loretta Young. Edward III pardoned the six brave burghers of Calais because Queen Philippa was in love with Eustace de St. Pierre. Richard III murdered the little Princes in the Tower because he had a grudge against Queen Margaret and the two other hags who prance through Shakespeare's play on the subject. Henry VIII is too easy. Lady Jane Grey is all about Nova Pilbeam, and Queen Elizabeth is principally known as having run the Little Theatre of the period. If I do not continue in this way, it is because my knowledge of history stops at this point.

In my young days I went to three schools, and history, in so far as I made acquaintance with it, began with the Battle of Hastings, and ended on that snowy morning when Charles I walked out of a window in Whitehall to be executed. I suppose the four Georges were dealt with at one period or another in the curriculum of these schools; I only know that I never encountered them. I once saw a play by Mr. Clifford Bax which was set in the period of George I, and all I gathered was that a nobleman of the period escaped execution owing to a wife who wittily pretended to have toothache. If I remember aright, the only people of importance in this reign were this Lord and Lady Nithsdale. As for the other Georges, I have never had the slightest notion why the English should be fighting the French at Quebec, the Scots at Culloden, the Turks at Navarino, or the French again at Dettingen. To this day Oudenarde and Malplaquet are merely names in crossword puzzles, and I have never yet been able to find out what teams were playing at Austerlitz and Marengo. The reader may ask what all this has to do with *The Charge of the Light Brigade* at the Carlton. The answer is that it has at least as much to do with that film as that film has to do with what I believe to have been an historical event. Let me make it clear that I am not posing as an authority on that event. I have looked up *Little Arthur*, and find an illustration entitled "The Charge of the *Heavy* Brigade," without any word in the text concerning these hearties.

Let me rather state what I saw and what I gathered of history at the Carlton. There was a very Beautiful Officer in the English Army in India who was in love with his Colonel's daughter. Unfortunately, during her fiancé's absence on some expedition she fell in love with his younger brother, and this led to many long and painful scenes in ball-rooms, conservatories, and tents. About an hour and a half after the beginning of the film, the Beautiful Officer found himself shut up in what appeared to be the same fort which did duty in *Beau Geste*. He and his men were beleaguered by the same Arabs masquerading as Indians and commanded by the Rajah in *The Green Goddess*, obviously acted by George Arliss's younger brother. After a deal of falling from Tarpeian rocks rising sheer from the plain, the English escaped because the Beautiful Officer, disguised, but with the legs of his British uniform still showing, had impersonated the Indian leader and ordered the Indians to retire. Later on they came back and overwhelmed the English, but said they would allow them to go home with honours of war and a safe conduct for their women and children, because the Beautiful Officer had shot a leopard which was about to maul the Rajah when he tumbled out of his howdah! (Does the reader ask what all this has to do with the Charge of the Light Brigade? He must wait another ten seconds, and reflect that at the Carlton I had to wait nearly two hours!) No sooner had the women and children marched out of the fort than the Rajah massacred them, which definitely marked him as a dirty dog. Presently the 27th Lancers, still including the Beautiful Officer, found themselves at the British Army Headquarters in the Crimea. For at ten minutes to eleven it was allowed to leak out that England and Russia were at war. Lord Raglan told the Colonel, with whose daughter the Beautiful Officer was still in love, that he must withdraw the Light Brigade. (I suppose that by this time the Colonel had become a Brigadier, entitling him to give orders to other Colonels.) Anyhow, he dictated the dispatch to my friend, Nigel Bruce, who was in command of the Light Brigade, though more fitted by nature for the Heavy Brigade. Here the Beautiful Officer stepped in. He had learned that the Rajah was in command of the Russian guns, and here it seemed was a chance for the 27th Lancers to avenge that massacre. Besides, was he not personally tired of life through having resigned the Colonel's, now Brigadier's, daughter to his young brother who by this time had joined the Lancers? So he destroyed the Brigadier's dispatch and substituted another ordering the Brigade not to retreat but to advance. He then carried the dispatch in person to Mr. Bruce, and sent his brother back to the Brigadier with a note telling him what he had done, thus getting his brother safely out of that Charge, at the head of which the Beautiful Officer proceeded to place himself.

The reader knows the rest, or at least he may be presumed to know Lord Tennyson's verses. If anybody blundered it was Warner Brothers. To take up a whole evening with a preposterous farrago of outworn Bengal-Lancer stuff, and then tack the famous Charge on to it, is as unpardonable as to weave a romance around Annie Laurie and wind it up with the Massacre of Glencoe.

The Charge itself has been magnificently filmed, and, indeed, the last twenty minutes are as hair-raising as anything I have ever seen in a cinema. But so, of course, might be the Massacre of Glencoe at the end of the film about Annie Laurie. Nine-tenths of the Carlton film is costly, demoded balderdash, for the reasons I have been at such pains to state. Errol Flynn makes a beautiful Beautiful Officer, and acts neither better nor worse than the beautiful horse which he rides so beautifully. Neither, in the theatrical sense, can be said to act at all; the art of this order of film-acting is to be your beautiful self whether you possess two legs or four. As for the Colonel's daughter, I have nothing to say against pretty Olivia de Havilland as an expositress of chaste nitwittery.

Looking at this film in general, all I feel inclined to say by way of summing-up is that I can think of no better way of spending the time between 10.45 p.m. and 11.15 p.m.

52

"CAMILLE"

1937

MISS GARBO has appeared in *La Dame aux Camélias,* and the performance must be a challenge to all the older critics. To the young gentlemen who were appointed film critics the day they first got into trousers it cannot be a challenge, because they have no recollection of anything wherewith to compare it. On the subject of Sarah Bernhardt I am alleged to be untrustworthy, and indeed I make no bones about saying that no actress that I have ever seen approached within ten thousand miles of her. And I do not believe that any actress to come will approach within fifty thousand! Therefore, this article will contain no word of what I personally thought about Sarah's Marguérite, though the performance is as vivid to me to-day as when, close on fifty years ago, I ran away from home to see it. But I shall give here one or two passages in the hope that our little Oxford suck-a-thumbs may get some notion of what Sarah was like. The first is from Mr. Maurice Baring:

> When I have seen the parts that Sarah Bernhardt made her own performed by lesser artists, I have wondered what happens to the play. If it was classical, *Phèdre,* for instance, one wondered where all the glory that was Greece, and all the grandeur that was Versailles, and all the music that was Racine had gone to: one longed in vain for those haunting, thirsty eyes that sent an electric current through the whole theatre, for that voice that made you think the words were being spoken for the first time; for those gestures which were too swift to analyse, for that harmony and rhythm in utterance, movement, speech and silence, crescendo and diminuendo, speed and pause and delay, that combined to produce and build something as concrete as a beautiful frieze or statue, as logical and ordered and disciplined as a great fugue, and as intangible as the gleam of sunshine on a wave or the reflection of a rainbow in the clouds.

Will young Oxford write this about Miss Dietrich or even Miss Harding? Two other aspects of Sarah might interest our young Solons. The first is shown in a passage from Sarcey's *La Comédie-Française à Londres.* "Nothing," says Sarcey, "can convey any idea of the infatuation she has aroused. It amounts to madness. When she is about to appear a quiver runs through the audience; she appears, and an Ah! of joy and rapture is heard on all sides. The house listens with rapt attention, bodies bent forward, glasses glued to eyes; they will not lose a word, and only when she has finished break into a fury of applause. Outside the theatre they speak of no one else." Does any film actress monopolise conversation outside the cinemas of to-day?

Of Sarah's Marguérite Gautier, C. E. Montague wrote close on forty years ago:

> Of Mme. Bernhardt's acting it is enough to say to those who know it that it has lost nothing of its incomparable grace and delicacy. It is impossible to describe the value and interest which the actress's delivery lends to passages with no great quality of their own. Uttered by her, such sentences as "on nous abandonne et les longues soirées succèdent aux longs jours," or "ainsi, quoi qu'elle fasse, la créature tombée ne se relèvera jamais," sink into the mind and remain vibrating there, like commonplace words set to the finest music. It is not that her delivery presents them in high relief. As elocution among actors goes, comparatively little relief or sharpness of edge is given to any of her passages. Rather she contrives to envelop whole scenes in a softening and blurring haze of diffused tenderness, the effect of the caressing voice carried on and rendered continuous by marvellous fertility in expression and gesture. The writing and re-writing of the farewell letter to Armand, the more restrained passages of the dialogue with the elder Duval, and, again, the more subdued passages of the conflict of agonising passions in the fourth act—these were fine enough, but one almost forgot their excellence in the supreme pathos of the scene of reconciliation. We can remember no more deeply touching moment at the theatre than that at which Marguérite rises from the sofa just before her death and tries to walk a few steps with a pitiful attempt to be strong and at ease, like a child that hopes it can go alone. At the wistful fingering of Nichette's bridal veil, at the repetition by heart of the letter from Armand's father, and at the gesture with which Marguérite runs to Armand, crying, "Oh! ce n'est pas toi; il est impossible que Dieu soit si bon," Mme. Bernhardt again reached almost the highest point of achievement. But the whole performance was wonderfully fine.

With all this in mind, I still say that Miss Garbo's performance as Marguérite, now to be seen at the Empire, is extremely fine. It nowhere moved me, but only for the reason that Arctic explorers are not going to find an English winter cold. But for other recollections I might have said that the performance was superb, particularly so in view of the fact that the re-fashioners of the story have imposed upon her an almost grotesquely American pair of Duvals. I am amazed at the ingenuity with which scenario-mongers will take a good story and spoil it. The elder Duval's plea that Marguérite shall sacrifice herself is made on behalf of the daughter who is going to be married; the film makes the daughter married already! In the play, Armand comes back to a deserted country house. The film substitutes for this a shot of Garbo traipsing on foot at night across the fields to the Château of the Comte de Varville! The death scene is cut to ribbons, and nowhere in the film is Marguérite allowed to deliver herself of that Dumasian ethic whose kernel is: "Ainsi, quoi qu'elle fasse, la créature tombée ne se relèvera jamais! Dieu lui pardonnera peut-être, mais le monde sera inflexible!" The youngest of my colleagues, Mr. Paul Dehn, appears not to have perceived that the piece is essentially concerned with Dumasian ethic, and that its atmosphere should be wholly that of the patchouli'd boudoir of the 'fifties. His complaint is that not enough of it happens out of doors!

> When the picture's atmosphere seems frowsty and fusty for lack of an airing; when tantalising glimpses of a meadow, a mountain, a cottage garden, a country lane are whipped off the screen with the peevish insistence of your self-styled invalid who refuses to sit in a draught—there is just cause for complaint.

It is true that there are meadows and so forth. But what meadows! Meadows painted with more lady-smocks and cuckoo-buds than Shakespeare ever dreamed of, and thicker with asphodel than a page of early Milton. Meadows so clustered with lambs and doves that Miss Garbo can hardly thread her way through them. In the original, old Duval comes to plead with Marguérite for his daughter's wedding. In the film he finds Marguérite attending a bees' wedding with a bee-keeper's veil over her head and shoulders. I gather that this open-air part of the film was honey to Mr. Dehn, who gives it as his considered opinion that this is probably Garbo's worst picture! Perhaps it is permissible for a critic who has seen more performances of the play than some of his colleagues number years to say that Miss Garbo's portrayal of a classic part is very good indeed.

53

THAT DREYFUS AFFAIR!

1937

BIOGRAPHY is all the rage just now, whether in plays or films. Queen Victoria, Parnell, Gladstone, Pasteur, Clemenceau—there is no end to them. And now we have Zola in *The Life of Emile Zola* at the Carlton. It was not to be expected that the film industry could avoid making Zola the centre of the Dreyfus Case. He was not the centre. People say: "No, of course not! Dreyfus was the centre and Zola was the hero!" Zola was not the hero of the Dreyfus Case, simply because the case did not permit of a hero. Zola was a magnificent ornament who suffered a good deal of spiritual pain and the physical discomfort of being obliged to flee the country. The only hero in the whole thing was the abstract figure of Justice, which took a lot of buffeting to start with, but triumphed in the end. It is astonishing how little people to-day know of the case which once shook the whole civilised world. I once submitted a play on the subject—and cannot refrain from pointing out the odd coincidence that this piece is actually being performed at the Q Theatre in the very week in which these lines appear!—as I was saying, I once submitted a play on the subject, based on the admirable drama of Hans Rehfisch and Wilhelm Herzog, to a well-known theatre manager, who replied: "My dear Agate, I know nothing about the Dreyfus Case. I have never been interested in it. I gather from your play, which I return, that certain Frenchmen once conspired to play a dirty trick on a man named Dreyfus." Since everybody is now flocking to the Carlton to see the Zola film—though I cannot imagine anybody flocking anywhere to see a Dreyfus play!—it may be of some purpose to say in a few words what the Dreyfus Case was about.

The crime which is known as the "Affaire Dreyfus" was brought about by the desperate attempts of General Mercier, the French Minister for War, to repair his political stupidities. It was redeemed by the steadfastness of Colonel Picquart. Before the "Affaire Dreyfus" was the "Affaire Turpin." Turpin, who had invented Melinite, became a spy. During his imprisonment for spying he announced another great discovery. Mercier relied upon what he called his "artillery sense" to reject the alleged discovery. Mercier's opponents in the French Chamber said that, while Turpin ought to be shot, spying had made no difference to his inventive genius, and that not Turpin but the General who turned down his new invention without examining it was the traitor. Mercier was very nearly dismissed, and the whole of the Dreyfus Case grows out of his frantic desire for rehabilitation. For now the public vaguely suspected, and the French War Office knew for certain, that French military plans were being given away to Germany. It was essential to find a scapegoat. If Mercier could not find one he was ruined. On the other hand, if he could find one, then he would recover all he had lost over the "Affaire Turpin." He got in touch with Colonel Sandherr, chief of the Intelligence Department, who, knowing how the land lay with Mercier, began to nose through the army list of young officers for a possible traitor. Stopping at the name

Dreyfus, he saw a chance of killing three birds with one stone—quieting the public nerves, propitiating his superior, and glutting that anti-Semitism which in him, Sandherr, was a passion. For Dreyfus was a Jew!

The first Dreyfus trial and conviction took place in December, 1894. The trial split France into two factions. The question was not: "Is Dreyfus guilty or innocent?" The question was: "Are you anti-Dreyfus or pro-Dreyfus?" To be anti-Dreyfus meant that though you believed him to be innocent you wanted the punishment to stand because he was a Jew and you were anti-Semite. To be pro-Dreyfus meant that because Dreyfus was a Jew, and because your sympathies were pro-Jewish, you desired his release even though he were ten times guilty. But what agitated France was something deeper even than the question of Semitism or anti-Semitism. Could the French nation afford to admit that French officers had conspired to do and maintain an act of gross injustice? The War Office said that Dreyfus, as a soldier, must be content to die like any other soldier in the cause of the Army's honour. Colonel Picquart said that honour based on a life was not honour and could not be defended.

The film at the Carlton does generously by this great theme. There is an unforgettable portrait of Dreyfus by Mr. Joseph Schildkraut, and most of the other famous figures are credibly presented. The courtroom scenes are brilliantly drawn, and the picture ends with a magnificent shot of Zola's lying in state. The last words are Anatole France's: "He was a moment in the conscience of his age." Which is a truly remarkable sentiment for a popular film. Zola is very well played by Mr. Paul Muni, who gives the testy ordinariness of the man wanting to go on leading his ordinary life as a writer, and without any desire to mount the high horse and prance about the battlefields of liberty. Zola's speech in his own defence is admirably delivered. But I was very much disappointed with his reading of the celebrated "J'accuse!" letter to the President in the office of *L'Aurore*. Some few days ago an unknown friend sent me a copy of the famous number of January 13, 1898, and, at the risk of again being personal, I shall confess that it was a romantic moment when I left this film to collect this faded challenge from the picture-framer's. But that is by the way. What the film could not do was to tell us the end of the story in so far as it concerns the chief villain, Count Esterhazy. Esterhazy admitted that he had written the *bordereau,* but declared that he had done so by the orders of a superior officer for the purpose of incriminating one who was already known to be a traitor. He then came to England and retired to Harpenden, in Hertfordshire, where he lived for seventeen years, dying in May, 1923. He lived as a recluse and kept more and more to his own house and garden in the last few years of his life. It is odd to think that the last echoes of that Affaire which shook France to her foundation and made the whole world rumble should have been heard in an English village.

54

"DEAD END"

1937

I AM in a little difficulty in writing about *Dead End*, the new film at the Gaumont, because my recollections of the play as I saw it in America kept coming between me and the picture. It is just possible that this impression was made not so much by the play itself as by the fact that it was among the first pieces I saw in that new and amazing country. I am, therefore, perhaps not so trustworthy a guide as I normally hope to be. It is certain that the film has made a great impression on some people who have not seen the play. That sensitive plant, Mr. Sydney Carroll, has been struck all of a heap by it:

> This is indeed a masterly production; but its theme is so disturbing, its scenes are so sordid and frightening that only in a limited sense can it be called entertainment. But it is one of those films that *must* be seen. Technically perfect, its photography shows a fine sense of the dramatic possibilities of shadows and gloom contrasted with sunlight.

Miss Lejeune is not so deeply affected:

> The film has all the qualities of honest intention, and one must respect it, but as a piece of film-making it is not wholly persuasive. We not have seen, in England, the play on which it is based, but a hint of theatre inhibition, without the flesh-and-blood urgency of the theatre, still hangs about it.

Oddly enough, the piece as it was played in New York was much more intimate than the film. There was no drop curtain, so that walking into the theatre was like being transported into the slum in which the action proceeded. There was only one set which had been there since the play started two years previously. All streets in New York end in the river, so that every street is a dead end. The spectator sitting in the stalls was separated from the mimic events by a width of water corresponding to the well of the orchestra, at the bottom of which the river was supposed to be flowing. Into this well the human wharf-rats continually dived to the accompaniment of thrown-up spray, while the plop and gurgle of the muddy water was heard throughout.

Perhaps it would be as well to tell the story briefly. Essentially it is an American version of Galsworthy's *The Silver Box*. Owing to the fact that the water-side commands a magnificent view, rich apartment-houses have been built up immediately behind the slums which congregate at their foot. The result is that a rich little boy lives cheek by jowl with the bunch of embryonic gangsters anywhere round about ten to fourteen years of age. The young scamps lure the rich boy into a cellar, beat him up, and steal his watch, and the ringleader, being apprehended, sticks a knife into the arm of the rich boy's father. To give full value to the message of the play a gangster is introduced as an example of the criminal flower of which these children are the buds. This is Baby-Face Martin, who was once a street-urchin even as these. With eight murders to his credit, and badly wanted by the police, he falls a victim to that sentimentality which in the time of Dumas *fils* was the note of the courtesan and to-day is the note of the gangster. He revisits New York in order to see his mother and the girl with whom years before he was in love. I confess I never quite believed this, though fully understanding the dictum that a play has to be got going somehow. Here we hit upon something which is the reverse of the Pathetic Fallacy. This is that gangsterism does not change the face of nature for gangsters. Nor does it change the face of much else, that which is chiefly altered being their own villainous masks, since there is always the plastic surgeon to help defeat the police. But sky and sea, hill and dale, look very much the same to a man who has committed a murder as to one who hasn't; the sun shines equally on the just and the unjust. What I am trying to say is that gangsters have their illusions the same as you and I. Perhaps Baby-Face Martin had seen too many films in which grey-haired mothers stroke the cheeks of repentant blackguards and sweethearts waiting for their lovers squander their sweetness on the desert air. But no! Baby-Face Martin's mother, denouncing him as a murderer, bids him get out of her sight and die; his girl has taken to the streets. On the night of this double disillusion the gangster is discovered by the police and killed. Everything concerning Martin, though exciting and affecting, is only an episode. The whole point of the play is what is to happen to the ringleader of the urchins. Here the rich boy's outraged father takes up the attitude of old Barthwick in the Galsworthy play: "I have no enmity to this boy—but other rich men's sons must be protected!" Wherefore the ringleader is sent to the reformatory, which is this play's metaphorical dead end. We know that when he comes out decency and he will turn their backs on each other.

The faults of the film are three in number. First, it has not the unity imposed by stage limitation; we feel that the director should have placed his camera firmly in one position and assembled his action in front of it. Second, it raises the Baby-Face Martin affair from the status of illustration to that of one of two principal themes. Third, the principal theme of responsibility to the criminal young is too much frittered away upon the idyllic sister of one of them. Sylvia Sidney is too much like Wordsworth's Lucy who, it will be remembered, dwelt among the untrodden ways. Whereas the girl in the play was a sweated sempstress working for a pittance in ways overtrodden. Humphrey Bogart as the gangster is not nearly as good as the actor I saw in America. But the wharf-rats, who are the same, were always and are still superb.

55

"STAGE DOOR"

1938

Stage Door, now showing at the Regal, is amusing, exciting, and *attendrissant,* each quality being introduced into the film with the mechanical precision of a chemist using a pipette. This was only to be expected, seeing that the authors are Miss Edna Ferber and Mr. George S. Kaufman. Miss Ferber is a writer to whom plots present no difficulty. Her brains teem with them, and it appears to be all one to her whether her stories concern the efforts of backwoodsmen to turn a barren plain into a city or the efforts of young women to turn themselves into actresses by ploughing the talentless field. With her, as they say in the Law Courts, is Mr. Kaufman, the greatest living wisecracker and the osteopath of plays that creak. There was a time when he and Mr. Marc Connelly were the theatre's Besant and Rice, and it would take too much space to give a list of their entertaining and nearly always successful productions, of which in this country *Merton of the Movies* and *Beggar on Horseback* are perhaps the best-remembered. I know nothing of Mr. Kaufman in person, but suspect him to be deeply sentimental, since only out of the rankest sentimentality could his alarming cynicism grow.

The story chosen by the present collaborators concerns life in a New York theatrical boarding-house, for which I think there is no equivalent in London. The place is a modest caravanserai where budding actresses eat and sleep while waiting to get their chance on the New York stage, and while they are waiting are coached by Miss Constance Collier. The latter claims to have been a success in the limitless past, and bases her claim on three newspaper cuttings reposing in her reticule. Lest I have no space to return to Miss Collier, let me say that her performance is of immense value, since it gives the film the steadying influence of a piece of deliberate acting as against that brilliant casting-to-type which, in the films, replaces acting. The three young ladies with whom we are principally concerned are Miss Katharine Hepburn, Miss Ginger Rogers, and Miss Andrea Leeds, and they are all planets circling round the central sun of an impresario played by Mr. Adolphe Menjou, who, by the way, has always been a much better actor than anybody has given him credit for. But though the planets all revolve round this impresario, they do so for different reasons. Miss Rogers has half a notion that she may be able to seduce Mr. Menjou, who, indeed, is on the point of falling for her when, owing to too much champagne, she lets out a flood of inanities which swamp even that expert roué's ardour. I now forgive Miss Rogers for the dreadful films in which she has appeared; in *Roberta* and others, except when she was dancing. I could at any time cheerfully have slaughtered her with the least humane of killers. Now something has happened to her, or, possibly, to her director, for her work throughout this film is a piece of brilliantly sustained comedy, including wit, fun, and a complete understanding of the situation. There is a scene where, with another girl, she does a double dancing turn, and here a less good actress, with Miss Rogers' reputation as a dancer, would either have danced her partner off the stage or given a grotesquely bad performance. To my infinite astonishment, Miss Rogers lets it be apparent that she just does not dance well enough. Miss Leeds's motive for revolving is that she wants to play the star part in which she was successfully tried out a year before, while Miss Hepburn is the daughter of a wheat king bent on throwing over her father's millions and conquering the stage by virtue of her own genius. But, alas, she hasn't any! What she possesses, of course, is all the other Hepburn qualities, and she makes contact with the impresario by bursting into his office and upbraiding him for letting Miss Leeds faint in his ante-room through malnutrition, which, Miss Rogers sapiently observes, is the Latin for "not eating." At that moment Mr. Menjou receives a mysterious offer. If Miss Hepburn is given the leading rôle in the new play, the money to finance it will be forthcoming. The financier, it need hardly be said, is Hepburn's father, who knows what a bad actress the girl is and hopes that by a flop she will return to the family wheat fields. Then extraordinary things begin to happen, and the film becomes wildly improbable. Hepburn gets the part, and on the first night little Miss Leeds, whose performance has been intensely moving throughout, commits suicide by throwing herself out of the window. The news is brought to Hepburn in her dressing-room, and she is so moved by it that, instead of being the infamously dud actress we saw at the dress rehearsal, she gives a performance for which a Katharine Cornell would give both her ears.

Indeed, she brings off several impromptu speeches, ending on her proper cue in the way that a violinist in a concerto will bring his cadenza into line with the resuming orchestra! On the strength of this performance Hepburn proceeds to become New York's leading actress, and I invite Miss Ferber to turn up *Dorian Gray* and see what happened to Sybil Vane. The latter, who has fallen in love with Dorian, says to him:

> To-night, for the first time in my life, I saw through the hollowness, the sham, the silliness of the empty pageant in which I had always played. To-night, for the first time, I became conscious that the Romeo was hideous, and old, and painted, that the moonlight in the orchard was false, that the scenery was vulgar, and that the words I had to speak were unreal, were not my words, were not what I wanted to say. You had brought me something higher, something of which all art is but a reflection.

What had happened, of course, was that Sybil had played Juliet and miserably failed. Now I suspect that Miss Ferber may very well not know that a bad and totally inexperienced actress playing under the stress of shock would give a worse performance than even her dearest enemies would think possible. I am quite certain that Mr. Kaufman knows this, and my view is that he gave in to Miss Ferber in the matter. But I cannot understand how Miss Ferber or any other collaborator persuaded him to renounce what would have been a master stroke. For even granting that Hepburn's one performance under stress of emotion was a success, what about all the others? No emotion when it is past will ever create technique where technique does not exist, and the witty thing would have been to show that successful first night followed by an appalling second! But then, I suppose, the film would have missed its message, that message being that the turning of Hepburn into a great actress has the power to console the departed spirit of little Miss Leeds. Which is the sheerest bilge!

56

"A YANK AT OXFORD"

1938

LET it be recorded that the midnight première of *A Yank at Oxford* at the Empire was an enormous success. But then everybody knew beforehand that it was going to be.

Leicester Square was closed from eight in the morning, the vicinity being kept clear by troops of cavalry at the trot, the canter and the gallop. Minute-guns went off throughout the day. Fanfares blew. Shakespeare's statue was removed, and in its place was erected an effigy of Mr. Louis B. Mayer. The Cabinet stopped writing notes to Hitler, Mussolini and Stalin in order to be present in force. The house manager, attired from head to foot in cloth of gold, handed a jewelled key to the Lord Mayor's coachman, who opened the proceedings. The foyer was a blaze of wit spoken and silent. Lady Wheelbarrow wore a new hat which completely occluded both eyes, and a veil long enough to kneel on. Lady Pushcart appeared decked with more gadgets than ever before. Beautiful Lady Truck entered alone, declining to have any of that ilk with anybody. Young Lord Pram, sucking the gold top of an ivory cane, took his seat as though the Empire were the House of Lords, which it very nearly was. Distinguished actresses holding sheafs of programmes in their flower-soft hands gave one looks, beatific or withering, according as one tended paper or mere half-crowns.

When the film was over we were put in wireless communication with Hollywood, and Mr. Louis B. Mayer told us how dear to his heart was the British film industry. Perhaps it was the lateness of the hour, perhaps it was the aftermath of an evening of flapdoodle, but I confess that, as Mr. Louis B. Mayer said this, a certain scepticism invaded my mind and refused to be shaken off. Out of what spirit of altruism had Hollywood sent over to this country its money, its genius for film-making and two of its biggest film stars—to wit, Mr. Robert Taylor and Mr. Lionel Barrymore? Somehow or other I just couldn't believe that the venture had been undertaken solely out of affection for the British film industry. What would real affection have set about doing? I think it would have said: "You Britishers want to make first-class pictures. We Americans have the money, the brains, the experience, let us say the knack, of making first-class pictures. Now let us fit our knack to your desire and see what the two of us can do. Your note is tradition; ours is go-getting. Your land is thick with ancient monuments—sometimes palpable as at Stonehenge, sometimes impalpable, yet ingrained and changeless, as in the manners and customs of your Universities. The American spirit has something which the English lacks. You cannot help living in the past; we who have no past cannot help living in the future. Between us we make the greatest race on earth. Let us together make a great picture worthy of our great and common race!" It was, therefore, a first-class notion to make a picture out of what happens when an American comes up against old England, and the fault I have to find with *A Yank at Oxford* is that it is from start to finish totally unworthy of what is set forth as the motive behind it.

Now let us get quite clear about this. I particularly wish it to be understood that I have no objection whatever to this film considered as slapstick.

I have no objection to seeing Oxford through the eyes of the Marx Brothers. *Charley's Aunt,* which also happens at Oxford, is my favourite farce in the theatre, and what is legitimate sauce in the theatre is legitimate sauce in the cinema. But consider the claims made for this film in the programme, which tells us that the young American finally captures the respect of Oxford, just as Oxford has already captured him: "For the sound of its bells will go with you, Sir, wherever you go, to the end of your life!" It goes on "That is why a great 'diplomatic première,' crowded with Cabinet Ministers, members of the Houses of Lords and Commons, Ambassadors, and all those who believe in the destiny of the English-speaking peoples, is taking place at the Empire Theatre to-night." J'ever read such nonsense? Did anybody ever dream of linking up peoples? If there is anything at all in this programme eloquence, why was the Vice-Chancellor of Oxford not invited? No one knows what the wild waves are saying. No one knows what the spires of Oxford are dreaming. But their dreams, I think, are something more than debagging, bump suppers and flirting with bedraggled Zuleika Dobsons in the form of booksellers' wives. If the spires of Oxford dream, surely it is because her young men are seeing visions. And I cannot think that they are the nightmares of *A Yank at Oxford*. Those spires must, indeed, have been dreaming when they countenanced this film. But perhaps they didn't countenance it. Where, I repeat, was the Vice-Chancellor? And is it true that Mr. Taylor, when he was over here to make the film, never went near Oxford?

"All this is very well," the reader may say, "but such a film as you have in mind couldn't have been made." And I ask why not? The consensus of opinion is that *Tom Brown's School Days* is a pretty good book. The page headed "Roasting a Fag" is at least as exciting as the debagging scene in this film. Yet the true note of the book is, I think, to be found in the passage in which Tom goes back to Rugby after the death of Arnold: "He raised himself up and looked round; and after a minute rose and walked humbly down to the lowest bench, and sat down on the very seat which he had occupied on his first Sunday at Rugby. And then the old memories rushed back again, but softened and subdued, and soothing him as he let himself be carried away by them. And he looked up at the great painted window above the altar, and remembered how when a little boy he used to try not to look through it at the elm trees and the rooks before the painted glass came—and the subscription for the painted glass, and the letter he wrote home for money to give to it. And there, down below, was the very name of the boy who sat on his right hand on that first day, scratched rudely in the oak panelling." The Rugby of Tom Hughes was the great School, and I maintain that the Oxford of this film, which is intended to draw together the English-speaking peoples, should have been the great University. There was room in the school-story for any amount of ragging; there would still have been room in the film for all that fun and excitement which is the essence of cinema. Hughes did not make the roasting of his hero the whole of his book; the debagging, the cheap flirtations, and the still cheaper athletics, in which the American wins a freshman's race in cap and gown and strokes the Oxford crew to victory while chatting to No. 7, are the whole of this film.

57

WHYMPER AND THE MATTERHORN

1938

HAVING no head for heights I am no climber. Being no climber I cannot see that anything is to be said for mountaineering, which does not even improve the breed of mountains. Yet such is the perversity of human nature that all my life I have been an avid reader of books about mountaineering. Now the most exciting of mountaineering stories has always been—and, whatever happens on Everest, will probably always remain—Whymper's account of the famous and tragic ascent of the Matterhorn in 1865. It all happened so long ago that all but specialists must have forgotten the details. And I think I shall best serve my readers this week by re-telling the story, partly in my own words, but chiefly in those of Whymper.

The whole story is shaped like a drama. It begins with a rivalry with the Italians who started on the 11th July to attack the unconquered peak from the Italian side, Whymper's party starting from Zermatt two days later. Whymper's original notion was to make the English attempt in company with Lord Francis Douglas and the guide Carrel. Carrel having been engaged by the Italians, Whymper then chose old Peter Taugwalder and his two sons. Dining at the Monte Rosa Hotel, Whymper and Lord Francis met the Rev. Charles Hudson, Vicar of Skillington in Lincolnshire, who had with him young Mr. Hadow and the guide Michael Croz: "We left the room to consult, and agreed it was undesirable that two independent parties should be on the mountain at the same time with the same object. Mr. Hudson was, therefore, invited to join us, and he accepted our proposal. Before admitting his friend—Mr. Hadow—I took the precaution to enquire what he had done in the Alps, and, as well as I remember, Mr. Hudson's reply was, 'Mr. Hadow has done Mont Blanc in less time than most men.' "

The narrative proper then begins with a passage which in any romantic novelist would be justly considered perfect: "We started from Zermatt on the 13th of July, 1865, at half-past five on a brilliant and perfectly cloudless morning. We were eight in number—Croz, old Peter and his two sons, Lord F. Douglas, Hadow, Hudson, and I. To ensure steady motion one tourist and one native walked together. The youngest Taugwalder fell to my share, and the lad marched well, proud to be on the expedition, and happy to show his powers." They found the general slope of the mountain difficult. This "was *less* than 40 deg., and snow had accumulated in, and had filled up, the interstices of the rock face, leaving only occasional fragments projecting here and there. These were at times covered with a thin film of ice, produced from the melting and refreezing of the snow. It was a place over which any fair mountaineer might pass in safety, and Mr. Hudson ascended this part, and, so far as I know, the entire mountain, without having the slightest assistance rendered to him upon any occasion. Sometimes, after I had taken a hand from Croz, or received a pull, I turned to offer the same to Hudson; but he invariably declined, saying it was not necessary. Mr. Hadow, however, was not accustomed to this kind of work, and required continual assistance." This difficult bit mastered, the summit was attained without much difficulty, and in his account of what they saw there Whymper grows almost lyrical: "There were the most rugged forms and the most graceful outlines—bold, perpendicular cliffs and gentle, undulating slopes; rocky mountains and snowy mountains, sombre and solemn, or glittering and white, with walls—turrets—pinnacles—pyramids—domes—cones—and spires! There was every combination that the world can give, and every contrast that the heart could desire. We remained on the summit for one hour—'one crowded hour of glorious life.'" And to crown their triumph, 1,250 ft. below them was the Italian party!

Then came the descent. One of the Taugwalder sons had not ascended the last part of the mountain, so that there were seven to make the descent: "Hudson and I again consulted as to the best and safest arrangement of the party. We agreed that it would be best for Croz to go first and Hadow second; Hudson, who was almost equal to a born mountaineer in sureness of foot, wished to be third; Lord Francis Douglas was placed next, and old Peter, the strongest of the remainder, after him." This left Whymper and young Taugwalder: "For some little distance we two followed the others, detached from them, and should have continued so had not Lord Francis Douglas asked me, about 3 p.m., to tie on to old Peter, as he feared, he said, that Taugwalder would not be able to hold his ground if a slip occurred." Then follows the account of the catastrophe, prefaced with another passage showing that Whymper, if he had not been a great climber, might have been a dramatist: "A few minutes later a sharp-eyed lad ran into the Monte Rosa Hotel saying that he had seen an avalanche fall from the summit of the Matterhorn on to the Matterhorngletscher. The boy was reproved for telling idle stories; he was right, nevertheless, and this was what he saw." Here follows Whymper's statement: "Michael Croz had laid aside his axe, and, in order to give Mr. Hadow greater security was taking hold of his legs, and putting his feet, one by one, into their proper positions. So far as I know, no one was actually descending. I cannot speak with certainty, because the two leading men were partially hidden from my sight by an intervening mass of rock, but it is my belief from the movements of their shoulders, that Croz, having done as I have said, was in the act of turning round, to go down a step or two himself, at this moment Mr. Hadow slipped, fell against him, and knocked him over. I heard one startled exclamation from Croz, then saw him and Mr Hadow flying downwards; in another moment Hudson was dragged from his steps, and Lord F. Douglas immediately after him. All this was the work of a moment. Immediately we heard Croz's exclamation, old Peter and I planted ourselves as firmly as the rocks would permit; the rope was taut between us, and the jerk came on us both as on one man. We held; but the rope broke midway between Taugwalder and Lord Francis Douglas. For a few seconds we saw our unfortunate companions sliding downwards on their backs and spreading out their hands endeavouring to save themselves. They passed from our sight uninjured, disappeared one by one, and then fell from precipice to precipice on to the Matterhorn-gletscher below, a distance of nearly 4,000 ft. in height."

I have not the space to describe how the two Taugwalders lost their nerve and could hardly be persuaded to cross the fatal place. There follows something in Whymper's account which is very important: "At last old Peter summoned up courage and changed his position to a rock to which he could fix the rope; the young man then descended, and we all stood together. Immediately we did so I asked for the rope which had given way, and found, to my surprise—indeed, to my horror—that it was the weakest of the three ropes. It was not brought, and should not have been employed, for the purpose for which it was used. It was old rope, and, compared with the others, was feeble. It was intended as a reserve in case we had to leave much rope behind, attached to rocks. I saw at once that a serious question was involved, and made him give me the end. It had broken in mid-air, and it did not appear to have sustained previous injury." It is ancient history now how old Taugwalder was accused of having *cut* the rope. Whymper on this point says: "Old Peter Taugwalder laboured for a long time under an unjust accusation. Notwithstanding repeated denials, even his comrades and neighbours at Zermatt persisted in asserting or insinuating that he *cut* the rope which led from him to Lord Francis Douglas. In regard to this infamous charge, I say that he *could* not do so at the moment of the slip, and that the end of the rope in my possession shows that he did not do so beforehand. There remains, however, the suspicious fact that the rope which broke was the thinnest and weakest one that we had. It is suspicious because it is unlikely that any of the four men in front would have selected an old and weak rope when there was abundance of new, and much stronger, rope to spare; and, on the other hand, because if Taugwalder thought that an accident was likely to happen it was to his interest to have the weaker rope where it was placed."

And there the matter could only be left. The film called *The Challenge* at the London Pavilion opens with the statement that free use has been made of these historical facts. In view of this statement I can only congratulate London Films on the great moderation in the amount of freedom they have used. The time is not yet when film audiences will accept a story like this entirely without embellishment, and therefore we have to put up with a good deal about Carrel and his efforts to vindicate Whymper. For in the film Whymper and old Taugwalder change places, so that it is the former who is accused of cutting the rope. In ordinary circumstances this liberty is permissible. What I have never been able to understand is that, in an expedition of this magnitude and danger, *any* weak rope should have been used for any purpose whatever. Nor can I quite understand why an almost wholly admirable film should be spoiled by absurdities of casting.

If it was worth while going to the trouble to engage a presumable Italian to play the Italian guide, why should that Italian guide's mother have Bayswater stamped all over her? Miss Mary Clare is a beautiful actress and a dear friend of mine. But that she has subsisted for sixty years on macaroni, which this mother must have done, I just don't believe. Nor do I believe that the guide's *fiancée* spoke pure Muswell Hill. Nor that the Swiss policeman and hotel-keeper were both born within the sound of Bow Bells.

Mr. Robert Douglas as Whymper acts very well. But what a nuisance it is knowing film actors! Mr. Douglas is married, as all the world knows, to the prettiest girl in Europe, and I just cannot believe that anybody married to that would have any truck with Matterhorns! The best performance in this highly exciting film is that of M. Luis Trenker as Carrel, and the best piece of verisimilitude is that of Mr. Frank Birch, who marvellously reproduces the lineaments of the Rev. Charles Hudson.

58

SOME MEMORIES

193

HOW far is it true that the young people of to-day care little for yesterda and not at all for the day before? If this is true, then it follows that you middle-aged writer of anything excepting novels cannot hope to interes any but the middle-aged. This sombre thought occurred to me as I sa watching the picture now showing at the Empire, Metro-Goldwyn-Mayer' version of *Frou-frou.* A point about these period plays, which have onl just become period, is the over-insistence on costume. Meilhac and Halév wrote their *Frou-frou* in 1869; the play was produced in London in th following year. I first saw Sarah Bernhardt in it, as nearly as I ca remember, round about 1890, and I cannot recall whether she played it a a costume-piece or not; I have a vivid recollection of her entrance in th first act *en Amazone,* and riding-habits don't alter much. As for the rest I have a detailed memory of Sarah's playing, but none whatever of th clothes in which she played. The impression I got from the film the othe day was that a number of people had got themselves up in the crinolin period, and that the whole thing was part of a fancy-dress ball. Neve in all my life have I seen so many staircases; nothing seemed to happe except on a staircase! The point, therefore, was not that Sartorys preferre the feather-headed sister to the sober-minded one, but which of the tw girls' crinolines ballooned the more effectively. More interesting than th film was the reaction of the audience, which declined to be moved eithe by the crinolines or the drama, tittering at the one and guffawing at th other. Yet seen in its true perspective, this piece about a doll-wife is a admirable one, since it is exactly the kind of thing which Ibsen in *A Doll' House* set out to demolish. Oddly enough, in the out-of-print little volum entitled *The Manchester Stage,* 1880-1900, W. T. Arnold's notice o Meilhac and Halévy's unique *succès de larmes* is immediately followe by Professor Oliver Elton's notice of Janet Achurch and Charles Charring ton in *A Doll's House.*

Arnold, whose notice of *Frou-frou* was written eight years before th first performance of any Ibsen play in this country, could still be move by the French play. It is significant that to Arnold, who was a ver sensitive critic, the play's emotion was still authentic in 1881. Or perhap the great Polish actress, Modjeska, made it seem so. It certainly seeme so in the previous year when Bernhardt played the part. Whether th modern film-goer is or is not interested in old plays, old performances and old criticisms seems to me to be something which the middle-aged critic must disregard, since to him they are of intense interest, and it is his first duty to be true to himself. Tucked away among my newspaper-cuttings is a notice written by C. E. Montague of Jane Hading's Manchester performance of *Frou-frou,* and it is of immense significance that in the intervening twenty-six years the dust had thickly accumulated on what was still a good though an entirely demoded theatre-piece. Montague writes:

> Perhaps there were a few persons in the audience last night who had also been in our Prince's Theatre on the midsummer evening in 1880 when *Frou-frou* was first played here by Mme. Bernhardt. One imagined them last night saying, "So this was the hand we were bluffed with," as they saw the deserted husband call in person to hand back to his wife her dowry—there was neither East nor West, post-office nor banker nor solicitor when two strong men or a strong man and a woman were wanted to stand face to face in the Dumasian and slightly post-Dumasian theatre for a good *scene-à-faire;* and again when the penitent wife looked in at her deserted husband, in the nick of time, to die in state on the drawing-room sofa, fortified by the last rites of the old Dumasian ethics: "Vous me pardonnez, n'est-ce pas?" "Ah! ce n'est pas à vous qu'il faut pardonner; c'est à moi," etc. One imagines the critical enthusiasm in 1869, and the honest pride of Meilhac and Halévy, when the dodge of making the wronged Sartorys first ask his wife for a glass of water and then spurn it on seeing two places laid at the table was first brought off. Last night M. Hauterive, as Sartorys, did the thing quite well, and, behold! we were no more moved than when our own sound-hearted scamps in sound melodrama take off their hats at the mention of their mothers, so fugitive is the effectiveness of even the cleverest new finds in theatrical "business."

Yes, I remember almost everything of Sarah's performance, which divided itself into three parts. The first was wholly given up to the charm of the tousled *étourdie,* and the fun of the rehearsal for those amateur theatricals in which Sarah gave a delightful imitation of an amateur. This was charm such as in all my theatre-going I have never encountered since. Even that uncharmed dragon, William Archer, could write of Sarah at this period: "She was certainly an exquisite creature," though he was careful to limit his praise to the period between the years 1875 and 1885 when the artist had attained full maturity and had not yet "coarsened her talent by the reckless overwork of her European and American tours." The second part was concentrated on the great quarrel scene between Frou-frou and the sober Louise, when the younger sister's replies rang out like pistol shots. I do not think I have ever heard a scene taken at such speed. If we are to believe Arnold, Modjeska speaking in a tongue foreign to her could not attain to this rapidity. The third peak in the performance was the death scene, and, as Arnold said in his essay on her Phèdre, "it is not contested that Mme. Bernhardt knows how to die." Even so, Arnold thought that in *Frou-frou* Modjeska's was the better dying: "Its great merit was the continued thought of the child at the dying woman's feet; Sarah Bernhardt forgot him too soon."

I cannot help it if these old comparisons are irking the reader. Was it Lamb who said that whenever a new book came out he read an old one? The fact that I am interested in the exploits of Mr. Bruen, the young Irish golfer, has not dimmed my interest in that greatest of all golfers, young Tom Morris, who died on Christmas Day, 1875, at the age of twenty-four. Modern actresses and film stars may come and go, and between the two essay the old parts. But their coming and their going, and above all their essaying, does not detract from my interest in their greater predecessors—Desclée who created this particular rôle, Bernhardt, Modjeska, and even Jane Hading. That is why I am still absorbed in these old criticisms. Arnold writes:

> It is true that Mme. Modjeska does not represent Frou-frou as a mere coquette, with little heart and no depth of feeling; but if she had done so, she would have disregarded the authors' most evident intentions, which are, surely, to paint a woman whose finer nature has been warped and overlaid by the successive spoiling of father, sister, and husband. It is brains that are wanting to Frou-frou, a clear eye to see where she is going, and a strong will to stop herself in time, and not at all tenderness of heart or depth of feeling. If Mme. Modjeska is wrong here, so was Sarah Bernhardt, and so, if we may trust tradition, was Aimée Desclée. If there is anything wanting in this part of the play, and very little indeed is wanting, it is because Mme. Modjeska is not quite *mignonne* enough for the part.

But enough of Arnold! If anything is wanting in the film—and a great deal is wanting!—it is because Miss Luise Rainer has none of the breeding of her predecessors and plays the part on two notes only. The first of these is a wholly conscientious assumption of a wholly non-existent irresponsibility, the only parallel for which on this side of the water would be if Miss Beatrix Lehmann's Electra suddenly took to making eyes! The second note is a gloom that even Miss Lehmann has never encompassed. Both parts are made to cohere by the use of an Austrian accent which Meilhac would have hated as much as Halévy, and vice versa. Sartorys is endowed y Mr. Melvyn Douglas with a pudding-like lack of interest, and the ruin f this fine old play is completed by the Louise whom the actress makes ot only a fright, but a comic fright, like one of Miss Edna May Oliver's uennas but without the distinction. To complete my discomfiture the hole thing has been transferred to Louisiana, if you please, with negro ervants and Frou-frou slapping the face of one of them and threatening er with a whipping. All in the best vein, I am to suppose, of *étourderie* as Ieilhac and Halévy conceived it!

59

WHAT IS A GOOD FILM?

1939

/HAT exactly does one mean when one says, "This is a good film"? At ie conclusion of *The Outsider,* the new film at the Regal, I sat for some me "blasted with ecstasy" at a conclusion so imbecile that the inmates f a lunatic asylum would not stand for it. And then I found myself telling ie management that I thought it was a very good film and that I should dvise my readers to see it. And so I do! Its concluding moment is of an liocy to make aborigines blush. But up to that moment it is an exciting nd even a compelling film. Let me go back to the beginning.

Miss Dorothy Brandon's play, when it was first put on at the St. James's 1923, made something of a sensation. Bone-setting was very much in ie air, and perhaps this is the place for a little story about a family prac-tioner who called in a specialist to a patient. The great man pronounced entence of immediate doom. A year later, the family doctor, meeting the pecialist in the street, told him that he had just returned from a luncheon arty held to celebrate the patient's complete recovery. "You must have iven him the wrong treatment!" said the great man icily. For, of course, iere is one thing which annoys the professional more than anything else. 'his is when, after he has failed at a job, some amateur comes along and ucceeds. Whereupon all that is left for the professional to do is to call the ther fellow a quack. Let me not, however, get side-tracked into a dis-ussion about professional status, which would be as much out of place in 'HE TATLER as film criticism would be in *The Lancet.* Lalage Sturdee had een a cripple from childhood, though nothing could have been more rippled about her than the pronunciation of her first name, a pronuncia-ion which defies phonetic spelling. I can only tell you that Lalage is iade to rhyme with "garage", with that word pronounced in the French ianner! Her mother dying when she was born, her father who was a distinguished physician went off to the East leaving his little daughter i the hands of the local bone-setter, who made a mess of the child's hip. An then the father came back to find that it was too late to do anything. Th most eminent surgeons were consulted and all shook their heads. So whe ever Dr. Sturdee gave a party, there was nothing left for Lalage (pronoun as previously, please!) except to sit at her grand piano and compose tun for sentimental operettes for which her fiancé, Basil, wrote the lyric Now about this time there was working in the East End of London a osteopath who, it seemed, had achieved some wonderful cures. This, course, greatly annoyed Harley Street, largely for the reason that th fellow wouldn't keep to the East End, but had the impudence to poach upo their preserves. Hips, thighs, tibias, fibulas which were to be reckone among Harley Street's oldest friends, deserted their former allegiance, pa one visit to Ragatzy, and being cured were seen no more. And Harle Street just could not bear this. It would not agree that Ragatzy was a jol good fellow, and it just couldn't bring itself to utter the words "Hip-hi hurrah!" Instead, Ragatzy had to be proscribed.

This is the place to say that one's sympathies in this matter were ve much with Harley Street. It is true that Mr. Frederick Leister, who pla Lalage's father, and Messrs. Kynaston Reeves, Edmond Breon, Ralp Truman, Walter Hudd, and Fewlass Llewellyn, playing the other doctor didn't look as though they were particularly dab hands at curing anyboc of anything. But at least they were the kind of consultants that no ma would object to seeing in his wife's bedroom. Whereas everything abo Ragatzy was objectionable, from his buttonhole to an oily manner con pounded in equal parts of the head waiter at his most subservient and th hairdresser's assistant at his cockiest. Mr. George Sanders, who pla Ragatzy marvellously, hits off the note. He makes Ragatzy common, y not too common. You feel that while the fellow's table manners are perfec he probably wears plush pyjamas. Now this gentleman has the notion th he can cure Lalage (don't let me down in the matter of pronunciatio please!). In his mind's eye he sees the newspaper headline: "Quac Succeeds Where Surgeon Fails." Besides, he has admired the young lady music in the theatres, and recognises that she has a soul! It would tak too long to tell how Ragatzy wins the girl's confidence and persuades he to undergo a year's treatment on his stretching apparatus. Finally she con sents, and as month succeeds month, we see her love for her fiancé weaken ing and her affection for Ragatzy increasing. And then the year is up, an all Harley Street is bidden to witness the great cure. It fails. Desperatel the quack calls upon her to march. Whereupon she drops to the floor. He lukewarm fiancé holds out his arms, and again she falls down. Then ther enters Lalage's father, who strides up to Ragatzy and strikes him on both cheeks. Whereupon Lalage comes cantering over the drawing-room floor saying, "Father, strike not the man I love!" or words to that effect. For love has conquered!

I don't remember that Miss Brandon's play ever attained such heights of bathos. Turning up my old notes I find that I actually took the play seriously: "The whole of the second act is a paraphrase into Samuel Butler of all that Juliet whispers on the balcony. And if the insistence upon sex is a trifle overdone, it must be looked upon as a backwash of that surge of emotion which went to the play's creation. The theme is one after Ibsen's own heart." And so on, and so forth. In the film there is no pretence at seriousness, the insistence being upon over-seriousness! Or have I missed some Great Truth? Is it possible that, if I am a cripple, I can take up my bed and walk if the place I am to walk to is my mistress's bedroom? But that if I am merely to go down to the office I must remain flat on my back? Whatever the answer to these questions, I have pleasure in certifying that *The Outsider* is a capital film which all readers of THE TATLER should visit. Accidentally, and not out of disrespect, I find that I have omitted to mention that Miss Mary Maguire plays Lalage. It should also, perhaps, be pointed out that this is an English film, made at Elstree, which makes its quality all the more remarkable.

60

THE TRUTH ABOUT "JAMAICA INN"

1939

READER, it is not often that I ask for sympathy! I do not ask it even now. What I suggest is that you should give intellectual consideration to the plight of one who, with a whole page of THE TATLER to fill, cannot speak his mind about the matter in hand. Or can he? The temptations to avoid truth-telling are many. I have a very considerable admiration for Miss Daphne du Maurier, the original inceptress of the spot of bother at the Regal Cinema. She is the author of what I regard as the most original, truth-telling, and accomplished biography of modern times, the book called *Gerald* which tells the life story of her father. Miss du Maurier is also, to judge from the novel called *Rebecca,* the possessor of the best-selling world's most valuable secret. This is the secret of how to be good, but not too good. I once asked the late A. B. Walkley to what he attributed the success of the French dramatist, Eugène Scribe. He replied: "Scribe always took great care never to be better than third-rate!" Miss du

Maurier's novels encircle the world; if they were a shade better they would hardly go round Clapham Common. This writer thinks, or pretends to think, what the vast generality of people who cannot write like to see set down in words. In an omnibus containing fourteen people, you will find that sixteen have read Miss du Maurier's novels, for that number includes the driver and the conductor! This is a talent for which I have the highest admiration and envy.

Consider, too, that Mr. Charles Laughton and half the cast of this film are personal friends of mine. How, then, can I be expected to speak my whole mind about this schoolboy nonsense? Let me see what somebody else has to say about the film of *Jamaica Inn,* and let that somebody be the gentleman in charge of this film's publicity. Here, in brief, is what the makers of this picture ask us to believe about it:

> Make way for Sir Humphrey Pengallan!—Laughton's greatest creation in Daphne du Maurier's sensational novel of which over a million copies have been sold—Unparalleled love romance—Tumultuous, flaming adventure—Absorbing romantic interest—A throbbing drama with colourful characters—Their lives and loves—Their hopes and dreams—A story with the lusty force of an Atlantic gale—Depicting the wild days when the Law reached no further than a musket shot—Wreckers led by a mad genius in Cornwall's lawless days—The most elaborate, expensive, and important picture yet made in Britain—It has the epic sweep of the master, Alfred Hitchcock, and is produced by the most famous of international producers, Erich Pommer.

Does Mayflower Pictures expect anybody but servant girls to be impressed by this? I cheerfully agree that every servant girl in the land will dote on this picture!

Yet I can see how the notion came about that the novel of *Jamaica Inn* might make a good film. There was the character of Sir Humphrey Pengallan, who, of course, is Stevenson's Weir of Hermiston, only drawn less well. There is enough of this character left—the implication of insanity and the snippets of quotation from Shakespeare, Burke, and Byron—to indicate that in the original Sir Humphrey is elaborately drawn. And then there was the Cornish coast, treacherous alike to sailing ships and scenario-mongers. Yes, it must all have promised extremely well! I think disillusion first set in with the first shot of Sir Humphrey's manor house. I do not know whether it was the layout, the size, the Dendy-Sadlerism, or the sheer glossiness of the apartments which accounted for my immediate and complete disbelief in Sir Humphrey and everything about him. Mr. Hitchcock should, before making this film, have reminded himself that the mark of the Englishman of the period with which the book deals, was not the dirt of the lower classes, but the grubbiness of the upper. Whatever the reason I had no belief that Mr. Laughton's Sir Humphrey was alive and doing this and that nefarious thing in Cornwall, in the way in which I believed in the theatre that his Man with Red Hair was actual and up to the monkey tricks indicated by Sir Hugh. The whole performance seemed to me to be "screen," by which I mean the film equivalent of "stagey." It had obviously been put together in the studio, at the same time as the eyebrows and the nose. Perhaps what most precluded my belief in the character was the actor's obvious delight in his own creation. One was conscious not of Sir Humphrey revelling in Sir Humphrey's gusto, but of Mr. Laughton revelling in Mr. Laughton's actorship. The result was that long before the end, Sir Humphrey, far from being *in* the picture, becomes an excrescence upon it. The smuggling scenes were good in a schoolboy sort of way. But frankly I am unable to believe in young ladies in evening dress scampering about the Cornish coast and hoisting warning signals in the teeth of a gale and a band of desperate smugglers. I came to dread every visible porthole, crevice, or other aperture lest Miss Maureen O'Hara should scream down it. Also I think that when two people emerge from the sea in which they have been swimming for twenty minutes, they should appear to be a little more than damp.

But the oddest thing about the direction was its strange air of unreality. Obviously real coaches-and-four were driven up to an inn which looked as though it had been painted on cardboard by an admirer of Vlaminck. And then what I shall call the spoofing was not too well done. It should not be manifest that ships driven on a hostile coast during a storm at night are really cockleshells being photographed in a bathroom. When the ship, being heroine-warned, went about turn, she took no more time in doing it than it takes to turn a paper boat. And then again, I really do think that a deck on which tons of water have just descended should not remain bone-dry! These things would not matter if what I believe to be the spirit of the novel had been transferred to the screen. In my view it wasn't. Indeed, I had the notion that the picture in its alternations between lonely house and smugglers' cove was a queer combination of *Wuthering Heights* and *Peter Pan.* Half of the best actors and actresses on our stage have been uselessly and expensively employed. For example, it does not need a Mary Jerrold to appear for ten seconds as a housekeeper and say: "This way, miss!" at a hundred pounds or so a minute. No, if this is "epic sweep" then give me a French picture where, with the help of an empty railway siding and his own full imagination, a Jean Gabin will give you a masterpiece.

61

A FILM OF PROVENCE

1939

THE critic of any of the arts is supposed to take a cold, clear, impartial view of any work presented for his consideration, independent of its subject-matter.

Whether the business of a play be the murder of an honoured guest, as in *Macbeth,* or the skittering about the stage of a featherbrain as in *Behold the Bride,* the critic's attention is supposed to be equally engaged. Whether a film is concerned with bird-life in Cornwall or the stage-door intrigues of chorines, he is supposed to be equally interested. I confess that this law always failed with me, or rather that I have failed in submitting to know it. There are parts of the world and parts of history which will always fill me with a passionate non-interest amounting to nausea and howsoever they are treated. Let any play, book, or film deal with Germany in the sixteenth, seventeenth, eighteenth centuries and I am immediately, as they say, sunk. At once I experience again the lacerating boredom of wading through Schiller's *History of the Thirty Years War* in my schooldays years and years ago. If anybody on the stage mentions the Elector of Saxony I know that I shall rush into the foyer and emit shrieks like a railway engine. It is exactly the same with novels about archbishops in Mexico, or vikings in Scandinavia, or cross-gartered Saxons in Early England. Obviously, then, I must be an unfair and even a bad judge of any plays or films where the subject-matter is violently antipathetic to my own appetite. On the other hand, there are plays and films which interest me perhaps more than they should, merely because of their subject-matter. Such a film is *La Femme du Boulanger* or *The Baker's Wife,* which has just been put on at the Berkeley Cinema. I sat through this long film entranced beyond lawful measure. The action takes place in Provence, in which earthly paradise I spent what I now know to have been one of the happiest periods of my life. The world was in the throes of the greatest of all wars, and there was I calmly buying hay for the cavalry, safe and sound in a corner of very heaven.

Of all the towns in Southern France, Arles, the centre of Marrows Vegetable, is the most celebrated, the oftenest visited, the most notably discussed. It is the paradise of the cheap philosopher. Does not the thunder of the Paris Express shake to its crazy foundations the ancient palace of Constantine? Is not the peace of the Alyscamps, that burying-place of Roman dead, violated seven days a week by the clamour of the goods yard and the clang of the giant workshop? Is not the sleepy Rhône bridged as unromantically as the Menai Straits? How reconcile antique beauty with electric light? And in these latter days how reconcile the Arlesienne of the pure Greek profile with the bullet-headed prisoner of war? Leaving this easy philosophy to take care of itself, let me at least say that Arles, the sentimental capital of Provence, is old in a sense undreamed of by those newcomers, the English. Henry James was wont to tease his American countrymen with our stately houses and immemorial butlers; well might he have used the cobblestones of Arles, along which he hobbled so painfully, to pelt us in our turn. We are, come to think of it, so desperately new. But Arles has no misgivings on the score of pedigree; her line comes down unbroken. The historian will tell you that through Arles Hannibal's Numidians marched to the sack of Italy, that within her walls a Roman Emperor had his palace, that during the governorship of Decimus Junius Brutus, a Greek designed and built the exquisite theatre, still to be seen. He will go on to tell you of the Amphitheatre, of the thickness of its walls, its diameter, its seating capacity. He will draw comparisons with the Colosseum at Rome. He will reconstruct for you the Vénus d'Arles, and discuss whether she may not be a reproduction of the lost Aphrodite of Praxiteles. If your historian have imagination he will tell you of the seas of blood that have flowed within the walls of the arena, and of horrors that belong more properly to the nightmare pages of a Huysmans than to sober history. If he have sentimental leanings, he will talk of Petrarch and Laura, Aucassin and Nicolette, and others of the world's famous lovers. Then he will grow lyrical over the famed Arlesienne beauty, and over the inability of alien blood to debase its coinage: "At Marseilles the Phœnicians may have planted their arsenals, founded their markets, trained their sailors. But at Arles they loved and bred. Here was the bosom upon which the weary seafarer reposed, and here paid back to posterity the debt he owed the woman of his choice." Thus ends my rhapsody!

The film about the Provençal baker takes place in any one of the little villages of which Arles is the capital. The story is simplicity itself. The village is torn with petty feuds and is unanimous only in its respect for the new baker and his bread baking. The quality of his bread is unapproachable. So is the beauty of his young wife. The whole village assembles each morning to receive its supply of the former and to get a glimpse of the latter. Unfortunately this complacent state of affairs does not last. The baker's wife falls head over ears in love with the young shepherd who comes to collect bread for the local marquis's castle. He elopes with her on the marquis's best horse. The baker is dazed with incredulity, and then stunned first with grief and second with self-consoling Pernod. He neglects his baking, and nothing can induce him to go near his oven. The bread supply of the village gives out. The marquis and the *curé* coax and wheedle in vain. Only the capture of the faithless wife can restore the baker to his sober senses and his oven. Everybody is despatched to find her, and she is found in an island in the middle of a marsh, quarrelling with her young lover and only too contritely anxious to be brought home again. The husband receives her without reproach, and the village once more has its unexampled bread. I cannot tell what impression this simple story made upon my colleagues, a handful of whom were present at thc private showing. Were they perhaps, despite their knowledge of French, a little incommoded by the Provençal accent? But to me that accent is as familiar as bread and butter. I suppose that I must in my life have heard four times as much Provençal spoken as pure French, and I shall confess to sitting back and revelling at the Berkeley, always providing that revelling can go hand in hand with complete nostalgia. This, of course, could not have happened without the perfection of acting. This the film receives, down to its tiniest part, and so beautifully did M. Raimu play the baker that when I came out into the open air the sun itself seemed to belong not to London but to Arles, that mistress of the imagination never to be forsworn.

62

UP-TO-DATE BALZAC

1939

TWENTIETH-Century-Fox will doubtless be surprised to learn that their brilliant farce at the New Gallery, *A Girl Must Live,* harks straight back to Balzac. The model is that famous novel entitled *Splendeurs et Misères des Courtisanes,* and that section of it whose title translated into English is "The Price Old Men Pay for Love." This has a tremendous scene in which the young and exquisite Esther Gobseck is at last left alone with the grotesque and sixty-six-year-old Baron Nucingen. Now that I come to think of it, that sentence is a gross misstatement of the facts. Actually Nucingen is alone with Esther; but she, poor girl, is alone with her memories. Balzac must describe what follows. The baron fell to his knees. Esther made no sign beyond giving him her hands, though she did not, as it were, know the sex of the monster who, pretending that her feet were cold, began to chafe them. This scene, in which from time to time burning tears fell on the head of the baron while he was industriously undertaking to restore warmth to those little feet, lasted from midnight until two o'clock in the morning. Presently Esther managed to make good her escape, and the baron was left to spend the remainder of the night on a comfortless sofa, only to be aroused shortly after sunrise by the officers of the law coming to arrest Esther for debt. The door of Esther's room opened, and in the doorway stood this unwilling courtesan, whose beauty, says Balzac, would have confounded the angel Raphael. In through the street door proceeded to roll a spate of human mud, advancing "not upon feet but paws." Then, apparently from nowhere, appeared the villainous procuress who rejoiced in the name of Europe. She put a stop to the activities of the creditor with a *coup de savate.* But the flood was only momentarily checked, and Esther would have been bundled off to prison had it not been for the baron, who proceeded piteously to write a cheque for the trifling sum of 312,000 francs and some odd centimes. Even so, his abortive evening was not yet entirely paid for. Turning to his men, all of whom squinted abominably, and some of whom lacked a nose, the bailiff-in-chief, grinning from ear to ear, proceeded to haggle with the baron about the gratuity which should content his assistants. "How much," he said brutally, "for this scum?" The core of the scene is, of course, tragic; if it can be called comic, it is comic in the manner of to-day's great French painter, Rouault, and of our old English painter, Hogarth. Only a French film could, I think, do this scene justice. And presumably this is not the spirit in which the makers of *A Girl Must Live* have approached the same theme.

The English film lowers the subject into the key of buffoonery, with the important justification that the buffoonery throughout is unendingly witty. The Nucingen on this occasion is Mr. George Robey, a wealthy furrier who is induced to back a musical comedy, the inducement being that he shall a say in the choice of the chorus-girls with all the rewards and emoluments attaching to so onerous and responsible a task! And at once he gets into the clutches of Miss Renée Houston and Miss Lilli Palmer, who put up a battle in comparison with which a duel between hornets would be stingless. Whether lady hornets have stings is a matter for the entomologist and as such beneath the consideration of a film critic! And then, suddenly, and to him quite inexplicably, Mr. Robey finds himself dropped. Why? Because an earl, forthrightly played by Mr. Hugh Sinclair, has hove into view from Australia, where he has been bushranging. It is Renée who first spots the earl, and between Southampton and Waterloo she succeeds in digging her claws into him. Renée's success rouses Lilli to battle which she proceeds to wage with both words and crockery. The scene in the bedroom, where every available missile is dispatched with unerring aim, has not been bettered, and perhaps not equalled, since the first custard pie was thrown. But the all-in verbal wrestling is even better.

Renée is mistress of the affront direct and absolute, whereas Lilli proceeds by subtlety. For when Mr. Robey tells Lilli that he hopes Renée will be able to keep her appointment for supper, Lilli says with angelic sweetness: "She will, of course, dear! Provided she can get away from her boy friend!" And when Renée boasts to Lilli that the earl cannot take his eyes off her, Lilli replies: "You should realise, dear, that he hasn't seen any woman, white or black, for eleven years!" But there is also a third chorus-girl, Miss Margaret Lockwood, who is in reality a far worse gold-digger than the other two, for the reason that she pretends not to care for money, and who therefore wins the earl by dint of moping. The picture is further enlivened by a richly comic performance of a landlady by Miss Mary Clare, and a gorgeous presentation of a restless maid by Miss Kathleen Harrison. It is still further enlivened by a drinking scene between Mr. Naunton Wayne, as an unabashed and unabashable crook, and Mr. David Burns as a not-too-straight film producer who is doing his level best to coax the earl to back a picture in which he is interested. I have not for a very long time seen anything more delicious than the look on Mr. Burns's face when he says to Mr. Wayne: "D'you know, I don't think that that guy *wants* to lose his money!" There are some remarkable shots of the earl's ancestral castle, in which apparently there are twenty-four spare bedrooms ready, at a moment's notice, to accommodate twenty-four ladies of the chorus. And the mistress of this lovely home is Miss Helen Haye, who looks and behaves exactly as a countess must who at tea-time has discovered twenty-four wasps in the jam.

This delightful picture greatly raises my hopes for British films, and I was, quite frankly, resigned to expect nothing further from that quarter. I hear excellent reports also, of the new film starring Miss Gracie Fields. Can it be that things relating to British films genuinely are looking up at last? They have still, of course, a very long way to look up before they attain to the high mark of recent French comedies like *La Femme du Boulanger*. But if in the matter of comedy we can attain to the best Hollywood standard—and I cannot imagine Hollywood doing any better with *A Girl Must Live* than has been done by the blazingly clever cast at Islington—then perhaps we are not entirely to be despaired of in this tricky little matter of picture-making!

63

CRITIC IN ARMS

1940

I AM in a blazing temper. But first I must go back a bit, back to my visit to New York in 1937. Almost the first thing I saw there after I had landed was the musical comedy, *Babes in Arms,* at the Shubert Theatre. About this I wrote in my diary: "This is a fresh, inventive musical comedy played by a sixteen-year-old cast headed by Mitzi Green and Duke McHale. The girl is clever, and the boy is a budding Richard Bird who can sing and dance as well as act. I enjoyed every moment of this; the music by Lorenz Hart and Richard Rodgers is in a fascinating idiom which is theirs and nobody else's. Haunting! The show cost comparatively little to stage—fifty-five thousand dollars only—and could be put on in London for a quarter of that sum. But I doubt whether it would be a profitable experiment. Seeing that it has been put together with many brains, I foresee flattering notices and empty houses. London likes its musical comedy to be solid, substantial, and thick; *Babes in Arms* is airy and fanciful, and the scenery is of the sketchiest. This is as it should be, since the whole notion is that a lot of actors' orphans will be sent to work on the land if they don't make good with a revue of their own concocting. The bill for the kids' scenery is forty-two dollars, which Sam, son of the orphanage master, puts up in return for forty-nine per cent of the profits. 'Just like the real thing.' " And I find that on leaving New York I wrote that among the high spots of my visit had been "the lilt of Hart and Rodgers' score, which has danced its way through everything I have seen and given this hard-boiled city a dreamlike quality." I brought home with me four of the records of the tunes in this show, but to my chagrin could not procure the delightful little dance tune called "Imagine." This had so fascinated me that I wrote to Hart and Rodgers and asked if no record had been made of it. They replied that a record would be made at once for my especial benefit, and a fortnight later I received this record. To ensure against the record getting broken I sent it to H.M.V. who very kindly made two or three extra copies for me. Now I think that the foregoing sets forth with sufficient plainness the fact that I fell head over heels in love with this naïve little piece, and clearly indicates the eagerness with which I was looking forward to seeing a film version of it. Well, I have seen the film version of *Babes in Arms* now showing at the Empire. And, as I say, I am in a blazing temper!

I was, I confess, a little uneasy at the notion that the boy babe was to be played by Mickey Rooney, all the more dismayed because I am a great admirer of this young gentleman who, when he likes, has more power and pathos than almost anybody else on the screen to-day. But wasn't it just possible that virtuosity as great as his might wreck the little musical comedy in the way that, I suggest, Toscanini might wreck a performance of Haydn's Toy Symphony? Well, the show was wrecked right enough, but long before Mickey had anything to do with it! It was wrecked by the failure of the transmuting agency to realise that to take a little piece whose note is modesty and then swell it out a kind of bloated magnificence is the one sure way of wrecking that little piece.

Let me explain. In the original the boys and girls are the inmates of a school for the orphan children of vaudeville artistes. They want to be vaudeville artistes themselves, whereas Authority prefers that they should work on the land. Finally, a bargain is reached. If the children can, out of their own wit and ingenuity, produce a piece of any merit, the land threat shall be withdrawn and arrangements made for the children to go into "the profession." And, of course, the great part of the musical comedy is taken up with the bringing-into-being of the kids' revue. Since all that they can raise in the way of production capital is forty-two dollars, they make the scenery out of cardboard and the costumes out of window curtains and lampshades. Now let us see what becomes of all this in the film. To begin with, all the parents are brought back to life so that the kids are orphans no longer. It is true that the parents are failures, and that the land threat is held out to the children unless they can make good quickly. And how do they proceed to make good? Well, first Mickey heads a torchlight procession through the town, there being an unlimited supply of kerosene torches miraculously to hand. Next, in place of the original piano, a babies' orchestra is hired, an out-of-door theatre is rented, and a show is put on where the production expenses cannot have been a cent under ten thousand dollars. The show is interrupted by a hurricane, and after some sentimentalities a Broadway producer invites Mickey to bring the whole production to New York. Whereupon it at once becomes indistinguishable from any other Hollywood musical. There is a great deal of music, none of which, with the exception of "Where and When," was in the original musical comedy. At least, I did not recognise any of it, and I do know that with one exception none of the records of the original in my possession appears in the film.

It goes without saying that there is a lot of extraneous Rooneyism, and we are made aware that Master Mickey can play several musical instruments, impersonate several film stars, and black his face to give a reasonably good interpretation of a nigger minstrel. I genuinely grieve for all this. I feel that this brilliant boy is being pushed on far too fast, and that in a year or two he will be just a squeezed orange. If there is any wisdom in this talented young actor's make-up or in those who are in control of him, provided he is controllable, he will pack up while the going is good—for surely he has made sufficient fortune!—and come back to the screen in a few years' time, not as the engaging hobbledehoy but as the grown man. What he should certainly not be asked to do at any time or phase is what he does in the present film—sing a pæan to America in the best Martin Chuzzlewit manner thanking Providence for having taken that great country under its especial care and for bestowing upon it, if not a Nelson, at least a Nelson Eddy!

64

VINTAGE GUITRY

1940

HOW sick one gets of the film's eternal wisecracking! And how delightful it is to move once again in a world of well-bred wit! In *Ils Etaient Neuf Célibataires,* now showing at Studio One, M. Sacha Guitry plays a boulevardier who is not quite a gentleman but is certainly not anything else—he wears the clothes of a crook—vivid yellow tie against sea-blue shirt—and yet carries them off perfectly. Jean is a crook, but one of the straightest possible kind. He describes himself as an insinuator! Money can only circulate by changing hands. Very well then! Jean insinuates his own pair of hands between the pair that gives and the pair that receives, and deducts a modest commission. But for the moment his tricks of insinuation have failed him; there is nothing doing on the boulevards or anywhere else. Then one day, sitting in a café expounding the philosophy of living by one's wits, he is interrupted by a newspaper-vendor crying the latest edict: All foreigners must at once leave Paris and persuade their own countries to give them hospitality. The consternation is general, from the Russian countess at the next table to the Italian waiter serving Jean.

Let me break off here to say how good even the newsvendor is in this film! He is old as are all French paper-sellers, and as a Frenchman it is up to him to voice his endorsement of French policy in this matter of expulsion. The Government may be "*sale*"—one of the privileges of being a Frenchman is that of always being able to vilify the government in power!—but in this matter it has done right. Bustled out through the swing door, he is by the very impetus of his ejection whirled back into the café where he at once resumes his tirade.

And now Jean puts on his thinking-cap. Foreign women are to be allowed to stay in France if they are able to find French husbands. "*Tiens, une idée!*" In a trice Jean has rented an empty villa outside which he proceeds to erect the sign, "Home For Old Bachelors." The opening day arrives, and Monsieur le Directeur sits at his desk prepared to receive applicants. Nine present themselves, and with French logic the Directeur says: "*C'est juste! Il y a exactement neuf lits!*" All nine of the old men turn out to be spars from the ocean of Parisian distress, and all still retain a measure of that dignity which is so distinguishing a mark of the French character. Each one is beautifully differentiated, and their names are delightful—Athanase, Adolphe, Adhémar, Alexandre, Amédée, Agénor, Anatole, Aristide. Then come the women who desire husbands in name only, and here the comedy is brilliantly restrained and nowhere allowed to overflow into farce. Seven matches are arranged, and seven weddings take place. Two of the old bachelors complain that no brides have been allotted to them. Whereupon Jean shrugs his shoulders and continuing in his unassailable logic says that since this is a home for bachelors it is essential that some must remain in his establishment. And then the bridegrooms fail to keep their bargain, each one turning up at the moment when he is least wanted.

All but one make nuisances of themselves, and the exception is Athanase. His reasons may be found, strangely enough and of all places in the world, in Mr. Masefield's *The Everlasting Mercy:*

Perhaps when man has entered in
His perfect city free from sin,
The campers will come past the walls
With old lame horses full of galls,
And waggons hung about with withies,
And burning coke in tinkers' stithies,
And see the golden town and choose,
And think the wild too good to lose,
And camp outside as these camped then
With wonder at the entering men.

Athanase admits that a warm bed is something and good food something more. But he realises that he will be hampered by what another school of humour calls an "everloving wife," and by two daughters whose husbands are policemen. Shall I, reflects the old rogue, ever be able to take the air between my two sons-in-law without feeling that I am under arrest? No! For him the wild, meaning the freedom of the Paris streets, is just too good a thing to lose.

I shall have space for only one more of these husbands. This is Adhémar, who is married to what the English programme calls, with delicious prudery, the owner of a lingerie shop. Those of my readers who have been to the Redfern Gallery to see the Montague Shearman Collection of modern pictures may have noted a tiny Goerg entitled "Jugement de Paris." If they saw this picture they must still remember that awful, appraising Eye. May I be very personal for a moment and confess that between this sentence and the last one I went to the telephone and bought the picture? Mlle. Marguérite Pierrey, who impersonates the Eye, is like sixteen Maupassant stories about "lingerie establishments" all rolled into one. There is an enchanting moment when Adhémar, welcoming a dozen or so of what he presumes to be stepdaughters, is astonished to discover that one is black. "That one of my predecessors," he says, "was, I presume, a colonial?" Madame smiles, and Adhémar continues: "One of our French possessions, I hope?" At that moment the valet-de-chambre, not to say doorkeeper, announces two gentlemen. Whereupon we are switched on to the adventure of one of the other husbands.

The things I most admire about this film are its entire refusal to have anything to do with clowning and the extraordinary deftness with which all unpleasantness is skirted. To the French there is no deftness about it, for as a nation they just do not make mistakes of taste. As I have already indicated, the film is perfectly cast and perfectly acted in every part, with a very fine performance by M. Max Dearly. Sacha himself, rightly relying on his own unerring judgment, has seen that the piece of acting he himself contributes to the film must not be more than a witty footnote to it. The bachelors are the story, and Jean is merely the commentator. But we feel throughout that his is the master-hand that makes these old and creaking but nowhere unamusing puppets dance.

65

A GREAT COMEDIAN

1940

I SOMETIMES think that the wise critic of any of the arts should begin every article with the Latin tag: "*De gustibus non est disputandum.*" Nowhere does this apply more forcibly than to comedians, and particularly to low comedians. The first point to be made about low comedians is the impossibility of proving that they are funny. All that you can do is to state the fact that they make you laugh, either ordinately or inordinately, and leave it at that. I remember settling down to read one of the late

A. B. Walkley's Wednesday articles. The subject was Grock, and the article began: "There must be a philosophy of clowns." And at once I knew that the famous critic was, in common parlance, sunk! For, of course, there mustn't be anything of the sort. In his attempt to *prove* the comicality of the great clown Walkley quoted Croce, Victor Hugo, Thomas Love Peacock, Jean Paul Richter, Aristotle, Dieterich, and Sainte-Beuve. Amid the display of erudition occurs this passage. Walkley is talking about the type of clown to which Grock belongs, and he says: "It is genial and macabre, owlishly stupid and Macchiavellianly astute, platypode and feather-light, cacophonous and divinely musical. Grock's first act is a practical antithesis. A strange creature with a very high and very bald cranium (you think of what Fitzgerald said of James Spedding's: 'No wonder no hair can grow at such an altitude!') and in very baggy breeches waddles in with an enormous portmanteau—which proves to contain a fiddle no larger than your hand. The creature looks more simian than human, but is graciously affable—another Sir Oran Haut-ton, in fact, with fiddle substituted for Sir Oran's flute and French horn."

And yet, you know, I doubt whether these fireworks illuminate anything more than the bare statement that Grock, whose personal appearance all readers know, used to come on to the stage carrying a very large bag containing the smallest possible fiddle. I remember a marvellous passage in which Jean Lorrain writing in the year 1900 describes the appearance of Little Tich at the London Olympia. Here again a magnificent writer finds it necessary for his parallels to draw upon Dickens, Constantin Guys, Daumier, and Goya. But the fact remains that a wonderful piece of descriptive reporting tells us little more than that Little Tich as a Spanish danseuse with a camellia behind his ear was very, very funny. In saying this I feel that I am in a way betraying my craft. It may be that the dramatic critics are unable to add to what I should like to call the verisimilitude of great clowns or great comedians during their lifetime, and the lifetime of those who remember them. We, living to-day, know all about Mr. Robey and no quotations from Brunetière, Novalis, and Leopardi are going to add to our understanding of his quiddity. But a generation is being born which conceivably will never have seen Mr. Robey. For them it is well that a C. E. Montague could write: "Last night he came on the stage first as that veteran theme of the halls, the middle-aged toper in black, frock-coated, tieless and collarless, leering with imbecile knowingness, Stiggins and Bardolph and Ally Sloper in one, his face 'all bubukles and whelks and flames of fire.' He ended as the equally familiar old woman of the same repertory, also of bibulous aspect, also half-knowing and half-crazy, a scold, farcical with relics of vanity, ugly as a gargoyle. Nothing could be staler than the subjects, nothing more fresh or fuller of gusto than their treatment. What he sang was nothing; you might have left it out without much lessening the fun .... You may call his topics stale or trivial, the mere words insignificant, the humour metallic, rasping, or worse, but the art, within its limits, is unsurpassable in its brilliant elliptical terseness, the volumes it says in an instant, its suddenness, fire, and zest."

What, then, am I to say about W. C. Fields which shall in any way enlighten those to whom he is as funny as Ally Sloper and Mr. Micawber combined? Shall I begin with a quotation from *Ally Sloper's Half-holiday* which burned itself into my brain when I was a boy, and which I have never forgotten: "A dirty mind is a perpetual feast!"? But this quotation would be of maximum infelicity and less a reinforcement than a stab in the back. Any performance of Fields is a perpetual feast, and the whole of it proceeds out of a mind which is essentially clean. His riot of fun is of such vast extent that never under any circumstances does he find it necessary to approach the borderline of squeamishness. There is a shot in *My Little Chickadee* at the Odeon in which Mae West puts him to bed with a goat in place of his intended bride. I cannot imagine any other comedian who would not make this scene either unsavoury or unfunny. The goat bleats, and her bleatings are interpreted by the more than bibulous bridegroom as the natural expression of feminine modesty. And just as you wonder at what point the censor is going to intervene, the goat leaps out of bed, and Fields also descends to terra firma, except that he finds himself treading upon a Red Indian brave, the custodian of the goat and who has as little logical place in this drama as has Queequeg in the tale of *Moby Dick*. And so the nonsense proceeds, illogical if you like but with a mad vein of Fieldsian logic running through it. Sitting down to cards he says: "Any game that is worth playing is worth cheating at!" His opponent asks: "Would you call poker a game of chance?" And Fields replies: "Not as I play it!"

I have recently been privileged to read a new book by Fields published in America but not here. It is called *Fields for President* and the author's logicality is well conveyed in his advice to business men which, being translated into English, runs as follows:

(1) Find out how much they've got.

(2) Get it.

(3) Get out.

In the film is also Miss West, who continues the mixture as before. In my opinion Fields completely overplays her, stealing every foot of the film down to the last word: "If you're ever in the Grampians, come up and see me!" And Miss West can only nod assent.

66

TO LIKE, OR TO DISLIKE?

1941

MY excellent and fair-minded colleague, Miss Lejeune, has been telling us that either you like or dislike Miss Katharine Hepburn just as you like or dislike Mr. Crosby, Mr. Cagney and the Marx Brothers. I feel that here is a half-truth to which I must devote half a page. Let us begin with Mr Crosby. Obviously you cannot like an artist who has reduced singing to the bayings of a love-sick bloodhound. But equally obviously you, being a craftsman in your own profession, cannot dislike a performer who, with an accuracy exceeding any physician's, has put his finger bang on the sentimental pulse of the uneducated world, roughly ninety-eight per cent of this globe's white population. From which it follows that, being a logical person, you must *half-like* Mr. Crosby. Mr. Cagney? If you hold that gangsters must never have baby faces and are ordained by Nature to resemble rats with double squints—why then you won't "like" this fine actor because you will regard his gangster assumptions as radically false. But if, on entering the cinema, you bethink yourself of Shakespeare's "There's no art to tell the mind's construction in the face," you will, I suggest, pull yourself together with the reflection that liking is one thing and critical appreciation another. The Marx Brothers? But in my view there is only one Marx Brother, and to have a grouch against Groucho is conceivable only on the theory that you are anti-Jewish. In which case, of course, you must have excessively disliked Sarah Bernhardt, and are beyond the pale. Or can it be that you have no ear for wit? Personally, after many years of steeling myself against my likes and schooling myself against my dislikes, I find that I have arrived at a state where I eliminate the individual and am swayed only by the artist. Then you must be more than human, says the captious reader. I am. The critic who is human is a walking contemptibility. He has no right to his free seat and should be queueing up at the box-office with the vulgar.

There, I freely admit, be niceties unperceived of the herd which, having parted with its greasy pence, holds itself at liberty to fall, or refrain from falling, for a film star's hair, dimples, waistline, or, if male, moustache, torso, biceps. The temptation in Katharine Hepburn's case has always been unusually strong. I well remember the shock, the delighted shock, I experienced at her first appearance. Here was a young woman possessed not of no looks to speak of, but of looks nobody would willingly speak about—a cheek-bone like a death's-head allied to a manner as sinister and aggresive as crossbones. Then this new discovery began to act, and as the film 'Morning Glory) wore on one began to perceive that the ungracious esture was the clothing for undefeatable spirit. Here, one said to oneself, vas the heroine of any Brontë novel, and the heaven-, or perhaps one hould say, hell-sent representative of the daemonic Emily herself. To have aid that afternoon that one liked or disliked the new actress would have een foolish; one does not like or dislike the forces of Nature. And then, fter a moving performance as Jo in *Little Women* the angry fire and ullen flame died down, and Hepburn—for all women are feminines in he last resort—took to vying with the Shearers, Wrays, and other of film-lom's milk-white does.

The milky way is traversed again in *Philadelphia Story* (Empire) in which Hepburn pretends to be the invincible ensnarer of the male, the ntire sex being represented as powerless in her toils. We see her on horse-back and off, out of bathing pools and in, drunk and sober, and alleged o be carrying off these vagaries with a charm and brilliance which would eclipse Shakespeare's Rosalind and Meredith's Clara Middleton put ogether. They sufficed to overthrow Cary Grant, but not before he had given her—why not this way round for a change?—a daughter precocious enough at the age of twelve to spy on her mother and priggish enough to blab. And now, respectably divorced, she is about to wreck another man's career by marrying him when James Stewart, a socialite reporter, turns up and by his scowls, largely helped by his commonness, quite vanquishes her. Whereby we get to the familair situation of the detestable girl whom nobody will marry. And if the film ended here it would be admirable; justice would be executed upon yet another detestable hussy. But now it turns out that we are supposed not to detest Hepburn but to find her enchanting to the point of ravishment. That the young woman's selfishness, arrogance, pertness and spiritual vulgarity are skin-deep only and that when you get to the true Hepburn bone you will find truth and loyalty and kindness and gentility. A combination of Imogen and Lorna Doone! And it appears that Cary Grant has known this all along, and that it was for knowing it that he was paid 50,000 dollars, or whatever he gets for wearing soft collars while every other man in the picture is decapitating himself with starch. Well, I just don't believe any of it. Hepburn as Joan of Arc waving her oriflamme and charging the English, nostrils quivering to match her horse's—yes, there is the true Hepburn. I see her again as any of the unpleasanter Aeschylean or Euripidean heroines, sword-struck and flame-consumed. But as a society pet enticing a hard-boiled reporter into a bathing pool and a midnight game of hide-and-seek among the nenuphars —the answer to this one is just plain No.

However, there is this much to be said for this film, that it is witty and goes at a tremendous pace. So fast, indeed, that I could not follow all its multitudinous wisecracking.

I sometimes wonder whether a new language may not be growing up of which old fogeys are insufficiently aware. I know that the other afternoon the cinema frequently rang with delighted laughter at sallies of which I was totally unable to perceive the drift.

I did, however, now and again catch something I could make head and tail of. As when the reporter said to the female of his kind: "Why do they have a telephone to the stables?" And received the reply: "So that they can talk to the horses without bringing them into the house." I would have added a rider to this—something about for fear of corrupting them.

The result of my cogitations? That I neither like nor dislike Miss Hepburn as the result of this film any more than I liked or disliked her before. I still think that in the right film she is a first-rate performer, and that when she is unsuited she is like nothing on earth. At least like nothing that I can recognise as existing on this earth.

67

A BRILLIANT MUSICAL

1941

THE number of times that I have enthused over a musical comedy as performed in the theatre could be numbered on the fingers of one hand, less the thumb and counting the little finger as non-existent. In fact, I have to go back to the days of *The Merry Widow* to find a musical show which has not choked me with its mock sentiment and genuine mindlessness welded to the consistency of dental putty. Such is the false impression left upon me by what Mrs. Amanda Ros would have described as maw-filling wads of nothingness. In the matter of what the cinema calls a musical I cannot remember that I have ever enthused. The reason, I think, has lain in the idiotic notion that the thing requires a plot, which means dialogue. If only the characters in a musical would dance and sing, and sing and dance, and never stop even for breath! For breath to them is fatal, since breath puts it in the power of their monkey brains to simulate human speech!

Turning up my old notebooks, I find that I wrote in February 1936:

> I last saw Miss Rogers in a film called *Roberta,* which—I strive to say it calmly and without excess of emphasis—bored me more than any public entertainment I have ever seen. You see, I have no

objection to cheerful, competent, neat-looking little chorus-girls. What I object to is the quality of glittering inanity which Miss Rogers took to herself in that film. Once bitten, twice shy, and I refrained from seeing *Top Hat* lest the spectacle should be repeated. *A fortiori*, I have declined to see *In Person*, which, I understand, is all about Miss Rogers, undiluted by Fred Astaire.

In the days of *Roberta*, Ginger Rogers was no more than a musical-omedy artist peeling the musical-comedy stuff off her arms and legs. But ought to have persisted and divined the genuine artist beneath the mere icker-up of heels, the woman of intelligence whose first step towards idding herself of the musical-comedy shackles and becoming a consider-ble actress was precisely that of cutting herself loose from that pathetic eetotum, that James Welch *manqué*, Fred Astaire. So much to explain my oathing of musical comedy on the stage, and the musical in the cinema.

It will be realised from the foregoing, and by the rarer sort of reader who ollows an argument instead of skipping it, that I addressed myself to *Down Argentine Way* (Regal), with misgivings strongly tinctured with ncipient nausea. For one thing, I dislike Technicolor in which all pinks esemble raspberry sauce, reds turn to sealing-wax, blues shriek of the washtub, and yellows become Yorkshire pudding. Again, I am not, alas, an admirer of Don Ameche, whose film heroes seem to me to reek of the barber's chair, though I can never decide whether they are sitters in it or standers behind. Miss Betty Grable? "Aren't you getting into deep waters?" said Miss Grable, looking into Don Ameche's hazel optics. Realising that the label for this kind of film heroine is "sans taste, plus eyes, plus teeth, plus everything," I felt like shouting No. For ten minutes I was comatose of mind and melancholy of spirit. Entertainment had died out of the world and, I felt, would never be born again. Was there hope in that question of a horse, the kind of animal that wins a race after tailing the field by ten lengths with a couple of furlongs to go? Perhaps. And then, to my agreeable surprise, the film began to be witty, largely in the person of an actor called Leonid Kinskey impersonating the more raffish sort of South American guide. The taxi-driver who takes him and his clients round the town is his brother-in-law, the head waiter at a dubious joint is his ex-brother-in-law, and it is their illicit commissions which prevent this top-hatted, kid-gloved scoundrel's sister from over-taxing her strength by taking in too much washing! Even on the race-track the precious fellow has a cousin and an uncle who will stoop to anything, and do. Here, then, was a character after the hearts of Maupassant and Damon Runyon, brothers under their highly different literary skins. "J'en chortle," said Stevenson of Mr. Shaw's Admirable Bashville. And at Mr. Kinskey I chortled my fill.

But that was not all. This character established, the picture began to go with a swing, gathering pace with the nods and becks of that overgrown poplar, Charlotte Greenwoud, the extravagances of that dynamic diseuse, Carmen Miranda—rather more Mérimée's heroine than Shakespeare's!—and the whirlwind tapdancing of the Nicholas Brothers. This last is something to give balletomanes pause. It is impossible, and its achievement brings forth applause rarely heard in the living theatre. Add some shots which are less crowd scenes than the canvases of a great master, some gay and delightful music, gathering verve, moving to a climax in which the horse referred to above wins by the neck his dishonest jockey has nearly dislocated in his effort to pull him and sell the race—and the result is a brilliant affair I could have sat through again then and there. I even got used to—in fact, I ended by revelling in—the colour. When the house is drowning itself in tears it is no good for the superior critic to say that the piece is not pathetic. Equally, when it is holding its sides it is useless for the supercilious fellow to pretend that the thing is not funny. The real difficulty occurs when the film cannot make up its mind whether its basis is light or shade.

In the theatre I have never believed in the genre known as comedy-thriller. I have never been able to see that you can laugh your head off and at the same time expect your hair to stand on end. In other words, I am an old fogey who believes that the first business of a work of art is to be consistent with itself. On the other hand, there are some films which do not pretend to be works of art, and perhaps *Trail of the Vigilantes* (Odeon) is one of them. Anyhow, this film, which has been described as a horse opera or cod Western, is extremely amusing provided you don't take your Westerns seriously, which I do. But even this did not obscure the great merit of a gloriously comic performance by Mischa Auer.

68

"LOVE ON THE DOLE"

1941

NEVER, in my writing life, have I known anybody make reference to a charming little book by Halévy called *Madame et Monsieur Cardinal*. These are the ultra-respectable parents of a fourteen-year-old ballet dancer whose job is to relieve the tedium of *Faust, Guillaume Tell*, and other masterpieces, and make an evening at the Opera tolerable for elderly gentlemen of depraved taste. Don't blame me, reader; I am recording, not inventing, the manners of Paris in the 'sixties.

Virginie having attained the age of fifteen, it happened one day that a millionaire who was a marquis but no gentleman made certain proposals detrimental to the honour of, but otherwise extremely favourable to, the Cardinal ménage. Up rose that outraged *père de famille*, Monsieur Cardinal. "I decline, Monsieur le Marquis, to permit discussion of such things in my house!" "But," objected the Marquis, "if Virginie and I are to be happy and I am to be allowed to contribute to the general Expenses . . . ." Monsieur Cardinal's wrath was terrible to behold. He rose from his chair, saying: "I do not understand the meaning of such language. It is not proper that I should understand it. Besides, I have an appointment at four o'clock which I am anxious not to miss. In the circumstances permit me, Monsieur le Marquis, to wish you not good day but au revoir." The reader has, of course, seen the point—that Halévy's anecdote is the Aristophanic or comic version of Walter Greenwood's Aristotelian or tragic story, now turned into a film, *Love on the Dole*. The novel was good, the play was excellent, and the film showing at the Odeon is half-way between the two.

So far as I can judge. . . . But hold on a bit. If I cannot judge of this film as a piece of photographic realism, who can? I was born within view of Hankey Park where the scene is laid. As an apprentice to the cotton trade I worked in my father's mill on a set of looms across the alley from those run by a lass quite as pretty as Deborah Kerr, and as the son of the boss I fancied myself along the lines of the Marquis in Halévy's story. The lass's name was Florrie . . . . But as Swinburne sings:

> You have forgotten my kisses,
> And I have forgotten your name.

For there were no kisses; ours was an eye flirtation. I was desperately shy —we never spoke, I never knew her surname and I certainly never kissed her. If I had known then what I think now! She pined, was sent away to the seaside and came back to marry a hefty young tackler (a foreman, or loom-supervisor). I ran across one of her sons a year or two ago. He was a blacksmith at Runcorn with a fine army record and six children. But all this is wandering from the point. What are the fruitless amours of an embryo film critic to the rabble? Or rather, to the distinguished readers doing him the honour of persual forty years later. The point is my single qualification, my unique ability to declare this film true or the reverse. (Miss Lejeune was born near Hankey Park but did not, I think, work in a mill.) Well, I pronounce the film to be as near the reality as the business of entertainment permits. Its chief faults are that Sally's mother (Mary Merrall) is too lady-like, a little too near Mrs. Micawber, and that Sally herself is not hard enough. Part of the brilliance, accidental or otherwise, of Wendy Hiller's performance in the stage play lay in the subtle implication that, despite Wordsworthian nonsense with the Labour agitator in the leafy purlieus of Boggart Hole Clough, she was of the fibre to support with some equanimity a fate worse than death. And the moralists in the audience had the satisfaction of believing that in a fortnight or so her protector would discover that betrayed innocence had turned his life into a far from merry hell. Deborah Kerr suggests nothing of this, and her performance is not within a mile of Wendy Hiller's. But it is a charming piece of work by a very pretty and promising beginner, so pretty and so promising that already there is the familiar yapping about "a new star." When I start my School for Film Critics the first lesson I shall strive to inculcate will be that no single play ever made an actress, with the possible exception of Mrs. Patrick Campbell, and that the reason a single film can make a star is that because while a star actress on the stage proper must shine in a whole galaxy of parts, the definition of a film star is any personable young woman who can goo-goo herself into success overnight. The best performance in the film comes from Geoffrey Hibbert as Sally's young brother. But surely a point is missed here? Both Harry's father and Harry's mother would have seen the lad in Halifax rather than take the bread out of their mouths to buy him a new suit to go courting in. The point is the emergence from boyhood's knickerbockers to manhood's long trousers—a budding process far more significant than the feminine change from wearing the hair down to putting it up, especially in these days when woman's only concern with her tresses is whether she shall have them tangerine, marmalade, red setter, or the golden variety of cocker spaniel. Hibbert's performance is excellent, though not so moving as Alex Grandison's in the stage play. I have never heard of Grandison since, and I warn young Hibbert that, if he is to become a real film actor, he will have to do a lot more than succeed in a part which plays itself. However, he has done very well for a beginning. There are first-class performances by Maire O'Neill, Marie Ault and two other actresses unidentifiable in the absence of a programme. George Carney and Clifford Evans do well, too. John Baxter has directed grandly, though I think he should have given us a shot of Sally at her work in the mill and coming home to tea with her hair all covered with cotton fluff. But perhaps times have changed since I ran four looms. Perhaps to-day's mill-hand wears some sort of contraption to protect her chevelure.

69

WINGS OVER AMERICA

1941

ABEL HERMANT, the witty critic of *Le Temps,* wrote a number of novels which he hoped might serve to reconstruct the history of our times. Future historians might do worse than consider the literary matter vouchsafed by the film companies of 1941. Paramount, for example, issues a broadsheet with reference to *I Wanted Wings,* the new picture now in flight at the Plaza and Carlton theatres. In this we read that Veronica Lake, "who is headed towards stardom with the speed of a rocket, weighs just ninety-eight pounds, but has the energy of an exploding bomb." Since she was born in Lake Placid, New York, she must have come to the surface with unprecedented splash. "When she accompanied a friend to a studio for a test, a director offered her a rôle, which she turned down because she had no acting experience." Gosh, likwise Golly! "Later, when she did get some, she returned with new confidence and the ambition to be a picture actress." Golly, likewise Gosh! Miss Lake is of the super-vamp type, modelling herself on the withdrawn exquisiteness of a Claire Luce, but compelled by the exigencies of the plot to turn herself into a Claire Lucifer. She croons, her eyes swim with desire, she wears flaxen tresses in the Garbo manner, and at the critical moment is to be found cluttering up the bomb-rack of a flying fortress.

I Wanted Wings would be a first-class picture if the directors had cut out (*a*) the women, (*b*) the aeroplanes. I frankly decline to believe that the air training of American pilots is conducted along such lines that cabaret singers can at will put spokes in their propellers. This film's story is sempiternal. The brave young pilot, Jeff Young, puts on a show of bravado which he by no means feels. As complement to him is Al Ludlow, who is a real coward, but nerves himself up to feats of valour beyond the capacity of his colleagues. And, of course, while Jeff is a howling cad, Al is a chevalier *avec beaucoup de peur mais sans aucune reproche.* Jeff gets himself into a mess with a blonde harridan who, having read Hardy's *Jude the Obscure,* brings off Arabella's old trick of pretending to be in trouble. Whereupon Al promptly marries the baggage, so that his pal can get his wings. It seems, and I do not believe it, that in the American Air Arm fatherhood outside marriage is a bar to a commission.

The late C. E. Montague summed up Al's type to perfection:

> This type, in its general lines, is that of the man who is not, as we say, a bad chap after all; the man who, again, is more wide-awake

than he seems; the man who may not have much gift of the gab, but is sure to come well through a scrimmage; the man who does not wear his heart on his sleeve, preferring to wear there a heart much less good than his own, so that when he turns out an unparalleled brick the cynical observer of human nature is knocked all of a heap; the man who, morally, is a regular lion of generosity, usually crouched, it is true, but quite prepared to do terrific springs of self-devotion if the occasion for them be sufficiently fantastic—mentally, too, a perfect mortar, or sunk mine of gumption, with a sluggish fuse to it, slow to take light, but going off at last in veritable prodigies of mother-wit and horse-sense and other forms of practical wisdom; the man who "has his faults," but still—well, if he drinks he is "nobody's enemy but his own," and at those next-morning hours when a nature radically bad would be ringing for soda-water, he is delighted to be shot or guillotined for the advantage of comparative strangers; he may not keep appointments, or pay his tailor, or do his work, and, of course, he is not a "plaster saint;" but then he "cannot bear to see a woman cry," and at any hour of the day or night he is game to adopt a baby, or soothe death-beds, or renounce, for reasons wildly insubstantial, the satisfaction of the cravings of his honest heart.

Now you are not to deduce from the foregoing that *I Wanted Wings* is a bad picture. It is not. It is a magnificent picture at all times when the women keep out of it. I say "women" because in this sort of drama there is always a good girl waiting, when the moment arrives, to clasp the shop-soiled hero to her milk-white bosom. I repeat that apart from feminine intrusion this picture is brilliant. The flying sequences are superb, and I was immensely thrilled in spite of the fact that a ten-minute flip at Peacehaven constitutes all I know or want to know of aerial navigation. Will the film ever grow up? I doubt it. Will it ever exceed the mentality of the fourth form? Again I doubt it. "He passes away under a cloud, inscrutable at heart, forgotten, unforgiven, and excessively romantic," was written of a greater coward than Jeff. This picture's hero passes away under Los Angeles skies, to be remembered ever, forgiven, and school-girlishly romantic. "He goes away from a living woman to celebrate his pitiless wedding with a shadowy ideal of conduct," wrote Conrad of Lord Jim. The film world knows this to be bosh. Jeff Young doubles, or rather trebles, the girl, the wedding, and a first-class certificate for conduct. In other words he scrapes through the court martial.

Ray Milland as Jeff gives a handsome performance, William Holden, Wayne Morris, and Brian Donlevy are superb, and the planes are even better. The girls, Veronica Lake and Constance Moore, are just in the way.

However, I recognise that in this matter I am fighting a lone battle. I realise that four-fifths of any cinema audience is feminine, and that to my fair readers the revolvings of the passion-impelled heart are of more importance than the revolutions of the petrol-driven engine. I have not the least doubt that to the feminine mind the flying parts of this film will seem an unwarrantable intrusion on more important matters.

70

CAN LITTLE ACTRESSES BE GREAT?

1941

IT is odd that the well-known sporting maxim—"A good big 'un will always beat a good little 'un"—should be unknown to the younger generation of theatre and film critics. It is absurd to think that a dozen of Tchehov's short stories are the equivalent of a novel like Tolstoi's *War and Peace;* they cannot be, because they necessarily lack architecture. St. Peter's at Rome is a greater achievement than the tiniest Trianon at Versailles, exquisite though that may be. More of mind and spirit goes to the fashioning of *King Lear* than to the loveliest of Shakespeare's lyrics. The little things do not demand the *longue haleine.* But it was left to connoisseurs of the race-course and the boxing-ring to lay down the law that, other things being equal, it is size that counts. Thinking over the great actresses of the past one is struck by a property common to them all—the property of not being little. They were not giantesses perhaps, but they could play Lady Macbeth. Consider the famous entry of Mrs. Siddons in Franklin's tragedy, *The Earl of Warwick.* At the back of the stage was a large archway, through which appeared the captive Marguerite of Anjou, preceded by four guards, who divided two by two on each side, leaving the opening clear. Instantly on their separating the actress burst upon the view and stood in the centre of the arch, motionless. "So electrifying was the unexpected impression," writes George Barclay, who played the King, "that I stood for a moment breathless. But the effect extended beyond me; the audience had full participation of its power; and the continued applause that followed gave me time to recover and speculate upon the manner in which such an extraordinary effect had been made. I could not but gaze upon her attentively. Her head was erect, and the fire of her brilliant eyes darted directly upon mine. Her wrists were bound with chains, which hung suspended from her arms, that were dropped loosely on each side; nor had she, on her entrance, used any action beyond her *rapid walk* and *sudden stop,* within the extensive archway, which she really *seemed to fill.*" Now consider any of the little actresses whom during the last ten years we old play-goers have been asked to accept as great. I put it to you, reader, that the impression they would produce would be not of filling an archway but of emptying it! The reason is a physical one, having nothing to do with talent. The impression of littleness is inescapable when the actresses conveying it are of key-hole size.

Given that the English stage has known a span some thirty times greater than the talkies, it follows that a life-size and fully-fledged actress like, say, Joan Crawford, is the film equivalent of Mrs. Siddons and almost as much out of fashion. To-day we are offered chits with big voices, and chits with no voices at all gambolling in *Rebecca,* playing at calf-love with Mickey Rooney, adolescence the theme, and the material pap. Now I will never agree to call a hillock a mountain, a pony a horse, or a fly-weight a heavy-weight. I will not call charming little girls great actresses on the strength of their having made a success of something written round their lack of experience as well as inches.

The trouble with our young critics is their inability to realise the harm they do. It is, of course, largely a matter of the age's vanity. To-day motor-cars, speed-boats, aeroplanes travel faster than ever before, and our young people just cannot bear to think that previous ages have excelled theirs in any respect whatsoever. It offends their vanity that to-day's actor possesses every quality except that of greatness. Even more so in the case of pretty little actresses, whose prettiness is a part of their littleness. When Miss Bergner came over here and exhibited her knees in a pathetic melodrama about a dead baby a young critic with a considerable following wrote: "She is of the stuff, I suspect, of the immortals—Mrs. Siddons, Rachel and Duse." That was six years ago, and what, pray, has this brilliant little actress in miniature since done to justify the grandiose argument?

The same preposterous claim was made for Miss Barbara Mullen, a little Irish girl with a talent for portraying the homelier kind of Scotch lassie. *Jeannie,* the play in which she flabbergasted junior reporters, is the intellectual and emotional equivalent of *Sweet Lavender,* and to hail an actress as great on the strength of Pinero's waifery-and-strayage was just not done in the days of my critical apprenticeship. We knew how to wait. Miss Mullen does a little thing charmingly, but she has still to prove that she can play anything except the pawkier heroines of Sir James Barrie or, what is perhaps worse, of that almost forgotten novelist, George Macdonald. Hear now the whole crux of the matter. People ask me why I have "got my knife" into this or that young actress. I haven't. I am out scalping for the immature critics who cannot see a gooseberry without hailing it as a giant. The picture itself (Leicester Square) is mildly pleasant, and throughout one has an equal urge to stay in the cinema and depart therefrom. First, Mr. Albert Lieven, who plays the bogus Viennese count, steals the film from Miss Mullen. Then Mr. Michael Redgrave steals it from Mr. Lieven, and finally Miss Kay Hammond purloins it from under the noses of all three. And now, perhaps, if Miss Mullen is the great actress we have been led to suppose, will she kindly give us a glimpse of her Rosalind, Cordelia, Lady Teazle, Nora, Hedda, and so on? The choice is wide enough, and a great actress will impose her own parts. Stage and screen wait, and so do I.

71

LET US MEANDER

1941

THOUSANDS of years ago there was a district in Asia Minor called Phrygia, and in it there was a river named Meander. It is, of course, possible that the country and the river are still there. This river declined to keep straight on and indulged in innumerable twists and turnings. From it we derive the English word "meander." Coleridge set his sacred River Alph "meandering with a mazy motion." Then a very bad poet, one Robert Montgomery, got hold of the word and talked of streams "meandering level with their fount." Whereupon the great Macaulay sourly observed that "no stream meanders, or can possibly meander, level with its fount." I don't remember any further use of the word in literature until we come to *David Copperfield*, on the second page of which an old lady objects to mariners who have the impiety and presumption to go "meandering" about the world. "Let us have no meandering!" was her phrase. As a film critic I am inclined to say "Let us have meandering" because.... Well, because it is, or may be, a way of not giving offence. And sometimes, dear reader, somebody produces a film to which the critic particularly wants not to be rude. In that case, says the logical reader, why not choose another film to write about? To which the answer is that that might involve being ruder.

Turning over Oscar Wilde's *Intentions* the other day I came across the following:

> Criticism is no more to be judged by any low standard of imitation or resemblance than is the work of poet or sculptor. The critic occupies the same relation to the work of art that he criticises as the artist does to the visible world of form and colour, or the unseen world of passion and of thought. He does not even require for the perfection of his art the finest materials. Anything will suit his purpose. And just as out of the

sordid and sentimental amours of the silly wife of a small country doctor in the squalid village of Yonville-l'Abbaye, near Rouen, Gustave Flaubert was able to create a classic, and make a masterpiece of style, so, from subjects of little or no importance, such as the pictures in this year's Royal Academy, or in any year's Royal Academy for that matter, Mr. Lewis Morris's poems, M. Ohnet's novels, or the plays of Mr. Henry Arthur Jones, the true critic can, if it be his pleasure so to direct or waste his faculty of contemplation, produce work that will be flawless in beauty and instinct with intellectual subtlety.

Why not? To an artist so creative as the critic, what does subject-matter signify?

In other words I am this week to build a masterpiece of criticism upon the film at the Leicester Square Theatre entitled *Forty Thousand Horsemen.* It just can't be done, since the orientation of that masterpiece, even if one could achieve it, must be towards rudeness. Rather would one err in the direction of courtesy and lenience towards this first full-length Australian film, which was preceded by a luncheon of as much magnificence as consorts with the times. There was Australian burgundy, while for those of weaker stomach there was, as the girl in the Southend wine shop said: "A French wine of similar type." There were eminent gentlemen to address us. And here, let me give a hint to all eminent speechifiers addressing a purely journalistic gathering. This is to make it snappy. It is unnecessary to tell a journalist anything twice: he has got it down before you have finished saying it once. Being himself an adept at compression—if he were not he would not keep his job—he resents repetition. I once asked a famous K.C. why Marshall Hall, to whom I had been listening that day, made every point four times. He said: "We all do it, and Marshall is no exception. The first time you say a thing the average juryman doesn't know you're talking. The second time he knows somebody is talking. The third time he discovers you are talking to him. At the fourth repetition he realises what you, Counsel, are saying to him, Juryman. "But film critics are a jury of different calibre. Will all eminent speechifiers remember this in future?

The intention behind *Forty Thousand Horsemen* was to show us the extraordinary bravery of the Australian Cavalry during the last war. And thus to enable us to understand the gallantry and dash of their sons, now the mechanised units of the Libyan Desert. Once more I open the little book called *Intentions* and I read: "I said to you some time ago that it was far more difficult to talk about a thing than to do it." That, of course, was the bosh of the period. It is, and always was, much easier to write beautifully about, say, a sewing machine than to make one. Old Man Hugo couldn't have mown two inches of a field of hay without amputating both feet. Whereas he could write:

> Quel dieu, quel moissonneur de l'éternel été
> Avait, en s'en allant, négligemment jeté
> Cette faucille d'or dans le champ des étoiles,

without mulcting his verse of a syllable.

Anybody can talk nobly about a film aspiring to embody Australian gallantry. The difficulty is when the aspiration stops and the actual job starts. In the Leicester Square picture the men were there, and the horses were there. What was wanted was a scenario-writer of talent and a director of something more than talent.

What we finally saw was a weak version of *Beau Geste* with a dreadful love story about a girl of seventeen who cuts her hair short and is immediately mistaken for a boy by the entire cavalry brigade. Did these bush-rangers come, then, from a bush so excessively out of range that they had never seen a girl before? Didn't they know that no girl can run without knocking her knees and slapping her tummy? Do you remember, reader, the last sentence in Olive Schreiner's *Story of an African Farm*? "But the chickens were wiser." In this film the horses and even the camels were wiser.

72

A NOTE ON REALISM

1941

WHAT an odd thing is realism in art! Put a real horse on the stage, and the two-legged actors are at once annihilated. In the old melodrama called *The Lyons Mail* there was a scene in which Irving used to rifle the pockets of the dead post-boy, tumbled from the post-chaise drawn by a sorry nag whose quarters alone were visible, the rest being hidden in the wings. And I remember how it took all the power of a really great actor to vie with the actuality of those hocks. As against this I remember the back-drop to some forgotten Russian ballet, where the artist had sought to show a gay spark driving a gig in the Bois de Boulogne. The reins finished in mid-air somewhere in the neighbourhood of the horse's withers, and reached to no bit, for the reason that there was no bit in the animal's mouth to reach to. There were no traces, which meant that the gig could not have been drawn; even if it could it must have collapsed, since there was no axle-tree to keep the wheels together. Yet one accepted the design as wholly adequate; here was a swell driving a gig in the Bois de Boulogne.

That it is acceptance and not reality that matters, was a late discovery in the English theatre which had gloried for too long in Tom Robertson's real doors and real mantelpieces. Some of us can remember the mountains of salt pretending to be snow in which Irving fought that duel in *The Corsican Brothers*, and it is within comparatively modern recollection how, on the first night of *The Garden of Allah*, people sitting in the front rows of the stalls were almost blinded by the real sand of that desert storm. All that was the wrong kind of realism. But there is a right kind. The very existence of the light comedy has always been staked upon the weather being fine. You know the kind of thing I mean. The curtain goes up to reveal Lady Marshmallow's chintz-covered drawing-room. This is surrounded by french windows to enable the sunlight to pour into the room from at least three sides. Through the window R. those in the theatre seated L. have a view of the Wold of Surrey as far as Box Hill. Through the window L. those seated R. can see the Weald of Sussex rhododendron-clumped as far as Chanctonbury Ring. Through the centre windows, for the benefit of those seated C., the Forest of Savernake hotly shimmers. Enter Dame Marie Tempest twirling a parasol. I remember the surprise and delight with which I saw the curtain rise on the second act of Dorothy Massingham's play, *The Lake*. The scene was a marquee, and the occasion the wedding of the heroine. The day, it seemed, had turned out wet, and the guests arrived looking like bedraggled birds of paradise. This was better than realism; it was immense fun. It was fun to see how popular actresses look when they are not being photographed and must, like their more ordinary sisters, contend with the rigour of an English summer. But this piece of right-minded realism was an exception, and the English theatre still remained a place where falls not hail, or rain, or any snow.

Enfin Hollywood vint; and the point about the whole art of the cinema was seen to be its adherence to reality. By some stroke of divination Hollywood perceived that in a medium where all was photographic, no actor could look so much like, say, a taxi-driver as a man who earned his living driving a taxi. As for the décor, no trouble and no expense was too great. Millions of dollars were spent in arranging that the furniture and plate at a banquet of the Borgias should be exact replicas of the properties used by that agreeable family. Must the scene take place at the North Pole, then Hollywood would equip an expedition for the purpose of recording something for which an artist would have used the local golf course and some tons of cotton wool. And the rainstorms! Never has there been such rain as that with which the windscreen-wipers of Hollywood have contended.

And then Hollywood's realism began to weaken. Young ladies whom we had seen soaked to the skin one minute would appear in bone-dry organdie the next. A frail heroine would emerge from the jungle after a life-and-death struggle with a gorilla looking as if she had just come out of a beauty parlour. The explanation, of course, is that the average feminine film-goer cares everything for frocks and nothing for feasibility. Then came that picture, or series of pictures, in which a young woman is gifted with a Voice, and, emerging from the Middle West, at five minutes' notice and without rehearsal goes on for Violetta at the Metropolitan Opera House. The reason, again, is that the public, impassioned for its Grace Moores, Jeannette Macdonalds and Deanna Durbins, prefers the triumph of its singing heroines to the reflection that untrained young women don't achieve such things.

Irene Dunne, the heroine of *Unfinished Business* (Leicester Square), hailed from a small town in Ohio, and her ambition in life was to go places and do things. Arrived in New York she got a situation at a telephone exchange, and her first job, if you please, was to sing a birthday greeting through the telephone to the owner of a smart night-club called the Koh-i-noor. It seemed that she had a Voice. Whereby she was taken on at the night-club, and to the tune of "Ta-ra-ra-boom-de-ay" (the verse, not the chorus) warbled to customers calling up:

> This is New York six-o-four,
> You're speaking to the Koh-i-noor.

Like a musical TIM. Presently she married Robert Montgomery, to efface the memory of Preston Foster whom she really loved. Going out of Robert's life, she was brought in again when he went to the opera and saw her on the stage not as prima donna but as a humble member of the chorus. *Salut au Monde*, yawped Walt Whitman; I emit the same barbaric noise and salute Hollywood for having realised that it is only a very exceptional telephone-operator who has enough talent to get into the chorus. And now, please, may we have that film about the aspirant for film honours who, turned down by Hollywood, hasn't got what it takes to peel them off the arm?

73

THREE GOOD FILMS

1941

WHAT is a good film? I think that one of the ways to answer this question is to transpose it and ask: What is a good picture? Meaning the thing which is painted by hand and hangs on a wall. It is a good picture if, all things considered, you prefer it to the bare wall. "But," say you, being argumentative, "even a bad picture may be better than empty space." Exactly, my dear sir—in that sense the bad picture becomes a good picture. So it is with films. Would I rather go on watching a film than emerge into a December fog, trudge through the rain to my club, and yawn while retired gynæcologists swap stories older than the Womb of Time? In that case the film is a good one.

Let me apply this rule to three films I saw on one day last week. The first one was called *Suspicion* (Odeon), and I strongly suspect that this film is good enough absolutely. It asks us to imagine that Cary Grant is a charming and well-bred English ne'er-do-well moving in good society. Whereas he isn't anything of the kind; his shoulders have the American campus written all over them, and his manners have obviously been learnt in some Palais de Danse. Also he says "fix" when he means "arrange." However, he is likeable enough for us to take him at the film-director's valuation, and as I have said so often, a film has got to be got going somehow. Cary falls in love with Joan Fontaine, who is the daughter of General Sir Cedric Hardwicke and Dame May Whitty. These three characters are authentic with the exception of two very small matters. One is that even to-day young women brought up as ladies do not receive telegrams in the presence of their mothers without revealing their contents. The other is that an English girl, speaking on the telephone, does not use the phrase "thank you for calling me," when she means "thank you for ringing me up." A trifling fee of, say, £5,000 would put any Hollywood director wise on these tiny points. But Mr. Alfred Hitchcock is not a Hollywood director but an English director who happens to be in Hollywood. Which just shows how Hollywood's communications corrupt English manners. Apart from these minute slips the film is admirable. It has plenty of deftly-arranged suspense. Cary has embezzled £2,000 which he must repay or go to jail. And we will skate over the fact that our English embezzlees are not normally satisfied with restitution and an apology. How is he going to get the money? By killing that most genial of murderees, Nigel Bruce? By poisoning Joan, now his wife, whose insurance money should yield him the necessary packet? We see him fiddling about with a glass of milk. What does this mean? The reader who sees this film will thank me for not telling him what happens.

If Joan Fontaine does not presently attain real stardom, this is because she looks, behaves and dresses like that extraordinarily unfashionable thing, a lady. And by that I mean the properly nurtured daughter of gentlefolk. Whether her unspoiled looks, natural charm and very considerable acting abilities will compensate for the absence of lacquered nails, smeared mouth, and all the dreary messes of the beauty parlour, the public must decide. I have often heard other critics talk of the Hitchcock Touch, and wondered what they meant by it. There is a moment in this picture when detectives call on Joan, and one of them cannot take his eyes from a modernist painting which Mr. Hitchcock has thoughtfully hung in the Grant-Fontaine lounge hall. The interview concluded, the young split lags behind for yet another look at this, to him, riddle-cum-abortion. If this is a specimen of the famous Touch—and it is very amusing—then I forgive this clever director for the tiny lapses referred to above.

I can never resist bosh if it is delirious enough. *Sundown* (Gaumont) is a story of adventure in a far-flung post of Empire, where the only industry appears to be gun-running. The plot is a strange mixture of *Sanders of the River* and Rider Haggard's *She*. The enchantress in question is a heavily-lidded desert-rose in whose veins runs the blood, it ultimately turns out, not of the Abyssinian Border but of Surbiton's herbaceous ditto. She was kidnapped at the age of two, poor darling, and her name is not Zia but, one guesses, Ethel. In the end a gallant major, well played by George Sanders, dies saying to his friend: "My dear fellow, the time has now come when I must tell you that I am the son of a bishop. Hang on to two things, old boy, the Church and the Army. Together they will save England." At this point we hear the yodelling of the Metro-Goldwyn-Meyerbeer Choir, presumably borrowed for the occasion. The scene changes to London where, in a roofless cathedral rather larger than St. Paul's, Bishop Cedric Hardwicke tells the congregation that there is a corner of a field in Somaliland which is for ever England. Whereupon the critics assembled for this trade show made melancholy but unerring bee-lines for the buffet.

The third picture was *Moon Over Miami* (Odeon), one minute of which, showing a female garage hand servicing a car with song and dance, drove me into the street. And there, queuing up in the wet and the fog, I saw scores of people who had obviously done an even harder day's work than I had, and were looking for that relaxation of which I had just had too much. It is here that the relativity of picture-judging comes in. These young people were obviously going to enjoy holding hands in the peach-coloured darkness and feeling the waves of Technicolor flow over them. And I realise that film critics are not the persons to judge of pictures like this. Only very, very rarely are we to be seen holding each other's hands.

74

WHY MUST THEY HAVE ACTORS?

194

IN 1937, on my one and only visit to New York, I fell in with that butterfly of criticism, George Jean Nathan. It occurs to me that the following entry in my diary may be of some interest:

> George Jean Nathan called to take me out for cocktails. As I do not want to drink too much—for what little drink there is in America is immensely potent—I order tea and crumpets, and get some very poor tea and very mean crumpets. The place is expensive, and I note one or two film stars who look exactly like white toy poms. They are accompanied, and obviously of the highest respectability, though only Peter Arno could do justice to their utter inability to open their mouths, and, when they do, to produce anything resembling human speech.

A little later this entry occurs:

> Nathan called this afternoon to take me to tea with Lillian Gish. She came into the room looking exactly as she did in *Way Down East*. A sad, pinched little face, with woebegone eyes looking out from under a hat like a squashed Chinese pagoda. A trim, tiny figure very plainly dressed; the whole apparition strangely reminiscent of Vesta Tilley. Since she left films she has played Shakespeare, Tchehov, and Dumas fils: "I came from the theatre, and I am glad to go back to it." Nathan has a theory that acting has nothing to do with the film or the film with acting, and that the proper function of the screen is to exploit the exuberant vitality of the Robert Taylors and Loretta Youngs, and discard all players as soon as they cease to exuberate. He thinks Lillian was the last screen actress.

I do not believe this. Bette Davis is a good film actress, and whether she can act on the stage is not the point. Nor do I believe, as I have been jealously told, that Davis is only a good actress because of the skill with which her directors push her about, and the virtuosity with which she is photographed after being pushed about.

I know some English film stars who, if they were prodded till they were blue in the back and their directors black in the face, would still not get as far as being bad actresses. There are film stars in this country who, if they were stood on their heads and shot by a photographer hanging by his toes from a trapeze, would still not be actresses at all. Either you can play golf or you can't, and no amount of coaching will turn a non-golfer into a golfer. Either you can act or you can't, and that is all there is to be said about acting.

At the same time, Nathan hit the nail somewhere near the head when he hinted that the function of the cinema is to purvey realism rather than art. From the earliest theatrical times of which we in this country have any record, the whole trend of the movement for the popularisation of the drama has been to get further away from imagination and draw nearer to reality. In the Elizabethan days the spectator imagined everything—the dramatist merely had to say "A Wood" or "A Market Place," and so it became. Some centuries passed, and then Tom Robertson arrived with his real doors, real door-knobs, real mantelpieces and real overmantels. After him came the Shakespeare producers with their massive and cumbrous sets, matting to represent grass, real running water and fairies that pretended to fly. And all the time the great British public, while learning to use its eyes, was forgetting how to use its ears. Then came the silent cinema, and with it the apotheosis of the goggle-eyed gaze and the atrophy of the ear. Whether the spoken film and the wireless will undo the mischief I don't know, though I must doubt it. To begin with, the language spoken on the Hollywood screen is the flattest that has ever emanated from the mind and tongue of man. Whatever the film, the dialogue is mostly an abysmal concatenation. "What's on your mind, sister?" "Baby, you've got me wrong!" "Boy, you sure said it." It is not an exaggeration to claim that the average Hollywood film gets along with fewer words than were known to an English agricultural labourer in the time of William the Conqueror. But that is by the way. I go back to my original proposition, which has this rider: that the average audience will tolerate ear-interruption but not anything that breaks in on eye-absorption. In the theatre the other evening Mr. Wolfit's soliloquies in *Hamlet*, spoken in a voice of great resonance, were interrupted by coughs throughout. Next day, in similar weather, I saw a film in which during the more exciting sequences of action, there being little or no dialogue to listen to, the house was dead still. Allied to this is the well-known fact, that while stage audiences are always fidgety, cinema audiences are invariably well behaved. Which again makes my case, meaning that in the opinion of the audience what is being said, but not what is being seen, can be safely interrupted.

Nathan's view of the nature of the film was strongly borne in upon me at the showing of *The Sea Wolf* (Warner's). This turned out to be an admirable picture, though a little divided against itself. It tried to combine the old familiar yarn about piratical blood ships with the psychological drama of the sea-captain who is a monster one minute and reads Milton the next. The film, however, did pretty well with two contending worlds, and there were two or three sequences in which the dialogue was entirely respectworthy. But I was sorry not to see those two hundred lashes in Technicolor.

On the other hand—and this is more or less Nathan's point—I felt as I watched this film that it would have been better art if the artists employed had been less good. I couldn't help reflecting that here in the parts of the captain, the drunken doctor, and the kidnapped novelist were those three excellent players, Edward G. Robinson, Gene Lockhart and Alexander Knox, and comparing their present assumptions with other metamorphoses.

Quickly the percipient reader says: "Must you not do this in the theatre and do you mind?" The answer is that in the theatre everything is on the plane of make-believe, which includes the actors, whereas in the cinema the plane is that of the real—the ship is real, floating on a real sea in real weather. The fog effects in this film are tremendous.

What then have we to do with people who are *acting*, in other words playing at being real? The ideal thing would have been a captain, doctor, and author we had never seen before and should never see again! Much more could be written on this subject, but my space is at an end.

75

HELL AND HOLLYWOOD

1942

WHAT would you do, reader, if the Devil offered you seven years of riches and power in return for the eternal custody of your soul? The first thing I should do would be to bargain for ten years on the principle laid down by Mrs. Erlynne in Wilde's *Lady Windermere's Fan* that "margin is everything." Marlowe's Mephistophiles allowed Faustus *twenty-four* years of fun. About Goethe's allowance I don't remember, even if I ever knew. That I shall ever know is improbable. As a boy I was forced to read *Wilhelm Meister*, which masterpiece, far duller than anything my friend Charles Morgan has conceived at his most spiritual, closed Goethe to me for ever.

And this brings us back to our question. What, reader, would you do with seven years of unlimited opportunity? It depends, of course, who you are.

Now Marlowe's Faustus was a German; it was therefore natural that his first wish should be for a Frau to keep house for him. But then, think of his second, third and fourth demands. These were for three books. The first a book of "spells and incantations" for the raising of spirits, the second a volume in which to read the "characters and planets of the heavens," the third a tome in which to see "all plants, herbs and trees that grow upon the earth." These three wishes seem to me to be singularly futile. Refraining from the easy joke, I confess that I am not anxious to raise any spirits except my own. I am no star-gazer. I have already learned all that I want to know, and perhaps more, about vegetation, from Mr. Middleton.

Among the mentionable things I should proceed to do would be the following:

1. Flout my friend Keith Douglas and, double-crossing Sir Henry Wood and the public-spirited B.B.C., engage the Philharmonic Orchestra and hire the Albert Hall for seven years for the sole purpose of vetoing, prohibiting and tabooing any performance of the Tschaikowsky Violin Concerto, the Rachmaninoff Second Piano Concerto, Wotan's Farewell, Elizabeth's Greeting, Bizet's Symphony, any Hungarian Rhapsody, and all British music since Elgar except Walton's *Façade.*

2. Fly to Hollywood for the purpose of seeing whether that Mecca of the manicurist and the mannequin is as hopelessly vulgar, silly, and subnormal as I take it to be.

3. In the absence of a third wish I should take the Albert Hall, posthumously, for a further three years.

The foregoing is intended as a preamble to the announcement that in *All that Money Can Buy* (Regal) Hollywood has boldly ventured into something which is neither vulgar nor silly. It has tackled the Faust legend and, for once in a way, it has tackled a serious subject intelligently. One of the rules of criticism—which, by the way, too few critics know—is that in writing about the abstruse and obscure you must take care that your writing is straightforward and simple. Whereas when your subject is plain and clear Meredith cannot be too subtle or Henry James too involved. I reel when I think of what Mr. Orson Welles would have done with the Faust legend. The world still debates whether the contraption called Rosebud in *Citizen Kane* was actual or symbolic. And I can quite imagine Mr. Welles trying to persuade me that while the soul is material the body is metaphysical. William Dieterle, the director of this film, falls into no such error. Realising that he must sell fantasy to the audiences of Minneapolis and Runcorn, Pittsburg and Huddersfield, he takes care that that fantasy shall be rather plainer than a pikestaff.

Jabez Stone (James Craig) is a young New Hampshire farmer living a hundred years ago. He is hard up and must sell next year's seed to pay off the mortgage on the farm. And, of course, to sell seed is to a farmer as abhorrent as it would be for a writer to part with his ideas. It and they are the germ of the future. And then the Devil appears. He looks like an old tramp, but we know it is the Devil because he appears in a blue haze—blessedly this picture is *not* in Technicolor—and because when he wants to light his cigar he summons lightning from the atmosphere. It should be said at this point that this Devil is a cheery, comic, mediæval fellow, thus keeping us unpretentiously in touch with what other times have thought about the Prince of Darkness. Even Goethe—since books which one has resolutely closed have a habit of opening of themselves—had the sense to make Mephistophiles witty, amusing and even something of a buffoon. Mr. Walter Huston's Devil is a really brilliant performance. This clever actor makes the fellow at once likeable and loathsome—a droll combination of pure logic and stark unreason, the sort of character that might have evolved if Barrie and Sheridan le Fanu had put their heads together. Since he is a farmer the young man's notions of power are purely bucolic. He must have the biggest farm and the biggest house. And the Devil takes care that in the new housemaid (Simone Simon) he shall have a mistress as alluring as Helen of Troy would have been had she known about Parisian *chic*. I think perhaps that the house is a mistake. The outside looks just the sort of thing a New Hampshire farmer would have thought fine a hundred years ago. It is just an outsize shack. The inside, alas, is Hollywood at its most stupefying. Hang it, there were not so many chandeliers in all New York.

Over against this Devil is set the great figure of Daniel Webster, the famous lawyer-politician, whose job it is to wrestle for the soul of Jabez. That fine actor Edward Arnold puts his back, his eyebrows and all the resources of his art into the tremendously unequal struggle. He contests the validity of the bond, demands that the case be tried by a jury. The Devil agrees, and produces from the nether regions a collection of traitors, renegades and murderers famous in American history. For a long time it is Pull Devil—Pull Webster. But the jury has its sentimental side. Its members admit that they too would have welcomed a second chance. And, of course, Jabez is returned to wife and kiddie and the free American air.

This is not quite the end, the clever director keeping sentiment in its place and preferring to wind up in the key of comedy. The final shot shows the Tramp crossing Jabez off his books as a loss, and turning up his private directory for the names of the next candidate for damnation. And the searching finger points, dear reader, at YOU.

76

PAULETTE, CLAUDETTE, MARLENE

1942

ACCORDING to the informative, not to say garrulous, programme circulated at the Press show, *Reap the Wild Wind* (Plaza)

"deals with America's fight to whip a little island empire of pirate wreckers who ruled the stategic Florida keys a century ago. That was before the railroad era, when the sea route upon which these wreckers preyed was the lifeline of the nation, linking the rich Mississippi Valley with industrial New England. The period is 1840, and the story has a curiously pointed bearing upon history now in the making. It tells of the freedom of the seas, of ships and storms and the salvage trade, of men and women. It moves from Charleston, the elegant, to Key West, palm-fanned and polyglot capital of the Florida keys, laden with the loot of a thousand wrecks; from there to sea, under sail; finally down to the coral-decked sea floor. The picture takes its title from the business of salvage masters, who, fighting hurricanes to save lives and cargoes from wrecked ships, literally reap their harvest from the wild wind."

Actually the film is all about Paulette Goddard, which is very nice for (*a*) P.G., and (*b*) P.G.'s fans. What a busy girl is Paulette, and how she enjoys taking the centre of the stage, and drawing attention to herself, and giving herself airs, and generally behaving, doubtless in strict accordance with the director's instructions, like an upper housemaid who can't decide between the footman and the second chauffeur. Is the date 1840? Yes, but the mincings and floutings, the head-tossing and hoity-toitings are immune from period restriction. Paulette, in this film, takes part in a fight with a murderous lot of sailors, dismantles a schooner's rigging with a hatchet, is spanked and thrown overboard, and never stops talking in that unmelodious voice of which she alone never tires. There came a moment when it seemed likely that the two men who were tearing themselves in half for her—actually she was tearing herself in two for one of them—that Ray Milland and John Wayne would be shanghai'ed on to a whaler, which seemed to offer respite from Miss Goddard. But we had reckoned without Cecil B. De Mille, whose production this is, and who apparently holds that any foot of celluloid that is not devoted to Paulette's beck, nod, smile, or little finger is a foot wasted. If you happen to like Paulette you will, of course, like this film very much. You may, however, resent the end where a giant squid, which is an octopus only more so, steals the picture from Paulette.

Reap the Wild Wind is in Technicolor, and also, I submit, in Techninoise—which means too much of both colour and noise. It may be that in a storm at sea you can't make yourself heard. But why shout so loud that, *in the cinema,* nobody can hear a word you say? I found the first ten minutes of this picture quite unbearable. And why engage to play rival rôles two film actors as much alike as Milland and Payne? From beginning to end I never knew whether the young man for whom Paulette was doing her stuff was the rough diamond who loved her or the husky she loved.

A complete contrast is *Remember the Day* (Odeon) which is sloppily sentimental throughout. This is a film in which every one is in love; a young schoolmaster and schoolmistress with each other, a little boy with the schoolmistress, and a little girl with the little boy. The period is that of the last war, and we see the lovers parted and the husband killed in action. Then the widow grows older, goes on teaching and takes to spectacles. Later, somewhere near our own time, she hears that the little boy who once adored her is now become a great man, yea, is in the running for nothing less than the Presidency of the United States. I must confess that the orgy of sentiment having by this time worn a little thin, I thought this dazzling climax to the little boy's career a bit thick; but it served the purpose of reintroducing him as a tall handsome man with, of course, a beauteous wife. In fact, the little girl grown up. For the cinema, though not in the strictest sense Darwinian, yet believes in the survival of the fittest.

For those who like what is popularly known as "a good cry" this hour and-a-half of undiluted sob-stuff will please; though I cannot quite subscribe to the ecstatic yawps on the programme describing this harmless little love story as one "destined to be one of the screen's greatest dramas" and "a picture of such depth, such feeling, such wide emotional scope that it cannot fail to have universal audience appeal." But the acting is excellent. Once again Claudette Colbert is her clever, witty and typically Parisian self: indeed, there are moments in this film when she reminds one of any French actress and thus gives us a glimmer of that distinction, at once so brittle and so elegant, which is characteristic of the France that was and will be again. The boy is admirably portrayed by Master Douglas Craft, who has the toughness and some of the charm of the earlier Mickey Rooney. It is a pity these clever children grow up: Peter Pan ought to have told us how to prevent it.

Man Power (Warner) is a re-statement of that old thing about the pure-minded café-singer, in a clip-joint, who falls for the sentimental, chivalrous, middle-aged man who wants to make a good girl of her, but falls in a prosaic and strictly sensible way. In a year or two there will be nothing before her except the streets or the water-side brothel; she gives herself in exchange for security, not happiness. But then, of course, she falls in love, and who should the man be but her husband's best friend? But the young woman's natural decency being postulated, it follows that we are in for a hell of an emotional disturbance—the new passion and the desire to give the husband a square deal. As old as the hills? Probably. And certainly as old as that good play, *They Knew What They Wanted.*

In a film of this sort the point is not the plot but the actors. Hollywood is full of noodles and ninnies who would have made this well-worn stuff utterly boring. Not so Edward G. Robinson (good) and George Raft (better), whose performances have that kind of compulsion which makes you think that you are seeing them for the first time. Marlene is the third in this admirable trio, and with an extraordinary sense of theatre—or film—she is content to play her rôle at half-cock, as it were. The part is that of a rather dull draggle-tail, and Marlene is content to give it just as much glamour as it will stand and no more. What a good actress! The story is set amid the telegraph poles and wires of California, which permits of an ending Zolaesque in its realism and brutality.

77

THE ANSWER IS: YES, MR. LUBITSCH!

1942

FOR years the film critics have amazed me by claiming to tell by looking at a film who has directed the picture. This had always seemed to me to be as fantastic as to claim that if at a classical concert you were to put a screen round the conductor you would know who is wagging the stick. On Wednesday last, Mr. Moiseiwitsch, taking one bite at three cherries, performed Beethoven's Concertos Nos. 3, 4 and 5, the conductors being Mr. Basil Cameron, Mr. Keith Douglas, and Sir Adrian Boult. If any musical critic is going to step forward and say that blindfolded he could have told which conductor was conducting which concerto I just wouldn't believe him. I also believe that if Mr. Moiseiwitsch had been indisposed and his place taken by Pouishnoff, Miss Myra Hess, and Mr. Clifford Curzon, none of the critics, blindfolded, would have been any the wiser.

However, I may be wrong. There was a time when I knew a René Clair picture, because the houses slanted and bowed to one another across the street. Now that Clair has given this up and his buildings have returned to the perpendicular, there is no reason why I should be able to tell his picture from anybody else's. On the other hand I think I might tell an Orson Welles's picture. At least whenever I see a shot which may be (*a*) a piece of buttered teacake, or (*b*) a tramcar, or (*c*) a picturisation of the heroine's soul-state—why then I shall confidently diagnose this master. And I begin to think it possible to recognise the work of Ernst Lubitsch. Why? Because it is witty. But with this qualification, that I shall only be able to distinguish the witty Lubitsch from the unwitty others so long as the others remain unwitty.

That *To Be or Not To Be* (Gaumont) is witty is incontestable. And by gosh, it had to be. At the beginning of the picture I was a little worried about the propriety of using the agony of Warsaw as a background for farce. But we see almost nothing of the agony, and there is a great deal of very amusing farce. And I am not ashamed to say that this film offends my sense of the proprieties far less than most films using the war as a background for heavy emotionalism. Lubitsch's wit is at any rate first-rate of its kind, while most of the emotionalism paraded in our war films contrives to be both laboured and catchpenny.

The film had to be witty to obtain our consent to a number of incredible things, which if the wit had ever ceased, we should never have believed. We should not have believed, for instance, that those typical flowers of Hollywood, Jack Benny and Carole Lombard, were Poles. That the Gestapo is so loosely conducted that an actor can wander about bamboozling authority and impersonating at will a Nazi spy and a Gestapo chief familiar to every one. The art of farce does not consist in plunging your characters into monstrous predicaments from which no ingenuity can extricate them. The art of farce consists in the ingenuity with which the farce-maker is able to get his characters out of situations from which, without that ingenuity, they could not be extricated. In the wildest farces of Labiche—incidentally the best farces ever written—it is just possible to believe that this husband did in such and such manner hoodwink that wife. And the art of the master is shown when the successful extrication from one scrape merely serves to plunge the hero into another. Judged by this standard *To Be or Not To Be* is a failure. But it is a failure redeemed by somebody's, and presumably Lubitsch's, wit. Jack Benny as the ham actor asks the Gestapo chief whether he has ever seen Tura, the great Polish tragedian. "Haf I not?" says the Nazi. "And vot he did to Shakespeare, ve Germans are doing to Poland!" This brought the house down. There is a charming performance by Carole Lombard, which is, alas, the last we shall have from this gifted player. The Nazis are superbly played, and part of German punishment after the war might consist in forcing the Germans to see films like this which expose the modern German spirit in all its bestial absurdity.

The Lubitsch film, though based on an indiscretion, is undoubtedly a work of art. *One Foot in Heaven* (Warner), based on the simple-minded message of Joseph, Silas and any other Hocking, is a work of just nothing at all. It tells how a Methodist parson makes headway against the greed, scandal-mongering, and all the petty vices of a one-horse American town. How he succeeds and gets a little older, how he succeeds some more and gets a little older still. How, one day, he gets rid of the preposterous and wheezy choir of antiquated beldams and puffed-up churls and replaces them by the children who, unknown to their parents, have been rehearsing Humperdinck's *Hansel and Gretel.* This, if you please, in the dead core and centre of America's Middle West round about the end of the last war! There is another charming scene which takes place on Armistice Night. The crowd comes to the minister's home to tell him the great news. There are signs of jollity, quickly and sternly repressed by the minister who bids his people kneel down and pray, which they do, in a heavy snowstorm!

Eventually the town decides that it has had enough of its parson and conspires to get rid of him by pretending that his schoolboy son has been surprised in too intimate conversation with a young girl pupil in the same class. This turning out to be wholly untrue and therefore pure slander, the minister satisfies his revenge by blackmailing the gossips into building a new church, with a slap-up organ and a carillon of bells imported from Switzerland. The picture ends with the good, earnest fellow manipulating the carillon with tears of joy rolling down his conscientious cheeks. Ends, did I say? Not quite. We are to understand that the new church and the organ and the bells and the social centre and the new parsonage will all be handed over to a successor, while Fredric March, with Martha Scott in loyal support, transplant themselves to Iowa, where a humble little church is in difficulties. Whereat the cynical, hard-bitten, *male* film critics filed out holding, like Walrus and Carpenter, their pocket handerchiefs before their streaming eyes.

78

BLIND SPOTS AND "BAMBI"

1942

NOBODY, to my knowledge, has ever written an essay on blind spots. Perhaps for the reason that there is nothing to be said about them. Or very little. But there is one point to be made about them, and if ever I write the essay I shall make it. On second thoughts why wait for the essay? Let me make it now. The point is the inherent unfairness of the blind-spotter. Over and over again you hear people say: "I detest so-and-so; he is one of my blind spots." You never hear anybody say: "I adore so-and-so; he is a blind spot with me." Logically, people should have no opinion about a blind spot. Yet the human mind takes very little account of logic, and I confess that in my case these areas of non-visibility are so many foci of detestation.

Among my blind spots are books about middle Europe in the seventeenth century, the result of schoolboy ploughing through Schiller's interminable *Thirty Years War*. All novels about latter-day middle Europe by authors with names like Feuchtwanger. So great is this phobia that for many years I shied at any concert presided over by Furtwängler! All British music with the exception of Sullivan and Elgar, all swing music, all crooners, all radio comedians and all the Marx Brothers with the exception of Groucho. Where is this getting us?—asks the reader. It is getting us, dear reader, to the art of Walt Disney.

Blind spots in the amateur do no harm to anybody. But they are excessively dangerous to the critic, who should always be on his guard against them. On the other hand he must beware of mistaking for blind spots the things he legitimately dislikes. If he fails to observe the nice distinction here, he and his criticism go down into a mushy swamp of universal praise. One golden rule emerges. This is that any artist or work of art which is approved by highbrows and lowbrows alike is not to be condemned because it does not happen to strike on a particular critic's box. If that critic does not find something to admire in the artist or the work, then he has hit upon something which he must recognise as a blind spot. Walt Disney, for whose early work I conceived something approaching a passion, has become with me a blind spot through what I can only call over-saturation. Conscious of this, realising that another load of Disney was like adding coals to a full cellar, yet resolved to be utterly critical, I hied me to the New Gallery to see *Bambi*. I was not helped by the preliminary matter.

First we had a Ministry of Information film in which sailors of the allied nations, gathered round a bar, clinked their canakins and proceeded to reconstruct Europe on federal lines. Which lines I am prepared to believe possible when Mr. Churchill tells me he is seeing eye to eye with Mr. Gandhi and Mr. de Valera. Yes, reader, I am aware that this page in THE TATLER is not the place for political discussion. But I submit that the M.o.I. began it, and that the proper business of the Ministry in the matter of the cinema is the distribution of informative films, and not the dissemination of propagandist and highly controversial matter. Next we had a long and boring film about bird life, then something longer and only slightly less boring about bees, accompanied by Mendelssohn's music for the nuptials of those insects played at half the proper speed. Roundabout here was an appalling short in which the vocal members of a jazz band looking like bruisers on the active list gave a perfect imitation of Good Time Charley's quartet in Damon Runyon's *The Lily of St. Pierre.* After which the band discoursed a variety of music reminding me of that music-seller's window at Swiss Cottage which every day for months has offered me choice of Tschaikowsky's Piano Concerto No. 1, Richard Addinsell's "Warsaw" Piano Concerto, a song called "Jealousy" with Hutch's photo on the cover, and something called "Booglie Wooglie Piggy." The News followed.

These excerpts lasting one hour and twenty-five minutes, it may be gathered that I was not in the mood for Bambi, Namby, Pamby, or even a thriller about Helen Lambie. The curtains parted once more, and while we were being told who was responsible for the film's plumbing, etc., a well-meaning friend of mine, who is a frenzied Disney fan, took occasion to say: "You know, James, Disney is more than a magician. He is a seer and a preacher without pulpit. He does what no other living artist seems able to do. He transports you into a world of beauty, phantasy and fun. Like the best of dreams but lasting longer, more vivid, more real. He is the Crome of the screen, and more. He can be at once as macabre as Hieronymus Bosch and as elegant as Corot. He is an inspiration, an exhilaration and a sublimation of earthly experience." Here the valued friend stopped for breath, and before I had time to growl "He's a blind spot with me," I found myself in an enchanted and enchanting world.

And that is all about this film. It realised for me the wonderful ending to the Goncourts' *Manette Salomon* which I roughly translate: "Sometimes in the lightsome hours of dawn, hours of dew-drenched clarity, of morning innocence recalling the childhood of the world under a sky from which the birds have brushed away the stars, in the verdant tenderness of May, in the solitude of green streets, of arbours preluding human abodes, in the midst of creatures familiar and unafraid as in the first days of Creation—Anatole tasted the joys of Eden, and was filled as by Divine bounty wit the bliss of Man face to face with the vestality of Nature."

79

CUSTOM CAN STALE

194

IS there a book entitled *Guide to Blind Film-goers*? I am not speaking c those multitudinous magazines which tell you with gloating detail all th open secrets of the film stars' careers, where they were born, how man times they were divorced, how many dollars they pretend to earn, an what they are going to do when their public retires from them. No, th book I mean would be a straightforward study of filmology containin a classification of the most popular types of picture. These, the studen would spell out in braille, would be divided into three main groups—th war film, the domestic, and the crook film. He would read who excel in each of these departments and what he sounds like, so that he coul recognise by ear, say, John Wayne in the first category, Walter Pidgeon i the second, and Humphrey Bogart in the third.

A man lacking all five senses would still have no difficulty with *Larcen inc.* (Warner), which is pure crook film from start to finish. It eve includes two species of crooks, the comic and slapstick type, and th morose and sinister kind. A crook in the second category appears in hushed atmosphere; the others shudder, they are frightened of him, an terrified of the violence, murder probably, written in his every gesture The story of the present film is founded on the revenge of one of thi type. We see him first in Sing-Sing, a retreat which maiden ladies of goo repute are getting to know better than the back of their hand. An orgy o that, to me, completely incomprehensible game called baseball is in pro gress; the prisoners are so well in flesh as to suggest an unhappy com parison between war rationing and prison diet. This picture caters for al tastes. It begins with farce, goes on to knockabout, has an episode of near tragedy, and ends again in the region of the wholly and wildly improbable It centres round three merry crooks and a saturnine one, who, in the Guid above mentioned, would fit automatically into the gangster category. Th merry crooks comprise "Pressure" Maxwell, a man of grand ideas who ir the past has done great things with slot-machines, dog-race tracks an what not, and a large brainless creature known as Jug Martin. When thi pair started walking down the street after their release I thought we were in for a re-telling of that better film—*Of Mice and Men.* But no: they encounter another old pal, a stout gentleman called Weepy Davis, and henceforth they become Three Musketeers of the Underworld, always under the leadership of the resolute and cocksure Pressure. Jug and Weepy are small-minded crooks, content with such chicken-feed as getting knocked down by passing cars, and knocking off things from counters. But it is they who do the work: Pressure directs and takes the profits, having perhaps read the work of Karl Marx and learnt the secret of capitalism.

Then the terrible Leo appears. Cretins born blind, deaf, dumb, without arms and with one leg only would know how Pressure steals Leo's prison-conceived idea and battens on it. I confess my confidence in Pressure was shaken when I saw how terribly afraid he and his brother Musketeers were of the vengeful little rat, how sweat poured from their brows, how their hands shook and their very feet quaked. Much as Athos and Porthos would have felt if they had double-crossed Aramis. But the cloud lifts and it is all great fun and first-class entertainment. The story may be childish: but does the cinema ever cater for intelligences above the age of, say, fourteen? (Answer: Yes, in *Citizen Kane,* where you are presumed to be so adult that you read symbolism into a black pudding.) The situations are so impossible that one ceases to relate the incidents to anything in real life: but it all goes with such a swing that one accepts these fantastic creatures, laughs, and leaves the picture-house in the best of tempers. Let me congratulate the authors, arrangers and all the other cooks and bottle-washers, on a story which throughout is excellent cinema. Whether it is "cinematic" it is not for the vulgar, unaesthetic, male critic to decide. The dialogue is brilliantly economical: this sort of Hollywood wit has the crackle of stage-thunder.

And the acting is superb. Nothing could be better in this kind than Edward G. Robinson's performance as Pressure, his calm insouciance, his unbaffled and unblushing cheek. A master-crook in every sense of the word till cornered: and then, like a man who, being knocked down, gets up again, he brushes the dust off his clothes and walks away, once more cock of the walk. Broderick Crawford as Jug is good, but that rich comedian Edward Brophy is even better: his slinky bonhomie, that unctuous and villainous grin, are a perpetual delight. And as the macabre crook Leo, Anthony Quinn give a first-class performance. The two females in the story are unimportant, and Jane Wyman and Barbara Jo Allen make the most of their happily infrequent appearances.

In the theatre I allow no playwright to re-tell me that one about the beautiful girl who sprains her ankle and is carried into a country cottage in time to prevent the good-looking cad in tennis flannels from blowing out his brains. The author can tell the story; I go to sleep until it is over. In the theatre I have observed this rule for the last ten years. I hereby give notice that henceforth I allow no film-producer to tell me again that old one about the momentarily disgruntled wife who runs into a nice young man in the Pullman car, finds herself swept on to his yacht, and doesn't misbehave for the reason that nobody can make love and be seasick at the same time. When this film unrolls itself I go to sleep. I don't care who directed *Palm Beach Story* (Plaza). I don't care whether he made the cameraman look down on Vallee and Colbert from the top of the yacht's funnel or keek up at them from the stoke-hole. I just don't want ever again to see Claudette in two minds about two men whatever the directing angle. Cannot somebody, somewhere, think of some other subject for this quite good actress? But that's only my personal low view. The highbrow critics will certainly hail this film as Preston Sturges's equivalent to the polychromaticism of a Bach fugue.

80

THE THUG AS HERO

1942

IT must be some forty years since I sat on an uncomfortable bench in the schoolroom where the Manchester Playgoers' Club held its meetings, and heard the late C. E. Montague read his paper entitled "The Wholesome Play." Of this essay it may be said that all dramatic critics worth their salt know it by heart; conversely, those who do not know it . . . . but perhaps that would be too sweeping. It was afterwards printed in a little book entitled *Dramatic Values*, a volume which I keep chained to my bookshelf since thievish friends are no respecters of books out of print and unprocurable. I have often thought it would be well worth while to set up a stand in Hyde Park on Sunday evenings and read a section a week. A pleasant fancy, and one which I should long ago have put into practice but for fear of the park authorities, who would doubtless consider Montague's sentiments on the nature of dramatic wholesomeness to be subversive in the extreme.

Montague is discussing the type of hero who, throughout the ages and from the birth of drama up to that of the authors of *Bootle's Baby* and *The Scarlet Pimpernel*, has been dear to the general heart. He writes:

The type is of that of the man who is not, as we say, a bad chap after all; the man who does not wear his heart on his sleeve, preferring to wear there a heart much less good than his own; the man who, morally, is a regular lion of generosity, usually crouched, it is true, but quite prepared to do terrific springs of self-devotion if the occasion for them be sufficiently fantastic . . . the man who "has his faults," but still—well, if he drinks he is "nobody's enemy but his own," and at those next-morning hours when a nature radically bad would be simply ringing for soda-water, he is delighted to be shot or guillotined for the advantage of comparative strangers; he may not keep appointments, or pay his tailor, or do his work, and, of course, he is not a "plaster saint," but then he "cannot bear to see a woman cry," and at any hour of the day or night he is game to adopt a baby, or soothe death-beds, or renounce, for reasons wildly insubstantial, the satisfaction of the cravings of his honest heart.

Well, there you have it. But not all of it. For to this must be added the question of the happy ending. Sir Arthur Pinero's first serious play was *The Profligate.* At the end of this drama a young man who had led the kind of career which as a matter of scientific fact ends in catastrophe and death, did end in this manner. But the theatre-managers, knowing their public, would have none of it. Montague writes:

So Sir Arthur Pinero re-wrote the last scene, and the lot of his young debauchee was improved from a horrible death to life and happiness with a charming wife, a clean slate, and a brand-new character. For this is the happy ending dearest to the sanitarian—that known causes should not have their known effects; above all, that in last acts any leopards which gain the play-goer's regard should be left rigged out in snowy, curly lambs' wool, and nice Ethiopians go off at the end as blonds with straight, tow-coloured hair.

But what would my old friend and mentor have said, could he have foreseen the film? You know the kind of thing I mean. Some rat of the underworld, having earned the chair some half-dozen times and escaped, comes by a change of heart after the film has been running, say, an hour and three-quarters. Shakespeare, who knew all about villains, realised that changes of heart just don't happen. Nightly at the Piccadilly, Macbeth is telling us:

For mine own good,
All causes shall give way: I am in blood
Stepp'd in so far that, should I wade no more,
Returning were as tedious as go o'er:

But what is nature to the makers of films? Consider your Hollywood thug who has gained the audience's regard on the strength of a twisted smile and a note of pathos in the hoarse voice. He has become "sympathetic." Somebody else being about to take the rap for a crime of which he is guilty, the thug, who has never been able to see a woman cry, though he may give her a sock on the jaw from time to time, now cannot bear to see an innocent man take his place in the condemned cell. Particularly if the innocent man is a total stranger to him. So he gives himself up. You can see him doing this any day in any cinema, and you have been seeing him do it any time during the last ten years. I have just come away from seeing Humphrey Bogart do it in *The Big Shot* (Gaumont).

This is a wildly improbable picture containing even more than the usual quota of fights and murders customary in a gangster film. Indeed, most of the people in it die, including the Big Shot (Bogart), his mistress (glamorous Irene Manning), the wicked solicitor (Stanley Ridges), the convict hoofer (Chick Chandler), and many others. The high spot of the film is a superb car chase, Bogart and his girl pursued by the police along a snow-covered thoroughfare longer than the Cromwell Road and even more exciting. But the improbability! And the characters! Never outside a lunatic asylum did any human beings, crook or otherwise, ever act in this sub-human and wholly illogical way. I will not believe that a salesman committing perjury to provide an alibi for a gangster would forget to warn his girl, who, of course, innocently gives him away in court. I believe most things about motor-salesmen, but not this. Do I believe that a prison housing "lifers" is the scene of elaborate music-hall shows? That its yards are the setting for agreeable conversazione with an atmosphere like that of an English suburban lawn-tennis club? Perhaps I do. But I flatly decline to believe that even an American jail can be quite so easy to escape from.

Humphrey Bogart makes it all credible. Bogart is always the same, but he always delights me. He has charm and he doesn't waste energy by pretending to act. He has a sinister-rueful countenance which acts for him. He has an exciting personality and lets it do the work. His expression never changes, whether he is looking on his mistress, the dead body of a man he has murdered, or a blackbeetle. He acts even less than Leslie Howard. And I like him.

81

WHO READS FILM CRITICISM?

1942

WHY have our highbrow critics failed to perceive that the entire charm of the cinema lies in its quality of being ephemeral? Sit through a serious play in the theatre, and you will undergo an experience which lasts. Certainly until you get home, sometimes all next day, and sometimes for the rest of your life! I can think of pieces of acting forty years ago the memory of which thrills me to this very day. As against this I can think of no screen performance from which I have not recovered before I have retrieved my hat. Once in the street I forget not only the title of the film but also what the story has been about. And as far as the names of the screen players are concerned, they are what Ethel Monticue called "piffle before the wind." Well, I suppose I just differ from the rest of the human race in this. There exists a strange kind of animal to be seen daily in bus and tube, whom I hear telling a friend things like this: "If you ask me, dear, I think 'er best part was in *What Men Adore.* I saw it last month—Saterday night it was—with Ada at the Grand Palace. You know, when John Macmussel takes 'er in 'is arms and crushes 'er lips . . . . oh, Ada and me cried ever so."

The foregoing has been brought about by a letter from a publisher containing an offer of so much cash that I didn't know whether to classify it as bullion or specie. But of course there was a snag. He wanted a book. The idea was, that I might like to re-publish a selection of my film criticisms. I confess that I found this notion utterly staggering. Remember, there are only two kinds of film criticism. There is the sort the highbrows write, all about camera-angles and montage, the sub-conscious and the sub-fusc. This is read by unwashed Bloomsburyites wearing thin beards and corduroy trousers, drinking Russian tea through straws in some damp, underground hole, miscalled a café. The other kind of criticism is the sort I purvey. This is read entirely by women whose hair appears to have become entangled with the chandeliers of beauty parlours. I should be horrified to think that this stuff of mine—admirably readable though it may be while you are being Eugène'd and Ardenated—is perused by you, dear lady, when you have done with titivating and have regained your normal mind. But to re-capture these soap-bubbles and print them and bind them in a book—no, a thousand times no! *Où sont les neiges d'antan?* The answer is that they are jolly well where they ought to be, in the limbo of the past. Who remembers the performances by these old screen players?

Was there not somebody called Vilma Banky? Yes. But was this a man or a woman? And does anybody nowadays care a hoot how he or she played, and in what films he or she appeared? Were they silent or were they talkies? As Vilma is now, so will Mr. X and Miss Y be in another twenty years—forgotten.

I must confess to toying a little with the publisher's idea. You see, I have preserved all my film criticisms, hundreds of them, neatly pasted in several bound volumes. And weakly do I confess that there are quite a number of things I should like to reproduce. There is my remark about Norma Shearer: "She has now acquired so much poise that she cannot walk, and is become so soignée she can no longer sit." Or "My particular dislike of Jew-baiting in Germany is that it is going to lead to a great many more films extolling that people at unbearable length." When *Abraham Lincoln* was screened the producer made Lincoln say after the famous Gettysburg speech: "Thank you." "Which," I commented, "is like listening to Bach's *Toccata and Fugue* and then hearing the organist blow his nose." About Garbo laughing: "She opens her mouth wide and goes through the motions of laughter. But it is mirthless laughter, like the yawning of a horse." "Let me ask whether Walt Disney by being more ocular has become more jocular." "Her exquisite face is as expressionless and has become as familiar as a wallpaper." "The film shattered one of my fondest hopes. For years I have wanted to see Joan Crawford in a gas mask." And lastly the criticism of a cinema pianist to which I shall award the honour of an inset:

> When I arrived a pianist was thumping out something that sounded like goodish Grieg. But before I had deposited my hat, the player's material had undergone sudden and violent descent to what one might call tripe *à la mode de* Saint-Saëns.

The best film this week is *Across the Pacific* at the Regal. This is a really magnificent spy-picture with a first-class self-presentation by Humphrey Bogart. And something in the way of playing even better by Sydney Greenstreet as a renegade American who has gone over to the Japanese. Here is also my favourite screen actress, Mary Astor, though her part is so bad that it would have been worth her while to buy herself out of it! *The Forest Rangers* at the Plaza is all about Paulette Goddard and a forest fire. And a lot more about Paulette, which is excellent if you happen to like Paulette! In case you don't, I think there should have been a little more fire. I thought I glimpsed Fred MacMurray somewhere in the picture, but I couldn't be quite sure as I was far too dazzled by Paulette's teeth, which, as ever, dominate the entire screen.

82

ANNOUNCING THE DILYSIANS

1942

An extract from a letter:

> On Thursday afternoon I went to see the Noel Coward film. Isn't it both trivial and horrid? Absolute lack of imagination in handling, and no drama at all. *Cavalcade* all over again. Very cheap and very nasty. Any sausage manufacturer could have done it as well: not a single solitary ha'porth of artistry. I never saw so clearly that film actors were puppets and could do no more than was set down for them by the director. As for the Dunkirk survivors: what a scene that should have been, and by Heaven, will be one day, in the right hands! Of course I wept at once and continuously . . . .

My correspondent, whom I take to be a woman, is obviously one of those highbrows *dont je raffole.* In other words, I suspect her of being a Dilysian. My cherished colleague, who henceforth gives her name to the abstruse coterie, wrote a Sunday or two ago:

> But to instance a scrap of literature embedded in a film is beside the point; if the film has its own validity as an art it must affect us by its own methods, which are basically, though not exclusively, visual.

Our Arch-Dilysian goes on:

> The pictorial effect in *Green Pastures* of the hands touching Moses's shoulder in farewell is more moving than speech.

What a bungler then was Shakespeare! What a time-waster to bother with that speech beginning: "It is the cause, it is the cause, my soul"—with all that rigmarole about quenching flaming ministers. Unless I am being wildly unfair, we shall presently be reading: "The pictorial effect in *Green Eyed Monster* of Othello's fingers snuffing the candle is more moving than any speech of Shakespeare."

Yes, I am afraid *In Which We Serve* is woefully deficient in visual tomfoolery. When the men in the water cling to a raft it is obviously a raft they are clinging to and not a sledge or other dubious object. Or should I write, symbol of dubiety? When you see the sailor going home in a third-class railway compartment it is obviously a third-class railway compartment he is going home in. When the soldiers from Dunkirk line up on the quay they are obviously "browned-off," utterly, entirely and completely browned off. There has been discussion recently by some of our graver innocents as to the origin of the soldiers' phrase so well-known to the mounted regiments before the present war. And I suggest that the exact equivalent of the cavalryman's expression of ennui is to be found in Zola's *Nana.* The scene is the Café des Variétés; at one of whose marble-topped tables is sitting Satin, the little *rouleuse du boulevard.* Zola writes:

> Mais elle etait si voyou, qu'on s'amusait à la faire causer. Et le journaliste, haussant la voix:-
> "Que fais-tu donc là, Satin?"
> "Je m'emmerde," répondit Saint tranquillement, sans bouger.

Just as Satin sat at her little table, calm and unfussed, boring herself to death—Smollett would not have boggled at a more literal translation—so the troops in Noel's picture stand at some semblance of attention, calm, unfussing, and bored with death. And really I do not see how the Dilysians are going to find a visual image to improve upon Mr. Coward's unadorned statement of fact.

Fortunately my correspondent's last sentence gives her and the Dilysians away in handfuls. She confesses that she wept, and that seems to me to be the be-all and end-all of any picture which sets out to make people weep. When I see a film so put together that reading a notice of it you imagine you have strayed into the wrong column and an article about some Surréaliste exhibition at the Lefèvre Galleries, why then I realise that this film will make me laugh, not weep.

Let me now turn to something which very nearly made me weep and not laugh. This is *The Road to Morocco* (Plaza), the programme of which contains the following remarkable note, the appositeness of which I will not stress:

> Every once in a while, movie-makers remember their medium's voiceless beginning and revive for a scene or two the art of pantomime. Often these scenes are among the best in the picture, which must prove something. Maybe what it proves is that films always were and always will be based on visual appeal.

The programme continues:

> Bing Crosby and Bob Hope, in *Road to Morocco,* play a dual pantomime scene which rivals their brightest exchanges of dialogue for laughter. They are dining 'on the cuff" in a small Moroccan café, when a fierce-looking native at the bar signals to Bing. That worthy strolls over to him and negotiates a business deal. The deal consists of selling

Bob to the native for two hundred dollars. All arrangements are made in sign language. Bing explains Bob's best muscular points with gestures, and haggles over the price the same way. At first the object of the sale goes on eating. Then, as he watches proceedings at the bar, he registers concern and, finally, downright protest. Considerable footage is given to the scene and not a word is spoken throughout.

I am not sure that this film does not make the best of both worlds, that of the Dilysians, and mine. There comes a moment when a camel puts its head through the wall of a tent and with his chin touching Bing's shoulder, says: "This is the screwiest picture I was ever in." Perhaps some day this intelligent animal will be given a chance in the highbrow films; let me assure him that he will find them far screwier than this one. Incidentally I found Bob's material hopelessly unfunny, Bing's melodies even trashier than usual, while Dorothy Lamour wandered through the picture looking and being glum.

What about *The War Against Mrs. Hadley* (Empire)? It was Dick Phenyl who said that: "No man is quite so sober as the individual who is occasionally otherwise. All his acuteness is concentrated upon his brief lucid intervals, and in those intervals his acuteness is devilish." But Dick's acuteness at its highest was as nothing compared with that of the Dilysians when they are not Dilysiating. The Head of the new order describes the Empire film as "a new phase in which Hollywood, having done with the brave British, now shows the American matron finding there is a war on, my dear." I couldn't agree more.

83

TO PAY OR NOT TO PAY

1942

SATURDAY morning at Briny Bay. You must know that it rained and rained and rained. Well, after a time one gets tired of walking up and down the wrong side of the promenade in a mackintosh talking to aloof little dogs who really don't want to be talked to. You can't ask your hotel porter more than fifteen times in one morning if he thinks it's going to clear up. In short, I was bored. So, to relieve the boredom, I thought I would go to the pictures.

The point I want to make is the difference between normal and professional film-going. It is the same, I understand, with the normal reader of novels and the professional reviewer. As a critic I spend the afternoon finding faults in something approaching a masterpiece and being very cross about those faults. And then, later in the evening, I will curl up in bed and read with infinite pleasure a story of how the Duchess of Kennington's long-lost daughter with the Oval face would have been strangled with a banjo-string by a Chinese thug on a palm beach in Florida if the equally long-lost son of the Earl of St. Pancras hadn't swum to her rescue through a shark-infested sea.

Well, there's a moral to all this. And that moral is that the professional critic, if by the nature of things he cannot drop his profession altogether, should wear it as lightly as possible. Dramatic critics think, of course, that after the performance of a new play the world can hardly breathe until it has read what they have to say about that play. They wonder, indeed, how it can sleep. Some foolish actors take them so seriously that after a first-night they don't go to bed until the morning papers have come out. Fancy sitting up all night to read a long account of the plot of the play—which they know much better than the critic—to see at the end of the notice: "Among others in an excellent cast was Mr. Macready Jones"!

But let me get back to the film I saw at Briny Bay. It began with a charming schoolgirl riding a bicycle and singing in choice Italian that aria from which *Two Lovely Black Eyes* was filched. Perhaps I wasn't quite as enchanted as the Bedlington terrier accommodated in a basket in front of the bicycle. Anyhow, I was filled with the sense of young America and the carefree charm of its small towns. Here let me say that I have no doubt that an American Thomas Hardy would find as much crime lurking in the hedgerows of an American small town as in your idyllic English village. But let that pass. Presently it appeared that the little girl had a Mamma who was Kay Francis, complete with nostalgia and pearls. Nostalgia was for a divorced husband languishing in gaol on account of somebody who had become shot after trying to frame the husband for a job of which he was innocent. But Kay was on the way to acquiring a second husband, a nice man who proceeded to give the little girl a new piano and her young brother a speed-boat. Then the first husband became pardoned and turned up to tune the old piano. And to him the little daughter, who, of course, didn't recognise her father, warbled *Una Voce* complete with cadenzas, and Daddy got his son, who likewise failed to recognise him, out of a terrible scrape with a knife-throwing Wop.

And all this time the school concert, or jamboree or something of the sort, was drawing near. But before it happened there was a turn in the plot whereby the little girl put out to sea in her brother's speed-boat and, a storm coming on, had to be rescued by Daddy, who turned out to be a first-class swimmer. Nothing being so good for the voice as immersion in a rough sea, the child next day made a terrific success at the school concert —which, by the way, was broadcast—and sang that *Second Hungarian Rhapsody* to the accompaniment of some two score mouth-organs and piano-accordions. And the end of it all was that, to everyone's surprise, Kay re-married Daddy, and the kind gentleman in the tuxedo slipped out of her life poorer only for one baby grand and one speed-boat. Incidentally, if little Gloria Warren sang the song entitled *Always In My Heart* once, she sang it a dozen times. Yet I give readers of THE TATLER my word that for the rest of the week-end I went about crooning—yes, positively crooning—some monstrous drivel to the effect that

Can't say exactly when,
But I know we'll meet again,
And, darling, tho' we part,
You'll be always in my heart.

The point, you see, was that I PAID FOR ADMISSION.

The following Monday I hied me to the Odeon to see *The Pied Piper*. As I did not pay to be let in, I naturally assumed my sternest critical integrity. It seemed to me that the first part of the picture was utterly charming with its strange combination of fun and pathos, a mixture against which the most hardened film-goer is still defenceless. I liked the way in which the children began to accrue insensibly, like the crescendo of orchestration in Bolero's *Ravel*. You may judge of the state of emotion in the house when I swear that these are the words I caught from my neighbour as he sought his handkerchief. But then the film changed its quality and turned into one of those stories of pull-Nazi pull-victim. The German officer was brilliantly played, but one has begun to see enough of the browbeating of heroic Britons by bullying Prussians. As far as my memory serves, Monty Woolley collected five children only, and I wanted to see him collect at least fifty. I am afraid I didn't believe in the anxiety of the officer to see his semi-Jewish niece conveyed to safety; as a good Nazi he would have throttled her with his own hands. Or in that scene in which he came down to the beach to see the children to the boat which was taking them to England. How much more amusing if there had been some three score little rats, and if, taking a leaf out of that magnificent film, *Emil and the Detectives*, they had at the last moment kidnapped the wicked Hun and taken him to England!

However, let me repeat that I had not paid for admission. Had I done so I should doubtless have found the film superb. Even so, I went out into the street and added to the gaiety of the blackout by humming my version of Ravel's *Bolero*.

84

STRICKLAND AND WOMEN

1943

The Moon and Sixpence (Odeon), the film made out of Somerset Maugham's novel about Gauguin, has two main themes. The first is that old thing about the non-obligation of the artist to conform to everyday morals; the second is that even older thing: Should artists marry? I remember when I was a boy being enormously impressed with George Moore's "What matters the slaughter of ten thousand virgins if they provide Delacroix [I think it was] with a fine canvas?" It was about this time that Wilde was writing: "No artist has ethical sympathies." "Vice and virtue are to the artist materials for an art." I remember how, reading this, vicious little schoolboys gave fresh rein to their vices under the delusion that they were turning themselves into artists. Later I remember how Montague tried to demolish the pernicious but amusing nonsense in a single sentence. "Wilde, when slowly dying of a retributive disease, with all his splendid gifts already dead before his body, was still chattering about the amplitude of the career of moral uncontrol." Unfortunately for Montague's argument the disease from which Wilde died was retributive only in the time-sense; twenty years later the medical profession had made the discovery which would have saved him, body, mind and perhaps even soul. Gauguin did not die of a disease which he contracted in the South Sea Islands but of one which he caught in Marseilles and afterwards spread among the innocent islanders. And I suggest that it would take a greater pen than Wilde's, or a greater brush than Gauguin's to make a pretty picture out of *that* kettle of fish.

However, I must confine myself to the actual picture which is more concerned with Strickland-Gauguin living than with S.-G. dying. I was sensible that the audience was far more staggered than I could hope to be by the artist's views on women. The film-goers round about me, mostly young people, have had it drummed into them through hundreds of pictures that women are rarefied beings to be set on a pedestal, and on whom men are privileged to bestow diamond bracelets, furs and chocolates, in return for an occasional kiss. Such an audience as this, then, could never have regarded women in any other light than fascinating, if capricious, goddesses, who in some extraordinary metabiological way transmute themselves in middle life into model mothers and later into those silvery old ladies with mob-caps whom we all adore. What, then, could such an audience think of Mrs. Strickland, who, when she thought her husband left her for another woman, refused to divorce him, but was quite willing to do so when she learned that his new mistress was only his art!

Long before Maugham wrote his novel, one Henrik Ibsen, in the play called *Hedda Gabler*, had dealt with the subject of women's indifference to art. In that play Ibsen showed how Hedda was willing to go through fire for the writer Lövborg, provided it was she who inspired his great book. And how equally ready she was, when the great book turned out to have been inspired by another woman, to put the manuscript of the now-detested book *into* the fire. "I am burning your child, Thea," she cried, her face twisted with rage and revenge. "Your child and Lövborg's." From which it follows that Hedda cared nothing about the book *qua* book. Strickland ran away from Mrs. S., not because he had ceased to love her—as a matter of fact he had never begun—but because he and his new mistress could not cohabit under the same roof as that icy virago. Art, you see, is an abstract subject, and women, on the whole, are not interested in abstract subjects. Listen to the average woman talking—what does she talk about? According to her age and social position, she talks about clothes, hats, make-up, servants, her menfolk, her children and rationing. No woman, talking about the theatre, bothers what the play is about: she is too much concerned with her adoration of Miss A or her detestation of Miss B. Now an artist who is really absorbed in his art—whether he is painter, poet or musician—is never thinking about anything else, however much he may pretend. If people must chatter to him about art, or his art, neither of which he wants to discuss—then he insists that they should at any rate chatter intelligently. And as women seldom do this—and why should they be intelligent about something which bores them?—your artist avoids female society, and if he is married, inevitably, sooner or later, runs away from his wife. Thus Strickland's action was entirely logical, and the film, so far as I was concerned, was preaching to the converted.

Should artists never marry, then? Bad artists yes; good ones no, unless like Blake they take to themselves a drudge. Decidedly the best way is Strickland's—a pretty, fifteen-year-old, not-too-dark Islander to act as model, cook and mistress. And if the child cannot speak English? Enchanting! Was there not once a French maiden who, advertising for a husband, supplemented her meagre *dot* with the phrase "pas de piano"? Would the child of fifteen have ceased to please at twenty? It was to be presumed that she had younger sisters. See Maupassant on the subject *(Les Sœurs Rondoli)*. Yes, I hold that Strickland's case was entirely logical and needs no excusing. Is there a rather nasty bit where the other Englishwoman he possessed goes off and hangs herself? The answer to that is that she possessed him, and that women who behave like millstones must take the consequences. But it is foolish of me to expect women to see anything of the sort; the conception is abstract and as such beyond their province. And why shouldn't it be? Women have the monopoly of beauty, charm and fascination, and that's enough.

A colleague is surprised at the choice of George Sanders for Strickland. He would have been my first choice in view of his quality of callous banter; I agree that he rises surprisingly well to the bigger task of suggesting the great artist. On the other hand I should not have chosen Herbert Marshall for the narrator; his note is too much that of honest, gentlemanly stupidity. Had I been United Artists I should have spent another hundred thousand dollars or so on luring Willie Maugham himself to link up the story. Perhaps they did; perhaps that old bird was too wily for them. Anyhow, it is an admirable film until the end, when it lapses into Technicolor and techni-pathos. What one wanted to hear was Strickland deciding in the last stages of leprosy whether the game had been worth the candle. The world has decided Yes. What did Strickland think?

85

PLAYING THE FOOL

1943

THE jamboree at the Regal in honour of the Free French made me ashamed of being British. It all goes back to a passage in Henry Morley's *Journal of a London Playgoer*. Morley was writing in 1858 about the difference between the attitude to serious drama of the French and ourselves: "There must be a deeper earnestness than plays can demand, in whatever serious thing Englishmen are to look at without exercise of that sense of the humorous which is part of their life; so natural a part that every man is in every grade of society regarded as a bore who lacks it; and the very phrase with thousands even among our educated men for not finding a thing acceptable is 'seeing no fun' in it." The proceedings last night began with a first-class news-film about Mr. Churchill's visit to the Near East, to be followed presently by the singing of a Workers' Choir and a first-rate "short" depicting the recent activities of the French on land, on sea and in the air. All this should and would have been a dignified proceeding; but the management, distrusting our ability to remain serious, thought fit to introduce a Donald Duck item which would have been inappropriate, even if it had been amusing. But it was not in the least amusing. And it was received by the highly distinguished audience in almost complete silence.

Then came the big thing of the evening, *To-morrow We Live,* a film about occupied France which never moved beyond Surbiton, except possibly for an excursion to Balham. I am getting tired of these schoolboy stories, a mixture of good Wallace rising to poor Henty, in which the hero escapes from the Nazi headquarters by catching on to the chandelier and swinging himself through the window to freedom and a waiting motor-boat at the cost of a gentlemanly cut on the forehead about an inch and a half long, while the British air-arm intervenes to prevent pursuit. And I certainly don't believe in the mayor's daughter who flirts with the German commandant, and from a secret signal-box changes the points and sends an ammunition train to disaster. And the Englishness of the characters—Streatham written all over them! Godfrey Tearle, as the French mayor, leads a party of martyrs to the place of execution with the unruffled suavity of an English country gentleman showing his guests the way to the dining-room. The only character who was remotely French was the baker's wife, played by Yvonne Arnaud, who is French. The Nazis were much better because most of them were played by Germans. Why not use French actors to play French parts? An English actor with his "Mossoo This," and "Madarm That," remains inescapably English; a French actor, however broken his English, remains indubitably French. The distinguished guests were very polite about it all afterwards; what they must have thought is another matter. I can't imagine Russians showing rubbish of this order. Indeed, I am beginning to wonder whether the British are, in fact, the salt of the earth. Alternatively, whether that salt is a good thing to be. I often feel that I should like to paraphrase the immortal lines of Keats so that they run:

> "Ugliness is dirt, dirt ugliness"—that is all
> Ye know on earth, and all ye need to know.

On this occasion the town of Pittsburg is my excuse. I have never heard an American speak of Pittsburg; perhaps he never does. I hasten to say that there are towns in England over which the English draw a discreet veil. Whenever I think of Pittsburg—which is as little as I can contrive—it is always in connection with Eleonora Duse who died there. She called Pittsburg "la plus hideuse ville du monde." One remembers too that Irving said that it was "hell with the lid off."

By the way, will the fudge about Duse never cease? I have just been looking at Arthur Symons's *Life, Study* or what you will, and I read once again about Duse reaching

> . . . a supremacy in art, so divine in her pure humanity, so mystic in the spiritual sense of the word, and so pathetic in her humility, which

has rarely if ever been equalled, and which could never or rarely be surpassed.

And Symons also quotes with approval another disciple:

> She was doubly the chalice. To the mystery and exaltation of her art were added a strange element of aloofness, which made her a great person in the cast of another drama which we call Life.

Let us see now how Duse comported herself in that other "drama which we call Life." On the same page I read:

> A banquet was given after her last performance, by the Italians residing in New York, in Duse's honour, at which the whole company was present, but the guest of honour's place was vacant. She refused; she knew what a vexation it would be to hear the speeches, so she remained alone in the hotel with a book, which was much more to her taste.

Are we to see in this gross and grave discourtesy to her hosts, who were also her compatriots, an example of Duse's spiritual mysticism or unsurpassable humility? Or are we to detect in that piece of extravagant rudeness an instance of that "strange element of aloofness"?

You are to learn, reader, that there is also an element of aloofness in your film critic. Marlene may not be, in the words of a neglected poet, "my woe, my early light, my music dying." But at least I will not see "those lily brows, that cherry nose, those cowslip cheeks" blackened and smudged by coal dust. A little bird having warned me that in *Pittsburg* Marlene plays a miner's doxy, I decided that so far as I was concerned, this picture must get along without me.

86

THREE FILMS

1943

WILL somebody please tell me who is Mr. William Saroyan and what he has written? The author of a recently published book on the American critic George Jean Nathan remarks: "Nathan has discovered or has been among the first to lend impetus to the reception of such widely different dramatists as Eugene O'Neill, Sean O'Casey, the earlier Paul Vincent Carroll, and William Saroyan." Well, that's good company. I ask for further knowledge of this gentleman because *The Human Comedy* (Empire) intrigues me. How can a man dare to take such a title, and, under this title, produce such childish balderdash as nine-tenths of this film turns out to be? In comparison with the picture which has been made out of Mr. Saroyan's story, Louisa M. Alcott's *Little Women and Good Wives* is a masterpiece of towering intellectuality. Methinks a better title for the film would have been *Little Men and Good Husbands* since it is all about American youth, and how if in a war some are killed it is in order that those who come through the war may lead sweeter and nobler lives and raise sweeter and nobler children.

The film begins semi-mystically. Macauley *père* has been dead two years, but is still conscious of what is happening on earth. Apparently he put no money by and was uninsured. Which was rather hard lines on his wife, his three sons and his daughter. The eldest son Marcus joining up, the Macauleys' income suddenly depends on the second son Homer (Mickey Rooney) who, according to my friend Synopsis, "attends High School in the day, but is hired as a night-messenger boy at the town telegraph office." To which all I can say is that telegraph boys in American small towns must be thunderingly well paid! But why the need to lay the whole burden on Mickey's shoulders? Why doesn't the daughter give up college and take a job of typing? Why doesn't Mrs. Macauley quit sitting around twanging the harp and start doing a little choring? Fay Bainter, sweeping the strings instead of floors, and through them delivering homilies to the five-year-old Ulysses Macauley couched at her feet and in imminent danger of having his nose amputated by the pedals—this forms a scene of stupendous bathos unparalleled in all my film experience.

There is a great deal about an old telegraphist, played by Frank Morgan, who spends his time getting drunk, getting sober, philosophising, moralising, and attending to his job—all in that order and with his job a good way last. There is a great deal about the eldest son, who is killed, and his friend who is not and is eventually taken into the bosom of the Macauley family. And a lot about how America's expensive little hussies have hearts of gold, and people who dress for dinner are not essentially better than postmen who don't wear ties. And where does Mickey Rooney come in? He is just the telegraph boy who knows what is in people's telegrams and whose honest face breaks into smiles or runs over with tears as the occasion demands. In other words, Homer is a great little hand at rejoicing with them that do rejoice and weeping with them that weep. Now I wonder! Is it possible that Saroyan, when he wrote his novel, had in mind the twelfth chapter of St. Paul's Epistle to the Romans? There is a great deal of sermonising in the film, all of it drawn from this famous chapter. You are shocked perhaps, and ask how a great piece of literature and a silly film can say the same thing? The phenomenon is not new, as any student of tracts and oleographs and bad "sacred" music is aware. There must be some explanation, apart from the superb acting by Mickey Rooney, why so preposterous a film should at times move us so deeply. I can only take it that the eternal values remain eternal in spite of Hollywood's efforts to cheapen them.

No film attains a greater degree of intellectual bankruptcy than one which takes a block of flats, or an omnibus, or a telephone box, or a pawnshop, or a Turkish bath, and builds a story round the frequenters of these establishments. *For Ever and a Day* (Leicester Square) is such a film. It is all about a house built in the first years of the last century. Indeed, we are told that the house is a living entity and not a mere collection of bricks and mortar. But even if so much be conceded the history of the house can only be told in terms of its tenants, and from this depends the saga of some four to five generations. All this can be very effective on the stage in such a play as *Milestones*. It was effective in *Cavalcade*, and it was effective again in the Orson Welles film of *The Magnificent Ambersons*. But note that in the case of the two plays and the film one controlling mind was in charge. In the present film seven directors are let loose. With the result that the thing has no unity because it has no mind. The first part is like a story in an old-fashioned Christmas Annual. As usual the dresses are overdone to the point when the director chokes himself with period-consciousness. There is plenty of evidence that whoever made this part of the film has not "lived" it. The young girl has been abducted, and her guardian and his attorney come to retrieve her. Do they come in a barouche? No. They come in a tandem-drawn gig with the box seat occupied by the two gentlemen and the groom perched in the dickey. *Where did they propose to put the young lady if she had consented to come back?* Why, in a subsequent section, does the coal-man in 1897 talk like the 1867 Sam Gerridge in Robertson's *Caste*? Again because the director has not "lived" his period. Towards the end there is a scene of genuine emotion beautifully played by Gladys Cooper and Roland Young. Subject, the loss of a son in wartime. And I can only imagine that by some happy accident the director of this knows something about the matter with which he has been entrusted.

To sum up, one of the most brilliant casts of modern times has been assembled to bolster up one of the poorest pictures. Why have R.K.O. Radio Pictures Ltd. nobody to tell them when Cedric Hardwicke is unfunny and Charles Laughton just plain bad? And couldn't they have sprung another fiver to hire an artist who could paint Aubrey Smith to look like Aubrey

Smith and not W. C. Fields? Yes, I know that this film has been made in a good cause and that the actors gave their services. I am not thereby deterred from saying what I think about it. The better the cause, the better the thing in its aid should be done!

After this pyramidal mush *China* (Plaza) seemed a most exciting, turbulent affair. This "Eastern" differs little from the average "Western" in this respect—there are the same number of roughs, toughs, fights, escapes and rescues. And always the same beautiful, virtuous and heroic heroine. Alan has his usual rôle of the hard-boiled Ladd with the heart of gold. Loretta Young is an American college teacher escorting a number of Chinese girl students to Chung King (I think). Alan, who is in charge of a lorry and is induced by Loretta to carry, somewhat unwillingly, her cargo of précieuses to their destination, wishes to make for Hong Kong (I believe). The tension which must be supposed to prevail among the audience as to whether these girlies reach Chung or are landed at Hong, provides most of the interest of the film. Which, if I may say so, is not, to put it mildly, of the very highest kind. But then it all happens rather too far away to be quite my cup of tea.

87

THE QUESTION OF STANDARD

1943

HAVING spent a dreary morning reviewing one of those feminine ebullitions which I call "bosom-claspers" I went in the afternoon to see Metro-Goldwyn-Mayer's latest film, *Du Barry was a Lady* (Empire). This will no doubt be a great success, but it is simply not my kind of film. I hated it when I saw it as a stage play and I disliked the film version even more. It seemed to me to be common in sentiment and cheap in humour. This, however, was not the opinion of the young airman on leave who accompanied me; he said I just don't understand swing, and that what to me seems a filthy and discordant noise is the most delightful music to him and his friends. Well, I suppose I am incorrigible; I judge by the standard of the educated public, forgetting that no cinema audience has the beginnings of an educated taste. From which I suppose Euclid would have argued that this is a super-excellent film.

Desmond MacCarthy hit the nail on the head when he wrote on a recent Sunday in *A Letter to a Common Reader:* "But when we [the highbrows] want to relax over a book, we can't get distraction or entertainment from the tosh you read. The habit of attending to the written word is too strong, and of thinking what's what as we go along." This applies equally to the cinema. I would rather spend two hours scrubbing floors or peeling potatoes than sit through a film like the *Du Barry* nonsense. The answer to that, of course, is that I am not a scrubber of floors or a peeler of potatoes. and that the people who are normally engaged in these humdrum occupations find that romantic which I find merely vulgar. Well, I don't think vulgarity of this kind is good for the cinema classes, and if I had any share in making the new world I should first of all establish a Censorship of Taste. How, then, would I propose that the lower classes fill in that time which my censorship would empty, since the taste of the masses is insusceptible of improvement? I should restore the old English sports and amusements, bear-baiting and cock-fighting, wrestling, boxing with naked fists, and open-air dancing. I would increase the strength of beer while lessening its price. I would let every man drink as much as he could decently carry. I would restore the pre-pre-war opening and closing times. I would consider restoring public executions, which are far less demoralising than most films. The spectacle may be revolting, but at least the revolt would be against the horrific. There is no cheap sentiment about a hanging. Remember that the age which permitted this produced Spenser and Marlowe, Ben Jonson and Shakespeare. And what, pray, has this age of the mushy novel, the cinema and the wireless produced? Nothing but bosom-claspers, film stars and crooners. Bah!

When *Du Barry was a Lady* was produced as a stage play I find that I wrote: "The romantic part of the entertainment is provided by Miss Frances Day, who seeks to show that the most exquisite of France's peccant ladies had really been of the grab-all-and-give-nothing order .... Much fun is made out of the scene in which the King is shot in the back by the Dauphin, whose principal hobby is playing at bows and arrows. The doctor called in to extract the arrow begins the operation by inspecting his royal master's tonsils. But alas, this touch of Sganarelle is but momentary, and we pass to lesser humours. Is it very funny when a drunken bar-tender dreams he is a French king, saying, 'Dooshess, how d'ya like this joint?' The dresses and décor are superb, though it might be held that this isn't the moment for superbity .... I cannot remember a piece which has struck me as being possessed of so little charm, so little taste, and so much inanity." All this in the film was even worse. An enormous amount of money must have been spent, only to emphasise what I wrote about the play. In fact, as the more subtle of my readers may have gathered, I disliked it very much.

It really seems as though there might be something in the rumour about the slump in film-going. Why shouldn't there be? The cinema during the last year or so has shown, with one or two exceptions, extraordinary poverty of invention. Over and over again, and *ad nauseam,* the films tell the same old tale. *Crash Dive* (Tivoli) is just another version of that old one about the unsophisticated maiden who is engaged to the sober-sided Lieutenant-Commander but who finds herself attracted by some dashing and younger Lieutenant. She resists, of course. But just as constant water-drops wear away a stone, so will gallantry, aided by a little persistence, wear down the most obdurate female heart. And, of course, the Lieutenant is appointed to serve on the same boat under the Lieutenant-Commander, and of course neither knows of the other's love affair; the elder officer may, at the most, suspect the younger of certain shore flirtations; the younger may hazard that the elder has some suitable girl in tow. But neither ever suspects that they can be in love with the same girl. Until, still of course, the day arrives when the Lieutenant-Comm. says: "Elmer, meet my fi-ancy." And who should the fi-ancy turn out to be but the Loot's sweetie-pie? There is no time for explanations, because at that moment comes a message that the boat has been ordered to Java or Jamaica or Joppa. On the bridge that night the Lieutenant says: "Sir, in that matter of Miss Antigone Pfotz I must explain that . . ." Whereupon his commanding officer stops him and says with some severity: "Lootenant Elmer M. Highball, the deck of the *Walt Whitman* is no place for the discussion of private and personal matters. When we reach land I shall be glad to hear your explanations, if you have any to offer . . . . In the meantime does not that craft which I have just espied on the horizon look to you remarkably like the *Prinz Eugen?*" In the present case the job facing the *Walt Whitman* (which is a submarine) is the spying-out and destruction of a Nazi submarine base. Whereupon we get a repetition of the raid on the Lofoten Islands, except that eight men blow up the local oil-tanks, gasometers, ammunition dumps, barracks and what-not all inside half an hour. Now I just don't believe that any eight men could do this in the case of a fully defended enemy base. Perhaps I ought to say I don't believe it as a matter of fact. In Technicolor I am prepared to believe anything.

I thought Dana Andrews excellent as the Lieutenant-Commander and Tyrone Power very good as his larkish self, and there is a first-rate performance by James Gleason. Anne Baxter dithers agreeably between her two beaux, and there is always Dame May Whitty poised augustly in the offing. But the film as a whole is run away with by Ben Carter as the negro sailor, Oliver Cromwell Jones.

88

BOSH AND TOSH

1943

LADY Eleanor Smith is an excellent novelist, who can tell a good tale whether it be about ballerinas or circus-riders. She moves easily from country to country and period to period, and has all those graces of style which, when the yarn she happens to be pitching is not particularly new, conceal the fact. In the cinema the graces are bound to disappear, with the result that nothing is left except the bare bones of the story. I can imagine that *The Man in Grey* (Gaumont, Haymarket, and Marble Arch Pavilion) is an excellent novel. How comes it, then, that there was not a moment in the film version of her book when I would not have gladly dived for my hat? Can it be that at 10.45 in the morning one just does not feel in the romantic vein? But let the reader judge.

The Hon. Clarissa Richmond (Phyllis Calvert), a blonde beauty round about the beginning of the last century, is the star pupil at Miss Patchett's academy at Bath. Also at the school is Miss Hester Shaw (Margaret Lockwood), a good-looking brunette belonging to an impoverished family and accepted as a charity pupil. Presently Hester finds she has had enough of Miss Patchett and her charity and runs away with a young Ensign who, we hear, comes later to a sticky end. Clarissa also leaves the academy, becomes one of London's most dashing débutantes, and is sought in marriage by the rich but infamous Marquis of Rohan (James Mason), whose tastes run to duelling, dog-fights and gambling. He is not in love with Clarissa but wants an heir. Indeed, I can imagine Lady Eleanor making the scene of his proposal quite amusing. I can imagine his lordship saying (putting the words of Millamant into the mouth of the naughty marquis): "Good Clarissa, don't let us be familiar or fond, nor kiss before folks, like my Lady Fadler and Sir Francis; nor go to Hyde Park together the first Sunday in a new chariot, to provoke eyes and whispers, and then never to be seen there together again—as if we were proud of one another the first week and ashamed of one another ever after. Let us never visit together, nor go to a play together; but let us be very strange and well-bred. Let us be as strange as if we had been married a great while, and as well-bred as if we were not married at all." What the marquis says is: "We shall live at my house in Grosvenor Square. You will go your way and I with your permission will go mine, and in this manner you will find marriage quite agreeable."

An incident now follows which I find very difficult to follow. Clarissa, hearing that her old school friend, Hester, is an actress playing at St. Albans, sets off in her coach to see her. The coach is held up by a dashing young man named Rokeby (Stewart Granger), whom she first takes to be a highwayman but who actually is the leading actor in Hester's troupe and who, in modern parlance, wants a lift. Has he fallen off his horse? Has his coach foundered? Anyhow, they arrive at St. Albans together, and Clarissa arrives at the theatre just in time to see her travelling companion begin Othello's speech: "It is the cause." Which presents us with a nice problem. Did the company start *Othello* with the last act? If not, what is Clarissa doing during the other four? Has she stopped at the inn to order supper and accommodation? Even so, she must be an unusual nitwit to travel all the way from London merely to see her friend smothered!

A young friend tells me that at this point my attention wandered, and that the journey to St. Albans was only decided on at the last moment. I accept this. *But who deputised for Rokeby during the first four acts? And what was he doing on the road miles from the theatre when he should have been in his dressing-room making-up for his part?* I ask these questions in view of the fact that the people engaged to make this picture include a director, an editor, a cutter, a period adviser, an adapter, and an art director. Why not add to these functionaries someone whose business it is to see that the story holds water? After the show Clarissa insists on taking Hester back to town to live with her for no conceivable reason, whereupon, to cut a long film short, the marquis falls in love with the actress, and the actress murders her benefactress and is promptly thrashed to death by the marquis.

Well, dear reader, Regency or no Regency, this is too tall a story for me. But will it be too tall a story for overseas troops, dusky warriors from Idaho, sailors who have spent months in the crow's nest, WAAFs on leave, and London's floating population generally? I imagine not. There is a lot of noise and bustle, and whenever the word "coach" is mentioned you see the wheels go round. The women's dresses are lovely, there is a glimpse of Vauxhall Gardens and even the Prince Regent puts in an appearance. Everybody in England appears to be in the cast, and Mesdames Calvert and Lockwood vie with each other as to who can achieve the naicest Kensington accent. In short, I imagine that this film will make a lot of money. Women, of course, will see anything. But I advise my male readers to dine well beforehand, with lashings of liqueur brandy, and to take with them a cigar of Churchillian proportions.

After lunch I hied me to the Pavilion to see *Undercover*. In this a number of our charming and familiar native actors run up and down Box Hill and the Hog's Back pretending to be guerrillas in Yugo-Slavia. Here is John

Clements putting up a vigorous pretence of being called Milosh Petrovitch, Stephen Murray asking us to believe that he is called Dr. Stevan Petrovitch, and Tom Walls tipping us the wink that he is not our old friend, but Kossan Petrovitch the father of the other two, and ready to be executed at a moment's notice if he can serve his country thereby. Godfrey Tearle, as the Nazi General, looks about as German as Aubrey Smith. But need I continue? I just didn't believe a word of it. Do I mean that British actors should not attempt to portray Yugo-Slavians? No. When, in the play *The Moon is Down* Lewis Casson plays the part of the Norwegian mayor, I am willing to make the pretence that the mayor is Norwegian, and I make that pretence because there is something in the play worth listening to. In other words, Steinbeck's piece has something to say, whereas *Undercover* has nothing to say. It tells how Yugo-Slavian guerrillas, very much in the English Saturday-afternoon spirit, set about making themselves nuisances to invaders. And, of course, successful nuisances. Is the safe running of a railway line and the preservation of a tunnel essential to the Nazis? Then you arrange for one of your heroes to instal himself in a first-class carriage, having placed in his suit-case a bomb timed to explode so that it blows up hero, train, tunnel and Uncle Tom Cobley and all. Does nobody search the luggage? Yes, but it is a rule in this kind of film that no Nazi shall ever find what he is looking for. Do the guerrillas want to destroy a lot of Nazis? If so, it's quite simple. They open fire from a farm-house from which they then allow themselves to be ejected. Whereupon the Nazis take possession and are blown to blazes, the idea that the place can be mined not having occurred to them. The synopsis says that "any similarity to any incident is coincidental." I agree.

89

ADULT AND JUVENILE

1943

OUT of the blue or the cellars of Studio One, which amounts to very much the same thing, comes *Derrière la Façade,* a small French film so good that it takes all Hollywood's monster productions between finger and thumb and puts them into a sack, which it then deposits in the Atlantic half-way between Hollywood and the port of entry into this country. I saw this film the day after I had seen the play called *Arsenic and Old Lace,* and was irresistibly driven to the conclusion that the French film is for the adult mind and the American play for the juvenile. The stage thriller has only one point to make, and it makes it over and over again. This point is that comicality which ensues when people "go off the handle." There are lots of examples of it in real life. Flowers of modesty who start swearing like troopers, lifelong celibates making beelines for establishments in which inhibitions are little rated, elderly vestals exhibiting a dexterity with the phial which would stagger the Brinvilliers herself—all these things are very funny, provided always that you think lunacy funny. As I sat watching this play I wondered whether it would not have afforded more adult entertainment if the author had shown us those seeds of rebellion lying *perdu* at the back to the most circumspect consciousness. How the nicest girls sometimes find themselves wishing they could swear like troopers, how pastors find their minds straying into the company of lost sheep for quite considerable distances, how old ladies straight out of Mrs. Gaskell's *Cranford* are not so far from giving murder a thought as they are generally supposed.

Arsenic and Old Lace says, in effect: See what absurd things people will do when they are mad. *Derrière la Façade* shows that there is an angle from which every one of us can be made out to be mad and, therefore, absurd. Entirely lacking in Hollywood boisterousness this brilliant picture is witty all the way through, from Elvire Popesco's eyebrows to Erich von Stroheim's toecaps. The story concerns a large block of apartments whose proprietress is found murdered in the lift. The investigating police are portentous and absurd, and as they raid the house each apartment reveals some little drama in its appropriate aspect of absurdity. There are more brains, elegance, wit and charm in a hundred feet of this film than in ten thousand feet sent over by Hollywood. It gets to work quickly, says all it has to say in an hour and a quarter, and then shuts up. There is a fine performance by Jules Berry, and the acting of Gaby Morlay, Gabriel Dorziat and Marguérite Moreno is outstanding. And I hope that these names include that of the really brilliant actress who plays the plain and neglected wife. The admirable production is by Yves Mirande. And now will Hollywood kindly grow up?

I say this because, judging from *For Me and My Gal*, which Metro-Goldwyn-Mayer are presenting at the Empire, this maturity has not yet come upon the American film world. When, O when, will Hollywood find a fresh, or half-fresh, or even a twenty-per-cent fresh story? Here is that venerable tale once again about the girl in love with the boy who doesn't know it, and the boy carried away by a fine lady, and the fine lady who just accepts a boy's flattery and doesn't care for the boy really, and of course there is the scene between Girl No. 1 (I love him) and Girl No. 2 (I don't love him), and equally of course the good and faithful No. 1

gets the boy in the end. Ever heard any of this before? Or of the setting in a music-hall, where Boy and Girl are partners in a song-and-dance act, and the fine lady is a music-hall singer who never appears without an obbligato of twenty pseudo-Magyar fiddlers? She has fifty steps to come down when she appears, singing of course, and a dressing-room like that of an operatic diva, and a flat in which the champagne and bowls of caviare just lie about like ash-trays. This celebrity is portrayed by clever Marta Eggerth, who sings more high notes than I have heard for years, although the quality of the music she sings is not of quite so high a description, including as it does a long paraphrase of Strauss Waltzes whose manifold variations and divagations put Godowsky's symphonic metamorphoses to shame.

The action of the film takes place round about the last war, and I was amused to hear the woman sitting next to me say to her friend: "Doesn't that war seem *terribly old-fashioned*?" In a sense I suppose it was: the uniforms seemed so odd, and the songs seemed to have lost so much of their old grip and verve. But it was nice to see the dear old war once again, in which, I noted with satisfaction, the American Army played not only the chief, but as it seemed, the entire part. For I did not see or hear one British soldier anywhere: not even in the scenes laid in what used to be called Gay Paree. Well, well, well . . . . if one may be permitted so daring a phrase. I noted a player new to me, one Gene Kelly. To this young man I doff my hat and cry bravo. He can act, he has charm, he has personality. He has an arresting smile composite in its ingredients, being made up as to three-quarters of the early Godfrey Tearle and one quarter of our Noel when he is feeling pleased with the world. Our dear Judy Garland is his dancing-and-singing partner, the good and faithful violet who weeps and blushes unseen: and how good *she* is! She is no Venus, let us admit—but how delightful is her smile, how genuine her emotion, how sure her timing, and how brilliantly she brings off her effects with a ping, and often with a pong. And I liked Richard Quine as her brother, although his speaking part consists of about four sentences. An American Barkis, not that any of my younger readers will have the remotest idea of what I am alluding to!

Finally I would say that in this film, which plays for over two hours, there is great diversity of material. There is fun, pathos, slapstick, love, kisses, tears, the old smell of sawdust, and the old sound of wedding bells. You pays your money and you takes your choice. I paid no money, needless to say, but I happened on a dollop of good thing.

90

LET'S GO HIGHBROW

1943

AND now, my chickabiddies, let's go highbrow. Here is the Great Eisenstein in a book called *The Film Sense*. Let me remind readers, who may possibly have forgotten, that Sergei M. Eisenstein was the internationally-known creator of *Potemkin*, *Ten Days That Shook the World*, and *Alexander Nevsky*. Reading this book has made me feel as though somebody with a genius for torture had stood me on my head for six hours in the middle of the Sahara Desert under a blazing sun with a Catherine wheel tied to each foot.

Eisenstein begins by quoting from somebody even more abstruse, one M. Zhirmunsky:

> Any non-coincidence of the syntactic articulation with the metrical is an artistic deliberate dissonance, which reaches its resolution at the point where, after a series of non-coincidences, the syntactic pause at last coincides with the bounds of the rhythmic series.

Then there is Mr. Lanz who informs us:

> . . . . strictly speaking, one does not "hear" a melody. We are able or unable to follow it, which means that we either have or have not the ability to organise the tones into a higher unity . . . .

And here is our old friend Lafcadio Hearn, who says:

> The public can't be supposed to know that you think the letter A is blush-crimson, and the letter E pale sky-blue. They can't be supposed to know that you think KH wears a beard and a turban; that initial N is a mature Greek with wrinkles . . . .

Then M. René Guillerée, who writes:

> Antique perspective presented us with geometrical concepts of objects—as they could be seen only by an ideal eye. Our perspective shows us objects as we see them with both eyes—gropingly. We no longer construct the visual world with an acute angle, converging on the horizon. We open up this angle, pulling representation against us, upon us, toward us . . . . We take part in the world. That is why we are not afraid to use close-up . . . .

And here is a passage from a novel by Pavlenko:

> And, you know, I wrote and wrote, I listened and made notes, compared, collated. One day the old man was playing something great, inspired, joyous, encouraging, and I guessed at once what it connoted: it meant rapture. He finished the piece and threw me a note. It appeared that he

had been playing Saint-Saens' *Danse Macabre*, a theme of terror and horror. And I realised three things: first, that my colonel didn't understand a thing about music, second, that he was as stupid as a cork, and third, that only by smithing does one become a smith.

But perhaps, my ducklings, you have had enough of quotations and would like to hear a passage of pure Eisenstein:

> Let us speak of the solution to the question of correspondence in silent montage. Here the effect comes not from the simple sequence of the film strips, but from their actual *simultaneity*, resulting from the impression derived from one strip being mentally superimposed over the following strip. The technique of "double-exposure" has merely materialised this basic phenomenon of cinematic perception. We shall see that a similar superimposition occurs even at the *highest stage* of montage development—audio-visual montage. The "double-exposed" image is just as inherently characteristic of audio-visual montage as it is for all other cinematic phenomena.

Have you ever thought, my poppets, what you let yourselves in for when you go to the pictures? In the meantime I could wish that somebody would revive the three Russian films named above. What is behind their making I shall leave to those esoteric ladies with whom this humble scribe would not dream of competing.

The title of 20th-Century-Fox's new film *Holy Matrimony* (Tivoli), "from the novel of Arnold Bennett," gave me no enlightenment as to which novel, until the curtains parted and the familiar spectacle of the famous painter pretending to be his valet, marrying a worthy woman of the valet class, being confronted later with the valet's own wife and the valet's three large and minatory sons—plus the contretemps, misunderstandings, complications and explanations inherent in such a Gilbertian story—revealed itself as our old friend *Buried Alive*, later to be made into that obstinate theatrical success called *The Great Adventure* with which the memory of Henry Ainley will be for ever associated.

A pleasant hour and a half, and very well produced and acted. Monty Woolley as the painter dots every *i* and crosses every *t* as is his wont; and, as ever, his diction is perfect and he wears his beard as if he were used to it—as if he liked it, in fact. I thought Gracie Fields rather squandered on the colourless part of the worthy wife, speaking in this film a nondescript English, neither Cockney, provincial nor King's. Why could not the producer have persuaded Gracie to give us the part in her incomparable native Lancashire? Laird Cregar produces another of his polished performances, Una O'Connor is pathetically funny, and Alan Mowbray and

George Zucco are full of zest. The film is excellent "period," and the dresses are a sheer delight. Which set me pondering—will the whirligig of time bring a revival of those rich, superbly-turned-out frocks, those noble patrician hats? No. And for the reason that the little besoms of to-day wouldn't know how to carry them off. Anything not absurd would look absurd perched on that uniform, ridiculous vacuity.

91

I BLUFF, THOU BLUFFEST . . .

1943

REALISING that nobody is so gammonable as your highbrow film critic, Mr. Orson Welles continues to bluff. On the occasion of *Journey Into Fear* (Astoria) THE TATLER proposes to "call" Mr. Welles. What, in this picture, does he hold? Mr. Welles's cards being put upon the table, they appear to consist of a mildly interesting story rather below the Phillips Oppenheim level. Now let me abandon the poker analogy. On what exactly does Mr. Welles rely? First, on the spectator's insufficient holding in logic. A subtle argument is an argument difficult to follow. But a muddled trend of events is also difficult to follow. Therefore, says Mr. Welles, whatever is muddled must be subtle. Yes, this idol of the highbrows is no master of the "undistributed middle." Did not our highest-browed critic claim great virtue for *Citizen Kane* on the ground that nobody knew that the object burnt in the first shot was a sledge? Did not Mr. Welles's representative over here say that every American would know it was a sledge and that it was an oversight on Mr. Welles's part not to realise that English audiences were unfamiliar with sledges? Was that highbrow critic abashed at this frank admission? Not at all. Was there any retraction? No. We were still to see in our doubts about the object a symbol of that twilight in which you and I, dear reader, dimly know each other.

The story of Mr. Welles's latest film would not begin to be interesting if it were told in a straightforward manner. Therefore Mr. Welles must tell it unintelligibly, relying on us to interpret that unintelligibility as subtlety. An American engineer wants to get out of Turkey with some valuable secrets. The Nazis wish to prevent this and decide to murder him. Then why doesn't the American engineer go to the American Consul? And why doesn't the American Consul put him on an American boat in care of the captain? Or on an American plane in charge of a trustworthy pilot? Instead the silly fellow puts himself in the care of a couple of cabaret performers, takes a Levantine cargo boat and finally lands up at Batum where he has a revolver duel with the two murderers who have dogged him throughout the picture. He satisfactorily disposes of both of them. But there is a third person who, also becoming shot, falls backwards through a window and whose identity is as obscure to me as that of the Third Murderer in *Macbeth.* And here we hit on one of the cards in Mr. Welles's hand—the card of obscurity. It is too dark to see who is this third murderer. But then it has been too dark throughout to see who anybody is. And the noise! Not since the early days of the spoken film have I heard all the characters in a picture bellow like sea-lions. This, of course, made it very difficult to hear what was said. (The same phenomenon can still be observed at every railway terminus and at most Tube stations.) Not being a technician I am unable to say whether the fault is that of reception or transmission. I know only that I am a regular visitor to the Astoria, and that this is the first time I have had any difficulty in hearing.

Where Mr. Welles shows himself a past master at bluffing the highbrows is in the exploitation of their gullibility in the matter of the "cinematic." It is for this reason that you see his figures in mirrors, at the ends of corridors, through port-holes or descending sides of liners at impossible angles. This is why, when a horse comes into the picture, all you are allowed to see is its belly. It is not what the characters are doing that matters, but the fact that the spectator sees them at a distance, out of the corner of his eye, sideways, upside down, and, of course, always in the dark; even the cabaret scene takes place by the light of what appears to be a farthing dip. This picture has been enormously praised because the rain gets on to the glasses of the chief murderer—a simple fact which every golfer who wears spectacles has known since he teed up his first ball. I am therefore but moderately impressed with it. What intrigues me much more is why the murderer should have waited for a thunderstorm and a seventh-story window-ledge in Batum to do that for which he had scores of opportunities on the ground floor on any fine day in Istanbul. As for terror and suspense, I didn't find in the whole of this pretentious piece of hugaboo a single moment of near-trepidation. In fact I found it all intensely boring, and but for the sharp elbows of my neighbours I might easily have gone to sleep. The notabilities in this film are Joseph Cotten, Orson Welles himself, and Dolores del Rio. Presumably they act well. It was too dark to see.

Now, Voyager (Warner) is a cheery little trifle lasting two hours and a quarter; the subject is nervous breakdown. It appears that the last unwanted child of a marriage is necessarily plain, and liable, when bullied by her mother, to become a candidate for a sanatorium. Charlotte Vale is the unwanted child who goes to the sanatorium, from which she emerges not only cured but beautiful! She falls in love with a married man, goes bats again, and on learning that the man has a daughter bullied by her mother as she formerly was, returns to the Home where she finds the child. Nursing the kid back to health she forgets her own *malaise* and finally becomes head nurse at the establishment, which she proceeds to endow with some of the fortune she has inherited from her mother. (Why the second sadistic mother couldn't die and leave the way clear for the unhappy lovers was a mystery.) Instead they decided that if they couldn't have the moon they must put up with the stars. Meaning week-ends at Palm Beach? No, reader. This is an intensely proper film. Bette Davis is excellent as the *belle laide*. Paul Henreid is the unhappy husband. I take him to be an Austrian, as he speaks basic Walbrook quite perfectly. Anybody who has lived at Swiss Cottage will know what I mean. There is a first-rate performance by Gladys Cooper as the tyrannical mother, and Claude Rains once more shows his capacity for being better than the film. The music is said to be by Max Steiner, though I think acknowledgements should have been made to Tschaikowsky and Wagner. The picture shows a certain dalliance with the Orson Welles method, since in her first shot we see Bette's legs descending an elaborate staircase. But they haven't got it right. You can actually distinguish between Bette's legs and the balusters. This, of course, is because Warner's director has a preference for lighting his subjects. In the Welles penumbra you wouldn't have been able to tell flesh from marble.

You may or not think that *Hi Diddle Diddle* (New Gallery) is an amusing frisk. The only certain thing to be said about it is that it was an enormous mistake to bring back Pola Negri, who is an extremely accomplished actress and moreover a grown woman. And for the very good reason that in both capacities she makes rings round the incompetent and undersized ninnies who pass for screen stars to-day.

92

NOT UP MY STREET

1943

LET me say that I saw *Behind the Rising Sun* (Tivoli) under ideal conditions. To begin with, the performance I attended was not one of those post-breakfast celebrations for which one has to rise shortly after cockcrow. It began at the reasonable post-prandial hour of eight p.m. The film was preceded by a soul-destroying "short"—provided anything can be called short which lasts sixty intolerable minutes. I cannot think that this nonsense would have been seeable even if one had been surrounded by beakers of champagne with usherettes spraying one with frangipani and odalisques tickling the soles of one's feet—amenities which are not forthcoming at this otherwise delightful house. When the "short" was finally over I felt that I was in a mood to enjoy anything. Was there not promise of atrocities? And just as some people flock to a street accident, so I cannot resist the spectacle of Nazis suspending tedious bores by their tiresome beards. I am fascinated, although I don't want these horrors to happen. No one will accuse people who rush to a street accident of wanting some old woman to be run over; nothing will keep them from rushing. I once knew a charming lady who disapproved of mouse-traps on the ground that they were rude to mice. Yet she confessed to me that she never saw an aeroplane without hoping it would crash. Since I never met a being whose inclinations tended less to murder, I must suspect an instance of that irresistible appetite for sensation of which many otherwise blameless persons are the victims. Let me say at once that the atrocities in the Japanese film have been exaggerated, and that there is no necessity to bring smelling-salts.

The drama is really a psychological one. It relates how a young Jap westernised by an American University to the point of calling his father "Pop" and mastering the intricacies of baseball, or whatever it is that they teach at American Universities—and let me say at once that my entire knowledge of the curriculum of these institutions is derived from Hollywood—returns to the bosom of his family and on the outbreak of the war between America and Japan becomes more Japanese than Japan's Emperor. Now it seems to me—and the point is one to which I shall return in connection with another picture—that this film's management made a major blunder in the choice of the actor to play the principal character; a blunder from which the film never recovers. What was postulated was a young man, imbued with the Japanese ideology, who had acquired a thin veneer of western thinking which cracked at the first pressure put upon it. What we were given was a fresh, good-looking young American, the hero of any film about football, and looking, thinking and talking like an American though faintly orientalised by the make-up man. The result was a complete disaster shown in many little ways.

I do not believe the young Jap would forget to remove his shoes before entering his father's house, particularly when he has just seen his father doing the same thing. There is a terrific fight between an American boxer and a six-foot master of jiu-jitsu who, by his code, is allowed to kick.

I do not believe that the boxer would have lasted a round, let alone recovered from the succession of goal-scoring assaults below the belt, the first of which would have put him out of action. Yet the film has some nice irony. There is a long love-affair between the young Jap and a typist of his own race. She takes him to see her people who, to do honour to their new son-in-law and to provide him with a slap-up wedding breakfast, have sold their younger daughter to the yellow slave traffic. The typist thinks this will never do; the young Jap holds that in consenting to be sold the younger daughter has done nobly. Is it cynical to suggest that almost any young girl would consider almost any life better than existence on a dull farm with parents who have never heard of the radio? Finally, we get to the tortures, and in the end the Americans bomb Tokyo so that everybody escapes, though whether the younger daughter goes back to the farm is a point not made clear. The one figure of interest was the young Jap's father, who became more and more convinced that Japanese fascism is a mistake. Had the whole of the film been on this high level I should have spoken differently of it. Alas, most of it is romantic hoodlum masquerading as world politics.

It may be argued about the foregoing that if Hollywood had got hold of a young Japanese actor, the choice would have been unpopular. But surely Mr. Goldwyn, when he started to make *North Star* (London Pavilion and Regal, Marble Arch), could have put his hand on some Russian actors. And Russians are popular enough. It is no good telling me that Marina, Kolya, Dr. Kurin, Karp and Sophia are the inhabitants of a little village in the neighbourhood of Kiev. My eyes and ears, without the programme, tell me they are Anne Baxter, Dana Andrews, Walter Huston, Walter Brennan and Ann Harding. They tell me, further, that all these artists are behaving, talking and thinking at their most American. And the tedium! It takes this film very nearly one hour to get going, and again one of the most wearisome hours in my experience. An hour filled with the depiction of American village life with picnics in the woods, rustic courtships and so on. If you had told me that the village in question was situated half-way between New York and Philadelphia I should have believed it. Putting American villagers into Russian costume and calling them by Russian names, while making them inexpertly go through the motions of Russian dancing, is never going to deceive this old bird. My friend and colleague, D. B. Wyndham Lewis, has often alluded to "the homely Island pan," meaning the typical British face, and I hope I am not straining international courtesy when I suggest that there is such a thing as the homely American pan. This picture is full of it, with the result that all verisimilitude vanished. Surely it should not have been beyond Hollywood's powers to get hold of Slavonic actors? Presently the Germans arrive, headed by Erich von Stroheim. Now von S. has saved many a picture before, and will save many again. But not even his brilliant performance could do anything with this one. In the end the villagers burned what they could of their village and formed themselves into a guerrilla band. After which they outwitted the Germans, and with a few clubs and an odd rifle or two drove off the magnificently-equipped invaders. Actually, of course, the Germans would have rounded up the guerrillas, burned what was left of the village and hanged among the ruins the owners of the aforesaid homely American pans. Surely it is time to call a halt in these war pictures. If one cannot, at least one can insist that they should bear some kind of relation to the real thing. I am astonished beyond words to discover that the author of this bosh—sorry, I mean the original story and screen play—is Lillian Hellman.

93

SOME HINTS TO THE CRITICS' CIRCLE

1944

INSPIRED by my old friend and revered colleague, Sydney Carroll, who weighed in during the Christmas holidays with a column article on a new play which he admitted he had not seen, I propose to write something about: (*a*) a film which I propose not to see, (*b*) one which I could not see, and (*c*) one which I did see. Sydney based his criticism of Terry Rattigan's *While the Sun Shines* upon things written about this engaging farce by people who had seen it; I shall do the same with *Jane Eyre* (Odeon). Beginning at the popular end of the critical stick I found one film reviewer who thought that Charlotte Brontë's novel was about a black-browed gentleman who bigamously married his servant. Another popular film critic, who also announced that he had not read the book, let it be seen that if had read it he should have pronounced it rubbish. Neither of these gossipy gentlemen appeared to have the slightest notion that the thing on which the film had been based is still one of the glories of English literature. Now the fact that a book from which a picture is taken may be a masterpiece does not matter; the only points to be considered in the present connection are whether such a book tells a good story, and whether that story can be told cinematically. Still it is well for the film critic to be aware that there is a masterpiece in the offing, so to speak. Which, of course, raises a broader issue; this is whether film critics should be literate or illiterate. Possibly this is to encroach on the province of the Critics' Circle, who may, for all I know, hold the view that the first qualification of a critic is to bring to the art he criticises what is known in Fleet Street as a fresh mind, that is, a mind totally innocent of any of that education which, in an earlier age, was held to be essential to a critic. Thus untrammelled and unshackled the free spirit.... Yes, reader dear, I could make out an excellent case for the Critic as Boor.

At the other end of the stick my young friend and revered colleague, Miss Dilys Powell, told me all I wanted to know about this film. And I can guess that she placed it exactly. Now let me go away from Charlotte for a moment and pay a call on another maiden lady who wrote novels, a lady of the name of Jane Austen. Among this writer's unfinished tales is one called *The Watsons.* In this there is a passage in which Lord Osborne expatiates on the merits of half-boots. The scene is an afternoon visit after a ball. Lord Osborne hopes that Emma has not caught cold, and relapses into silence. After much hard labour of mind he recommends half-boots for walking in dirty weather, and expresses the opinion that ladies should ride whether they can afford it or not. There is some discussion of this, followed by a second relapse into silence. Rising to take 's leave, his lordship "recommended exercise in defiance of dirt; spoke again in praise of half-boots; begged that his sister might be allowed to send Emma the name of her shoemaker."

The late A. B. Walkley's comment on this was: "There is only one peer in Jane's novels, Lord Osborne, and he is an empty ass. 'Spoke again in praise of half-boots' settled *him.*" This phrase of A. B. W. should be in more general use. Dear Dilys's "*Jane Eyre* is not innocent of monotony" settles this film as far as I am concerned. It hints, in a whisper to be heard from one end of Leicester Square to the other, that the film is dull. And if there is one thing I will not put up with at the pictures it is dullness. In a theatre, yes, for one of the conditions of first-rate art is that it does not exclude dullness. The mind must have its resting-places—a fact which, in their respective spheres, Michael Angelo and Shakespeare, Goethe and Beethoven have all known and recognised. Show me a work which is all sparkle, and I will show you a *little* work, perfect if you like but still not of the great order. We should not palliate a moment of dullness in, say, *Fledermaus;* we are grateful for such moments in the *Ring.* But here again is matter less perhaps for this page than for the august deliberation of the Critics' Circle.

And now to return to my friend Sydney, with whom we began. I am surprised that my colleague should believe and reaffirm that hoary nonsense which pretends that good actors by their good acting can persuade a critic that a bad play or film is in fact a good play or film. This is nonsense. It is only the bad critics who are so deluded; I challenge Sydney to produce a single instance in which Shaw, Walkley, or Max has been persuaded by good acting to mistake nonsense for sense. I challenge him to produce a single instance from the columns of the *Sunday Times* in support of his theory during the last twenty years. In the converse case it is the bad critic and not the good who is prevented from seeing the quality of a good play by the inefficiency of the actors. I challenge Sydney . . . . But I am probably wasting my time. When it is pointed out to him my old friend will realise as quickly as anybody that he has been writing Christmas nonsense.

What exactly is meant by "the Nelson touch"? I have always taken it to mean valorous disobedience of orders, congratulations and honour if the thing comes off and a court-martial if it doesn't. The new film at the Leicester Square is called *The Nelson Touch* presumably because it is all about sticking to orders, come what come may. Still it takes more than titular contradiction to spoil a good picture, and this is a very good one. (I know, because this is the film I was lucky enough to see.) I don't profess to have the slightest knowledge of naval affairs, but here, it seems to me, is a first-hand representation of what goes on in a corvette. This picture cannot be accused of being literary, and has none of that self-consciousness which, it is pardonable to say at this distance of time, prevented Coward's *In Which We Serve* from being a complete success. The only false touch I noticed occurs at the very end. It seems that the six ships which the corvette, though badly limping, brings safely to port, wish to salute her. The crew of the corvette are lined up, and their eyes become what third-rate novelists call "suspiciously moist." One of the men says out of the corner of his mouth: "I wonder whether we shall be patched up in time to take them back again." And his chum replies: "If not, then there'll be others." This, of course, is the purest patriotic bunkum. The conversation of sailors nearing port can have only one printable subject: "Will The Pubs Have Run Out Of Wallop?"

I invite the Critics' Circle to exercise some control over the hats of their women critics. At the press show of *Cry Havoc* (Empire) my view was almost entirely occluded by a hat which appeared to consist of a large pork pie surmounted by a small pork pie on the top of which a dicky-bird was perched, spreading tail-feathers for victory. This preposterous fowl filled two-thirds of the screen, leaving one-sixth at either edge, so that I felt like one hearing a film on the wireless. From the dialogue I gathered that *Cry Havoc* is a tragedy, despite the fact that it is conveyed in familiar exchanges like "Skip it!" "I'm nuts on the guy," and "That dame sure has it in for me." Presently, to my everlasting shame and disgrace, I found I was falling asleep, possibly the result of sixteen consecutive hours of vigil at other and, I think I must say, less lugubrious entertainments. When I awoke I found my coat sleeve drenched with the tears of a friend whose view, since he was sitting behind a short and conveniently bald-headed critic, had not been impeded. I gathered from him that he had been moved by a noble story of nursing in Bataan. I therefore invite readers of THE TATLER to view this picture for themselves, and form their own opinion about it. I do not admit that my opinion can ever be untrustworthy; I take my stand in the present instance on the firm ground that as I was prevented from seeing the picture I have no opinion. Will the Critics' Circle take some steps in the matter of feminine headgear, please? There are two other methods of dealing with this nuisance. One is that an attendant should be employed to deal with offenders, if necessary by force. The other is that these small private theatres should have their floors raked.

94

HORRID SUSPICION

1944

IN Mr. Sacheverell Sitwell's new and exquisite extravaganza, fantasia, rhapsody, symphonic poem—entitled *Splendours and Miseries*—occurs a passage which I venture to think could be adapted to the film "musical." Mr. Sitwell is writing about Madeleine Smith who, in 1857, was tried for murdering her paramour by giving him arsenic, her motive being to enable herself to turn respectable and marry a Mr. Minnoch. The verdict was the Scotch one of non-proven, which means that half the jury thought she did it and the other half thought she didn't. All sorts of fantastic theories were advanced at the time, and of these Mr. Sitwell makes a list. The first is the Maybrick defence, that L'Angelier (the lover) died as the result of a long course of arsenic self-administered. The second, that his passion for Madeleine was such that he drank the cocoa which his mistress handed to him knowing it was poisoned. Third, that he dropped arsenic into the cocoa without Madeleine knowing it. Whatever the fact, Madeleine got away with it and, five years later, married a Mr. Wardell, a designer employed by William Morris. She was often drawn by Rossetti as the Magdalene, and had the pleasure, we are told, of listening at her own dinner-table some thirty years later to a discussion on the Maybrick case. Madeleine retired to Leek in Staffordshire, went to the United States, and in 1914 married an American, who appears to have left her poorly off. Anyhow, she thought of going into pictures, a suggestion which I have no doubt Hollywood would have accepted had she still been young and pretty. She died in 1927 at the age of ninety-two, saying nothing to nobody, and thus rivalling in secrecy the famous American non-provenite, Mary Borden. For myself I have always thought that the interest of the case has been exaggerated, and brought about through the fact that she is the only murderess who has come down to posterity wearing a sailor-hat.

Mr. Sitwell states that Madeleine becomes an obsession with all who read about her. I understand this obsession; I myself have never stopped thinking about the Wallace case and trying to make the scale come down on one side or the other. But our memorialist goes further; he pretends that Madeleine haunts any music heard "during that time," and that that music will suggest her strange history for ever. Mr. Sitwell means, of course, not the music of 1857, at which date he was not born, but the music he was hearing at the time of his first introduction to the case. Personally I should hate to think that the publication of Madeleine's crime in the Famous Trial Series coincided with my first hearing of *Rosenkavalier*. Or that I must for ever associate the Marschallin with a dubious little creature wearing a straw boater. However this may be, Mr. Sitwell writes:

> Madeleine Smith is for ever associated in my mind with the Liebeslieder Waltzer of Brahms which, as far as my imagination is concerned, she may be said to haunt. In the same fashion, the exquisitely graceful and lovely piano Quartet in G minor, K. 478, of Mozart, was spoiled for me, when I most loved it, by Hitler's murder of Roehm and his friends on the dreadful 30 June, 1934. In different vein, Chopin's Mazurka in C sharp minor, No. 3, played in incredible and supernatural nuance of touch by Horowitz, makes me think of the Talking Mongoose of Cashen's Gap. Most lovers of music will have known similar sensations.

And now comes my point. What of to-day, when Hitler is murdering more Poles than ever before and when that little rat Goebbels is chattering away faster than the most accomplished mongoose—are these dreadful things to be for ever associated in our minds with the theme songs of *The Girls He Left Behind* (Gaumont, Haymarket, and Marble Arch Pavilion) and the strains of Benny Goodman's band? The next few months are to see the launching of the greatest invasion force in history. Are we to associate this with Alice Faye crooning:

A journey to a star
Will not be very far
As long as I'm alone with you.

Or the departure of the greatest army ever sent overseas with the same young woman wailing:

No love, no nuthin',
Till ma baby comes home.

Yes, and the B.B.C. will make sure that we do by dinning these lamentable ditties into us night after night. What? During the invasion? Yes. During the invasion.

The plot? All about an army sergeant torn between two girls, his home-town mousey-pousy—Walkley's term—and a back-stage roguey-poguey. The conversation between the American sergeant and the roguey-poguey goes something like this:

R.-P. Say, you wanna hear me sing sometime, dontcher?
A.S. Yeah.
R.-P. Could be.
A.S. Start in, sister.
R.-P. All right, soldier, you win.

Of Alice Faye's talent and charm I do not pretend to be a judge. There are some who put her above Betty Grable, some who put her below; I join neither school of thought. On behalf of James Ellison who plays the sergeant, I resent Hollywood's habit of presenting the typical American as a fifty-fifty per cent combination of bounce and cretinism. Carmen Miranda is becoming more and more like Mickey Rooney, and the best performance, as usual, is given by the unstarred Charlotte Greenwood, who, as a legitimate actress, makes nonsense of these screen pretenders. It now remains to be said that the picture, which is in Technicolor, is the acme of the sumptuous and the apex of the grandiose. There is a garden-party in a setting which suggests that at any moment Norma Shearer herself is going to appear as Juliet. There is a sequence in which a number of giant bananas take on the quality of so many Platonic ideas. There is a finale in which the heads of all the principals are intended to swim about in a ruby deliquescence like that of the best American sunsets. Actually they only look like the plaster casts of heads guillotine-served under Robespierre, and reposing on red velvet. Fortunately the Terror lasts a comparatively short time—not more than an hour and three-quarters from start to finish. And pray what is all this expense of effort about? It is about that sheer pointless inanity which is less than nothing. It is strange, said Chesterton, that an age with nothing to say should have invented the loudspeaker. In my view it is equally strange that the age which has invented Technicolor should have nothing to paint.

What the foregoing amounts to is that Tom, Dick and Harry, together with their girls, will vote this "musical" first-class. I have a suspicion that I enjoyed bits of it myself. In a sneaking, shame-faced sort of way.

95

NO AND YES

1944

I TAKE the following from the *Daily Herald* for Tuesday, June 13:

> Hundreds of American assault troops are now reported to have lost their lives in gaining the mile-and-a-half beach sector near Vierville. An army major in charge of burying the dead on this beach says that he estimated some 750 bodies were recovered, while probably an equal number were washed away by the succeeding high tide. The troops came in at low tide on D-Day. "The American people ought to see this," he said grimly, indicating rows of bodies stretching for several hundred yards.—Reuter.

Within half an hour of reading this I was sitting at the press view of *Up in Arms* (Empire), a musical about the war. And here, if you please, is the "literature" on the subject duly handed out to me:

> Tailored for the box-office, the first musical from the expert Goldwyn source for five years, *Up in Arms* marks the notable return of the producer to a field in which he released such triumphs as *Whoopee*, *The Kid From Spain*, and *The Goldwyn Follies*. The result of his experience is a film in Technicolor outstanding for surprise, catchy music, hilarious comedy, and beautiful presentation and personnel. Two of New York's brightest musical-comedy and night-club stars make their screen débuts in the picture. They are the brilliant Danny Kaye, who draws star billing, and Constance Dowling, the latter being co-featured with Dinah Shore and Dana Andrews. Kaye, undoubtedly Broadway's most sensational comedian of recent seasons, goes all out in two outstanding speciality acts for the show—his "Lobby Number" satirising screen musical comedies, and his "Melody in 4-F" with which he nightly stopped the show in *Let's Face It* on the American stage. Dinah Shore sings two special numbers in her famous style. A big ensemble number is "All Out for Freedom," Glittering production scenes stud the *Up in*

Arms presentation, particularly a shipboard "jive session" and a lavish dream sequence staged in a pastel-hued drug store seemingly as spacious as the Wembley Stadium. The whole show is embellished with three dozen of Hollywood's most glamorous beauties who actually enhance the Technicolor of the production.

I cannot think of anything more unfortunate than that this nonsense should have been put on at this moment. I have to say further that I do not believe that the vulgarity of mind which can turn the war into a musical is typically American.

A highly-placed American officer with whom I discussed the matter said that wartime Hollywood had become a pain in the neck to all decent-thinking Americans, and that the boys themselves, meaning the troops, were not amused. And why should soldiers taking the war seriously—and those beaches are a deadly serious business—be tickled at the notion of stowing away cuties in the baggage of detachments leaving for this country? Even on its own plane I found the show dreadful beyond words. So much so that when a crooner with a voice like a sea-sick kitten put over a number with the burden "This Is the End of Me," the devoted and long-suffering critic of this paper took the hint and departed.

The above objections do not apply to the new Charles K. Feldman production, *Follow the Boys* (Leicester Square). This is almost entirely concerned with entertainments for the American troops, partly in camps, partly on the air, organised by what Friend Synopsis calls the "Hollywood Victory Committee." Here is an idea at which nobody can cavil, and as we only see units of the U.S.A. forces in the guise of rapturous audience, there can be no talk of degradation. In other words, the film is legitimate entertainment and as such beyond reproach. But not, alas, beyond criticism! The film is a long hotch-potch of performers, dance-bands, dancers, music-hall performers, singers, comedians and concerted vocal numbers, held together by the thinnest of stories. We will, if you please, take the performers first.

There is a varied and distinguished list of these, not far different from those galaxies of music-hall stars which were seen nightly in London's West-End music-halls many years ago. Jeannette Macdonald sings for us; a pity that her song is so very banal, both in words and music. Then we get a great surprise. A first-class conjurer appears, and with him a beautiful woman who is sawn in half, after which the lower half of her body dances off while the upper half smiles at us from the wings. Well, what of it, you ask? Hold on a minute. The magician is Orson Welles, and the lady is Marlene Dietrich herself! Then W. C. Fields gives us some superb clowning with a billiard table. Sophie Tucker, looking as robust as ever, treats us to a patriotic song, the gestures as large, the diction as flawless as ever. The Andrews Sisters sing their usual incomprehensible nonsense provoking applause that a Melba or a Tetrazzini might have envied. Arthur Rubinstein plays the "Liebestraum," marvellously of course and making it sound almost like a new piece, which is all to its advantage. And then, the endless band: Ted Lewis, Freddy Slack, Charlie Spivak, Louis Jordan, all playing what sounded to me like the same tune played by the same instruments in the same tempo. Common music in common time, as a witty neighbour remarked.

And the story? Well, it concerns George Raft—who calls himself Tony West in the film and is one of the chief organisers of these U.S.A. Forces shows—and his dancing partner and subsequent wife, Vera Zorina, who calls herself Gloria Vance. Tony neglects Gloria, being wrapped up in the production of stars. Gloria becomes a mother, having refused to see Tony for—well, it can't be for over a year, can it?—and will probably never dance with him again as he is killed on a ship torpedoed by the Japanese on the way to Australia whither he is conducting a cargo of stars. We are pleased to tell you that the stars are all saved, though what happened to the lifeboat when Sophie Tucker was hauled into it, I shudder to think. So there you are. And if you like this style of entertainment, *Follow the Boys* is just your cup of tea. Personally after an hour and a half of it I found myself incapable of following anything whatsoever.

96

THE FOUR WHO WERE HANGED

1944

Justice Is Coming. This news-reel, issued by the Soviet Film Agency and now showing at the Tatler Theatre, is entirely sickening and should be exhibited all over the country. It might act as a counterblast to those consciously or subconsciously pro-Nazi films which invite us to sympathise with an escaping German, or show us groups of Nazi officers concentrating not on camps but on Schubert. The present picture is concerned with some of the symphonies which the Nazis have not left unfinished. Three hundred children whose bones breaking through their skin show that they were starved to death. Six hundred bodies of men and women burnt to death. Civilians, whose only crime was that they belonged to another race, thrown into gas-vans and driven around until they were poisoned by the carbon-monoxide from the exhaust-pipe emptying itself into the van. Let us face it. We in this country know very little of the horrors of war, nothing whatever of what it means to live or endure existence in an occupied country. We have had our blitzes and our bombings, and have withstood them. But we do not know—and please God we never shall know—what emotions we should experience if in, say, Reading or Derby thirty thousand decent-living people were conscientiously murdered. This picture shows us a mother and two children burnt to death by the Germans; and it is darkly hinted that there are worse things than being burnt to death. What is to be done with those responsible for these filthy atrocities?

The criminals brought to justice in this news-reel are four in number. We see the actual trial, and the way of it is this. First the prosecutor puts a question in Russian which is translated into German by an interpreter. We hear the accused reply in German which the interpreter puts back into Russian. And we, sitting in the theatre, hear above the other speakers the rendering of all this into English. And I have enough knowledge of German, if not of Russian, to appreciate the integrity of the English version. Of the four prisoners three are German, the fourth is a Russian traitor. The first to be examined is Captain Wilhelm Langfeld of the German Intelligence. To me he does not look the officer-type; he is obviously uneducated and has none of the gloss which these swine use to cover up their brutality. He admits to ordering the killing of one hundred civilians. The next is Rheinhardt Retzlav of the Gestapo. This precious fellow has a mouth like a shark, no chin and a forehead straight out of Lombroso. He admits to pushing the citizens of Kharkov into the murder-van. The third is Leutnant Hans Ritz of the S.S. He is a blond, rather sheepish-looking young man who might be a shop-assistant or something equally harmless. We learn, however, that he is a sadist of exquisite depravity. He confesses to having slaughtered women and children with his own hand. Perhaps I don't feel so vindictive about the fourth, one Michael Bulanov; this is a decent-looking fellow and might be mistaken for any Russian concert-pianist. Given the choice between driving a murder-van and being put into one and driven around—which of us is going to swear that he would not have saved his own skin since refusing to save it would not have helped anyone else? In other words I'm rather sorry for Bulanov, who at any rate has the decency to admit that he has been a coward. It is the other three upon whom one concentrates. Well, of course they have got to hang, and they do hang. But their hanging leaves us with a sense of frustration. After all, they were only carrying out orders, and the highest in rank among them is only a captain. What we want to get at is the Colonels and the Generals and the people above Colonels and Generals.

It never does to neglect "unser" Shakespeare. Well, let us see what "unser" Shakespeare has to say on the subject of people like Hitler and Himmler, Goering and Goebbels. Here again I am inclined to make distinctions. I am willing to believe that Hitler is an ecstatic madman, Himmler a sadistic brute, and Goering an overfed fathead. I don't feel that any of these three is what I should call educated. But Goebbels is a different case. He has brains and education. He has been a journalist and has committed the one crime which no journalist will ever forgive—he has tampered with the truth.

But perhaps this is my personal quarrel with Goebbels. Let us consider the horrible quartet as a whole and hear what "unser" Shakespeare thought on the subject of vengeance. First Othello's

> I would have him nine years a-killing.

Next his

> O, that the slave had forty thousand lives!
> One is too poor, too weak for my revenge.

And again

> Had all his hairs been lives, my great revenge
> Had stomach for them all.

The trouble is that Hitler and Himmler, Goering and the little Doctor have only four lives between them. So I take another play of Shakespeare, that of *Macbeth*, and turn to the lines in which Macduff invites Macbeth to surrender and promises him his life:

> Then yield thee, coward,
> And live to be the show and gaze' o' the time.
> We'll have thee, as our monsters are,
> Painted upon a pole, and underwrit,
> "Here may you see the tyrant."

My own way with the quartet would be to turn them into a travelling circus and send them round the once-occupied countries, each immured in a bullet-proof glass cage. These cages would be nicely warmed because each of the quartet would be naked with his uniform and decorations fastened to the glass at the back of the cage. Over the whole show would be emblazoned: Here may you see the *Herrenvolk*! The captives would be given plenty to eat and drink. But they would be compelled to listen, day in and day out, unceasingly and endlessly, to the torrents of their own eloquence reproduced by exceedingly loud speakers and diversified only by selections from *Mein Kampf* and the more idiotic bits of Nietzsche. The circus would, of course, be entirely managed, run and policed by Jews whose Jewishness could be seen a mile away. And here an even brighter idea strikes me. This is to send the quartet, not to the once-occupied countries, but to their own! It would be appropriate if the show were to start from that beer cellar in Munich.

97

A LETTER TO MERVYN McPHERSON

1944

DEAR MERVYN,

If only Hollywood would not overboost its wares! If *An American Romance* had come to me in the ordinary way I should have said it was a nice, well-intentioned, dull, and over-long picture of the steel, motor and aeroplane industries. But the picture didn't come to me untrumpeted and unfanfared. The day before I saw it I received a letter from you headed in red ink: "Answer to your prayer! THE REAL AMERICA COMES TO LIFE ON THE SCREEN." And then in black ink: "Surely this is the answer to the critic's prayer for a picture about America, made in America, not just the America of the bijou residence with thirty-nine bedrooms and three swimming pools, or the America of the gangster, or the co-ed, or the sublimated swingster, but the America of the poor immigrants whom the United States took in, and who in return made those United States the richest and greatest industrial country in the world."

In one respect, dear Mervyn, you were right. I have long wanted a picture about America as it really is. In other words, a picturisation of something you will find in Whitman's *Collect:*

> When I pass to and fro, different latitudes, different seasons, beholding the crowds of the great cities, New York, Boston, Philadelphia, Cincinnati, Chicago, St. Louis, San Francisco, New Orleans, Baltimore—when I mix with these interminable swarms of alert, turbulent, good-natured, independent citizens, mechanics, young persons—at the idea of this mass of men, so fresh and free, so loving and so proud, a singular awe falls on me. I feel, with dejection and amazement, that among the geniuses and talented writers or speakers, few or none have yet really spoken to this people, created a single *image-making work* [italics mine] for them, or absorbed the central spirit and the idiosyncracies which are theirs—and which, thus, in highest ranges, so far remain entirely uncelebrated, unexpressed.

I thought from your letter that you had at last found for us this "image-making work." Again:

> Indeed, the peculiar glory of our lands, I have come to see, or expect to see, not in their geographical or republican greatness, not wealth or

products [italics mine], nor military or naval power, nor special, eminent names in any department, to shine with, or outshine, foreign special names in similar departments—but more and more in a vaster, saner, more surrounding Comradeship, uniting closer and closer not only the American States, but all nations, and all humanity. That, O poets! is not that a theme worth chanting, striving for?

Would not that, O Mervyn, have been a film worth making and boosting? I looked for a film about the American Romance and you give me one about an American industry.

It is true that you write: "This tale of a self-made man and a self-made nation takes Steve Dangos (Brian Donlevy) through the forty-six most crowded and pregnant years in all history, from 1898 to 1944. It takes him through the pioneer years of the mammoth American steel industry; from steel to 'flivvers'; from those to the 'streamlined monarchs of the road'; and from automobiles to Flying Fortresses."

I think, dear Mervyn, that you have been led away by King Vidor, who has spent ten years on conceiving something that any competent hack could have conceived in ten minutes. In my view it is just not true to say that behind this film's flivvers and Fortresses are the human souls of the hero, his family and his friends. They seem to me to be mere figures taken from a card-index, and I feel that I know no more about them at the end of the picture than I did at the beginning. *They just don't live*, as the dramatic critics say. The whole picture boils down, I submit, to a row about the employees' right to a voice in the industry to which they are giving their lives.

Let me end by offering you three crumbs of comfort. First crumb: I am not mechanically minded. I cannot and will not drive a motor-car. I don't in the least care how they are made. I have never been to the motor show. I refuse to go in a plane. A film about hair-pins would interest me as much as one about flivvers and Fortresses. Second crumb: In spite of my non-interest in the subject I didn't feel the picture had lasted two hours and a half. Third crumb: I thought it all technically magnificent.

Yours ever,

JAMES AGATE.

P.S. You noticed, of course, four omissions from the American hot-pot? There was no mention of Germans, Wops, Negroes, and British. To judge from this picture, the American *plat* consists entirely of a couple of Slav onions and some gravy.

98

SOME CUTTING REMARKS

1944

WHAT'S all this fuss about cutting? My revered colleague. Dilys Powell, recently wrote about the new film at the Plaza:

> Again and again throughout the film we find this over-all movement within the scene: figures gathering for a speech, arguments behind the scenes in an election campaign, a voters' meeting. It must not, of course, blind us to the ferocious efficiency of the cutting. In *Hail The Conquering Hero* every scene, every gesture is broken off when its point has been made and not a fraction of a second later; the aside is cut at the precise moment when it has become intelligible. Let us look into this matter of cutting.

Nine-tenths of novel-writing is a waste of time because nine-tenths of novels are written for old ladies in Buxton or Cheltenham who have nothing to do but bulge in the bow-windows of private hotels with the circulating library's latest novel. This has to be long in order to spare the old ladies the too-frequent trudge to the library. Whether they know it or not, the maxim of the popular novelist must ever be: Twaddle To Save Waddle. That is why you read this sort of thing:

> Lord Eustace descended slowly from the limousine.
>
> "I shall not want you again, Skeggs," he said.
>
> "Very good, my lord," said the chauffeur, touching his cap with a gesture in which a discreet sympathy was discernible. He knew all about the trouble with her ladyship.
>
> Lord Eustace ascended the steps. There were seven of them; there had been seven of them since his earliest infancy. He remembered that his nurse had dropped him on the third step—or was it the fourth? Which accounted for the slight curvature in his spine.
>
> "Her ladyship in?" he asked. And sympathy was again visible in the grizzled butler's reply. "In the blue room, my lord." Were we more flippant we might hint to the reader that however blue her ladyship's boudoir, her husband was feeling bluer still.
>
> Wending his way through endless corridors which had once rung with the steps of his Norman ancestors, Lord Eustace entered that one of her boudoirs which his wife affected on Wednesdays. Tea had obviously just been served, but he waved away the proffered crumpet with a bitter sneer. "We have sterner matters to discuss, Alethea," he hissed. "I refer,

of course, to your infatuation for young Gonzales Bensusan, which has become the talk of the Club."

"Don't," she said—and every word was like a poniard driven home by a hand of ice—"Don't be ridiculous!"

In the novel this sort of stuff is all very well, and if I were condemned to spend my life gazing out of bow-windows, I should probably read this sort of stuff. In the film it would be utterly tedious. And this is where I take it that good cutting comes in. You don't see Lord Eustace tramp those endless corridors, mount those steps, descend from that limousine or even get into it. You cut from the moment when Lord Eustace hears a fellow-member at the Club stop dead in the middle of a sentence concerning his wife. The next shot shows the lady telling her husband not to be ridiculous. And the next? This, of course, shows the stain on the wall caused by the dish of crumpets which so narrowly missed his lordship's head.

Curious art, the secret of which, if I read my colleague aright, is not putting in but leaving out! It is as though Wagner had handed *Tristan* to some cutter and said: "Take your scissors, boy, and turn this into a masterpiece." What I can't understand is why film directors take the trouble to photograph so much that they know they're going to cut out. Of course, Preston Sturges's cutting is excellent. But why make so much fuss about it? Nobody should be allowed to make a film unless he can cut with the ferocious efficiency with which this film has been cut. Is it suggested that in that case most films would come to an end after some twenty minutes? *Tant mieux,* as our neighbours wittily say.

The story of the little squirt who is boosted into a hero must, by the time these lines are printed, have gone round London. This film cocks a magnificent snook at small-town patriotism. Nothing is forgotten. The flag-waving, the processions, the irrepressible brass band, the pompous officials, the ridiculous women with their super-absurd hats, the bouquet-presenting child—everything is there. The result is an hour and a half of unforgettable laughter. In the end the film dwindles into sentimentality, very much as though in *Le Rosier de Madame Husson* the young man had repented and resumed his innocence. However, up to the last quarter of an hour, the film is superb, and even with the final lapse is ten times better than anything that has come out of Hollywood for years. How good an actor young Eddie Bracken is we shall, of course, not know until he appears in a rôle which is not sure-fire from the first cut to the last.

I laughed myself silly at *The Climax* (Odeon), although this story of operatic singers in what are presumably the 'seventies is intended to be taken seriously. The chief figure is a wicked doctor, Hohner (Boris Karloff), who murders the opera star, Marcellina, because he is jealous of her voice. As he explains in that slow, sinister way that Boris has, her nightly bawling to anyone who can pay for a ticket robs him of that exclusive love which should be devoted to him alone. But M. doesn't love him at all, so he strangles her and hides her corpse for ten years in what Friend Synopsis tells me is a subterranean room, though the doctor always has to mount steps of monumental height to reach it. Now appears another Voice, that of a young girl who is only a student. Angela (Susanna Foster) is at once engaged to appear in a curious opera where she makes her début singing Chopin's so-called Minute-Valse and going up to what sounded to me like an E in alt. But the doctor, who doesn't approve of these capers, hypnotises Angela and robs her of her voice, so that at the next rehearsal, she stops short on a mere high C and stands there mute and motionless; for all the world like the doll in *Tales of Hoffman* when the mechanism has run down. But good must needs triumph over evil, and here is good personified in the composer Franz (Turhan Bey) who counter-hypnotises Angela, so that she gets her voice back. Whereupon she appears in a revival of some great masterpiece in which the chorus sings Schubert's *Marche Militaire* all through. Needless to say, the doctor is unmasked—by his own housekeeper, who has taken board and wages for ten years in the hope of denouncing him—after which he inadvertently sets fire to the "subterranean" corpse and to himself. Whereupon Angela in the ecstasy of freedom mounts to apices of sound which turn Mozart's Queen of Night into an Ada Crossley.

This is only a little of this glorious, intoxicating nonsense. You should watch the antics of the king who, seemingly some nine years old, goes to the Opera every night and sits in the front of his box with a body-guard of Goeringesque generals. Or the unnamed prompter who unfolds a score the size of a Shakespeare First Folio but never seems to find the right place. Or the opera singers themselves, all of whom seem to consist exclusively of sopranos and tenors. But the Technicolor is very well managed, with here and there a touch of Orson-Wellesian crepuscularity. As for Boris, with his funeral face and his graveyard voice, I now cannot rest till I see him as Hamlet.

99

FRATERNITY SQUARE

1945

THE much-heralded *I Live In Grosvenor Square* has arrived at last and is safely and, I may say, successfully housed in those twin mansions the Warner and the Empire. The pre-trumpeting of a picture always fills me with misgiving. When I am told, for example, that Miss D's part in the new film "is the greatest, most dramatic, most thrilling rôle ever undertaken by any actress" I yawn. Because I just know it isn't. But *I Live,* etc., is not at all bad. It certainly has some glaring faults, and perhaps it were best to deal with these first. It is much too long. And what, pray, is it all about? Simply the vagaries of an aristocratic miss (Anna Neagle) divided between her affection for an American sergeant (Dean Jagger), who is billeted in her grandfather's house in Grosvenor Square, and a man of her own class, an officer and prospective politician (Rex Harrison). The old, old stuff! The heroine's trepidations—("I do like you, Johnnie, honest to goodness I do") —her hesitations—("I thought I loved Peter, but I was wrong, it's you I love")—her fluctuations—("I do love Peter after all, though I did think it was Johnnie I loved"). Can anything be more tiresome and more boring? I know, I know—the average film-goer adores this theme and all its variations, and will sit for hours open-mouthed in admiration and wonder at these fatuous little Madam Can't-Make-Up-Their-Minds.

But of course the two hours are not entirely filled with these amorous combinations and permutations—there are other things. There is the Duke of Exmoor, for instance, who is played by Robert Morley and is a very good-natured, good-humoured, good-hearted duke indeed, always handing cups of tea to what he is humorously pleased to call his "paying guests," giving presents—I knew at one point for certain that he would fish out some Last War relic and present it to one of the Yanks with the usual tearful "This belonged to my son—I am sure you would like to have it"—to which the Yank replies that he has no words with which to express his thanks—and hasn't! The Duke seems to spend most of his time trimming hedges and driving about in what to me looked like a misshapen wheelbarrow. That is the Duke; of which I permit myself to remark with no disrespect that he appears to be by Tom Robertson out of Ouida Corelli. Then there is the housekeeper (Nancy Price). Here, I think, is the place to point out what I hold to be another of the faults of this picture. All the characters are so good and kind, so well-bred, so generous, so hospitable. Even Nancy, who certainly starts off by giving the frozen mitt to Dean Jagger, thaws, and in the later shots is all smiles and saccharine, presiding at her seventy-second birthday party, given in her honour by the P.G.'s who, of course, sing that, to us, slightly silly tune without which no American natal feast would be complete. And then there is the Duke's cousin (Irene Vanbrugh) who is urbanity itself. There is Dean's buddy (sorry, I can't remember his name) who is fidelity itself. There is Rex's rival parliamentary candidate, who is noble-heartedness itself. There is a delightful Colonel. There are two golden-hearted girls in a train. There is a butler of overpowering ancestry and charm. Everyone is delightful, everyone pays compliments, everyone is out for a good time, gives a good time, has a good time. In fact, it's like being cooped up for hours with endless Cheerybles, Tapleys, Cousin Feenixes (without the wit), and all the people whom you would run a mile to avoid. At times I prayed for an ounce of Bogart to sour my imagination.

I take it that the whole thing is an elaborate effort to promote goodwill and understanding between the Americans and ourselves. Good! But must the management, in order to do this, give us quite such an improbable version of Engish town and country life during the war? Do the granddaughters of dukes really talk of "civvy street", and say "maybe" when they mean "perhaps"? Have British officers in wartime so much leisure that they can stump the country canvassing for votes? Do English Dukes take their titles from the village in which they happen to have an estate? (I know comparatively few Dukes.) Do singers at service clubs perform on a cottage piano, and do the guests lining the stairs sing the chorus of a song they have never heard before? Are the halls in Grosvenor Square the size of a concert-hall and the sitting-rooms the dimensions of Olympia? Like Rosa Dartle, I only ask for information. The dialogue seems to be a composite business. Part of it is quite smart, even to borrowing from Wilde ("Do you understand what you say?" "Yes, when I listen carefully"), and sometimes of that fearsome monosyllabic kind which I have heard called Basic American. The latter is the sort mainly adopted in the numerous love-scenes between Anna and her two swains.

But the film is well acted. Both Rex and Dean are excellent. Anna has little else to do but to be sweet, and sweet she duly is. If in the one scene where she could do a bit of real acting, she doesn't do it—well, there is probably an excellent reason for it. But truth compels me to say that the picture is dominated, held, and entirely run off with by Irene Vanbrugh and Nancy Price. When you hear those voices, watch those gestures, note the faultless timing, the elegance and the virtuosity attained by the simplest means—when either of these superb war-horses takes the stage we say:— She paweth in the valley and rejoiceth in her strength. She swalloweth the ground with fierceness and rage. She smelleth the battle afar off, the thunder of the leading man and the applause.

100

WHAT IS THE SCREEN FOR?

1945

THE Skibbereen Eagle, it will be remembered, had its eye on the Tsar of all the Russias, though whether His Imperial Majesty returned the compliment is open to doubt. THE TATLER has had its eye on Charles Laughton for some time and it begins to look as though that fine actor has been cocking an eye at THE TATLER. It has been held in this column that Laughton was not doing himself or his art justice in throwing both away on comic butlers, senile grandpas, and drooling ghosts. The view the writer has taken is that Laughton, when he left the stage, was a first-class character actor, and that when he adopted the screen as his medium he added to his genius for character a talent for melodrama. His Captain Bligh was magnificent and unforgettable. Never mind the faults of that film, the lagoons filled with Mr. Cochran's Young Ladies masquerading as bathing belles, and all the rest of the non-realism. Laughton made Bligh a grotesque and frightening figure. He does the same for Captain Kidd.

And now here is something that I offer for the consideration of our highbrows. Something culled from a writer now, alas, going out of fashion, largely, perhaps, because of the contempt he poured upon the intellectuals of his day, calling them persons "depressed by exceptionally æsthetic surroundings." The writer is Robert Louis Stevenson. He begins by telling his readers that drama is the poetry of conduct, romance the poetry of circumstance:

> There is a vast deal in life and letters both which is not immoral, but simply non-moral; which either does not regard the human will at all, or deals with it in obvious and healthy relations; where the interest turns, not upon what a man shall choose to do, but on how he manages to do it; not on the passionate slips and hesitations of the conscience, but on the problems of the body and of the practical intelligence, in clean, open-air adventure, the shock of arms or the diplomacy of life. With such material as this it is impossible to build a play, for the serious theatre exists solely on moral grounds, and is a standing proof of the dissemination of the human conscience. But it is possible to build, upon this ground, the most joyous of verses, and the most lively, beautiful, and buoyant tales.

And, I suggest, the best kind of film! Not for Stevenson that cinematic use of the camera whereby a young woman firmly crossing her ankles obviously means that she is abjuring marriage. Or some brawny wench, spitting on her large and sinewy hands, indicates that Polly Parsnip has taken the measure of the village blacksmith and is about to deal with him "according." Can it be doubted that if Stevenson had written for the screen his pictures would have dealt with ships and shipwrecks, bullyings and mutinies, pirates and the ends of planks and ropes? Or that his dialogue would have teemed with allusions to long-boats and jolly-boats? *Treasure Island* and *The Wrecker* are magnificent boys' books, and I think that Stevenson's films would have been boys' films. Further, I feel that Stevenson would have wanted all films to be boys' films. Certainly, *Captain Kidd* (London Pavilion) is first-rate entertainment for fourteen-year-olds, full of the hurly-hurly of the pirate seas in the days of William and Mary. (That the story is not easily disentangled rather adds to the charm.) Laughton is grand throughout; he shows again one of the first qualities of the great actor, whether of stage or screen—that power of compulsion which makes it impossible for you to take your eyes off him. And now I permit myself to make Hollywood a suggestion. This is that it should go to the nearest book-shop—are there book-shops in Hollywood?—dig up a copy of *Jonathan Wild* by that good scenario-writer, Henry Fielding, and present our Charles as that Truly Great Man.

There is nothing for fourteen-year-olds in Noel Coward's *Brief Encounter* (New Gallery). The story concerns a woman with a husband and two children who falls in love with a married doctor. "What happens to Laura and Alec might so easily happen to you or me," says Friend Synopsis. (But isn't the function of the screen to show what can't happen to you and me?) Synopsis goes on to remark that this "makes screen entertainment which is unusually arresting and full of drama and suspense." I wonder! Alec persuades Laura to meet him in a flat which is borrowed from a friend and then—I am still quoting Synopsis—"the unexpected return of the friend prevents anything worse than a humiliating flight for Laura." Worse? *Worse?* But surely this is the world of what a man or woman should choose to do. The world of the hesitating conscience. The world in which some things are moral and others immoral. The world for and by which Stevenson held that the theatre existed. I believe that if R.L.S. had been present at the New Gallery on Wednesday morning last, he would have protested that what he saw was theatre rather than film, and psychological novel rather than theatre. I have an inkling that Noel himself felt something of this, for if not why that very nearly full-length performance of the Rachmaninoff C minor Piano Concerto which pounds and drones and rattles in the background whenever the tedium becomes unbearable? Brilliant through Celia Johnson's performance is, this film without that music would just collapse. Let Mr. C. think on the frightful example he has set. Given the score of *Tristan,* the L.P.O., Beecham conducting, and an actress of C.J.'s ability, I know half a dozen Fleet Street hacks who could turn out a *Chance Meeting* which would be every bit as good as *Brief Encounter.* And Noel is no hack. He is very nearly a man of genius, and a man of near-genius should have done better.

101

THE LOST MILLION

1945

Caesar and Cleopatra cost over a million and a quarter pounds, took two and a half years to make, and well and truly bored one spectator for two and a half hours. Why film a play which has no action that matters, while such action as there is serves only as framework to the philosophic idea? What Caesar was doing in Egypt, whether he was trapping or entrapped, who rescued him and why—these things are a muddle and a bore. We are not interested because obviously Shaw was not interested. What fascinated him in his subject matter was the character of Julius Caesar, character shown not in action but in talk. And you cannot make a picture out of talk, however good that talk may be.

First a word about Caesar, this play's core, pivot, and *raison d'être.* Caesar is Mr. Shaw's hero because he is Shavian. His ideas are unclouded by idealism or any kind of romantic nonsense. He is, as Mommsen points out, a realist and a man of sense.

It is Caesar and nobody else who fascinates Mr. Shaw, and I suggest that he has made him too perfect. "I am he," says Caesar to the Sphinx, "of whose genius you are the symbol: part brute, part woman, and part god—nothing of man in me at all." And later, on being asked whether Caesar despairs: "He who has never hoped can never despair." I take this to be not perfect man but perfect fish. Caesar is first cousin to the He-Ancient in *Back to Methuselah,* and not even the people who murdered him could have wished him anything worse. It is not denied that Caesar is given wonderful things to say. Take, for example, the dialogue between Caesar and Cleopatra when the latter, having hired assassins to kill Pothinus, defends her crime on the grounds of lawful vengeance:

> Cleo: Listen to me, Caesar. If one man in all Alexandria can be found to say that I did wrong, I swear to have myself crucified on the door of the palace by my own slaves.

Caesar: If one man in all the world can be found, now or for ever, to *know* that you did wrong, that man will have either to conquer the world as I have, or be crucified by it.

This sublime exchange may or not be good theatre I am sure it is bad film because there is nothing in it for the eye. It is as effective read at home by the fireside.

The rôle of Cleopatra in play and film? Nothing that matters. She is not a gold-digger only because, being Queen of Egypt, she has no need to dig for gold. She shows no signs of the world figure she was to become, and Caesar's attitude towards her throughout is Pooh-Bah's, "Go away, little girl. Can't talk to little girl like you. Go away, there's a dear." Perhaps some day a dramatist will arise who will give us a play about the real Cleopatra. Mr. Shaw failed. Or perhaps it is the charming actresses who have enacted his Cleopatra who have failed, and first on the stage and now in the film have given us a charming little hoyden who can babble about murdering her brother without being believed. People have often asked how Shaw's Cleopatra came to grow up into Shakespeare's. The truth is that she didn't. History, declining to be romantic, gives the lie to Shakespeare and tells us that Cleopatra lured Antony to the Monument, and double-crossed the dead man after he had performed his half of their suicide pact, that she then offered herself to Octavius Caesar hoping to repeat her triumphs with Julius and Antony, and that it was only when Octavius turned her down that she decided to commit suicide. I am not disputing Shakespeare's right to beglamour historical fact; the point I want to establish is that Cleopatra was a slut whose essential sluttishness is still to be put forward. I agree that Mr. Pascal may plead that it is a little hard to demand that he should succeed where Shakespeare and Shaw failed.

But it is time to be getting back to the film. Sir Max Beerbohm, writing about this play in the first year of the present century and six years before its production, said this: "I wish very much that this play could be produced. But it would cost many thousands of pounds, and managers are coy of a vast production that is not the setting of some vast dramatic motive." I disagree. I see no reason why the production of this play should cost more than a few hundreds, just as I see no reason why a film of it should cost more than a few thousands. Mr. Shaw's whole theme is what goes on in Caesar's mind, and in what the girl-queen uses for mind. I see no point in making Alexandria a rose-red city half as old as Denham unless that city is going to serve some purpose. If, for example, the point of the play were the sacking of Alexandria with gates stove in by battering rams, and marble columns yielding to the foreheads of charging elephants. And then how unconvincing are these antique buildings! How inept that use of the camera which can find no beauty in the antique world! The costumes, too, are all obviously brand-new. Why wasn't somebody engaged to make them look soiled and grubby, as the American actor Mansfield did in his production of *Richard III*? It is the old story of æsthetic insincerity. Can any director imagine that Wigan, Accrington, Barnsley, Leatherhead, Portsmouth, Swindon really care to the extent of over a million pounds about the portrayal of Caesar's mentality? The answer is obviously No. Wherefore the vast sums expended on irrelevancies, the architecture of Alexandria and all those scampering armies? I can quite understand that the success of *Pygmalion* tempted Mr. Pascal to have another go. (Didn't this picture have a wholly irrelevant ball-scene?) Then why not *Androcles and the Lion*, where one would have tolerated as legitimate embroidery an hour and a half of fun in that Roman amphitheatre? Where gladiators could have fought and charioteers raced round the arena without drawing a word of protest from me. Two and a half hours over *Androcles* might, I think, have been well spent. Two and a half hours over *Caesar and Cleopatra* is just an hour and a half too long. Particularly when one reflects that all of the essential story could have been shot in the studio, plus a hundred square yards of the sandhills between Blackpool's South Shore and St. Annes. The sad truth is that, as Max perceived forty-four years agô, "most of the scenes are mere whimsical enbroidery, a riotous sequence of broadly humorous incidents." Or put it that this is a little play with one fine moment and a leaven of philosophy. In other words, choicely and pointedly not the thing to turn into a splurgy, splendiferous, magnoperative film.

Vivien Leigh as Cleopatra looks about as Egyptian as the Lass of Richmond Hill, but kittens it charmingly. Claude Rains plays Caesar like a fashionable psychiatrist dealing with trouble in some good Hollywood family; Flora Robson, as the nurse with the boring name, treats her charge as Mrs. Pipchin treated Paul Dombey; Stewart Granger plays Apollodorus with the air of Surbiton's lawn-tennis champion at his most dashing. The West End may be gammoned by this film; the suburbs and provinces will, in my opinion, not be taken in by the kind of thing D. W. Griffith did better half a century ago.

102

THREE DUDS

1946

What Next, Corporal Hargrove? (Empire). Corporal Hargrove has the job of cementing allied relations with French villagers. Before I dozed off I gathered that the ingenious fellow goes about extracting from the guileless peasants sums of money in return for a non-existent, madcap scheme to turn the village into a tourist centre. On their side the aforesaid peasants, who are very far from guileless, sell this cheat a map purporting to be that of a Paris cellar in which a consignment of valuable watches is hidden. Ultimately the corporal gets to Paris, and we are supposed to sympathise when the cellar turns out to be empty. And then I fell asleep. And dreamed a Mid-Winter Night's Dream. I was sitting in a New York theatre at the first-night of a fantasy by Thornton Wilder. But the remarkable thing was that the best performances came from the auditorium, the stalls being peopled by what our genteeler columnists call "well-known figures of stage and screen"—here Edward G. Robinson, there Myrna Loy. Suddenly the woman next to me opened her vanity bag, pulled out of it a straw-coloured moustache, and stuck it on her lip saying: "It's a pity one can't always wear one of these!" I looked closer and found it was Ina Claire. I turned to Humphrey Bogart on my other side and said: "Is this a genuine first-night?" He said: "Sure!" I said: "Will Miss Claire and all of you be here throughout the run?" He said: "Geez, we won't make it to-morrow night!" I said: "But the show depends on you." He said: "You goddam punk, don't you know the resources of this country are inexhaustible?" And then I woke up to find my old friend Mervyn McPherson beaming though his eyeglass as though his firm had produced a masterpiece. The trouble with dear Mac is that he ought to be presiding over U.N.O., where, I am persuaded, his charm would get anybody to agree to everything and everybody to agree to anything. In the world of the cinema he is lost, in the sense that he can't even bring off the feat of persuading simple me that this is anything but the silliest film ever. Let me put it that *What Next, Corporal Hargrove?* shouts for Techni-horror and William Bendix.

Saratoga Trunk (Warner). The author of the Book of Proverbs has described the four unknowable things. I think that to-day he would add a fifth—the way of a film magnate with the critics. There was a press show of this film in the second week in December, and I can only suppose that the reason for having another in the third week in January is that, on the earlier occasion, there was a clash of dates, since not even a film magnate can believe that a picture improves by being kept in a tin. However, strong in my sense of duty as always, I turned up for another basin-full. I found Gary Cooper still there, as tall and quizzical as ever and still wearing that sun-tanned smile and white cowboy hat which must surely make him laugh if he ever stops to think. There was Ingrid Bergman, alleged to be French, fussing over her dwarf attendant, Cupidon, in the very accents of Cora Pearl's

Je souis Kioupidonne, mon amor
Ah fait l'école bouissonière....

But what does to-day's cinema-goer know or care about *La Belle Hélène* and the Bouffes-Parisiens in the 'sixties? And why the hell should he? Well, he is a wise man who knows when he is beaten. I did not wait for the end when according to Synopsis, "a blood-stained figure lurches through the gaping crowd—Gary carrying Cupidon. And in that moment Ingrid realises there can be no other man." Pish! and likewise tush! In my poor view this film bellows for Techni-horror and Carmen Miranda.

Masquerade in Mexico (Plaza). Angel O'Reilly flies to Mexico City with a mysterious packet which, she discovers, contains a valuable diamond. She slips it into the pocket of Tom Grant, a fellow passenger, who is subsequently charged with the theft of the stone. By the time he proves his innocence, Angel is singing at a fashionable night-club. Tom persuades Angel to pretend she is in love with Manolo Segovia, a bull-fighter, of whom Tom's wife, Helen, is enamoured. Life becomes extremely complicated for everybody, particularly when the real diamond thief turns up, but eventually he is brought to justice, Manolo seeks fresh hunting ground, and Tom gets a divorce and marries the girl on the plane.

No, dear reader, I make no claim to be the originator of the foregoing piece of prose. Half-way through this film a friend whom I had bullied into coming with me said: "I wouldn't see any more of this if I were paid for it." I said: "I won't see any more of it, and I *am* paid for it." And we departed, leaving the Film Section of the Critics' Circle glued to the screen, struck to the very soul by the suspense, the conflict, the convolutions of the plot, the psychology of the bull-fighter, and the avoirdupois of the bull. This picture, or as much as I saw of it, yells for Techni-horror, which it doesn't get, and Dorothy Lamour, which it does. THE TATLER'S conscientious scribe is pleased to inform ladies now having their hair twiddled and their ears twaddled that Dorothy "makes her début as a dancer, sings a portion of the soprano sextet number of the opera, *Lucia di Lammermoor,* and has thirteen complete wardrobe changes, each one accompanied by a matching hair-do, in her rôle as an American showgirl who poses as a Spanish countess when she meets the sophisticated international set of Mexico City." That the ballet sequence "depicts in dance form episodes in the struggle of Mexico for independence." That Ann Dvorak "appears in the sequence as an Aztec princess, as Empress Charlotta, and as the symbolic representation of tyranny." Last I read that "Arturo de Cordova, the Latin-American romantic star, was called upon to give his best comedy performance in this film. The handsome Mexican-born actor plays a bull-fighter who fancies himself as a lady-killer as well as a bull-slayer." What I am looking for is a bull who fancies himself as a Cordova and Lamour-slaughterer. Not, of course, that off the set I would between the winds of heaven visit any of those cheeks too roughly.

103

WHAT ABOUT IT?

1946

THE notion has been put forward that because the exportation of British films would bring in American dollars it is the duty of British film critics to boost British pictures. Perhaps the Critics' Circle would like to say something about this? In the absence of any august pronouncement I have to declare that no considerations having to do with economics or international politics are going to weigh with me to the extent of a bus ticket. Selling films to compete in the American market is one thing; the making of intrinsically good films is another. It would be nice if "the pictures" and the art of the screen were as inseparable as Abbott and Costello. But they are not. They can be separated, with honour to each. No wise man would say that an artistic picture must not be produced because it is not a money-maker. And similarly, no wise man would ban a money-making picture on the ground that it is not intellectual. Was *The Wicked Lady* designed to titillate the ears of the groundlings? But Nature has given the groundlings ears, and they are entitled to have them titillated. I do not attack the makers of such pictures. Economic and political conditions doubtless demand that this country opposes to Hollywood's nincompoopery British nincompoopery of equal competence. I wish these commercial films well. But nothing is going to make me declare that because they do well at the box-office they are good films.

Here, as near as I remember, is the plot of a Hollywood film which had a great success in this country. The heroine was a blue-eyed, flaxen-haired daughter of Russia who spent her days manipulating a tractor on the broad fields of the Ukraine. But she had a soul for music, and her evenings were spent communing with the old Collardski and Collardski, which, with the samovar, constituted the farmstead's entire stock of furniture. Saving up the occasional roubles penuriously bestowed upon her by her stepmother she went for a holiday to Moscow, where Stokowski was starting a tour with the Boston Symphony Orchestra. And now our heroine embarked on a lot of stealing. She stole into a rehearsal of the Tschaikowsky Piano Concerto, at which José Iturbi was lending a hand. Immediately after the rehearsal she stole from the back of the hall to the piano and began to play the concerto by ear but with such mastery that the members of the orchestra, who had been thinking about lunch, re-opened their cases, took out their instruments, crept back to their desks and began to insinuate an accompaniment. Finally Stokowski tore back into the hall, threw off his astrakhan coat, astrakhan muffler, and astrakhan cap, and grabbed his conductor's baton. And then what happened? Iturbi contracted tonsillitis, and our heroine deputised and stole the concert. Did she become a famous concert pianist? No. She stole back to the Ukraine. Because there, ankle-deep in the rich soil, was a ploughboy waiting. It is true that he had hands the size of any six non-Communist blacksmiths'. True that there was a dreamy look in his eyes which the vulgar attributed to vodka. True that he didn't know Rimsky-Korsakoff from Gershwin. But he owned several versts of mud and two tractors, and his soul was pure.

Whereupon our English concocters of masterpieces, moved by the spirit of emulation, produced *The Seventh Veil* which, as near as I can remember, went like this. The heroine was again a young woman with a soul for music. She had also a guardian who was in love with her and, when she declined to solace his midnight hours with the slow movement of the Sonata Pathétique, smashed her knuckles with a walking-stick, whereby she spent the next six months undergoing a course of mental therapy until one day a famous hypnotist announced that she was cured. Whereupon she took her hands out of the plaster-of-Paris in which they had been encased for six months, rinsed them in hot water, and set out on a concert tour taking in Paris, Berlin, Budapest, Prague, Rome, the Aleutian Islands, Pearl Harbour and Seattle. At this last she received a cable insisting upon her immediate appearance in London. Flying back and arriving at the Albert Hall just as the L.S.O.—I recognised the leader—was tuning up for the Rachmaninoff Piano Concerto in C Minor, she treated the audience to two minutes of the first movement, cut the slow movement, and wound up with two minutes of the last movement. Sweeping up her gloves and a bunch of arum lilies, she then went out to supper with the dance-band leader, who was the real reason why she had refused to solace her guardian's midnight hours with the slow movement of the Sonata Pathétique. But she married James Mason in the end.

Now both these stories are tripe, and the trouble is that Hollywood makes bigger and better tripe than anything we can manage in this country. And for all sorts of imposing reasons. A concert tour of the principal American cities covers more ground than a tour of this country. Their concert-halls are vaster, and they have more young women who look as though they could play the piano. And, let us face it, they have a bigger and better choice of screen artists. This must be so, since acting is a temperamental and, therefore, a cosmopolitan art, whereas the British genius is for the phlegmatic and the insular. Whence it follows that when it comes to putting over rubbish, we shall be beaten one hundred times out of one hundred. Why, then, doesn't it occur to our film brains to turn disadvantage to advantage? When it comes to producing certain kinds of picture, the documentary, for example, we can leave Hollywood standing, because our natural taste instinctively avoids sentimentality. Nobody will argue that we have a William Bendix in this country, but consider his films! "We do not mention our ingénues; it would be brutal," wrote Max at the beginning of the century. For the same reason I do not mention our screen young ladies who all specialise in the adolescent. There is not a film actress in this country who could stand up to the heroine of *Dark Victory* or *The Little Foxes*. Or you might put it that while every English filmactor is a born Aubrey Tanqueray there is no English film actress who could look at Paula. Any effort to compete with Hollywood by throwing about more money and non-existent acting talent is doomed to fail. Where we can draw level is by using better material. And I suggest that we should begin slowly, making one good picture as against forty-nine like *The Seventh Veil* type, and not caring what that good picture grosses.

104

SEVERAL KINDS OF NONSENSE

1946

NOW, reader, take a long breath. Would you, being a man of business and fortyish, on being told by a detective that your wife had murdered three former husbands for their insurance money, and having yourself, at your wife's instigation, taken out an increased insurance policy, and, moreover, contracted the habit of receiving at her hands a white powder alleged to be bicarbonate of soda, but bringing on bouts of vomiting with all the symptoms attendant upon arsenic poisoning—would you, I ask, in these circumstances, tell the detective that he was no gentleman and order him out of the house? Would you, being the aforesaid noodle, have your suspicions aroused when the haddock which your wife was going to boil for your lunch with her own fair hands was devoured by the cat which, under your very nose, turned over on its back and died of acute poisoning? I think you might. But I don't think you would passionately embrace her, tell her that she had the ill-luck to be one of Nature's poisonous flowers, and suggest that she should forestall the arrival of the heavy-booted sentry by helping herself to the arsenic. That is what happens in *Bedelia* (Plaza), and it is all very, very silly.

It is the old question of turning your barely possible novel into your extremely improbable film. Both of Miss Caspary's tales, *Laura* and *Bedelia,* had a certain degree of persuasiveness in book-form. Reduction to the screen has meant in both cases that all those passages of quasi-rational mortar with which the authoress interlarded her non-rational bricks have had to be omitted. The function of mortar, an architectural chap (acknowledgments to D. B. Wyndham Lewis for the turn of phrase) once told me, is two-fold—to hold bricks together, and to keep them apart. In the present case the absence of mortar has failed equally to hold the bricks together, or to keep them apart from anything except nonsense.

How is *Bedelia* played? At a guess I should say very well indeed by Ian Hunter as the noodle, and reasonably well by Barry K. Barnes as the detective; this actor has at last shed some of that over-plus of gentility which has so often made his voice sound like cold cream. As for Bedelia herself, Margaret Lockwood may look like the poisonous flower, but to me never begins to suggest the serpent under it. This is yet another of those pictures which seem to call for rather more dramatic power than Lockwood is capable of.

Tailpiece to the foregoing: A Bournemouth friend of mine whose passion is Siamese cats tells me that his Bluebell, on the eve of certain happy events, put a paw on each of his knees and with her eyes made piteous appeal. "I knew what she was saying. She was imploring me not to call two of her kittens Laura and Bedelia."

There is dull nonsense and there is exciting nonsense. If *Bedelia* falls into the first category then I shall undoubtedly place *The Strange Love of Martha Ivers* (Carlton) in the second. This is a picture which has gone wrong because the makers of it haven't been able to decide exactly what picture they were making. Martha Ivers (Janis Wilson, afterwards Barbara Stanwyck) is the niece of a dragonsome aunt. The child makes frequent escapes, generally in the company of young Sam Masterson (Darryl Hickman, afterwards Van Heflin), but is always brought back to the auntuncular, if I may coin a word, mansion. Now Auntie has a loathing for cats, and one day Martha finds the old lady beating her, Martha's, pet pussy. So she snatches up some handy blunt instrument and bashes Auntie's head in, whereby Auntie dies.

Now there are living in the house one Mr. O'Neil (Roman Bohnen), a time-serving steward, and his little boy Walter (Mickey Kuhn, afterwards Kirk Douglas), the latter of whom was present at the murder. So the steward concocts a story. The two children are to say that they were standing on the stairs when they saw a tramp come in through the open door, do the deed and vanish. What of Master Sam, who was more or less on the scene at the time? Well, he's a straight kid, and won't say anything either way. And now it turns out that Auntie has left all her money to Martha. Wherefore, O'Neil *père* insists upon her marrying O'Neil *fils*. But why, since she loathes him? Because he terrifies her. Because in the meantime a man has been tried for the crime and been hanged, both Martha and Walter identifying him as the tramp they had previously sworn to. Years pass, and we learn that Martha has become a great business magnate and owns half the factories in the town, while she has pushed her husband, who incidentally drinks, into the post of District Attorney with an eye on ultimate Washington.

At this point the reader sits back and says, "What's the matter with that? Surely here's a theme—a strong woman and a weak man bound together by crime and loathing each other—which Ibsen would have delighted to use. And haven't we arrived at the exact point where the Old Man would have raised his curtain, trusting to tell the antecedent happenings in verbal flashbacks?" I agree. The trouble starts when Sam Masterson turns up again. Sam has a poor record. He has acquired money, though nobody knows how. He has made fortunes and gambled them away. He has been accused of murder, but successfully pleaded self-defence. At the moment he is engaged in reclaiming, or anyhow finding a bedroom for, Toni Marachek (Lizabeth Scott), a Lauren Bacall-ish young woman with an eye for a fur coat and a deft hand at stealing one. She is now out of gaol on probation. When Sam and Martha meet, deep calls unto deep. Or so we innocent spectators think. But Walter, in his capacity as District Attorney, knows better and suspects blackmail. What else can be Sam's motive for coming into their lives again? Whereupon, what might have been a good psychological drama of hate between husband and wife is turned into a violent and excessively complicated screen-drama. District Attorney sets his cops to beat up the blackmailer;

blackmailer isn't going to blackmail because he never saw Martha strike Auntie, having departed a few seconds before. And in any case he is much too busy deciding which of the two women he is most on fire about. Wife wants blackmailer to murder husband. And the fur-coat fancier? She is just around and about chucking a spanner into the works whenever she thinks she can get something out of it, maybe love. Whereby a film which has begun very excitingly peters out into a lot of dreary nonsense at the end of which husband and wife commit suicide, and blackmailer and thief set out for the future in the highest-powered car Hollywood can lay its hand on.

The best acting, in my humble opinion, comes from Kirk Douglas who, as the husband, really has a part to play and plays it. Next the two children, Janis Wilson and Darryl Hickman, who play the young Martha and the young Sam. Van Heflin is just the usual good-looking American, and we're going to see lots and lots of Lizabeth Scott, until Hollywood uncovers somebody with a more glamorous glottis. But I warn this young woman that if, in her next part, she uses the word "maybe" more than a hundred and fifty times I shall rise in my seat and bellow. Barbara Stanwyck? Well, you know what Barbara's like. Endless nose, endless breakfast, lunch, tea and dinner gowns, with a lot of *négligés* thrown in, and chunks of pretence about being the vortex to some tragic whirlpool.

It is astonishing how often Old Man Ibsen crops up. *Beware of Pity* (Leicester Square) bristles with the whiskers of that more than fretful Norwegian porcupine. Beware, Ibsen was always saying, of idealism, of doing the right thing at the wrong moment. *The Wild Duck* showed the harm that is done by blurting out the truth to people who are not ready for it, and I can see Ibsen fashioning a grim sermon on the misuse of pity. Title? *The Wild Goose,* of course.

Judging by the story of this film, Stefan Zweig is a sentimentalist of the first order. (Except that a novelist should never be judged by any film version of his work.) His thesis is that there are two kinds of pity, the easy sort which makes its bestower feel good, and the more difficult sort which demands that he who pities should make sacrifices on behalf of the object of his pity. And I think of an old Lancashire rhyme:

> Sympathy without relief
> Is like mustard without beef.

The name that Zweig gives to the nobler kind of pity is compassion. So far so good.

But from that to the moral of this picture is a far cry. A young Czechoslovakian officer meets a crippled girl to whom he shows the ordinary courtesies; she, of course, mistakes these for something more. She falls desperately in love with him, he weakly consents to some sort of engagement and then goes back on his promise. Whereupon she commits suicide. All this happens before the first World War, and the beginning and end of the picture show the officer proffering advice to a subaltern who has got himself into a similar difficulty at the end of the second World War. He tells the young man his own experience, how he had failed to "give," by which he means sacrifice himself, and how it is the duty of the subaltern to succeed where he failed. I can just imagine the savage fun Ibsen would have had with all this. Let us suppose that this marriage with love on one side only takes place. How long is it going to be before the wife realises that one of two things must happen? Either the husband is going to put up some show of affection for five nights in the week, on condition that he is allowed the other two off, or he will be wholly faithful until the sight of crutches drives him first into a nervous breakdown and then into an asylum. And I think Ibsen would have pointed out that the fault is not in the virtue of compassion, but in forcing that virtue upon the wrong kind of man. There is a certain kind of poor fish who enjoys being miserable. But to insist that a man who is fond of mountaineering should marry a girl he isn't attracted to just because she can't walk, seems to me to be nonsense.

However, this isn't the first time that nonsense has made an extremely interesting film, and it won't be the last. Beautifully acted by Lilli Palmer, Cedric Hardwicke, Ernest Thesiger, and Gladys Cooper, with a grand performance by Albert Lieven. (Well, perhaps not grand, but better than your British, glove-counterish leading man. Or leading gentleman, which is worse.) The direction by Maurice Elvey is superb, and I mean it. Blake made a great deal of fuss about seeing a World in a Grain of Sand. Mr. Elvey, with almost no fuss at all, has managed to see the mansions and barracks of Czechoslovakia in Islington, and her scarps and precipices in Cheddar Gorge.

105

THAT NAUGHTY ACADEMY!

1946

I AM a teeny-weeny bit peeved at the management of the Academy Theatre which this week is presenting a double bill—*The Forgotten Village* and *Frenzy*. I am peeved because the programme cites thirteen film critics in praise of the first film while ignoring your humble servant in THE TATLER. Which naturally sent me to my press-cutting book to see in what way I had offended. I found this:

> I went to *The Forgotten Village* prepared to snooze through some prickly, sun-drenched story of no interest. The picture was announced as being by John Steinbeck, who had written in the synopsis: "It means very little to know that a million Chinese are starving unless you know one Chinese who is starving." I entirely agree. To be perfectly candid, it would have meant very little to me if the picture intended to show the whole population of Mexico dying of tsetse-fly or humming-birditis. Now, after this preamble, let me say with maximum sincerity that I watched this picture, lasting an hour and ten minutes, in entire and complete absorption. It told again the old story of dirt, ignorance, prejudice and superstition, and showed how an entire village would rather its babies perished than that they should be saved by a vaccine drawn from a cow or a horse. (A few people in this enlightened country still hold this view, including, I understand, one extremely distinguished dramatist.) The photography was entirely remarkable, with none of that nonsense about using the cinema cinematically, the Mexican peasants acted with superb naturalness, and the film was blessedly silent save for some appropriate music and the story-telling of Burgess Meredith, who used so much tact that while one got the full sense of what he was saying one was quite unconscious that one was being spoken to.

No, reader, I am not quoting myself because I am lazy, but because I can't improve now upon what I wrote on May 17, 1944. And now for a little ancient history. Years ago I wrote about some actress that she was like "an Alp at dawn." After which I went on: "It is only proper to say that I can't remember ever having seen an Alp, and that it is many years since I beheld the dawn." I was horrified to find on the following Tuesday morning the walls of the theatre plastered with the words: "James Agate says, 'An Alp at Dawn.'" Reflecting on this I feel that the fault is not the Academy's but mine. That if in the notice of *The Forgotten Village* I had written some such phrase as "Popocatapetl at Dawn," I should have received the honours of quotation as freely as anybody else. It only remains for me to say that I still regard *The Forgotten Village* as a wonderfully moving little film, and exhort everybody to go and see it.

But I think it was a mistake to show this little masterpiece in front of *Frenzy*, since in my view the Swedish piece doesn't stand up to the comparison. Talking of comparisons it was rather fun comparing my Sunday monitresses. One said she was unable to see this film "without experiencing a certain genial glow; the sort of glow one gets from a dip in the sea, from hearing the overture to *The Marriage of Figaro* well played, or from the scent of miles of gorse on a hot spring day." The other was struck all of a Dilysian heap: "The character of the master, bullying at one moment, cringing and whimpering at the next, calculating his methods of torment, relishing his vicious triumphs, is completely expressed. Nobody would suggest that this is an everyday type; but then no more is Iago; the point is that on the screen the man is convincing, solid, a monster, but a flesh-and-blood monster who persuades by the very enormity of his madness. The playing of the part by Stig Järrel is a *tour de force;* this is a performance which makes the usual screen actors of the horrific look like something out of a charade."

But then I know what "got" the dear lady. "The visual detail, both of setting and of behaviour, is memorable: a lamp swinging on its flex as the boy stumbles through the dead girl's room . . . ." Wonderful what a Bit of String can do! Whereas I, realist and clodhopper, want to know what a tobacconist's assistant is doing with a flat as big as my own with innumerable doors and, in the matter of lighting, an electrician's paradise. And whether, in Sweden, shop-girls drink themselves to death at twenty? But then I am not intellectually gammonable. And being ungammonable I am afraid I think that *Frenzy* is a little bogus. I believe in a schoolmaster who cares nothing at all for women, but wants to lick the hides off the little beasts in front of him. And I am prepared to believe in a schoolmaster who likes tobacconists' assistants to the exclusion of school-room pleasantries. What I don't believe in is the sadistic usher who distributes his favours indifferently, and hums to himself *à la Floradora:*

Yes, I must thrash some one really,
And it might as well be you.

But let me leave the subject. Sadism is a deep and hidden thing, for ignorance of which, let me trust, I shall not be rebuked, as à Kempis says, at the day of judgment.

There are, however, declared and open matters in which civilisation stands in great danger of rebuke. These are crooning and jazz. Between which, however, I am prepared to make a nice, a very nice distinction. I hold that crooning is ultimately forgivable, but that jazz, swing, jive and all the rest of these filthy noises can never be taken out of the category of the abominable. After all, we have to remember that films like *Do You Love Me?* (Gaumont) are written for errand boys and nursemaids, junior clerks and typists. It is Dick Haymes who wants to know whether Maureen O'Hara loves him, and Dick, of course, is the well-known crooner. He is a nice, pleasant-looking, ugly fellow with a jowl like a rueful bulldog. But the moment he opens his glottis entire audiences swoon, with the exception of those who are thrown into epileptic fits. Well, it ill-becomes any film critic who has ever been inside a theatre to mount the high horse about this. Let me go back to the year 1879 and see what the great French critic, Sarcey, had to say about the first appearance in England of a young French actress, name of Sarah Bernhardt, and her reception by the London public of that day: "One critic cuts Rachel's throat and offers her up as a sacrifice to the new idol. Another declares Mlle Sarah Bernhardt to be not only the first of living actresses, but the greatest actress of all time. Between them they use all the adjectives there are and regret that the English language is so poor. When the new actress ceases to speak and gives way to another player they fall into a catalepsy."

Now let us hear a later English critic, Arthur Symons, one of the most cultured men that ever made part of a theatrical audience. Here is his picture of her: "Never have I forgotten the thrill that went all over me as she gave me her hand to kiss: which I did with all the fervour of my fiery youth. Her fingers were covered with rings, her long and slender fingers; the nails were dyed with red henna—which I saw afterwards in the East. She was then at the zenith of her fame and of her beauty. There was the 'golden voice', with the Jewish drawl over the syllables—a voice that penetrated one's very heart, as the aching notes of the violin can penetrate one's heart and one's nerves." And of her in another play, Harancourt's *La Passion de Jésus Christ,* in which she had to take the part of the Virgin Mary: "Suddenly Sarah appeared; gorgeous, covered with rich raiment, wearing all her jewels, painted and made up with her conscious art; wonderful, languid, languorous. She began; then, as always, her voice touched me, as if nerve thrilled nerve, and as if, as in Verlaine's superb phrase, *le contour subtil* of the voice were laid lingering on one's spinal cord." And then the audience began to hiss, the Parisians having some sort of muddled notion that the play was blasphemous and that the Virgin Mary should not be acted by a Jewess. There was a great commotion and finally Sarah withdrew like a furious tigress.

The point of the foregoing? The words "*le contour subtil* of the voice were laid lingering on one's spinal cord." It is only fair to Dick Haymes to grant that when he sings:

Do you love me,
Do you love me,
Do you love me,
Do you love me?
Tell me, do!

he impresses the unsophisticiated film-goers of to-day in the same way that Sarah impressed the London critics more than sixty years ago. And that when he sings:

Do I thrill you,
Do I thrill you,
Do I thrill you,
Do I thrill you,
Through and through?

he is having the same effect on the cinema-goer's spinal cord that Sarah had on that of Arthur Symons.

But for the modern jam session which in this film is made to follow immediately upon the last movement of Tschaikowsky's Fourth Symphony, I can find no excuse, any more than I can find words to describe the acting of Maureen O'Hara, who doesn't. Harry James can blow his own trumpet; I shan't. And Reginald Gardiner is badly treated by the camera, which makes him look, as Mrs. Patrick Campbell said of a rival beauty, as though he had two glass eyes.

106

SHAKESPEARE FOR THE MASSES

1946

THIS week I propose to discuss the first of a series of films by which Marylebone Film Productions hope to bring Shakespeare to the masses. I was horrified, confounded, not by the attempt but by the deed. First let me get rid of the popular misconception that there is no need to take Shakespeare to the masses because the masses lose no opportunity of flocking to Shakespeare of their own accord. Harold Hobson wrote in the *Sunday Times:*

> I am mildly puzzled by the notion that Shakespeare needs popularising with the general public. Few actors earned more from the general public than Irving did; and he got most of his two millions out of Shakespeare. But that was a long time ago? Very well then. Did Mr. Richardson's Falstaff, did Mr. Olivier's Richard III need popularising with the public, general or otherwise? The only problem the Old Vic had when it was playing Shakespeare in its last two seasons at the New Theatre was that so many people came that many of them couldn't get into the house. But Mr. Olivier and Mr. Richardson gave superb performances? Of course they did. Superb performances, not "popularising," are what Shakespeare needs . . . Shakespeare is already beyond all dispute or cavil the world's most popular dramatist. Mr. Rattigan and Mr. Coward have golden fingers, but the money their

admirable plays attract is a cabby's tip compared with what Shakespeare draws into the earth's box offices. No, the proper way of tackling Shakespeare is not to begin his pieces half-way through, and then miss out half of what is left in the fear that audiences can't be expected to stand more than a bit of him. Play him magnificently and they will take it on the chin.

With all due respect to an old and valued friend and a brilliant writer this is flat nonsense. The masses, always with the exception of the Old Vic faithfuls, do not flock to Shakespeare. What they flock to is Gielgud in something, and Richardson and Olivier in something else, and if it's Shakespeare it's just too bad. I quote from an old diary: "It is owing to Wolfit that for four weeks in succession, *en pleine guerre,* there have been four revivals of plays by Shakespeare played to full or nearly full houses. But this is no reason why the London play-goer should lay flattering unction to his soul in the matter of improved taste. D. W.'s manager telephoned me this morning to say that at each and every performance, Czechs, Poles, Norwegians, Belgians, and French had accounted for 50 per cent of the audience and sometimes 75 per cent. 'The rest have been Jews! Had we relied on Christians we should have played to empty benches.' What happened, pray, when Wolfit announced his *Lear* at the Scala? The theatre was empty until the *Sunday Times*' critic woke 'em up. Hobson talks of the drawing power of Rattigan and Coward, as to which I have to say that their drawing power is real. Coward's *Blithe Spirit* ran for five years and suffered three or four changes of cast; Heaven and John Parker alone know how long *Private Lives* ran. The original cast for the second of these was headed by Gertrude Lawrence and Coward himself: the piece is again running at the re-opened little Fortune Theatre *without these artists.* Can Hobson really believe that the first and second parts of Shakespeare's *Henry IV* could run for five years with actors of diminishing fame? As we used to say in Lancashire: "Have a bit of common!"

But to return to the other morning. I was horrified to see that Othello's colour was glossed over, and that there was no suggestion that Desdemona had married (*a*) a blackamoor, or (*b*) against her father's will. Horrified to find that the play started with one of Iago's most difficult soliloquies, full of metaphysical straining, and incomprehensible to anybody except practised Shakespearians. Horrified to see nothing of Cassio and Roderigo. Horrified when the business of the handkerchief was cut to an unintelligible two-thirds. Horrified that the audience was not told that the tragedy of Othello is that of a noble and simple soul undone by a subtle, scheming rascal. Horrified when they drowned Othello's closing speeches with the last movement of Tschaikowsky's Sixth Symphony. Horrified when Othello, instead of stifling Desdemona, strangled her. Horrified when Iago, instead of having the lean, sinister look which the *optique du théâtre* demands, was presented by an actor chubby of face, Falstaffianly stomached, and ready at any moment, one thought, to burst into an aria *à la* Caruso. Horrified when in enormous letters the screen announced "Iaggo," followed by the actor's name.

I confess that nothing would please me better than to make the short version of *Macbeth.* But I should have to be given a free hand. I hold that two things are essential in anybody who is going to film Shakespeare for the masses—reasonable understanding of Shakespeare and a comprehensive understanding of the masses. What is the little chit whom I overheard in the bus saying to her friend, "You wasn't taking us to the pictures Setterday, was you, 'Orace?"—what is Camden Town going to make of:

> Will all great Neptune's ocean wash this blood
> Clean from my hand? No; this my hand will rather
> The multitudinous seas incarnadine,
> Making the green one red.

Wherefore I should insist upon making the plot as plain as if it was something enacted by Alan Ladd and Veronica Lake. I should make it clear, probably by a commentator or conceivably a Reciter in the Obey manner, that *Macbeth* is a tragedy of retribution. Further, that the evil was not prompted by Lady Macbeth but originated in Macbeth's mind ("What beast was't then That made you break this enterprise to me?") long before the encounter with the Witches. Having established beyond any manner of doubt what was the core of the play—I should show the Witches as spirits abetting evil rather than instigating it—I should then trust to the poetry to get by, though I have almost no hope that it will. As the inventor of the law which I call the Non-Increasibility of Nothing I must believe in the Non-Educability of the Masses, whether by Shakespeare, Beethoven or anybody else. But I am a firm believer in the Forlorn Hope, and as such can only hope my chit in the bus will be able to conceive that somebody can incarnadine something beyond her multitudinous toe- and finger-nails.

Dr. Bowdler wrote in the preface to the first edition of his *Family Shakespeare:* "I can hardly imagine a more pleasing occupation for a winter's evening in the country, than for a father to read one of Shakespeare's plays to his family circle. My object is to enable him to do so without incurring the danger of falling unawares among words and expressions which are of such a nature as to raise a blush on the cheek of modesty, or render it necessary for the reader to pause, and examine the sequel, before he proceeds further in the entertainment of the evening." Yet Dr. B. could retain the line:

Villain, be sure thou prove my love a whore,

which the other morning's film altered to:

Villain, be sure thou prove my love is false.

Four-fifths of to-day's screen heroines are "gold-diggers", the modern euphemism for the old, robustious, Tearsheetish thing. The word is banned by the film censors, who have no objection to the pollution of young mind so long as young mind doesn't know what pollution is called.

But all that is by the way. The point, I repeat, is that whoever is going to make a film of, say, *Macbeth*, must be given an absolutely free hand. Nothing must be taken from his script and nothing added to it. He must be given a voice in the casting, and the power of veto. Whom would I personally cast for Macbeth? I can think of five actors whom I should very much like to see in the part. Basil Sydney, Leslie Banks, William Devlin, William Fox, and Esmond Knight. For Lady Macbeth I should unhesitatingly choose Sonia Dresdel. The critics are always complaining that a part is not worthy of Dresdel's powers. Well, here is a part that is! I am tired of Lady Macbeths who squirrelise the rôle after the likeness of Ibsen's Nora. I am tired, too, of those Lady M.'s who go through the tragedy with their eyes open but their sense shut, and are less than awake everywhere except in the sleep-walking scene. Almost any dull actor will do for Banquo, and there will be no nonsense about Lennox, Ross, Monteith, Angus, and Caithness. I should want about five supers to suggest guests at the banquet; these would afterwards turn themselves into Malcolm's army.

Curtains and a few bits of painted cardboard would suffice for the scenery. I should get as background music some nice, disgruntled Sibelius records turned down very low, and given as much intelligence and drive as, say, a caterer puts into his business, the whole thing could be shot in a week. No, I should not want to "produce." And if I know my Dresdel she would say to any cameraman with views about picturisation in the Dilysian mode, "Leave that damned thing where it is, and just turn the handle while I act. And no nonsense about photographing the candlestick. Who do you think is playing Lady Macbeth? Me or the candle?" Which would be very rude of Dresdel. But entirely right.

107

HEROES OF ARNHEM

1946

"They gave their bodies to the commonwealth and received, each for his own memory, praise that will never die, and with it the grandest of all sepulchres, not that in which their mortal bones are laid, but a home in the minds of men, where their glory remains fresh to stir to speech or action as the occasion comes by. For the whole earth is the sepulchre of famous men; and their story is not graven only on stone over their native earth, but lives on far away, without visible symbol, woven into the stuff of other men's lives."

PERICLES

SOME little time ago the makers of Basildon Bond notepaper held a competition for the Best Letter Written by a Member of the Forces during the recent war. The judges were Miss Margery Anderson, Commander Campbell, and the film critic of THE TATLER. The writer of the winning entry was the twenty-two-years-old

Pte. I. Rowbery 4928327
2nd S. Staffs Regt. (Signal Section)
Att. 1st Airborne Division.

He was killed at Arnhem.

Blighty.
(Some time ago)

Dear Mom,

Usually when I write a letter it is very much overdue, and I make every effort to get it away quickly. This letter, however, is different. It is a letter I hoped you would never receive, as it is just a verification of that terse, black-edged card which you received some time ago, and which has caused you so much grief. It is because of that grief that I wrote this letter, and by the time you have finished reading it I hope that it has done some good, and that I have not written it in vain. It is very difficult to write now of future things in the past tense, so I am returning to the present.

To-morrow we go into action. As yet we do not know exactly what our job will be, but no doubt it will be a dangerous one in which many lives will be lost—mine may be one of those lives.

Well, Mom, I am not afraid to die. I like this life, yes—for the past two years I have planned and dreamed and mapped out a perfect future for myself. I would have liked that future to materialise, but it is not what I will but what God wills, and if by sacrificing all this I leave the world slightly better than I found it I am perfectly willing to make that sacrifice. Don't get me wrong though, Mom, I am no flag-waving patriot, nor have I ever professed to be.

England's a great little country—the best there is—but I cannot honestly and sincerely say "That is worth fighting for." Nor can I fancy myself in the rôle of a gallant crusader fighting for the liberation of Europe. It would be a nice thought but I would only be kidding myself. No, Mom, my little world is centred around you and includes Dad, everyone at home, and my friends at W'ton—*That* is worth fighting for—and if by doing so it strengthens your security and improves your lot in any way, then it is worth dying for too.

Now this is where I come to the point of this letter. As I have already stated, I am not afraid to die and am perfectly willing to do so if by my doing so, you benefit in any way whatsoever. If you do not then my sacrifice is all in vain. Have you benefited, Mom, or have you cried and worried yourself sick? I fear it is the latter. Don't you see, Mom, that it will do me no good, and that in addition you are undoing all the good work I have tried to do. Grief is hypocritical, useless and unfair, and does neither you nor me any good.

I want no flowers, no epitaph, no tears. All I want is for you to remember me and feel proud of me, then I shall rest in peace knowing that I have done a good job. Death is nothing final or lasting, if it were there would be no point in living; it is just a stage in everyone's life. To some it comes early, to others late, but it must come to everyone sometime, and surely there is no better way of dying.

Besides, I have probably crammed more enjoyment into my 21 years than some manage to do in 80. My only regret is that I have not done as much for you as I would have liked to do. I loved you, Mom, you were the best Mother in the World, and what I failed to do in life I am trying to make up for in death, so please don't let me down, Mom, don't worry or fret, but smile, be proud and satisfied. I never had much money, but what little I have is all yours. Please don't be silly and sentimental about it, and don't try to spend it on me. Spend it on yourself or the kiddies, it will do some good that way. Remember that where I am I am quite O.K., and providing I know that you are not grieving over me I shall be perfectly happy.

Well, Mom, that is all, and I hope I have not written it all in vain.

Good-bye, and thanks for everything.

Your unworthy son,

IVOR

108

"THEIRS IS THE GLORY"

1946

THIS extraordinarily noble film, which deeply moved the audience at the Gaumont at its Press showing, has been conceived and executed with maximum dignity. The "literature" handed to the critics contained no more than the bare mention of the producing company, which is General Film Distributors, Ltd. Nothing about the director, and perhaps I shall not be shot if I say that this was Brian Desmond Hurst. Nothing about the composer of the admirable music, for which Guy Warwick should be given the credit. Only three of the participants—you would not call them actors—are named, and there would have been just as much reason to name three thousand.

The picture has been superbly made with a wonderful command of variety and of pictorial effect and no suggestion at any time that truth is being made to play second-fiddle to effectiveness. The major difficulty in any film of this kind is to let the spectator know what is happening, which seems to me to be equally true of the commander in the field. He may know what is happening, but I feel that he only just knows. This uncertainty, this fog of war, is given its exact value, and it is set in what I can only describe as a welter of luridity. The whole eight days' battle is, as Tennyson said,

> Wrapt in drifts of lurid smoke
> On the misty river-tide.

Now and again there are shots of great beauty, as when a snowstorm overtakes the summer sky and the flakes turn out to be parachutes, and the music tinkles as if Mr. Warwick had borrowed from Cyril Scott's "Rainbow Trout." And then begins that unequal contest in which some of the bravest men in history were defeated, not so much by a clever and courageous foe as by lack of food, lack of water, lack of sleep, and last, lack of ammunition.

Napoleon said that any army marches on its stomach. I think that Haig in the first World War, and Montgomery in the second, would agree that the British soldier lives by and on his sense of humour. I have no doubt that many a man spent those eight days at Arnhem in a mortal funk; I doubt whether a single man ceased to see the comic side of discomfort. This ranges from the dry humour of the high-ups to the Rabelaisian lubricity of the low-downs. One of this army's colonels is told by the Germans that if he doesn't evacuate the château now used as a hospital they will blast him out of it with their tanks. The colonel sends a message back if a single tank dares to come anywhere near him, he will blow it off the face of the earth with his anti-tank guns. The messenger departed, he turns to his adjutant and says, "No need to tell them that I haven't got any anti-tank guns!" But the German is persistent and orders the British to surrender and indicate same by waving a white handkerchief. "Blimey," says a Tommy, "white 'ankerchers arter six days of this muck? Wot does 'e tike us for—a lot o' bloomin' pansies?" And again, when a sergeant tumbles into a trench and the occupant says, "I say, Sarge, don't you go taking off your boots in my boodwah. Wot would the neighbours think?" And last, when the owner of a wireless set is told by his chums to tune in to dance music, and the best he can get is somebody singing "You'll be far better off when you're dead." And all around the bloody battle is raging—and an arm's-length or two away men are dying.

Two war correspondents make fine contributions. One is Alan Wood who says: "If in the years to come you meet a man who fought at Arnhem, take off your hat to him and buy him a drink—for his is the stuff of which England's greatness is made." Was he, perhaps, thinking of Shakespeare? The other correspondent is Stanley Maxted: "Their story will be told wherever men cherish deeds of good report—the story of those filthy, grimy, wonderful gentlemen who drop from the skies to fight where they stand . . ." Was he, perhaps, thinking of Pericles?

There is little more to be said. I repeat that this picture confers upon the film a dignity which one had thought to be the exclusive property of the tragic drama of the stage. Nothing is given less than its proper value, and nothing is over-stressed. I know no more moving scene than that in which the wife of the burgomaster of Oosterbeek reads the Ninety-first Psalm to wounded boys in whose eyes is mirrored the pestilence that walketh in darkness and the destruction that wasteth at noonday.

INDEX

(A) FILMS

(B) PLAYERS

(C) FILM DIRECTORS, PRODUCERS, AUTHORS

(D) SUBJECTS, AUTHORITIES, COMPOSERS, CRITICS, WAGS

(E) — AND SARAH BERNHARDT